THE COURT OF ADMIRALTY OF IRELAND, 1575–1893

# The Court of Admiralty of Ireland, 1575–1893

KEVIN COSTELLO

FOUR COURTS PRESS
*in association with*
THE IRISH LEGAL HISTORY SOCIETY

Typeset in 10.5pt on 12.5pt EhrhardtMt by
Carrigboy Typesetting Services for
FOUR COURTS PRESS LTD
7 Malpas Street, Dublin 8, Ireland
www.fourcourtspress.ie
*and in North America for*
FOUR COURTS PRESS
c/o ISBS, 920 N.E. 58th Avenue, Suite 300, Portland, OR 97213.

A catalogue record for this title is available
from the British Library.

ISBN 978–1–84682–243–8

Printed in England,
by MPG Books Ltd, Bodmin, Cornwall.

# Contents

# Illustrations

# Abbreviations

| | |
|---|---|
| *1828 Accounts* | Accounts relating to the Admiralty Court of Ireland, 1828 (HC 1828 (101) xxii.i) |
| Ad &El | Adolphus and Ellis reports. King's Bench. 1834–40 |
| *Alumni Dublinenses* | G.D. Burtchaell and T.U. Sadlier, *Alumni Dublinenses 1593–1860* (Dublin, 1935) |
| Bodl. | Bodleian Library |
| BL | British Library |
| Buls | Bulstrode's reports. King's Bench. 1610–26 |
| Burrell | William Burrell's reports. Admiralty. 1764–1840 |
| *Cal. anc. rec. Dub.* | *Calendar of the Ancient Records of Dublin*, ed. Sir J.T. Gilbert and Lady Gilbert, 19 vols (Dublin, 1889–1944) |
| *Cal. S.P. Dom.* | *Calendar of State Papers, Domestic* |
| *Cal. S.P. Ire.* | *Calendar of State Papers, Ireland* |
| C Rob | Christopher Robinson's reports. Admiralty. 1798–1808 |
| *3 Co Inst* | E. Coke, *Third Part of the Institutes of the Laws of England* (London, 1669) |
| *4 Co Inst* | E. Coke, *Fourth Part of the Institutes of the Laws of England* (London, 1644) |
| Co Rep | Edward Coke's reports. King's Bench. 1572–1616 |
| *Commons' jn* | *Journals of the House of Commons of the Kingdom of Ireland, 1631–1791* (Dublin, 1753–1791), reprinted and continued, 1631–1800 (Dublin 1796–1800) |
| *Compendious View* | A. Browne, *A compendious view of the civil law and of the law of admiralty, being the substance of a course of lectures read in the University of Dublin* (London, 1802) |
| Court of Admiralty Commission Report, 1864 | *Report of the Commissioners appointed to inquire into the High Court of Admiralty of Ireland* (HC 1864 [3343] xxix 219) |
| Court of Admiralty Depositions | *Calendar of material relating to Ireland from the High Court of Admiralty Depositions*, ed. J. Appleby (Dublin, 1992) |
| Council Book of Cork Corporation | *The Council Book of the Corporation of the City of Cork from 1609 to 1643 and from 1690 to 1800*, ed. R. Caulfield (Guildford, 1876) |
| Cro Jac | Croke's reports. King's Bench and Common Pleas. 1603–25 |
| Dods | Dodson reports. Admiralty. 1811–22 |
| *Eighteenth Report* | *Eighteenth Report of Commissioners on Duties, Salaries and Emoluments of Courts of Justice* (HC 1829 (5) iii 195) |
| ER | English Reports, 1210–1865 |
| *Fourth Report* | *Fourth Report of the Commissioners on the Courts of Justice* (HC (1818) (140) x. 557) |
| *FJ* | *Freeman's Journal* |
| Genealogical account of Ayreshire | G. Robertson, *A genealogical account of the principal families in Ayreshire, more particularly in Cunninghame* (Ayreshire, 1823) |

| | |
|---|---|
| Hag Adm | Haggard Reports. Admiralty. 1822–38 |
| *Hale and Fleetwood* | *Hale and Fleetwood on Admiralty Jurisdiction*, ed. M.J. Prichard & D.E.C. Yale (Selden Society, London, 2003) |
| HC | House of Commons papers |
| *History of the Irish Parliament* | *History of the Irish Parliament, 1692–1800: Commons, constituencies and statutes*, ed. E. Johnston-Liik (Belfast, 2002) |
| Hob | Hobart reports. 1603–25 |
| Ir Eq | Irish Reports. Equity series. 1867–78 |
| *Ir Jur* | *Irish Jurist* |
| *ILT & SJ* | *Irish Law Times and Solicitors' Journal* (Dublin 1867–) |
| ILTR | Irish Law Times Reports (in *ILT & SJ*) |
| Knapp | *Knapp's reports. Privy Council. 1829–36* |
| *Law and Custom of the Sea* | *Law and Custom of the Sea*, ed. R.G. Marsden, 2 vols (Navy Records Society, London, 1915–16) |
| Law Rec | Law Recorder. Ireland. 1827–36 |
| LR Ir | Law Reports. Ireland. 1878–93 |
| LT(NS) | Law Times (New Series) |
| *Liber munerum* | *Liber numerum publicorum Hiberniae*, ed. R. Lascelles (London, 1830) |
| *Life of Jenkins* | *The Life of Leoline Jenkins*, ed. W. Wynne, 2 vols (London, 1724) |
| *Lords' jn* | *Journal of the House of Lords of the Kingdom of Ireland* (8 vols, Dublin, 1782–1800) |
| McGill | McGill University Library |
| Mer | Merivale's reports. Chancery. 1815–17 |
| Mod | Modern reports. 1660–1755 |
| NAI | National Archives of Ireland |
| NAS | National Archives of Scotland |
| *NILQ* | *Northern Ireland Legal Quarterly* |
| *Ormonde Calendar* | *Calendar of the Manuscripts of the Marquis of Ormonde, K.P., preserved at Kilkenny Castle. New series*, ed. Caesar Litton Falkiner and F. Elrington Ball, 8 vols (HMC, London, 1902–20) |
| Owen | Owen's reports. Common Pleas. 1586–96 |
| P | Probate, Divorce and Admiralty, second series. 1891–1971 |
| Park | Parker's reports. Court of Exchequer. Revenue. 1743–67 |
| *Petty–Southwell Corr.* | *The Petty–Southwell Correspondence, 1676–1687*, ed. Marquis of Lansdowne (London, 1928) |
| PRONI | Public Records Office of Northern Ireland |
| Raym. | Raymond's reports. King's Bench and Common Pleas. 1695–1732 |
| RCB | Representative Church Body Ireland Library Archives |
| RIA | Royal Irish Academy |
| Rowe | Richard Rowe's reports. King's Bench. Ireland. 1799–1823 |
| *Rules for the adjudication of prizes 1665* | 'Rules for the Admiralty Court in the adjudication of prizes, 1665', in *Law and Custom of the Sea*, ed. M.G. Marsden (Navy Records Society, London, 1916) |
| *Rycaut's Memoranda* | 'Sir Paul Rycaut's Memoranda and Letters from Ireland, 1686–87', ed. P. Melvin, *Analecta Hibernica*, 27 (1972), 123 |
| Salk | Salkeld reports. 1689–1714 |

| | |
|---|---|
| *Select Committee* | *Report of the Select Committee appointed to take into consideration the Eighteenth Report of the Commissioners of Judicial Inquiry in Ireland, together with the depositions forwarded to those Commissioners by Sir Jonah Barrington, judge of the High Court of Admiralty in Ireland, and other papers connected with the conduct of Sir Jonah Barrington in the discharge of his judicial functions* (HC 1829 (293) iv. 1). |
| Show KB | Shower's reports. King's Bench. 1680–94 |
| Sp Ecc & Ad | Thomas Spinks' reports. Ecclesiastical and Admiralty. 1853–56 |
| *Statement by registrar* | *Statement by Registrar of High Court of Admiralty of England showing progress of Court, 1840–67; Memorandum on Jurisdiction and Practice* (HC 1867 (375) lvii) |
| *Strafford Letters* | *Letters and Dispatches of Thomas Earl of Strafforde*, ed. W. Knowler, 2 vols (London, 1739) |
| Swab | Swabey reports. Admiralty. 1855–59 |
| 'The Irish Admiralty' | Appleby J. & O'Dowd, M., 'The Irish Admiralty: its organisation and development, *c.*1570–1640', *Irish Historical Studies*, 24 (1985), 209 |
| TNA (PRO) | The National Archives, Public Records Office (England) |
| *Volley of Execrations* | *The letters and papers of John FitzGibbon, earl of Clare 1772–1802*, ed. D.A. Fleming and A.P.W. Malcomson (Dublin, 2005) |
| W Rob | William Robinson's reports. Admiralty. 1838–50 |

# Acknowledgments

Much of the research, on which this book was eventually based, was carried out during a year of leave, as a Senior Research Scholar, subvented by the Irish Research Council for the Humanities and Social Sciences. It is important to acknowledge the extent to which the support of the IRCHSS enabled the carrying out of this study.

I have been assisted with references provided by: Dr Sonia Anderson, Dr Vandra Costello, Mr Justice Adrian Hardiman, Daire Hogan, Dr James Kelly, Dr Elaine Murphy, Dr Peter Solar and D.E.C. Yale.

Professor Norma Dawson and James McGuire, literary editors of the Irish Legal History Society, gave up a great deal of their time in order to read and correct the manuscript prior to publication. Dr Donal Coffey provided valuable copy-editing assistance.

I owe a great debt of gratitude to W.N. Osborough. An outstanding scholar and stylist, it was he who suggested the topic of a history of the Court of Admiralty of Ireland. He read the text meticulously throughout its development and constantly brought pertinent references to my notice.

The staff of the National Library of Ireland, the Department of Early Printed Books in Trinity College Dublin, and the National Archives of Ireland have always been very helpful. Most of the research for the earlier part of this study was carried out in the National Archives at Kew, and I would like, in particular, to acknowledge my gratitude to the document production staff at the National Archives, one of the best administered institutions that I have encountered.

Help in locating, or in photographing, the images used in the book was provided by Racheal Richardson, Muiris Moynihan, Dr Peter Murray and Joe Woodward. I would also like to thank the anonymous owner of 'Cork Harbour 1738' for permission to use an image of the painting.

This book is dedicated to my daughter, Hope Amelia (Millie).

# Select glossary of admiralty-related legal terminology

advocate: a lawyer who argued suits in the admiralty and ecclesiastical courts.

anchorage: a toll paid for anchoring vessels, which in seventeenth- and early eighteenth-century Ireland was payable to the admiralty marshal. In return for receiving the toll, the admiralty marshal was required to maintain buoys and marks for the navigational safety of the port. In 1753 the Irish Court of Common Pleas held that the collection of the toll by the Admiralty in Dublin was illegal.

ballastage: a toll paid to the Admiralty by ships for the privilege of taking ballast. In Ireland ballastage was collected by the admiralty marshal. The Admiralty's right to ballastage in the port of Dublin port was superseded by the Dublin Ballast Act 1707.

bottomry: a transaction in which a ship master in a foreign port, in need of supplies or repairs in order to complete the journey, pledged the vessel as security for credit. Where the ship master defaulted on the terms of the bottomry bond (which usually involved a high rate of interest) the unpaid creditor could have the vessel seized by a court of admiralty situated in the country to which the vessel had returned.

civilian: a practitioner expert in the specialist (civil) law administered by the admiralty or ecclesiastical courts.

droits: perquisites entrusted to the lord admiral, such as wreck, royal fish, flotsam, jetsam, lagan, and pirates' goods. Courts of admiralty determined disputes relating to admiralty droits.

ferriage: the entitlement to regulate, and license, the provision of ferry services. In the early seventeenth century the Admiralty claimed the right of ferriage over maritime waters.

flotsam: goods thrown overboard in order to save a ship in danger and subsequently found at sea; a type of admiralty perquisite.

impugnant: the respondent in an admiralty or ecclesiastical suit.

*in rem*: the admiralty process under which the victim of a maritime wrong may have the vessel connected to the wrong, arrested and sold. This entitlement to take, and sell, the vessel *in specie* is particularly effective where the wrongdoer himself does not have sufficient assets to satisfy the claim, or has left the jurisdiction.

instance: the instance side of the court of admiralty was concerned with private injuries occurring at sea (such as a collision) or breaches of a maritime contract (such as a wages' contracts or bottomry bonds). The term is used in contrast to the other side of the court's business: prize.

jetsam: goods found floating on water; a type of admiralty perquisite.

lagan: goods tied to a float or buoy found on the sea; a type of admiralty perquisite.

letter of marque: a commission granted by the Crown authorizing the seizure of vessels or goods belonging to a hostile state, and immunizing the holder from prosecution for the seizure. The holder of a letter of marque was known as a privateer. Letters of marque were issued by the English Court of Admiralty; the Irish court was never authorized to issue letters of marque.

libel: the document instituting an admiralty suit and containing the promovent's allegations.

material-men: shipwrights who built or repaired vessels. According to admiralty legal theory, failure to pay for the repairs, or the supply of equipment, rendered the vessel amenable to arrest and adjudication by the Court of Admiralty. However, the courts of common law disputed the court's entitlement to hear material-men suits on the ground that such contracts were negotiated on land (and were, therefore, outside the jurisdiction of the Admiralty Court).

privateer: the holder of a letter of marque authorized to undertake the capture of enemy shipping.

prize: enemy vessels or goods, seized at sea during time of war by a legally authorized party. The sentence of a court of prize was necessary to give the captor title to the enemy vessel or goods. The issue of whether the Irish Court of Admiralty was authorized to act as a prize court was a constant subject of controversy in the seventeenth and eighteenth centuries. The conventional view was that a court of admiralty was only entitled to exercise prize jurisdiction where it had obtained a commission from the Crown entitling it to act in prize cases. Such prize commissions were only rarely granted to the Irish court.

proctor: a lawyer who managed suits in the admiralty and ecclesiastical courts.

prohibition: a writ prohibiting an inferior court, or institution, from exceeding its jurisdiction. The application for a prohibition was grounded upon a suggestion (or statement of grounds). The writ was most commonly issued against the Court of Admiralty by the Court of King's Bench (and sometimes, also, by the Court of Exchequer). A writ of prohibition could be lifted, and the suit returned to the Court of Admiralty, by a writ of consultation.

promovent: the promoter of an admiralty suit.

*quo warranto*: an action by which a person or institution holding an office or privilege was required to demonstrate the legality of the exercise by him of the contested privilege. In the seventeenth century the action was used to test the claims of corporations or landowners who claimed the right to exercise admiralty functions.

replevin: a remedy under which goods which had been seized by another could be re-delivered to the original possessor. In the seventeenth and eighteenth centuries it was widely used in Ireland by the owners of vessels, which had been arrested by a court of admiralty, to obtain re-delivery of the vessel. The party replevying was required to give security binding him to bring a legal action to establish his right to the goods which he had re-seized. Replevin was, along with prohibition, a common method of frustrating the processes of the Court of Admiralty.

reprisal: a licence authorising a subject who had suffered loss through the acts of the subjects to obtain reparation by capturing enemy shipping. The institution was becoming obsolete by the seventeenth century.

royal fish: creatures such as whales, sharks, and porpoises. At common law the right to seize royal fish originally belonged to the Crown; the Crown delegated this entitlement to the admiral, and the right to royal fish became a form of admiralty perquisite.

salvage: compensation paid to persons for voluntarily saving a ship or its cargo from destruction; or compensation for rescuing a vessel seized by an enemy vessel or by pirates. Disputes about the entitlement to, or quantum of, salvage compensation were determined by courts of admiralty.

sentence: the decision of a court of admiralty or ecclesiastical jurisdiction.

CHAPTER ONE

# Establishment, 1575–1660

INSTITUTIONAL HISTORY OF THE IRISH COURT OF
ADMIRALTY, 1575–1660

*The establishment of the Irish Court of Admiralty*

THE MODERN CYCLE OF ADMIRALTY judicature in Ireland began in August 1575 when the lord admiral of England, Edward Clinton, earl of Lincoln, appointed an English civil lawyer, Dr Ambrose Forth, to attend to 'civil and maritime disputes and business' in Ireland.[1] There already was a vice-admiral of Ireland. Gerald Fitzgerald, earl of Kildare, had served as vice-admiral of Ireland since 1564.[2] However, Edward Clinton seems to have decided that it was necessary to expand the operation by appointing a judge. There were a number of reasons why he may have considered that the existing admiralty machinery now required a judicial officer. One may have been the problems encountered in the prosecution of piracy in Ireland. In England the Piracy Act 1536[3] had superseded the old process by which pirates were tried according to civil law and had made piracy triable according to common law; however, the Piracy Act 1536 was not applicable to Ireland. The only alternative, therefore, was to try the case according to the course of the old pre-statutory civil law procedure. But this required a judge acquainted with the arcana of civil law procedure. In 1573 a commission from the Court of Admiralty was directed to the vice-admiral of Ireland, Gerald Fitzgerald, together with 'other whom he shall think meet'[4] to try Scottish pirates according to civil law procedure. Fitzgerald, who had no legal training, would not have been competent to administer a criminal trial conducted according to civil law principles, and the need to have a civil law judge competent to try pirates may have played a part in prompting the decision to establish an admiralty judge in Ireland. Secondly, the machinery for the collection of admiralty revenue in Ireland was incomplete without the presence of an admiralty court. Without an admiralty court there was no means of definitively settling disputes over the right to admiralty perquisites. The Admiralty had become unsettled by coastal landowners in Ireland making

---

1   7 Aug. 1575 (TNA (PRO), HCA 14/15, nos. 200, 201).
2   *Vice-Admirals of the Coast*, ed. J.C. Sainty (List and Index Society, London, 2007), p. 65.
3   28 Hen. VIII, c. 15 (Eng.), 1536.
4   1 June 1573, *Acts of the Privy Council, vol. viii, 1571–1575*, ed. J.R. Dasent (HMSO, 1894), p. 110.

legal claims to maritime wreckage and pirates' goods. A set of instructions directed to the Irish Admiralty in 1573 required the vice-admiral to investigate the claims of 'all gentlemen that shall claim by prerogatives to have all such goods, wrecks or pirates goods as shall come upon their land'.[5] The solution of these disputes necessitated the existence of an admiralty court, one of whose specialist functions was the resolution of competing claims to admiralty droits. Thirdly, the lord admiral may have been motivated by a concern to extend to the Irish maritime industry the much more effective enforcement processes of an admiralty court. A court of admiralty offered the litigant a procedural advantage unobtainable in the courts of common law: a judgment enforcement process which operated *in rem*, enabling judgment to be executed against the vessel of the defaulting party. The absence of a court of admiralty in Ireland meant that the most effective mechanism for ensuring that a vessel owner answered for his maritime wrongs was unavailable in Ireland. It may have been to remedy this comparative disadvantage that Edward Clinton decided to appoint a judge of admiralty for Ireland. Indeed this was the very reason mentioned by Ambrose Forth himself: in correspondence with Dr Julius Caesar in 1591, he recollected how 'my lord admiral … for the ease of the subject [had] his admiralty court established [in Ireland]'.[6]

Forth had been a fellow of Jesus College, Cambridge until 1573, when he swapped academic life for a career as a civil lawyer in Ireland. Forth was well connected at the English Court of Admiralty: his older brother, Robert Forth,[7] was a senior admiralty lawyer, who sometimes sat with David Lewes, the judge of the English High Court of Admiralty, and it is an obvious possibility that Ambrose's older brother may have had a part to play in his appointment as Irish judge. Sir Ambrose Forth[8] served as admiralty judge for thirty-five years, combining his office as admiralty judge with a general civilian practice. There had been significant support for promoting him to the office of master of the rolls in Ireland;[9] but he was overlooked and his practice remained confined to the civil law margins of the judicature; in addition to his post in the Admiralty Court he served as a judge of the Court of Prerogative.[10] Forth was something of a poor mouth;[11] but he did reasonably well out of his various offices, deriving earnings, in addition to those from his judicial posts, from his position as master of chancery, from a salary of £20 'yearly entertainment',[12] and from a grant of lands in Kells, Co. Meath, from

5    *c*.1573 (TNA (PRO), HCA 14/13, f. 141).
6    A. Forth to J. Caesar, 14 July 1591 (BL, Add. MS 12,503, f. 398). See generally, 'The Irish Admiralty'.
7    *Middlesex Pedigrees* (Harleian Society, lxv, 1869), p. 141. G.D. Squibb, *Doctors' Commons* (Oxford, 1977), p. 155.
8    Forth was knighted on 2 Aug. 1604; J.S. Brewer and W. Blunden (eds), *The Carew Manuscripts*, 6 vols (London, 1871), vi, p. 384.
9    Lord deputy to Lord Burghley, 30 Dec. 1592, *Cal. S.P. Ire. 1592–1596*, p. 42.
10   6 Dec. 1617 (TNA (PRO), SP 63/234, f. 130).
11   Writing to Lord Cecil in 1604, he described his address as 'my poor farm house at the Cabra near Dublin', 13 Apr. 1604 (TNA (PRO), SP 63/216, f. 43).
12   6 Dec. 1617 (TNA (PRO), SP 63/234, f. 130).

which he derived a rental income.[13] He almost certainly earned more as master in chancery and as judge of the Prerogative Court than he did as judge of the Court of Admiralty. When in 1610, following the death of Forth, a successor was being sought, the lord deputy described the Court of Admiralty of Ireland as an institution 'in respect the causes are like to be very rare and the benefit thereof little or nothing at all'.[14]

This lack of admiralty business can, in part, be explained by the inability of the court to operate in the principal seaports. Admiralty courts required access to maritime towns, their principal place of business. However, many Irish municipal corporations claimed rights to admiralty jurisdiction under their charters, and refused to recognize Forth's authority.[15] Forth wrote to the lord admiral, Charles Howard, asking him to prompt the lord deputy, Sir John Perrot, to intervene with Dublin Corporation and the other corporations resisting the authority of the court, suggesting that[16] 'the lord deputy's favour from time to time in assistance of your honourable ministers might greatly further the execution of the office, if it might please your honour, in private or by directions from the lords of the Council, to move him thereunto'. Perrot, over-sensitively, interpreted this as an allegation that he had been complicit in undermining the court, and bullied Forth into signing a humiliating public retraction withdrawing any suggestion that Perrot may not have been conscientious in his support of the court and the rights of the lord admiral. Forth supinely denied any suggestion that

> your lordship hath any ways stayed the proceedings of that court ... but contriwise I have found your lordship ... very favourably inclined to myself in private, and greatly countenancing and furthering me in my late travels through the several provinces of Connacht and Munster, and for my better execution of that office ... I must truly further certify that your lordship had by sharp punishment executed my orders against the offenders that had withstood me by fine and imprisonment.[17]

Business was also being diverted from the Irish court by the natural preference of litigants to sue in the better-established English Court of Admiralty. In the 1590s Ambrose Forth made a rather hopeless argument that the English court should cede cases to the Irish court where the litigants were Irish-based. In 1591, he petitioned Sir Julius Caesar on behalf of a Dublin merchant who had been ordered to appear before the court in London, that the trial be transferred to Ireland, the Dublin court being the *forum conveniens*:

---

13  Ibid. Forth's rental income from the lands in Kells was £30 per annum.
14  Lord deputy to the lord admiral, 4 June 1610 (Lambeth, Carew papers, MS 619, f.135).
15  See p. 20, below.
16  A. Forth to C. Howard, 25 Feb. 1586 (TNA (PRO), SP 63/128, f.118).
17  15 Apr. 1587 (TNA (PRO), SP 63/129, f. 96).

it is to be regarded how great the distance of the place is, how chargeable the travail, how poor and without money the whole people of Ireland are, which with other weighty considerations will move you ... [to] release the defendant from his appearance there and commit the plaintiff to pursue the defendant within the kingdom of Ireland.[18]

Although Forth never succeeded in making his court hugely busy, it is to his credit that he instituted both the national Court of Admiralty of Ireland and the Munster Court of Admiralty. He established admiralty law in Ireland, and administered it for over thirty years. He also managed to do so without attracting any of the charges of impropriety or laziness which blemished the reputations of the two men who would succeed him.

### Sir Adam Loftus' first period as judge (1612–19)

The career of Sir Adam Loftus, Sir Ambrose Forth's successor as judge, was divided into two periods. The first was a period of seven years beginning with the taking effect of his appointment by the earl of Nottingham late in 1612. Loftus' first tenure ended when, in 1619, he was dismissed, and Sir Lawrence Parsons replaced him.

Ambrose Forth had died in 1610.[19] In June of that year the chief governor, Sir Arthur Chichester, wrote to the lord admiral, describing the difficulty he had encountered in recruiting a person willing to take on the office:

according to your lord's pleasure on that behalf I have made enquiry and had conference with some that profess the knowledge of the civil law about a person fit to be made a judge of the admiralty here; but in respect the causes are like[ly] to be very rare ... I find no man of part or quality that doth make any accompt of it.[20]

He had, however, found one volunteer for the office: 'only Sir Adam Loftus, who is one of the masters of the chancery, and of the Privy Council here, is not altogether unwilling'. Acting on this recommendation, the earl of Nottingham directed the judge of the English High Court of Admiralty, Richard Trevor, to draw up a commission for Loftus 'a gentleman very well recommended to me by the lord deputy'.[21] Loftus and Forth were well acquainted. The early stage of Loftus' career had overlapped with Forth's: the two men worked together as masters in chancery,[22] and both had been knighted together at the same ceremony. But Loftus was the better-connected, and by the early seventeenth century Loftus' career had overtaken that of Forth, becoming judge of the martial court in 1597, and being appointed to the Privy Council in 1608.

18   A. Forth to J. Caesar, 14 July 1591 (BL, Add. MS 12,503, f. 398).
19   13 Jan 1610. *Alumni Cantabrigienses Part 1*, ed. J. Venn, 4 vols (London, 1922), i, 160.
20   A. Chichester to the earl of Nottingham, 4 June 1610 (Lambeth, Carew papers, MS 619, f. 135).
21   23 July 1612 (TNA (PRO), SP 63/245, f. 177).
22   TNA (PRO), SP 63/218, f. 29.

The court remained out of commission between the death of Forth in 1610 and the arrival of Loftus' warrant of appointment two years later. Eventually, in December 1612 the lord deputy, Sir Arthur Chichester, recorded that 'Mr Ellesworth hath now lastly brought over a commission by which Sir Adam Loftus is authorized to be judge of the Admiralty Court here, which had been without one a long time'.[23]

From the very beginning there were concerns in London about Loftus' commitment to the position. As early as the following year, 1613, the earl of Nottingham had lost patience with Loftus, and had issued a warrant for revocation of his appointment, reciting sarcastically that 'by reason of his many employments in the kingdom [Loftus] can hardly have leisure to attend the place'.[24] Nottingham cooled down and Loftus was continued as judge, but the complaints continued. In 1614, Adam Loftus was censured by the Admiralty for his failure to provide accounts of admiralty cases in Ireland; the lord deputy regretted that Loftus was not able to do Nottingham 'that acceptable and good service which he well can and otherwise effectually accomplish'.[25] In 1619 the duke of Buckingham was appointed to the office of lord admiral. This change of administration seems to have precipitated Loftus' dismissal. In June 1619, within six months of becoming lord admiral, Buckingham had moved against his Irish judge, issuing a warrant rescinding Loftus' appointment. Buckingham replaced Loftus with a man from within his own family circle, Sir Lawrence Parsons.[26]

## Sir Lawrence Parsons (1619–28)

Lawrence Parsons' career as judge of the Court of Admiralty of Ireland[27] was also undistinguished, and it ended in embarrassment. Parsons relied on surrogates to carry out the function on his behalf. The chief governor of Ireland, Viscount Falkland, complained that Parsons 'doth nothing himself in the business' but instead had 'a deputy perform the service for him'.[28] The extent of the instance business transacted by the court during this period continued to be insignificant. In 1629 Adam Loftus estimated the extent of the profit made by the court as

23  A. Chichester to the earl of Nottingham, 24 Dec. 1612, 'Letter Book of Sir Arthur Chichester', *Analecta Hibernica*, 8 (1938), pp 3, 68. William Ellesworth was the marshal of the Irish Court of Admiralty.

24  17 Nov. 1613, (TNA (PRO), HCA 49/106).

25  A. Chichester to the earl of Nottingham, 19 Dec. 1614, 'Letter Book of Sir Arthur Chichester', *Analecta Hibernica*, 8 (1938), p. 175.

26  'Whereas I have bestowed the place of judge of the admiralty in Ireland lately held by Sir Adam Loftus on Lawrence Parsons'. Buckingham to Henry Marten, 27 June 1619 (TNA (PRO), SP 63/245, f. 177). V. Treadwell in *Buckingham and Ireland, 1616–1628* (Dublin, 1998) suggests (at p. 326), that Parsons' jurisdiction was limited to Munster. However, Parsons' patent clearly constituted him 'judge of the Admiralty in Ireland' (TNA (PRO), SP 63/245, f. 177 (27 June 1619)).

27  Warrant for appointment dated 27 June 1619 (TNA (PRO), HCA 25/215).

28  Viscount Falkland to E. Nicholas, 17 May 1627 (TNA (PRO), SP 63/244, f. 285).

between five to ten pounds over the ten-year period during which Parsons served as judge.[29] Parsons' tenure was tainted by two allegations of corruption. In 1626 Parsons was charged with having appropriated admiralty perquistes.[30] The Admiralty in London directed the president of Munster, Sir Edward Villiers to investigate these corruption charges. Villiers' report was one of qualified acquittal only: having 'very punctually examined him' he had established that 'sometimes he might have helped himself to trifles and petty commodities'. However, Parsons had managed to evade the more serious charges: 'if he had done it in things of value and importance he had been so cautious and done it so warily as ('til I see his accounts) I cannot detect him'.[31]

Further serious allegations were made against Parsons the following year. In 1626 an English privateer, Captain Langford, had taken the *Vinecorne*, an alleged Spanish prize into Kinsale. The vice-admiral of Munster (and lord deputy of Ireland), Viscount Falkland, and Parsons had released the captured vessel. They had examined the bills of lading and heard the testimony of 'some Dutch merchants of worth living here' and unable (as they put it) 'to make flies appear camels in the case of the ships'[32] held that the goods were not Spanish prize and discharged the vessels.[33] However, according to some reports, money had changed hands: an admiralty official, Humphrey Jobson, swore an information accusing Sir Lawrence Parsons of having received bribes of between £2,000 and £3,000 from the owners for permitting the release of the vessel.[34]

In 1627, while Parsons was under investigation and out of the way, Loftus had taken control of the court and had unofficially resumed acting as *de facto* judge.[35] Loftus claimed that he had been appointed for life,[36] and that Parsons had no right to act as judge having 'entered upon that right of mine'.[37] The lord deputy, Viscount Falkland (who was also in dispute with Loftus) complained of Loftus'

---

29  A. Loftus to E. Nicholas, 29 Jan. 1629 (TNA (PRO), SP 63/248, f. 65).

30  The charge was investigated in the Star Chamber; he had been 'so censured in the Star Chamber as he is not fit'. E. Villiers to E. Nicholas, 8 Feb. 1626 (TNA (PRO), SP 63/242, f. 80).

31  E. Villiers to E. Nicholas and Buckingham, 27 Apr. 1626 (TNA (PRO), SP 63/242, f. 250).

32  Viscount Falkland to E. Nicholas, 8 Mar. 1627 (TNA (PRO), SP 63/244, f. 118).

33  'Proclamation by the lord deputy of Ireland setting free Henry Duke and his ship, 27 Jan. 1627' (TNA (PRO), SP 63/245, f. 67).

34  23 Apr. 1627 (TNA (PRO), SP 63/244, f. 222). Falkland, in turn, retaliated by committing Jobson to Dublin Castle and trying him at Castle Chamber for 'scandalous words and rotten aspirations'. Viscount Falkland to E. Nicholas, 15 Aug. 1627 (TNA (PRO), SP 63/245, f. 119). The outcome of the prosecution against Jobson cannot be determined.

35  It may be on account of this *de facto* exercise of the office that Loftus was at this period being referred to as 'chief judge of the Admiralty'; Henry Jobson to E. Nicholas, 20 Mar. 1627 (TNA (PRO), SP 63/244, f. 168).

36  The lord admiral's commission of 23 July 1612 appointed Loftus to the office of judge 'during his life' (TNA (PRO), SP 63/245, f. 177); A. Loftus to the lords of the Admiralty, 22 Nov. 1628 (TNA (PRO), SP 63/247, f. 264).

37  A. Loftus to E. Nicholas, 29 Feb. 1629 (TNA (PRO), SP 63/248, f. 65).

bullying Parsons into withdrawing from the court: 'Sir Lawrence Parsons, who is judge admiral of the kingdom under the admiral seal, but for that the lord chancellor had so much taken upon him to be judge, though lately disallowed by my lord and forbidden to exercise it, that Sir Lawrence is fearful to execute it'. Falkland requested the English admiralty official, Sir Edward Nicholas, to do something that may 'give [Parsons] courage to do his duty and make others to take notice of him to obey him'.[38] Loftus' occupation of the office was brought to an end when, as a result of the dispute between him and Falkland, he was summoned to appear in London, where he remained until late in 1628.[39] Meanwhile, in the same year, Parsons died.

Following Parsons' death, Viscount Falkland wrote to Sir Edward Nicholas, pressing him to nominate a replacement. Falkland noted the administrative difficulties caused by the want of an admiralty judge: 'by the decease of Sir Lawrence Parsons (who by patent from the late lord admiral held the office of judge of the Admiralty in this kingdom) the authority of the court … in the province of Munster being suspended, all suits and controversies depending therein are now at a stand'. Falkland, who, of course, disliked Loftus, was determined that Loftus not be re-appointed. Falkland proposed, as an alternative to Loftus, the English civilian Robert Travers. Travers had previously served as surrogate to Parsons, and Falkland recommended Travers as 'the fittest [that] can be appointed, being a man both sufficiently read in the civil law and already practised in the manner of proceedings in that court'.[40] On the other hand, Loftus, who had been apprised of the suggestion that Travers be appointed, was not prepared to give up his struggle to regain the office: 'yet I will defend my right against him though the profit of it exceedeth not an egg, neither is the business so great, or the causes incident to that place so many that one man may … have idle days'.[41]

Loftus succeeded in being re-appointed. Elated, he declared his intention to discharge the function conscientiously, and to restore the court's reputation following the damage done by Parsons' performance:

> It is very true that since Sir Lawrence Parsons first entered upon that right of mine, there hath not been very regular course observed, nor any form used in the proceedings, but all was voluntary depending upon pleasure. I shall use my best industry to rectify what hath been made crooked, and settle things in such good order as heretofore they hath been.[42]

38  Viscount Falkland to E. Nicholas, 17 May 1627 (TNA (PRO), SP 63/244, f. 285).
39  In May 1627 Loftus was called to London in consequence of 'certain differences between him and the lord deputy and the earl of Cork' (Dublin Corporation, Gilbert MS 169/2, ff 125, 193).
40  Viscount Falkland to E. Nicholas, 15 Sept. 1628 (TNA (PRO), SP 63/247, f. 148).
41  'An extract from a letter of the lord chancellor of Ireland, dated at Dublin 22 November 1628' (TNA (PRO), SP 63/247, f. 264).
42  A. Loftus to E. Nicholas, 29 Jan. 1629 (TNA (PRO), SP 63/248, f. 65).

*The Court of Admiralty, 1628–38, Loftus' second period*

The lord admiral may have regretted Loftus' re-appointment. Loftus' second period as judge began with a long struggle over his claim to exercise the power of appointment of admiralty marshal. In 1630 an English Admiralty official, Robert Smith,[43] who would turn out to be a very significant irritant to Loftus, arrived in Ireland. Sir Edward Nicholas, the secretary to the Admiralty, was a first-class administrator who had taken a very active interest in ensuring the full account-ability of the Irish admiralty. In the early 1630s Nicolas intensified this supervision by appointing Robert Smith, as his eyes and ears in Ireland. Smith, in turn, by reason of his closeness to Nicholas, was in a position to displace his Irish rivals as the principal beneficiary of admiralty patronage. In 1633, following the death of the marshal, William Ellesworth,[44] Smith was appointed by the lord admiral to fill the vacancy.[45] In the meantime, Loftus had made his own appointment to the office: a Dublin official named Salmon. Loftus refused to hand over the warrant of appointment and documentation relating to the perquisites of the office. The point of this struggle was less about the office of marshal and more about the ancillary office conventionally attached to that of marshal – the waterbailiff. The office of waterbailiff, with its entitlement to fees for levying the admiralty custom duties of anchorage and ballastage, was easily the most profitable of all of the admiralty offices. Smith petitioned the lords of the Admiralty complaining that he had been unable to 'obtain a sight and copy of the said Ellesworth's patent and such other writings, articles and orders as might conduce to the due performance of the office'. Ellesworth's widow had 'transferred the said writings into the hands of the lord chancellor of Ireland, who is judge of the Admiralty in that kingdom'.[46] As a result, he had been 'yet debarred thereof and the office executed by one Salmon by [Loftus'] appointment'.

The struggle to make Loftus comply lasted for eighteen months. In August 1633 the Admiralty directed the lord chancellor to hand over Ellesworth's patent and papers, to withdraw the office from Salmon, and to pay back all the profits that Salmon had earned. Smith reported that Loftus refused to comply with the Admiralty's directions, asserting his entitlement to make the appointment of marshal.[47] It was pointed out to Loftus that the Admiralty was doing no more than

---

43  In 1633 the Privy Council of England referred to Smith's 'good service and long attendance upon the affairs of the Admiralty and navy here'; English Privy Council to Loftus, 7 Aug. 1633 (TNA (PRO), SP 63/254, f. 100).

44  Ellesworth's warrant of appointment was dated 8 Feb. 1612/3 (TNA (PRO), HCA 49/106).

45  Warrant of appointment dated 1 June 1633 (TNA (PRO), HCA 25/215).

46  Petition of Robert Smith, 29 July 1633 (TNA (PRO), SP 63/254, f. 93).

47  R. Smith to the commissioners of Admiralty, Nov. 1633 (TNA (PRO), SP 63/254, f. 200). Smith claimed that the lord chancellor upon 'receipt of your lordships' said letters he himself had bestowed the office on one Salmon … by his patent of judge'. Smith added that '[Loftus] had neither warrant nor power to do, and so had not only encroached upon your lordship's place, and thereby created a precedent very prejudicial to the office of lord admiral which is now in your lordships, but frustrated your petitioner of the reward intended him …'

exerting power which it exercised over all of its judges, including the judge of the English court: 'we presume your lordship will not insist to some authority to do more than the judge of the admiralty here, under whom your lordship's place of judge of the admiralty there is subordinate, hath power to grant'.⁴⁸ Loftus counter-argued that Ellesworth 'being a person of an indigent estate [who had] spent much in this [*quo warranto*] suit' against Dublin,⁴⁹ was due compensation. He pointed out that, under the new arrangement with Salmon, it was envisaged that a portion of the fees would be used to compensate Ellesworth's family. He repeated his argument that the disposal of junior court offices belonged to him as the judge of the Admiralty Court in Ireland: 'the gift of all such offices as are necessary and subordinate unto this place do of right appertain to my nomination'.⁵⁰

With Loftus continuing to be impossible, the Admiralty, in July 1634, was forced to seek the intervention of the new lord deputy, the formidable Thomas Wentworth 'for it hath been always the wisdom of former times ... that the rules and government of the admiralty there, and the officers of the same, be kept altogether subordinate and conformable to the government and orders of the Admiralty here'.⁵¹ Loftus and Wentworth were, at that point, personally close. Smith reported that, when he had looked for the lord deputy, he had discovered that he was staying at Loftus' country retreat and that 'the lord deputy shows more respect in this kind to the lord chancellor than he does to any other noble man in the kingdom',⁵² and repeated rumours that 'there is a match concluding between Sir George Wentworth and the lord chancellor's daughter'. Wentworth, at first, interceded with the Admiralty on Loftus' behalf, observing that he found 'his lordship very sensible and indeed afflicted under the apprehension of your lordships displeasure'. He pointed out that the office of lord chancellor was relatively underpaid, and that Loftus had a legitimate claim to the more valuable admiralty offices.⁵³ The Admiralty, however, renewed their instruction on 4 November, and, this time Wentworth was more forceful, placing Smith in the office of waterbailiff and requiring Salmon to account for the profits he had received in the interval.⁵⁴

Loftus had confirmed his reputation as a difficult and, indeed, venal appointee. In addition to the trouble over the waterbailiff, a catalogue of adverse reports had built up. Loftus was reported as having refused to observe on 'slender pretences' a commission from the judge of the English Court of Admiralty, Sir Henry Marten, to restore to its owners a Dutch vessel, the *St Jacob*, which had been

---

48  Irish committee of the Privy Council to Loftus, 21 Dec. 1633 (TNA (PRO), SP 63/254, f. 202).
49  See p. 24 below.
50  A. Loftus to the commissioners of Admiralty, 18 Aug. 1634 (TNA (PRO), SP 63/254, f. 353).
51  Commissioners of Admiralty to T. Wentworth 12 July 1634 (TNA (PRO), SP 16/264, f. 41a).
52  3 Sept. 1634 (TNA (PRO), SP 63/254, f. 429).
53  T. Wentworth to the commissioners of Admiralty, 26 Aug. 1634 (TNA (PRO), SP 63/254, f. 374).
54  T. Wentworth to the commissioners of Admiralty, 22 Dec. 1634 (TNA (PRO), SP 63/254, f. 503; SP 63/254, f. 359).

detained on suspicion of piracy in Waterford.[55] The intervention of the Privy
Council was required in order to force Loftus to comply.[56] In 1630 a complaint was
made that Loftus was hearing a suit about the wrongful dispossession of a vessel
which had already been decided against the promovent by the Court of Admiralty
in London.[57] In 1631 Loftus issued a commission to the marshal and five others
for the disposal of a vessel seized in Galway. The admiralty marshal, William
Ellesworth, who executed the sale, was overheard saying that he must 'have the
Indian hides for the lord chancellor to make bellows for his iron works'.[58] Further,
disquiet was caused in London when it was discovered that Loftus was, in addition
to his office as judge, acting (and receiving profits) as vice-admiral of Leinster. The
Admiralty sought proof that he had been properly appointed to this administrative
vice-admiralty post, pointing out that it was unlikely that he would have been
appointed 'forasmuch as the said places are not compatible'. Loftus made no
reply.[59] In 1635 the Admiralty acceded to Loftus' request that his son Robert be
made vice-admiral of Leinster. During the meeting Sir Edward Nicholas, who was
well apprised of Loftus' activities, interlineated upon his papers: 'the lord
chancellor [Loftus] has not deserved so much respect from the lords'.[60]

The Admiralty was not alone in being dissatisfied with Loftus' performance.
Officials close to the king shared this perception. In 1628 Loftus had begun
entrusting the office of judge to a surrogate, the English civilian, Dr Alan Cooke
(known, apparently, by the nickname 'Alan Pouke').[61] In 1633 Charles I's secretary
of state, Sir John Coke, wrote to Wentworth commending Alan Cooke as a first-rate
civilian 'not inferior to any in that kingdom in his profession of the civil law' and
suggesting that Loftus be replaced by Cooke. Alan Cooke was now surrogate judge
of the court, 'and in that place (as I hear) hath done his majesty special service'.[62]
Coke hinted that it would be in the public interest if Wentworth was to take control
of the situation and secure Cooke's promotion to the position of judge:

55  'The humble petition of John Williamson', 4 Mar. 1634 (TNA (PRO), SP 16/262, ff 31, 36).
56  Privy Council to A. Loftus, 4 Mar. 1634 (TNA (PRO), SP 16/262, f. 36).
57  'The humble petition of Valentine Payne', 30 June 1630 (TNA (PRO), SP 16/169, f. 115).
58  Deposition of Peter St George, 18 Mar. 1636, *Court of Admiralty Depositions*, p. 244.
59  Commissioners of Admiralty to T. Wentworth, 4 Nov. 1634 (TNA (PRO), SP 16/264, f. 30).
60  4 Apr. 1635 (TNA (PRO), SP 16/286, f. 57).
61  Petition of Alan Cooke, 7 Mar. 1636 (TNA (PRO), SP 63/255, f. 199) referred to the fact that
    Cooke 'for eight [?] years past has executed the place of judicature of the admiralty of Ireland'.
    Cooke was referred to as surrogate to Adam Loftus in a document relating to an appeal to the
    English Court of Admiralty (TCD, MS 735, f. 56). The document is undated, but (since it refers
    to Northumberland as the lord admiral) it must have been drafted post-1636. By the late 1630s
    Alan Cooke shared the office of surrogate judge of the Court of Admiralty with William Hilton
    (*Cal. anc. rec. Dub.*, iii, p. 349). Alan Cooke was constituted a master in chancery in 1636: *Liber
    Munerum*, ii, p. 21.
62  10 July 1633, *Strafford Letters*, p. 92.

And though he be employed but as deputy to the lord chancellor, yet when you thoroughly consider the nature and extent of that place in the relation it hath both to strangers and to us, I suppose you shall hold it fit, that both the place and person shall depend more on the king's vice-regent than any other.

In 1638 Loftus was dismissed from the office of lord chancellor, imprisoned, and finally left for England. It was in this year that Loftus' association with the Court of Admiralty finally ended. Once Loftus left, the court fell into abeyance. In 1670 the duke of York described the court as having ceased operations in 1640.[63] In the 1640s the provincial Vice-Admiralty Courts of Leinster and Munster displaced the central Court of Admiralty of Ireland as the active admiralty judicature in Ireland. In 1642 the act book of the Court of Admiralty in London recorded two appeals from the provincial Court of Admiralty of Leinster.[64] There were none from the now defunct national court.

### The constitutional character of the Irish Court of Admiralty in the early Stuart period

From its foundation in 1575 until 1783 the Irish Court of Admiralty was the constitutional subordinate of the English High Court of Admiralty. This constitutional inferiority had two important consequences. First, the English court manifested its constitutional dominance by hearing appeals from Ireland.[65] Second, the English court was able to operate concurrently with the Irish court in Ireland. In 1612 a commission issued from the court in England to Edward Bradstone to enquire into a wreck which had been washed up off the Irish coast.[66] In 1634 the *Dolphin* of Southampton, which was docked at Kinsale, was arrested and appraised by virtue of a warrant from the English High Court of Admiralty.[67] In 1640 a bailiff nominated by the English court, John Cornish, related how he had been assisted by Dr Alan Cooke in executing a warrant issued by the English High Court of Admiralty for the arrest of a Wexford merchant, John Devonrax, in Ireland.[68]

However, this exercise by the English court of concurrent jurisdiction in Ireland was a cause of tension. In 1614 the lord deputy, Chichester, reported with some sympathy the complaint of Sir Adam Loftus that 'causes have been perforce withdrawn again continually out of his hands and jurisdiction, by virtue of such commissions and directions as have been sent unto him out of England, from time

63  TNA (PRO), ADM 2/1,755, f. 2.
64  *Thompson v. Lissett* (TNA (PRO), HCA 3/40, f. 670 (16 Aug. 1642)); *Re Thomas Watmouth* (TNA (PRO), HCA 3/40, f. 693 (18 Oct. 1642)).
65  *Croney v. Nugent*, 8 Nov. 1639 (TNA (PRO), HCA 3/37, f. 426v). See the cases cited at fn. 64 above.
66  Commission dated 12 June 1612 (TNA (PRO), HCA, 14/41, f. 145).
67  *Court of Admiralty Depositions*, pp 242–3.      68  Ibid., p. 282.

to time, in bar of his further proceedings in them'.[69] In the early 1630s the Admiralty insisted to Loftus that he was the constitutional subordinate of the judge of the English High Court of Admiralty.[70] In 1634 the lords of the Admiralty expressed surprise at the failure by Loftus to co-operate in the execution of a commission of restitution issued by the English Court of Admiralty, a tribunal to which 'the officers and jurisdiction of the Admiralty [of Ireland] are subordinate'.[71]

*Irish admiralty courts and the civil wars, 1641–53*

In October 1641 a Catholic uprising broke out in Ulster and spread rapidly. There followed eleven years, between 1641 and 1652, in which political power in Ireland was divided between the three participants in the Irish civil war: the Confederate Catholics, the Royalists under the marquess of Ormond, and the English parliamentary army. Each of these three forces had their own admiralty organization: the courts of admiralty originally established by the king's lord admiral were Royalist; the Confederates established a separate system of admiralty courts; later, the Parliamentary forces instituted their own admiralty judicature.

Dublin remained in Royalist hands until June 1647. Although the national Court of Admiralty of Ireland was in abeyance since 1640, the Admiralty Court of Leinster continued to function in Dublin. *Macredie v. Staples*,[72] a salvage case heard by the Leinster court in February 1647, provides a glimpse of the routine instance work being undertaken by that court during the late 1640s. Macredie had freighted a lighter called the *Speedwell* to transport coal from the *Fortune* of Dartmouth, then lying at Poolbeg, to the quay of Dublin port. On arriving, Macredie deposed, 'the said vessel was split to pieces' and as Macredie and his gabbard made to turn back 'the master and company of the said vessel the *Fortune* called the said Macredie, and his company in the said gabbard, and desired them to stay to help them to save [the cargo] … and to take the same aboard the said gabbard and to carry the same to the quay, and he should be paid his freight for the said voyage'. The libel (carefully inserting the recital essential to ensure that the court could not be deprived of jurisdiction by prohibition from the King's Bench)[73] alleged that this promise had been given *super altum mare*. The judge, William Hilton, decreed a sentence in favour of Macredie, directing the defendant to pay him 16s. 6d. The Leinster court was also undertaking that staple of admiralty court business – wages cases. In December 1643 the master and crew of the naval vessel, the *George* of Bristol, petitioned Dr Cooke in the provincial Court

---

69   A. Chichester to the earl of Nottingham, 19 Dec. 1614, 'Chichester letter-book', ed. R. Dudley Edwards, *Analecta Hibernica*, 8 (1938), p. 175.

70   Irish Committee of the Privy Council to Loftus, 21 Dec. 1633 (TNA (PRO), SP 63/254, f. 202).

71   Privy Council to A. Loftus, 4 Mar. 1634 (TNA (PRO), SP 16/262, f. 36). In 1637 a warrant was issued from the English High Court of Admiralty to arrest one William Hunt in County Cork. *Court of Admiralty Depositions*, p. 252.

72   Marsh's Library, MS Z.3.2.1(3), ff 4–21.          73  See p. 34 below.

of Leinster 'setting forth how that the said ship was so leaky as that she was not fit for service any longer, and that he and they wanted provision both of meat and money so that they were not any longer able to subsist'.[74] The lords justices intervened, directing the payment of the sailors' wages (together with conduct money for their return to Bristol).[75]

Operating concurrently with the Court of Admiralty of Leinster were two courts attached to the rival factions in the English civil war. The first, a Parliamentary admiralty court, operated in Kinsale from 1645 and was presided over by Robert Travers (who, in the 1620s, had acted as surrogate under Sir Lawrence Parsons). The second was the Confederate Court of Admiralty, which operated between 1642 and 1649, with James Cusack (who had earlier served as an officer to the Commission for Defective Titles) as judge.[76] The Confederate court, which sat at Galway, Wexford, and Waterford, appears to have functioned principally as a prize court, issuing letters of marque, and condemning prize captures.

The question of constitutional reform of the Court of Admiralty in Ireland, and, in particular, the issue of its constitutional subordination to the English court,[77] featured in each of the truces negotiated between the Royalists and the Confederates. In 1646 the articles of peace agreed with the Confederates included a provision which removed the right of the High Court of Admiralty in England to hear appeals from Ireland:[78] 'It is further concluded, accorded, and agreed by, and between, the parties aforesaid, that maritime causes be determined in this kingdom without driving merchants and others to appeal and seek justice elsewhere'. The appeal to the Court of Admiralty of England was to be abolished; instead the 'party grieved is to appeal to his majesty in the Chancery of Ireland'. This Irish sentence was 'to be definitive, and not to be questioned upon any further appeal, except it be in the Parliament of this kingdom if the Parliament be sitting; otherwise not'.[79] The demand was repeated in 1648, in the negotiations leading to the treaty of January 1649, together with the additional demand that there be a separate admiralty of Ireland. Ormond agreed to the demand for reform of the admiralty appeal:

74  *Ormond Calendar* (ii), p. 338.
75  But, alongside the more routine work, like that in the *Macredie* case, the Leinster court in the 1640s was also engaged in less typical functions, including adjudicating on captured Confederate prize vessels. Lords justices of Ireland to E. Nicholas, 13 Mar. 1643 (*Ormond Calendar* (ii), p. 242).
76  TNA (PRO), SP 63/260, f. 310. Cusack had been educated at the Middle Temple. In 1633 he had been made crown attorney to the Commission of Defective Titles. *Register of Admissions to the Middle Temple*, ed. Sturgess, 3 vols (London, 1949), i, p. 109; M. Ó Siochru, *Confederate Ireland, 1642–1649* (Dublin, 1999), p. 257. *Strafford Letters*, i, p. 83.
77  See p. 11 above.          78  Art. 22 (TNA (PRO), SP 63/261, ff 84, 90).
79  J.T. Gilbert, *History of the Irish Confederation and the war in Ireland*, 7 vols (Dublin, 1889), v, p. 300.

we consent that maritime causes may be determined in this kingdom without driving merchants or others to appeal and seek justice elsewhere, and if it shall fall out that there be cause of appeal, the party grieved is to appeal to his majesty in the chancery of Ireland, and the sentence thereupon to be given by the delegates to be definitive and not to be questioned upon any further appeal except it be in the Parliament of this kingdom, if the Parliament shall be then sitting, otherwise not.[80]

The declaration concluded by promising to place this constitutional reform on a statutory basis: 'this to be by Act of Parliament'. It is not easy to identify why the admiralty appeal to England was regarded as such a national grievance, or as a virtual *casus belli*. Appeals to the High Court of Admiralty were not common. The act book of the Court of Admiralty records five Irish appeals to London between 1639 and 1644; none are recorded for the period 1610 to 1639. At any rate, following the victory of the Parliamentarians, the Confederate demand for reform of the admiralty appeal was never implemented.

*Admiralty courts during the Commonwealth, 1653–60*

In 1647 Dublin surrendered to the Parliamentary forces. The Court of Admiralty of Leinster was suppressed. In 1651 the commissioners for the affairs of Ireland directed that admiralty jurisdiction be transferred to the Corporation of Dublin. The commissioners' direction opened with a recital recognizing that 'anciently the mayor and citizens of Dublin have claimed, and used to have cognizance of, all such pleas within the said bay, port and harbour'. It was ordered that 'until the Parliament of the commonwealth of England, or the said commissioners, shall otherwise give order therein' the 'mayor, recorder, aldermen and sheriffs of the city of Dublin, or any three or more of them' were to adjudicate of 'all pleas, debts, contracts, trespasses, batteries, breach of the peace, and all other offences done or committed upon the sea, or between high water and low water mark, and the same to hear and determine according to the law and custom of the sea'.[81]

However, the transfer to the mayor, aldermen, and sheriffs of Dublin was a transitional measure – 'until the Parliament of the commonwealth of England, or the said commissioners, shall otherwise give order therein' – pending the re-constitution of an admiralty court in Ireland. Within three years an admiralty court was once more functioning in Ireland and by 1654 Dr Dudley Loftus was acting as an admiralty judge in Ireland.[82] In 1656 Oliver Cromwell instructed the lord deputy to formally re-establish the Court of Admiralty under the great seal of Ireland.[83] The

---

80  Bodl., Carte MS 23, f. 138.                    81  NLI, MS 11,959, f. 15 (4 Oct. 1651).
82  BL., Add. MS 19,833, f. 4. Loftus was stated to be in receipt of a salary of £100.
83  In recognition of the civilian expertise of masters in chancery it was provided that the court 'in difficult cases was to be assisted by the judges or masters of chancery', 27 Mar. 1656, R. Dunlop, *Ireland under the Commonwealth*, 2 vols (Manchester, 1913), ii, pp 578–82.

Parliamentary Court of Admiralty sat at the King's Inns,[84] and occasionally sat as a divisional court: in 1655 the commissioners ordered that a petition be referred to the Court of Admiralty at Dublin presided over by Sir Gerard Lowther, Justice Donellan and Dudley Loftus.[85] In 1660 the General Convention of Ireland recommended the re-establishment of the system of provincial vice-admiralties.[86] This recommendation was implemented, and the provincial vice-admiralties, with ancillary courts, were re-constituted.

## PROVINCIAL COURTS OF ADMIRALTY IN IRELAND, 1600–45

### *The Court of Admiralty of Munster, 1608–43*

The Court of Admiralty of Munster was the earliest established provincial court of admiralty in Ireland. Henry Gosnold had been a student friend of Sir Francis Bacon while they both attended Gray's Inn, where Gosnold enjoyed a reputation as a wit. He was subsequently elected MP for Clonakilty, and was appointed a justice of the Presidency Court of Munster.[87] Gosnold appears to have been installed as admiralty judge in Munster by the first decade of the seventeenth century; in 1608 the chief baron of the Court of Exchequer in Ireland described Gosnold as 'judge or deputy judge of the Admiralty'.[88] The original constitutional basis of the Court of Admiralty of Munster appears to have been internal within the Irish Admiralty Court. Gosnold was a deputy established by the judge of the Irish Court of Admiralty in Dublin (rather than a judge commissioned by the lord admiral in London). In 1608 the chief baron of the Irish Court of Exchequer, Sir Humphrey Winch, described Gosnold as 'deputy judge of the Admiralty'. That description suggests that Gosnold acted as Forth's 'deputy' in Munster. The constitutional status of the Munster Court of Admiralty was more that of a satellite of the Irish Admiralty Court (rather than a direct English appointment). This was definitively confirmed in the 1630s by the lord deputy, Wentworth: in correspondence 'touching … the Vice-Admiralty of Munster', Wentworth wrote that in Munster 'before my time, and still continues settled therein, my lord chancellor as judge whose substitute is Mr Justice Gosnold'.[89]

---

84 There is a reference to the Court sitting in the King's Inns in the 1650s in *Fleming v. Lynch* (TNA (PRO), HCA 15/13).

85 'Roger Crimble: ordered that the above petition of Roger Crimble be referred to the Court of Admiralty at Dublin viz: Sir Gerard Lowther, Justice Donellan and Doctor Loftus, or any two of them to consider of the allegations … and further to proceed in the case according to law and the rule of the court … 28 June 1655' (NLI, MS 11,959, f. 498).

86 A. Clarke, *Prelude to restoration in Ireland* (Cambridge, 1999), p. 269.

87 L. Jardine and A. Stewart, *Hostage to fortune; the troubled life of Francis Bacon* (New York, 1999), p. 140.

88 Winch CB to Sir Arthur Chichester, 2 Apr. 1608 (TNA (PRO), SP 63/223, f. 150).

89 T. Wentworth to the commissioners of Admiralty, 20 Jan. 1636 (TNA (PRO), SP 63/256, f. 6).

After Lawrence Parsons had replaced Adam Loftus as judge of the Court of Admiralty, the position of Munster admiralty judge was delegated to the Oxford-educated civilian,[90] Robert Travers. In the 1620s Travers was the subject of a number of charges of corruption. The *Greyhound* from the United Provinces, had been seized by Captain Hill and taken into Kinsale as a prize. Travers, 'notwithstanding that he know the said ship and goods to belong to your supplicant, being not enemy with his majesty, did yet for a bribe of £60 give licence under the seal of the admiralty' for the sale of the goods.[91] Very damningly a committee of the Presidency of Munster found that the claim (that Travers had received £60 'as a gratification from the said Captain Hill for permission to make the said sale') to be true.[92] Travers had also been named in a complaint the previous year in which it was alleged that he had corruptly arrested a privateer from Weymouth, which had brought in a valuable Brazilian prize to Youghal; the arrest, it was suggested, was no more than a ruse designed to induce a bribe. Travers, it was alleged, 'wiled to draw some reward from the said factor'.[93] Travers was considered so discredited that in 1626 Sir Edward Villiers, the newly appointed lord president of Munster, was pleading for Gosnold's re-appointment[94] in place of the current, venal incumbent:

> yet still do I hold it necessary that that my lord should be served with better and upright officers than with such a one as now (by Sir Lawrence Parsons' appointment) doth wholly manage causes belonging to the Admiralty, and is such a man that for his misdemeanours had been censured in the Star Chamber, as is much to his lordship's dishonour to have him employed in a place of that trust.[95]

In the early 1630s,[96] following the death of Parsons, and the re-appointment of Adam Loftus, Gosnold resurfaced as judge of the Admiralty Court of Munster.[97] In 1636 the constitutional basis of the Munster Court changed from that of a satellite of the Irish Admiralty Court to one directly established by the lord admiral.[98] This required London to make a new appointment. Though it was

90  Archbishop of Canterbury to T. Wentworth, 29 Dec. 1638 (*Strafford Letters*, ii, p. 265); *Alumni Oxonienses 1500–1714*, ed. J. Foster, 3 vols (London, 1896), iii, p. 1053.
91  10 Jan. 1629 (TNA (PRO), SP 16/132, f. 2).
92  Certificate of lord president of Munster, 10 Jan. 1629 (TNA (PRO), SP 63/248, f. 9).
93  Travers, in his defence, objected that no letter of marque had been granted. 'The Humble Petition of John Hill', 15 Nov. 1628 (TNA (PRO), SP 16/120, f. 104).
94  E. Villiers to E. Nicholas, 8 Feb. 1626 (TNA (PRO), SP 63/242, f. 78).
95  E. Villiers to E. Nicholas, 28 Mar. 1626 (TNA (PRO), SP 63/242, f. 205).
96  Account of the vice-admiral of Munster, 1629–30 (TNA (PRO), HCA, 30/158).
97  TNA (PRO), SP 63/254, f. 214; T. Wentworth to the commissioners of Admiralty, 20 Jan. 1636 (TNA (PRO), SP 63/256, f. 6).
98  T. Wentworth to the commissioners of Admiralty, 20 Jan. 1636 (TNA (PRO), SP 63/256, f. 6).

suggested that the Admiralty secretary, Sir Edward Nicholas, may not have been 'so well satisfied in his abilities and carriage', Gosnold was retained.[99] Gosnold continued to serve into the early 1640s.[100] By the mid-1640s, when areas of Munster fell to the Parliamentary forces, Sir Robert Travers was rehabilitated as judge of the Parliamentary Court of Admiralty in Munster. Travers was back to his old tricks, once more taking an unhealthy interest in prize vessels taken into Munster.[101]

*The Courts of Admiralty of Leinster, Ulster and Connacht, 1635–43*

Prior to 1635 there had existed only one local court of admiralty in Ireland, the one which functioned in Munster. In the mid-1630s vice-admiralty courts were established in the remaining three provinces. In May 1635 the Admiralty had issued a set of 'Rules and Orders' designed to strengthen admiralty jurisdiction throughout England and Ireland.[102] This programme of reform included a scheme for the establishment of vice-admiralty courts. The vice-admirals of each of the provinces were written to and required to establish an instance court in every vice-admiralty. Vice-admirals were instructed to 'keep common courts for matters of justice between party and party'. Where the vice-admiral himself was not expert in law he was to nominate a 'discreet, learned, and experienced man in the civil laws'; alternatively 'for want of a civilian, one learned in the common laws of the realm'.[103] The vice-admiral was also instructed to appoint a registrar as well as 'an honest and sufficient man to be marshal' and to take care that 'courts of enquiry for the affairs of the Admiralty according to … his commission be every half year kept throughout every shire within the limits of his commission, at such convenient times and places'. The 1635 reforms resulted in the establishment of vice-admiralty courts in each of the four provinces. The constitutional basis of these four 'new' vice-admiralty courts was different to that of the pre-1635 Munster Court: the Munster Court had been established by Ambrose Forth as a satellite of the national Court of Admiralty of Ireland, and the judge of the Munster court was answerable to the judge of the Irish Court of Admiralty. Under the new vice-admiralty regime the judge was appointed by, and was answerable to, the lord admiral of England.

William Hilton (who had served as attorney of the province of Connacht, as a judge of the Court of Prerogative and Faculties, and subsequently as a baron of the Court of Exchequer)[104] was nominated local judge for the provinces of Ulster and Connacht.[105] In 1635 the English civilian Alan Cooke had sought 'the place of

---

99 Warrant of appointment dated 8 Oct. 1638 (TNA (PRO), HCA 25/215).

100 Gosnold is referred to as judge in *Battens*[?] *v. Lissett* (TNA (PRO), HCA 3/41, f. 218 (15 May 1643)).

101 *St Peter*, 1645 (TNA (PRO), HCA 13/60).

102 2 May 1635 (TNA (PRO), SP 16/264, f. 123).      103 Ibid.

104 *Cal. S.P. Ire. 1633–1647*, pp 111, 171.

105 G. St George to the commissioners of Admiralty, 30 Sept. 1635 (TNA (PRO), SP 63/255, f. 114); A. Chichester to the commissioners of Admiralty, 4 Oct. 1635 (TNA (PRO), SP 63/255,

judicature under the name of vice-admiral of Leinster it being the place of his abode'.[106] Cooke, who had acted as surrogate to Loftus in the national court, was appointed judge of the Admiralty of Leinster the following year.[107] By the 1640s the judge of Ulster and Connacht, William Hilton, was also acting as deputy judge of the Admiralty Court of Leinster under Dr Cooke. In 1647 Hilton succeeded Cooke as judge of the Leinster court. Hilton, who, by this stage administered admiralty law in three provinces, had become, in effect, the national admiralty judge.[108]

*Appeals from the courts of vice-admiralty*

Sir Leoline Jenkins, in correspondence with the duke of York in 1670, referred to the existence of a local court of appeal from provincial admiralty courts 'during the period of two judges successively the last of whom died about the year 1640'.[109] The court to which Jenkins was referring appears to have been a court of appeal in admiralty cases operating in Dublin, and similar to the court of delegates in ecclesiastical cases.[110] It functioned as an intermediary court of appeal, lying between the provincial vice-admiralty courts and the English court. The local court of appeal in Dublin saved suitors the expense of appeal to England, but it was inconsistent with the theory of the subordination of Irish admiralty courts to the High Court of Admiralty. Henry Gosnold, the judge of the Munster Admiralty Court, queried the wisdom of an Irish tribunal of appeal which avoided the direct supervision exercised by the English Admiralty Court – the effect of an 'appeal from the court of vice-admiralty to the King in chancery [was] to pass by the lord high admiral, as having no power to reform the error in his vice-admirals'.[111] However, this Irish court of admiralty appeal seems to have had a short existence. From the late 1630s onwards, appeals from local provincial courts begun to be taken directly to the High Court of Admiralty in London.[112]

f. 118). His warrant of appointment as judge of Ulster was dated 12 Nov. 1635, and as judge of Connacht was dated 30 Mar. 1636 (TNA (PRO), HCA 25/215).

106  Petition of Alan Cooke, 7 Mar. 1636 (TNA (PRO) SP 63/255, f. 199).

107  Warrant of appointment dated 8 Mar. 1636 (TNA (PRO), HCA 25/215).

108  TNA (PRO), HCA, 3/40, f. 670; TNA (PRO), HCA 3/40, f. 693. Hilton's warrant of appointment was dated 28 May 1647 (TNA (PRO), HCA 49/106).

109  In 1670, as the duke of York set about the reconstitution of the Irish Court of Admiralty, he sought the advice of Sir Leoline Jenkins as to whether there should be a system of appeal from the provincial courts to the court of appeal in Dublin (Jenkins to the duke of York, 23 June 1670, *Life of Jenkins*, ii, p. 675).

110  Appeal by Patrick Marley from decree of Dr Alan Cooke, 29 May 1639 (TCD, MS 735, f. 55).

111  'An answer to Judge Gosnold' (n.d) (Camb., Magdalene, Pepys MS 2,872, f. 212).

112  *Ballese v. Lissett* (TNA (PRO), HCA 3/41, f. 218 (May 1643)); *Thompson v. Lissett* (TNA (PRO), HCA 3/40, f. 670 (16 Aug. 1642)); *Thomas Watmouth* (TNA (PRO), HCA 3/40, f. 693 (18 Oct. 1642)).

REGISTRARS OF IRISH ADMIRALTY COURTS, 1585–1640

The function of registrar was described in the 'Rules and Orders' of 1635 as being to record 'presentments, acts and orders' and to keep books of record.[113] The registrar was also a source of intelligence on admiralty procedure and of scarce books on admiralty law. On the appointment of lord deputy Falkland as vice-admiral of Munster in 1619, the registrar was requested to make available 'a copy of the ordinary course of proceedings in sea causes, either civil or criminal (which last in cases of spoil or depredation is most usual) whereof the registrar of the admiralty do keep books and may be persuaded to yield copies'.[114]

In June 1585 Humphrey Staverton was appointed registrar of the Court of Admiralty of Ireland.[115] John Forth, possibly a relative of the late judge, was referred to as registrar of the court in the 1630s;[116] Forth died in 1636. In 1634 Thomas Wogan acted as registrar when the central Court of Admiralty held a court of enquiry in Ulster.[117] When in the late 1630s the national court was superseded by the Admiralty Court of Leinster, John Dunbarr acted as registrar of that court.[118]

The power of appointment of registrar of the Munster Admiralty Court had 'by ancient custom' been exercised by the provincial vice-admiral; as part of the process of centralization the duke of Buckingham insisted that the power be transferred to London.[119] In 1633 Falkland informed the Admiralty that the office of registrar of Munster was vacant; while acknowledging that constitutionally the right of appointment now rested in London, he reminded the lords of the practice of the Admiralty 'ever admitting of such as by his vice-admirals were recommended', and petitioned them to appoint Henry De Laune as registrar.[120] However, London insisted on exercising this function: in 1637 the Admiralty appointed Hogan Rookwood as registrar of the Munster Court.[121]

Samuel Franklin, who had served as a clerk to the queen's procurator of the Admiralty in England, had appeared in Dublin ('having been called by his friends to live there') and in 1636 was granted the position of registrar of the Leinster Admiralty Court.[122] Franklin's period of service in Ireland was short-lived. Having

113  2 May 1635 (TNA (PRO), SP 16/264, f. 123).

114  'Sir Edward Villiers' queries re Admiralty, 1619', n.d. (TNA (PRO), SP 63/223, f. 125).

115  TNA (PRO), HCA 25/1, Part II, f. 341.

116  15 Aug. 1634 (SP 63/254, f. 367). It was claimed that Loftus had appointed his own registrar in preference to that appointed by the lord admiral. R. Smith to E. Nicholas, 18 Sept. 1634 (TNA (PRO), SP 63/254, f. 446).

117  A. Chichester to the commissioners of Admiralty, 8 Oct. 1634 (TNA (PRO), SP 63/254, f. 458).

118  Warrant of appointment dated 15 Sept. 1638 (TNA (PRO), HCA 25/215).

119  Viscount Falkland to the commissioners of Admiralty, 14 June 1633 (TNA (PRO), SP 63/254, f. 78).

120  'An honest and very capable man', Viscount Falkland to the commissioners of Admiralty, 14 June 1633 (TNA (PRO), SP 63/254, f. 78).

121  Warrant of appointment 7 Jan 1637 (TNA (PRO), HCA 25/215)

122  'Petition of Samuel Franklin', 13 Feb. 1636 (TNA (PRO), SP 63/255, f. 188). Warrant of appointment dated 18 Feb. 1636 (TNA (PRO), HCA 25/215).

filled the office for two years he returned to England to practise as a proctor in the Court of Arches. Alan Cooke made use of John Dunbarr (apparently 'a man most sufficient and fit to be trusted with the place') as registrar in place of Franklin, and, on Cooke's recommendation, Dunbarr was formally appointed.[123]

In 1636 George St George recommended that the office of registrar of the Admiralty Court of Connacht be filled by one Thomas Campion. Campion was appointed but, St George reported, 'having had some occasion to use him, I find him altogether inexperienced', and recommended that the post be transferred to the English civilian Samuel Franklin[124] (who, at that point, also held the office of registrar of Leinster). William Brown was the replacement approved by London.[125]

### RIVALS FOR ADMIRALTY JURISDICTION: THE MUNICIPAL CORPORATIONS

In 1582 the judge of the Irish Admiralty Court, Dr Forth, complained about 'officers of certain corporations who, notwithstanding your Lordship's directions, [are] making their charters like cheveril stretch their grant of an inch to the length of an ell'.[126] Five years later the situation had not improved: in a letter to the lord admiral (Charles Howard), Forth complained that the 'officers within liberties … utterly refuse, either to intromit my ordinary authority or to plead and show their charters touching the admiral jurisdiction'.[127] The assertion of admiralty jurisdiction by municipal corporations was a constant grievance to the Admiralty. The difficulty was that these claims were not always illegitimate; the claims of some of these towns were sustained by royal charters explicitly granting admiralty jurisdiction.

The court's difficulties began in the principal city of the kingdom, Dublin. In 1582 Queen Elizabeth granted to the Corporation of Dublin a revised charter which entitled the mayor to exercise an admiralty jurisdiction between Arklow and the river Nanny in County Meath.[128] The charter emboldened the municipality to engage in a campaign throughout the 1580s to expel the court from Dublin. In 1586 a pirate called Edmond Wycombe, and two Dublin merchants who had traded with the pirate, had been committed to Dublin Castle by the Admiralty judge Dr Forth. Forth's order was countermanded and the prisoners discharged on the

---

123  A. Cooke to the duke of Northumberland, 23 Aug. 1638 (Alnwick Castle, Northumberland MS, vol. 14, f. 170). Dunbarr was appointed on 15 Sept. 1638 (TNA (PRO), HCA 25/215).

124  G. St George to the lords of the Admiralty, 20 May 1636 (TNA (PRO), SP 63/255, f. 325). 'Petition of Franklin', June 1636 (TNA (PRO), SP 63/255, f. 356). Appointment dated 25 June 1636 (TNA (PRO), HCA 25/215). In 1635, Henry le Squire was nominated registrar to the judge of the new Court of Admiralty of Ulster. The warrant of appointment is dated 1 Feb. 1639/40 (TNA (PRO), HCA 25/215).

125  Warrant of appointment dated 1 Feb. 1639/40 (PRO, HCA 25/215).

126  A. Forth to J. Perrot, 15 Apr. 1587 (TNA (PRO), SP 63/129, no. 41).

127  Ibid.                                    128  *Cal. anc. rec. Dub.*, i, pp 36, 37.

authority of the mayor of Dublin, Richard Rounsell.[129] A Dublin merchant, Sylvester Thunder, had been the victim of a more serious abuse by the Dublin administration. Thunder had obtained a warrant from Dr Forth under the seal of the Court of Admiralty for the seizure of the goods of two French merchants, who, it was alleged, were victualling a piracy enterprise in La Rochelle which had attacked his vessel. For the offence of using the process of the Irish Admiralty Court '[Thunder]had been committed to the Castle in Dublin by extraordinary means wrought by one Foster, alderman of Dublin, where he yet remain[ed] prisoner with irons upon him; without any proceedings in the Admiralty Court or any other court'.[130] At the same time, Dublin had established its own court of admiralty. In 1587 the corporation retained a civilian, Oliver Eustace (a 'student in the cyvall law') and charged him with administering the Corporation Admiralty Court which he was to 'set at good store' in return for the profits made by the court from fees, and a salary of £4 per annum.[131]

Under the charter granted by Elizabeth in 1578,[132] the mayor of Galway was constituted admiral 'within the port, bay, town, liberties, franchises, and suburbs of Galway aforesaid, and within and over the islands of Aran, and from the said islands to Galway aforesaid on each side of the water there'. The mayor was given jurisdiction to 'inquire, hear, determine, do, exercise and execute', while the lord admiral was expressly withdrawn from Galway: 'no admiral of us, our heirs or successors, shall have, or exercise, any power, authority or jurisdiction of admiral within the port, bay, liberty … franchises, suburbs, islands and places aforesaid'. The mayor was to receive for the use of the town 'all and singular wrecks of the sea, forfeitures, fines, amerciaments, redemptions, issues, commodities, advantages, emoluments and profits whatsoever … by reason of his admiralty or admiral's jurisdiction'. Galway appears to have taken the view, during the Spanish war, that the charter entitled it to adjudicate prize captures. In 1587 Forth requested the intervention of the lord admiral against the Corporation of Galway asking it 'to suffer neither the Portugal ship, nor any of the goods lately brought hither in way of prize by Captain Edward Banks' to be made amenable to process from the corporation.[133]

Galway reasserted its claim to process prize claims during the wars with France and Spain in the late 1620s. In 1627 George St George, the vice-admiral of Connacht, reported that he had not been able to execute a commission of appraisement and inventory of a French prize, the *Hope of Rouen*. The Galway merchants, whom he had appointed to assist him in appraising the prize, had not only refused to co-operate

129   A. Forth to C. Howard, 25 Feb. 1587 (TNA (PRO), SP 63/128, f. 118).
130   Petition of Sylvester Thunder addressed to Julius Caesar, n.d. (BL, Add. MS 12,503, f. 402).
131   *Cal. anc. rec. Dub.*, ii, pp 206–7.
132   J. Hardiman, *The history of the town of Galway* (Dublin, 1820), appendix, p. vi.
133   A. Forth to J. Perrot, 15 Apr. 1587 (TNA (PRO), SP 63/129, f. 96).

but also sent me into the town house before the mayor, and the rest of the corporation, to let me know that by a general clause of their charter they had full jurisdiction of admiralty granted to them and they acknowledge no admiral nor any power from that court but from the king himself, and although I told them I had a commission out of that court yet they ... told me that what that court had done was *coram non judice*.[134]

St George was forced to obtain the intervention of the lord deputy, and the prize was handed over to the Court of Admiralty. However, early the following year the corporation was granted a writ of prohibition from the King's Bench restraining the Admiralty Court from hearing the prize claim. St George reported that, having initially given signs of compliance, the corporation had 'flown from this course and have brought prohibition out of the King's Bench to stay the proceeding'.[135] St George warned that 'if this may pass there is no business for the jurisdiction of the Court of Admiralty' and advised that the lord admiral write to the chief justice: 'I believe he will soon recall his prohibition'. St George also mentioned to Edward Nicholas that the recorder of Galway, Henry Lynch, was at court seeking a renewal of the city's charter, and suggested that it would be an appropriate time to ensure that the admiralty portion of the charter was omitted.

Galway's defiance continued into the 1630s. In 1635 the English admiralty envoy, Robert Smyth, described how the mayor of Galway had prevented the admiralty marshal from executing the process of the English Admiralty Court within the town,[136] at first, he said, 'I was courteously used by the mayor, and by the recorder's advice, mr. mayor gave obedience to my grant and lord deputy's command, whereupon I made a deputy there with the consent of the vice-admiral, and acquainted the mayor therewith who seemed well pleased'. However, the corporation reverted to its previous position of hostility: 'after I was gone, there were several warrants issued out of the Admiralty of England to arrest a vessel, which lay there about four miles off Galway, called the *John and Dorothy* of London ... but the mayor, understanding of it ... would not permit my deputy to execute them but by his waterbailiff'.

The important maritime town of Wexford was also asserting its own admiralty pretensions. Theories as to the legal basis of the Wexford claim varied. On one view, it had acquired title by prescription. In the Chancery proceedings, *Furlong v. Codd* in 1591, the mayor of Wexford sought the restitution of a wreck. The mayor claimed that he was local admiral by custom, his chancery bill asserting that[137] 'he is admiral and his predecessors, sovereigns of the said town, have been time out of mind admirals of the sea within the franchises of the sea within the said town of

---

134   G. St George to E. Nicholas, 15 Nov. 1627 (TNA (PRO), SP 63/245, f. 223). E. Nicholas to G. St George, 9 Oct. 1627 (TNA (PRO), SP 14/215, f. 53).

135   G. St George to E. Nicholas, 18 Feb. 1628 (TNA (PRO), SP 63/246, f. 46).

136   R. Smyth to E. Nicholas, 15 Dec. 1635 (TNA (PRO), SP 63/255, f. 148).

137   NAI, Chancery bills, N 90.

Wexford'. He claimed that 'by virtue of his said office, time out of mind' he was entitled to 'all goods wrecked upon the sea and … wreck cast upon the land by the sea side'. The alternative theory was that the Corporation of Wexford had acquired title by virtue of a medieval charter. Dr Cooke, the surrogate judge of the Irish Court of Admiralty in the 1630s, reported that 'the town of Wexford challenge to be admirals, and thereby to have right unto wrecks, by a patent or grant made unto them from [lord Adomar de Valentia, earl of Valencia] sometime governor of that county'.[138]

The Corporation of Limerick was also truculent. In 1632 the vice-admiral of Munster, Viscount Falkland, was informed by his deputy that his attempt to take possession of two whales had 'met with such opposition' from the mayor of Limerick 'laying claim to them by virtue of his patents from his majesty, that I could not have the tenth part'.[139] Again, the resistance of the mayor of Limerick had a plausible legal foundation: the charter which had been granted to the corporation in 1609 by James I gave it the right to all royal fish as well as the powers of the Court of Admiralty of England and Ireland.[140] In 1638 the admiralty marshal complained that the mayor and bailiffs of Youghal 'who will not permit me to put in execution my patent notwithstanding I have my lord deputy's patent to that purpose, they pretending themselves to be admirals by grant from King Edward the fourth'.[141] The Corporation of Cork also asserted charter-based claims to an admiralty jurisdiction. In 1500 the charter of Henry VII had entrusted authority over Cork harbour in the Corporation of Cork.[142] This grant seems to have provided the legal basis of Cork's assertion of admiralty jurisdiction. In 1627 the corporation declared that 'by the charters of our sovereign lord the king, granted to this corporation, the mayor hath been always admiral within the harbour of Cork and the creeks and branches thereof'.[143]

The Crown continued to undermine the authority of the Admiralty Court in Ireland by making grants of admiralty to corporations and manorial lords into the seventeenth century. In 1610 the City of London sought, and was granted, the admiralty jurisdiction over the coast of Tyrconnell and Coleraine.[144] Earlier Sir

138  A. Cooke to the earl of Northumberland, 23 Aug. 1638 (Alnwick Castle, Northumberland MS, vol. 14, f. 170). In 1697 the corporation argued that the right to exercise admiralty jurisdiction derived from a charter dated 13 April in the 11th year of the reign of King Henry IV which recites a former charter granted by 'Adomar, sometime earl of Pembroke, and confirmed the same' (TNA (PRO), ADM 1/3665, f. 116).

139  T. Harris to Viscount Falkland, 26 Nov. 1632 (TNA (PRO), SP 63/253, f. 245).

140  The admiralty component of the charter of 3 Mar. 1609 is described in the *Report of the Commissioners appointed to inquire into municipal Corporations in Ireland* (HC 1835 (23) xxvii 1, 346).

141  R. Smith to E. Nicholas, 1 Feb. 1638 (TNA (PRO), SP 63/256, f. 187).

142  *Council Book of Cork Corporation*, p. xi.

143  25 Aug. 1627, ibid., p. 131. C. Smith, *The ancient and present state of the county and city of Cork* (Cork, 1815), ii, p. 358. On 24 Sept. 1638 the Corporation of Cork voted to reimburse Melcher Lavallyne for expenses incurred in employing 'an agent for Dublin, this next Michaelmas term to solicit for the Admiralty.' *Council Book of Cork Corporation*, p. 191.

144  *Cal. S.P. Ire. 1608–1610*, pp 350, 359–62.

Arthur Chichester had been granted the office of admiral of Lough Neagh.[145] In 1631 Charles I made a supplementary charter grant to the Corporation of Waterford, handing over to it in unequivocal terms the right to enjoy the traditional perquisites of the admiral (excluding only wreck and pirates' goods). Included in this very generous charter was the right to hold an admiralty court, as well as the power to license fishing and to impose a levy for the granting of fishing licences.[146] Waterford asserted its admiralty charter against the Confederate administration and attempted to establish an admiralty court in the town during the 1640s. The Confederate Council directed that 'the mayor and Corporation of Waterford be commanded not to interrupt the judge and officers of the admiralty established by the last assembly of the Confederate Catholics ... until the pretence of the corporation thereto receive a legal trial'.[147]

### Quo warranto *and the corporations*

In the first decade of the seventeenth century, in an effort to suppress these rival admiralty jurisdictions, *quo warranto* proceedings were initiated against the Corporation of Dublin. In 1606 the attorney general, Sir John Davies, issued an information in the King's Bench charging the corporation with 'exercising for ten years past the office of admiral between Arklow and Nany Water, having an admiralty court, appointing a water bailiff and taking customs'.[148] The corporation responded by pleading the 1582 grant made by Elizabeth, and contending that 'from the time of which the memory of man does not run to the contrary, the corporation and their predecessors have made and erected beacons in the water aforesaid and within the limits and bounds, and that they had received anchorage and beaconage from vessels which had come into and anchored within the water aforesaid'. The King's Bench held that the 'plea of the corporation of carrying aforesaid privileges and liberties is not sufficient in law'.[149] It emphatically ordered that those 'privileges and liberties' be 'seized into the king's hand and the corporation excluded from exercising these functions forever and that they shall be fined for their contempt in usurping these privileges and liberties'. In 1616 Dublin Corporation moved to have the judgment reversed by writ of error in the King's Bench in England.[150] However, the decision of the Irish court stood.[151] The *quo warranto* litigation did not, however, succeed in putting a stop to the claims of Dublin Corporation. In 1638 the judge of the Court of Admiralty of Leinster reported that the mayors of Dublin and Wexford 'take upon them by their

---

145  T.M. Healy, *Stolen waters* (London, 1913), pp 39, 157, 248, 265, 272.
146  *Magna Charta Libertatum Civitatis Waterford*, ed. T. Cunningham (Dublin, 1752), pp 72–4, 87.
147  Bodl., Carte MS 22, f. 473.                   148  RIA, Haliday MS, 12/E/2, f. 450.
149  Ibid.
150  *Cal anc. rec. Dub.*, iii, p. 68.
151  In 1634 Wentworth described the litigation as resulting in the recovery of the office of waterbailiff 'pretending to be within their charter'. T. Wentworth to the commissioners of Admiralty, 20 Dec. 1634 (TNA (PRO), SP 63/254, f. 503).

waterbailiffs to arrest ships and barques and to try all manner of actions properly belonging to the Admiralty Court'.[152] Later that year the court ordered the waterbailiff of Dublin (John Tetlowe) to be attached for contempt.[153] The corporation retaliated against this act of aggression by initiating prohibition proceedings against the court, and obtaining a writ of *habeas corpus cum causa* from the Court of Common Pleas for the release of Tetlowe.

In 1637 the Admiralty requested the judge of the English Admiralty Court, Henry Marten, to advise it on how to deal with the problem of the Irish maritime municipalities. Marten advised a re-commencement of the *quo warranto* strategy employed by Sir John Davies.[154] In 1638 the lord deputy, Thomas Wentworth, instructed the attorney general to initiate *quo warranto* proceedings against those corporations in Munster which challenged the judicial and administrative authority of the admiralty.[155] The attorney general was instructed to:[156]

> question by *quo warranto* all such charters of corporations and lords of lands and other persons as hold or claim any jurisdiction or right of admiralty in that kingdom by any other grant than lyeth from the lord high admiral under the seal of the Admiralty to end that the same may be brought back and restored again to the office of lord high admiral of England.[157]

The prosecution of these *quo warranto* proceedings was interrupted by the death of the attorney general, Sir Robert Osbaldeston. In 1640 Alan Cooke wrote to London with the news that 'the old attorney is dead' and requesting that his successor be encouraged to 'prosecute the *quo warrantos* already set in foot by his predecessor'.[158] However, the momentum seems to have slowed following the death of Osbaldeston.

Municipal corporations were not the only problem. Patents to manorial lords conferring admiralty rights also reduced the authority of the admiralty. The exercise of admiralty jurisdiction by private manorial lords had long been a problem: the admiralty judge Dr Cooke complained that 'every man which is but

152   A. Cooke to the earl of Northumberland, 23 Aug. 1638 (Alnwick, Northumberland MS, vol. 14, f. 170).

153   *Cal. anc. rec. Dub.*, iii, p. 349.

154   'That his majesty's pleasure may be signified to His Attorney General there by *quo warranto* to call into his Majesty's Majesty's Exchequer of Ireland such towns corporate and lords of manors there as claim either admiral … or droits of admiralty to make the right to the same appear'. H. Marten to the commissioners of Admiralty, 8 July 1637 (TNA (PRO), SP 63/256, f. 116).

155   R. Smith to E. Nicholas, 1 May 1638 (TNA (PRO), SP 63/256, f. 231).

156   24 Apr. 1639 ( TNA (PRO), SP 16/418, f. 111).

157   In 1643, upon the petition of Robert Smith, 'marshal and waterbailiff of the several vice-admiralties in the kingdom of Ireland', the speaker of the House of Commons was directed to write 'unto the mayor and sheriffs of the town of Youghal, thereby directing them either to suffer the petitioner Robert Smyth to enjoy the perquisite and profit of his place, as formerly he hath done, or otherwise to appear here and answer in writing by themselves'. *Commons' jn*, i, p. 312 (20 Apr. 1643).

158   A. Cooke to the commissioners of Admiralty, 19 Oct. 1640 (TNA (PRO), HCA 25/215).

a lord of the manor by the seaside challenge all manner of wrecks and droits'.[159] In 1632 the deputy vice-admiral for Munster identified the following landlords as exercising admiralty jurisdiction: the earl of Cork, Lord Coursey, the Powers, FitzGeralds, O'Donovans and O'Sullivans.[160] Cooke favoured a legal campaign impeaching the validity of such grants. These grants were, he argued, without any legal basis, merely 'usurped upon pretended customs in the time of rebellion'. Alternatively, if the lord deputy had made these grants, he did so without jurisdiction. The lord deputy had no power to issue such grants, for 'I made search of all the former deputies' grants, and there is not one word in the commission which gave them power to make any such grants'. Dr Cooke, 'speeding commission upon commission', had instituted inquiries into the validity of these patents. Dr Cooke's investigative activities had prompted retaliation – landlords whom he had targeted 'procured prohibitions or else presented petitions against me before the lord deputy or council'. A number of measures were adopted; first, Wentworth (who Dr Cooke praised as 'the only man who doth stand for his majesty's right therein'), in his role as commissioner of the 1634 Commission of Defective Titles,[161] suspended issuing patents confirming admiralty grants until the validity of the original grant was established by the Court of Admiralty.[162] Second, the commissioners established to sell lands at Londonderry were instructed not to give away any admiralty grants, particularly the rights of 'anchorage, ballastage and ferriage and the like below the first bridges'.[163] Third, the attorney general initiated actions by way of *quo warranto* against usurping landlords.[164] In 1639 the attorney general, Sir Robert Osbaldeston, brought a series of *quo warranto* proceedings. In the case of the information against Viscount Claneboy of the manor of Groomsporte in County Down, the Court of Exchequer ruled for the attorney general, declaring that Claneboy's grant did not justify him holding a local admiralty court.[165] However, not all of these expensive actions succeeded. The Talbots of Malahide had been granted the admiralty of Malahide in 1485;[166] in 1639 the Court of Exchequer upheld Richard Talbot's claim to the admiralty franchise of Malahide.[167]

159  Petition of Alan Cooke to the lord deputy (Alnwick Castle, Northumberland MS, vol. 14, f. 170).
160  H. De Lauen to Viscount Falkland, 16 Sept. 1632 (TNA (PRO), HCA 30/158).
161  H. Kearney, *Strafford in Ireland, 1633–1641* (Cambridge, 1959), pp 81–4.
162  Petition of Alan Cooke to the lord deputy (Alnwick Castle, Northumberland MS, vol. 14, f. 170).
163  24 Apr. 1639 (TNA (PRO), SP 16/418, f. 111).
164  Informations were also taken in Easter 1639 against Henry Cheevers for exercising the office of admiralty in the manors of Mountagne, Dublin and Banore, Co. Wexford (RIA, Haliday MS 12/E/2, f. 426).
165  *The Hamilton manuscripts*, ed. T.K. Lowry (Belfast, 1867), pp 30–1.
166  Grant to Thomas Talbot of the admiralty of Malahide, 1485 (Bodl., MS Talbot a 1); B. Donovan & D. Edwards (eds), *British sources for Irish history, 1485–1641* (Dublin, 1997), p. 234.
167  Ibid., p. 248.

## PRIZE LAW IN IRELAND, 1580–1660

*The wars with France and Spain, 1626–30*

The Irish Court of Admiralty was not empowered to hear prize suits. That power was reserved to the English Court of Admiralty alone. This central principle of Irish prize law was rehearsed in 1626 when the Munster Admiralty Court attempted to process a prize capture: Captain Launxton, a somewhat suspect English privateer, had arrived at Berehaven with a Spanish capture freighted with salt. There he met the deputy vice-admiral of Munster, William Hull.[168] Hull had entered into a convenient financial arrangement with the prize master that he could have the cargo condemned as prize in the Munster Admiralty Court and 'have sentence here out of this court for his better expedition' if he would pay the 'dues as are usually paid in England'.[169] Sir Edward Nicholas, secretary to the lord admiral (the duke of Buckingham) sought the advice of the judge of the High Court of Admiralty, Sir Henry Marten. Marten firmly instructed the lord admiral that the disposal of prize captured under a letter of marque at any other place than the High Court of Admiralty in London was 'expressly contrary to the orders of the lords, ancient customs of letters of marque, and the bonds entered into by all such who take out such commissions of reprisal'.[170] Clause 4 of the standard-form letters of marque issued to privateers against Spain clearly excluded the Irish court from prize jurisdiction: privateers were directed that 'no part of [any prize goods was to be] sold, spoiled, wasted or diminished until judgment hath first passed in the High Court of Admiralty [of England] that the said goods are lawful prize'.[171]

Although the rules for the disposal of prize deliberately excluded the Irish Court of Admiralty, the judge of the Irish court pressurized London to have the court's claim to exercise prize jurisdiction recognized. It was argued (an argument that was to be reprised repeatedly over the following two hundred years) that an extension of prize jurisdiction to Ireland would act as an incentive to the Irish maritime community to volunteer as privateers. In 1629 Adam Loftus requested permission to exercise prize jurisdiction in the case of a Dutch vessel, the *Three Kings*, arguing that if an order were given for 'her to be unloaded here, and judgment to be given upon her in the Admiralty Court' Irish privateers would be encouraged to join the war effort, and their captures would boost revenue:

> It would certainly give great contentment to the adventurers who are
> inhabitants of the kingdom; and it would be great encouragement to others
> of this land to follow their example and try their fortunes at sea, if they might

---

168  On Hull see 'The Irish Admiralty', pp 324–5.
169  W. Hull to Viscount Falkland, 24 Oct. 1626 (TNA (PRO), SP 63/243, f. 270).
170  E. Nicholas to Viscount Falkland, 18 Dec. 1626 (TNA (PRO), SP 63/243, f. 291). Nicholas expressed his conviction that Lauxton was a pirate and William Hull a 'countenancer of pirates'. (ibid.).
171  *Law and custom of the sea*, i, pp 410–13.

see cause to hope for liberty to bring their booty obtained by their charges as adventurers into their own homes, which could not but rebound to his majesty's great profit, both in his customs and his admiralty duties.[172]

Despite the legal understanding that it had no jurisdiction to do so, the Munster Court of Admiralty, run by Robert Travers, appears to have attempted to induce prize masters to undergo adjudication in Ireland. In 1628 an English prize master reported that, on returning home, he had put into Youghal 'where one Sir Robert Travers pretending much friendship to Symon Gibbons, the petitioner's factor, told him that he would spare him a journey for England and adjudge his prize here'. The prize master was sufficiently apprised of the conditions of the letter of marque to resist the invitation: 'but the said Gibbons replied that his merchant was bound in great bonds in the Admiralty Court in England to the contrary, and, refusing his entreaty, came to England'.[173]

Limited concessions were made to the strict prohibition against the exercise of prize jurisdiction by the Irish court. Occasionally, an exceptional commission might be issued to Ireland to adjudicate or assist in prize cases. In 1627 permission had been granted to the Irish court to condemn French vessels which had been seized in Munster ports under the embargo against the presence of enemy vessels in Irish ports.[174] In 1628 a commission for the appraisement of a prize which had been condemned in the English court was sent from London to be carried out by Irish admiralty officers.[175] In 1630 Loftus was authorized by the king to adjudicate in the case of the *St John d'Avangaliste*, a prize carrying Spanish goods which had been forced into the port of Dublin.[176] In 1626 the Irish court was allowed to adjudge the legality of the capture of an enemy vessel taken under a letter of

---

172  A. Loftus to the Privy Council, 30 June 1629 (TNA (PRO), SP 63/248, f. 216); a similar argument had been made in 1626 by Falkland: *Cal. S.P. Ire. 1626–1634*, p. 161.

173  'The humble petition of John Hill', 15 Nov. 1628 (TNA (PRO), SP 16/120, f. 104).

174  In correspondence with Nicholas, Falkland wrote that it was his understanding that if 'any questions arise here touching the property of ships or goods stayed here being French by virtue of direction for that embargo and yet claimed by others as pretended property, that the said proceedings and the dependings thereon should be tried in the Court of Admiralty here'. Viscount Falkland to E. Nicholas, 11 June 1627 (TNA (PRO), SP 63/245, f. 64).

175  St Ledger to H. Marten, 9 Oct. 1628 (TNA (PRO), SP 63/247, f. 178).

176  Lord treasurer to A. Loftus, 14 May 1630, transmitting the king's instruction to the judge of the Irish court to administer 'a legal adjudication and condemnation in the Court of Admiralty, and appraisement of the said goods, give order that all the goods be delivered to James Des Maistres to be sold and disposed of for his majesty's use and best advantage, taking a note and a particular inventory under his hand of the weight, quantity and quality of all such goods as he shall receive'. Loftus was instructed to be careful to ensure that the Crown would not be prejudiced in the event that an appeal succeeded and the goods were ordered to be restored (TNA (PRO), SP 63/250, f. 229). Loftus, though upset at the absence of any mention of compensation for the service, assured Dorchester that there would be 'a legal adjudication as soon and with as much expedition as the law will permit which is already begun'. A. Loftus to Lord Dorchester, 2 June 1630 (TNA (PRO), SP 63/250, f. 258).

reprisal. That case raised an important doctrinal issue of the law of reprisal. The problem concerned the issue of whether the terms of letters of reprisal authorized captures made within domestic ports. A Spanish vessel had been taken in the 'Baltimore road' by Sir William Hull and Walter Ellis, acting under the authority of letters of reprisal. The Munster vice-admiral, Falkland, sought the advice of William Clerke 'of Dublin, the civil lawyer'. Clerke advised that the capture was not authorized by the letters of reprisal: 'the prize being taken within the harbour … is perquisite of admiralty, and consequently of your lordships, and not to be allowed to the man of war'.[177] The legal basis of Clerke's conclusion was that the letter of reprisal only extended to captures on the high seas, and did not cover captures within domestic ports. A second opinion was requested from the judge of the English Court of Admiralty, Sir Henry Marten. Marten, in what was to become a leading opinion on this point, imperiously dismissed Clerke's argument:

> in truth I do not well understand the reasons which were used by him to maintain this his opinion, but I no way approve it. For, first, in taking this prize in Baltimore road, they had the express warrant of his majesty's commission to the lord admiral, and the lord admiral his commission to them, as is acknowledged by Mr Clerke in these words: 'To stay and apprehend the ships and goods of the said king of Spain and his subjects, wheresoever the same shall be found upon the seas or in any port or ports thereof, within or without his majesty's realms and dominions to answer their losses'. Secondly, it must be remembered that this commission is not of grace, but of justice; for it is intended that none have these letters of reprisal but such as have received loss and damage and wrongs … It is therefore a strange conceit, in my apprehension, to imagine that a subject wronged and damnified by the king of Spain, or his subjects, should not relieve or help himself by surprising the goods in his majesty's own dominions …[178]

*Prize jurisdiction during the civil war: the Royalist and Parliamentary admiralty courts*

Two Irish courts exercised prize jurisdiction concurrently during the Wars of the Three Kingdoms, 1641–9: the Royalists under Ormond in Dublin operated a prize court, while the Confederates supported their considerable privateering activities with prize courts on the south east coast and in Galway. Although the Parliamentary forces had established their own court of admiralty in Munster, they do not seem to have been permitted to exercise prize jurisdiction in Ireland.

The Dublin-based Court of Admiralty, which had previously been denied any role in the issuing of letters of marque, or in adjudicating prize disputes, was, for the first time, made a tribunal of prize administration.[179] In March 1643 the

---

177  De Laune to the lord deputy, 6 Aug. 1626 (TNA (PRO), SP 63/243, f. 67).

178  Opinion of H. Marten, 19 Sept. 1626 (TNA (PRO), SP 16/36, f. 30); SP 12/237, f. 18; *Law and custom of the sea*, i, pp 427–9.

179  The court also administered letters of marque: privateers in the service of the Crown would enter

Royalist naval pinnace, the *Swan*, captured as prize a ship called the *Magdalen*, 'laden with rebels' goods and bound for New Ross'. The captured vessel was brought to Dublin, condemned as prize, and the vessel and her lading were entrusted for disposal to Robert Smith, the admiralty marshal.[180] However, the importance of the court probably declined after the mid-1640s; from July 1644 the Parliamentary army placed Dublin under an effective blockade.[181] Men-of-war prevented Royalist ships entering or leaving the city, and Dublin ceased to be a viable destination for Royalists bringing in prizes for judicial condemnation. The existence of the Dublin Royalist prize court formally terminated when, in June 1647, the duke of Ormond surrendered the city to the Parliamentary forces.

During the civil war a Parliamentary admiralty court operated in parts of Munster. However, this court did not exercise prize jurisdiction. In July 1644 the

into the necessary bonds and receive their letters of marque from the court in Dublin. The standard-form Irish letter of marque issued by the Crown in 1644 prescribed in detail the procedure for the condemnation of prize captures:

We do give full power and authority unto him to enjoy as his proper goods all ships, goods, plate, arms, ammunition, victuals, pillage and spoil, which shall be so seized and taken by him and which by the definitive sentence of the Court of Admiralty in Dublin shall be pronounced and adjudged to be lawful prize, without any accompt whatsoever thereof to be made (reserving unto us the tenth part, accustomed in such cases to be paid into the said Court of Admiralty) to be disposed of by our said lord lieutenant general and council ... for the time being of that our kingdom of Ireland for the good thereof; provided always that whatsoever prize or prizes, goods or ammunition, or victuals, the said Captain Bradshaw shall take, he bring the same with all convenient speed (wind and weather serving) without breaking of bulk into that our said harbour of Dublin, and that he, the said Captain and other the chief officers of the said ship bring in upon oath a true and faithful inventory of the ship or ships, barques or other vessels, goods, moneys, plate, ammunition and victuals, which shall be taken from time to time by virtue and authority of this commission, and a true appraisement made thereof, and the same, together with all papers and writings found in any ship, or other vessel, so by him taken shall be carefully preserved, and two or three officers of every ship or other vessel so taken, shall be examined by the judge of the Court of Admiralty in Dublin, and the said examinations with the said papers, inventories, and appraisement shall be brought and shown unto our said lord lieutenant general, chief governor, or governors for the time being, to be by them considered of, and afterwards remanded into the registry of the said Court of Admiralty, to the end that the taking of the said ship or ships and goods may there be justified, or restitution made if there shall appear any just cause ... Provided also that the said Captain Bradshaw, the master, and two or three of the principal officers of the said ship shall, before their going to sea, enter into bond in the said Court of Admiralty in the sum of two thousand pounds sterling, unto our judge of our admiralty there to our use, that neither the said ship nor captain, master or company or any one or more of them shall, under colour or pretence of this our commission, rob, spoil and endamage any of our subjects, friends and allies, other than such particular person of his majesty's subjects, friends and allies as shall be found to have aided and relieved the said rebels, or shall be taken carrying arms, ammunitions or victuals to the said rebels or shall have committed piracy. Lastly we do hereby provide that this our commission shall endure no longer than during our good pleasure ...', *Ormonde Calendar* (i), p. 85.

180  Lords justices of Ireland to E. Nicholas, 13 Mar. 1643, ibid. (ii), p. 242.
181  Elaine Murphy, '"No affair before us of greater concern"; the war at sea in Ireland, 1641–1649' (PhD, TCD, 2007), pp 13, 132.

important Munster ports of Cork, Youghal and Kinsale defected, and allied
themselves to the Parliamentary side. Baron Broghill was appointed by Parliament
as vice-admiral of Munster in February 1645.[182] Sir Robert Travers, based in
Kinsale, served as judge of this Parliamentary admiralty court.[183] Broghill
contended without success that the Munster court should be allowed to function
as a prize court. The Munster court possessed, he argued, 'a full power of
judicature for all sea causes and prizes which shall be brought into this province in
the Admiralty Court here'.[184] Although complaints were made about the
inconvenience of bringing prizes over from Munster,[185] the prize court for Irish
captures remained the Court of Admiralty in London, which between 1643 and
1653, condemned over 800 prizes taken in Ireland.[186]

*Prize jurisdiction in the Confederate Court of Admiralty*

The Confederate administration was the real force in Irish privateering in the
1640s. In 1642 the General Assembly of Confederates resolved that the 'Supreme
Council shall have disposition and management of the Admiralty of the sea for
public use and service'.[187] This resolution provided the constitutional basis for the
establishment late in 1642 of the Confederate 'Admiralty Court of Ireland', and
the appointment of an Admiralty judge, James Cusack.[188] Letters of marque were
drafted by the Confederate admiralty and entrusted to envoys on the Continent,
Fathers Shee and Bourke.[189] Between December 1642 and February 1643 at least
twenty blank letters of marque were issued by Confederate agents.[190]

　　The quality of Confederate prize administration became a cause of concern and
was required to be reformed in the late 1640s. The original Confederate letter of
marque[191] was, by comparison with its Royalist equivalent,[192] crudely drafted. The
licence was vaguely defined as authorizing seizure of the 'vessels and goods of the
Parliamentary rebels and enemies of his Majesty carrying contraband'. There was

182　Ibid., p. 19.　　　　　　　　　　　　183　The *St Peter*, 1645 (TNA (PRO), HCA 13/60).

184　The *Flora*, 1646 (TNA (PRO), HCA 13/248).

185　In 1647 a request was made that the cargo of tobacco carried by the *John of London* which was
　　　under arrest in Cork be sold immediately because of the delay which would elapse before a trial
　　　could take place in the English Court of Admiralty. Petition of Daniel Kendell and others to
　　　Lord Inchiquinn, 21 Jan. 1647 (TNA (PRO), HCA 23/15).

186　Murphy, 'No affair before us of greater concern', pp 378–434.

187　John T. Gilbert (ed.), *History of the Irish Confederation and the war in Ireland, 1641–49*, 7 vols
　　　(Dublin, 1882–91), ii, p. 84.

188　Ibid., pp 96–7; 5 Mar. 1642 (TNA (PRO), SP 63/260, f. 310).

189　Gilbert (ed.), *History of the Irish Confederation*, ii, pp 125–6, 203–5, 261–3.

190　J.H. Ohlmeyer, 'Irish privateers during the Civil War, 1642–1650', *Mariners Mirror*, 76 (1990),
　　　119.

191　Commission issued by earl of Muskerry as 'High Admiral of Ireland' 18 Dec. 1848 (TNA
　　　(PRO), HCA 13/249, no. 156); J. Appleby, 'An Irish letter of marque, 1648', *Irish Sword*, 61
　　　(1983), 218.

192　See p. 30 above.

no express requirement that the prize master enter into bonds; no prohibition on breaking bulk; and no requirement for making an inventory or preserving documentation. Some of the decrees of the court were the cause of diplomatic complaint. In 1649 Michael Bolan, the mayor of Wexford, wrote to Ormond exonerating himself from a charge that the 'judgment is not legally given' in a prize case, the *Pleasure*, heard by him and the Confederate admiralty judge James Cusack.[193] Earlier the Spanish envoy to the Confederate Catholics complained that Captain John Brooks had taken, off the Canary Islands, two Spanish vessels bound for Bilbao and deposited the Spanish crew in the Portuguese island of Madiera. He had then taken the prize into Galway where, in the summer of 1642, he had obtained 'upon false surmises, a judgment in the Admiralty Court there the said ships and goods to be lawful prizes, he having suppressed all the dockets, bills of lading, charter parties, letters of advice and other evidences and writings that might discover the truth'.[194] In 1648 an effort was made to strengthen Confederate prize administration. Concerned that the judicial component of the prize process had broken down, a new Court of Admiralty was constituted by the allies:[195] 'There is an apparent necessity of settling an Admiralty Court and ordering of maritime causes in the seaports, harbours … '

The problem was that vessels were 'daily taken and brought into the several harbours as prizes by sundry persons who dispose of the same with their ladings without trial or adjudication'. In the absence of judicial condemnation, purchasers 'may not safely or securely buy such ships … until the same receive a legal trial or be adjudged lawful prize'. Dr Donough O'Keneally was appointed judge of the Court of Admiralty in the ports of Dungarvan, Youghal, Cork and Kinsale and in all other ports, havens, harbours and crooks from Dungarvan along the sea coast to the river Shannon. The new court was directed to act according to the rules of English prize doctrine, and to follow the 'laws and statutes of the courts of admiralty of the kingdoms of England and Ireland'. In addition to acting as a prize court, the new local admiralty court was entrusted with instance jurisdiction, having power to 'determine pleas or actions between party and parties'. The court was to be equipped with the usual personnel of a traditional admiralty court: a marshal, cryer, clerk and receiver.[196]

193  Bodl., Carte MS 24, f. 504.                    194  Bodl., Carte MS 14, f. 88.

195  'A draft of a commission for judges of the Admiralty in certain ports, 1648' (n.d.) (Bodl., Carte MS 23, f. 148).

196  In Galway the mayor, Richard Blake, Dominick Browne and Thomas Lynch were appointed to 'judge of prizes and cases arising thereupon in the ports and in the whole province of Connacht' (Bodl., Carte MS 23, f. 442).

THE IRISH COURT OF ADMIRALTY, INSTANCE JURISDICTION AND
INTER-CURIAL COMPETITION

In 1389 and 1391[197] the English parliament had enacted measures prohibiting the
lord high admiral from adjudicating disputes which occurred on land. The
admiral's judicial activities were restricted to 'thing[s] done upon the sea'. Reciting
that 'great and common clamour and complaint hath been oftentimes made before
this time and yet is, for that the admiral and their deputies hold their sessions
within divers places within the realm' the admiral was forbidden from hearing
disputes arising from transactions occurring on land: 'it is accorded and assented,
that the admirals and their deputies shall not meddle from henceforth of any thing
within the realm but only of a thing done upon the sea ...' The activities of the
lord admiral were the subject to an identical measure in Ireland; the English
admiralty statutes of Richard II were re-enacted in Ireland by the Dublin
parliament which convened in 1402.[198]

In the sixteenth century the statutes of Richard II were revived by the courts of
common law, and particularly by the Court of King's Bench, as the basis of a
campaign for the suppression of the growing civil maritime jurisdiction of the
English Court of Admiralty. In the early seventeenth century, the cause was led, in
particular, by Sir Edward Coke (whose treatment of the Court of Admiralty in
chapter 22 of his *Fourth Part of the Institutes* provided the principal source for the
common lawyers' objections). The statutes of Richard II, and their 'thing[s] done
upon the sea' restriction, provided the jurisdictional foundation for the anti-
admiralty case. According to Coke's formula 'by the law of the realm the Court of
Admiralty had no conusance, power or jurisdiction over any manner of contract,
plea or quarrel within any county of the realm ...'[199] The effect of this rule –
abbreviated as the 'locality' principle – was that the court had no jurisdiction over
disputes originating on land. It was limited to 'thing[s] done upon the sea'.

Of course, most varieties of commercial maritime litigation being undertaken
by the Admiralty Court in the Elizabethan period involved agreements negotiated
on land, and therefore failed the locality standard. The competence of the court to
entertain disputes between vessel owners and ships' provisioners ('material-men')
or shipwrights was compromised by the fact that the cause of action usually 'arose
within the county'. In *Leigh v. Burley*[200] a writ of prohibition was issued preventing
the English court from hearing an action taken by a shipwright, Leigh, who had
libelled Burley for defaulting on payment for sails supplied in the port of London.
The King's Bench held that the 'contract was made on land, and *infra corpus
comitatus*, and therefore the admiral can have no jurisdiction; for the statutes of the
13 and 15 of Richard II and 2 H. 4 cap. 11 are that the admiral shall not have

197   13 Ric. II, st. I, c. 5 (Eng.), 1389–90; 15 Ric. II, c. 3 (Eng.), 1391.
198   3 Hen. IV (Ire.), 1402. *Statutes and Ordinances and Acts of the Parliament of Ireland King John to
      Henry V*, ed. H.F. Berry (Dublin, 1907), p. 507.
199   (London, 1644), p. 134.                    200  (1609) Owen 123; 74 ER 946.

conusance but of things done *super altum mare*'. In 1632 the Company of
Seawrights petitioned the king against the shutting down of the court. They had:

> hitherto been always accustomed to have their suits decided in a speedy way
> in the Court of Admiralty, where the ships they build or repair are by arrest
> liable to make them satisfaction, but now by the grant of prohibitions in the
> King's Bench, the ship is discharged ...[201]

Litigation involving collisions, where the collision occurred within waters other
than the high seas, was also being withdrawn from the Court of Admiralty.[202] The
ground of the prohibition was, again, that the incident had occurred *infra corpus
comitatus*. The most important category of litigation affected by the prohibition
involved the breach of maritime contracts for the carriage of goods concluded in
overseas ports.[203] In *Thomlinson's* case, another extra-jurisdictional maritime
contract case, Coke CJ said:

> The Court of Admiralty hath no cognizance of things done beyond sea; this
> appears plainly by the statute 13 Rich. II, cap. 5, the words of which statute
> are that the admirals and their deputies shall not meddle from henceforth of
> any thing done within the realm, but only of a thing done upon the sea.[204]

It was not enough that the contract had been made on the sea, and that the court
did, in fact, have jurisdiction. There was a further condition. It was necessary that
the litigant also positively show that the court had jurisdiction; a prohibition might
issue where the fact of the cause of action having a marine location (occurring *super
altum mare*) was not explicitly recited on the libel: 'note that every libel in the
Admiralty doth, and must lay the cause of suit *super altum mare* ... for the
jurisdiction there grows not from the cause, but from the place'.[205]
    The locality doctrine meant that the Court of Admiralty could have nothing to do
with land-based disputes; the common lawyers had further reduced the court's
competence by extending the definition of 'land'. The law French wording of 15

---

201  *Cal. S.P. Dom.* 1631–1633, p. 517.
202  In *Violet v. Blague* (1617) Cro Jac 514; 79 ER 439 the King's Bench referred to an earlier case
     where a ship lying at anchor at Blackwall in London which had been damaged by another ship,
     and where proceedings for damages in the Admiralty Court had been prohibited.
203  4 *Co Inst*, pp 134–5: 'Bargains or contracts made beyond the seas, wherein the common law
     cannot administer justice (which is the effect of this article), do belong to the constable and
     marshal; for the jurisdiction of the admiral is wholly confined to the sea, which is out of any
     county. But if any indenture, bond, or other specialty, or any contract be made beyond sea for
     doing of any act or payment of any money within this realm, or otherwise, wherein the common
     law can administer justice and give ordinary remedy; in these cases neither the constable or
     marshal, nor the court of admiralty hath any jurisdiction'.
204  (1605) 12 Co Rep 104, 77 ER 1379; *Palmer v. Pope* (1611) Hob 212, 80 ER 359.
205  Per Coke CJ in *Palmer v. Pope* (1611) Hob 213; 80 ER 359.

Richard II, c. 3 allowed the admiral jurisdiction beneath '*les pountz … pluis pscheins al meer*'. The court's understanding was that its jurisdiction extended up to the first 'bridges' near the sea. However, in *Leigh v. Burleigh* the judges of Common Pleas held that the proper translation of 'pountz' was 'points' not 'bridges'.The effect of this interpretation was to abolish the right of the Court of Admiralty to act in disputes occurring in ports or in tidal rivers, for the limit of the court's jurisdiction was outside the borders set by the first points of land, and not the first bridges: 'that the 15 of Richard the 2 is mis-printed, viz. that the admiral shall have jurisdiction to the bridges; for the translator mistook bridges for points, that is to say, land's end'.[206]

The degradation of Admiralty authority was aggressively enforced by the writ of prohibition from the King's Bench. The writ could be obtained *ex parte* without scrutiny of the truth of the allegation founding the application for the writ. The party restrained by an irregularly obtained prohibition could admittedly have the prohibition lifted by obtaining a writ of consultation. But the fact of having, as a condition to maintaining an action in the Admiralty Court, to incur the risk of a prohibition, and then the expense and delay of obtaining a writ of consultation, may well have been a disincentive to litigants thinking of suing in that court. The judges of the Court of Admiralty also complained of defendants who waited until the proceedings in the Court of Admiralty had concluded, before then seeking prohibition from the King's Bench.[207]

These problems were not restricted to England. In Ireland the common law courts, which were fighting for maritime business, were issuing prohibitions in the same way as their English counterparts.[208] Even the Court of Chancery was involved. In *Codd v. Forth*[209] a prohibition was sought from the Chancery to prevent the Court of Admiralty hearing a case about the delivery of a consignment of cloth 'soasmuch as this is a transitory matter, and might very well have been

---

206  (1609) Owen 122; 74 ER 946.
207  The King's Bench in 1609 in *The Case of Admiralty* (1609) 12 Co Rep 77; 77 ER 1355 agreed not to issue prohibitions post-sentence. This was subject to the qualification that a prohibition might be issued where the applicant could offer positive proof 'by any matter in writing, or other good matter, that this was done upon land'.
208  The Court of Admiralty did not have exclusive jurisdiction over maritime causes. The courts of common law and chancery had also acquired jurisdiction over matters of maritime law. Litigants had, as Coke CJ put it, *electionem fori*. The records of the Irish Chancery indicate the degree to which plaintiffs preferred to pursue maritime cases in courts other than the Court of Admiralty. In *Browne v. Chevin* (NAI, Chancery bills, I.43) the plaintiff alleged that he had contracted with the defendant, a Drogheda merchant, to serve as a pilot on a voyage from Lisbon to Drogheda in consideration of £5 and rations of meat and drink, but that the vessel having been forced in to Galicia, the agreement had been renegotiated and the plaintiff had to diet himself. In *French v. Hay* (NAI, Chancery bills, B. 129) the plaintiff alleged that Hay, having been paid to carry the *St Michel* to Spain to purchase wine, had instead 'received of the king of Spain's freight for bringing some of his soldiers to the town of Kinsale' and had, contrary to the contract of affreightment, not purchased or returned the wines.
209  NAI, Chancery bills, J. 57.

tried at the common law as in the chancery'. In 1600 the Privy Council referred to
the prejudice to 'her majesty's own subjects, as well English as Irish' caused by the
King's Bench issuing writs of prohibition, implying that prohibitions were being
issued from the Irish courts of common law.[210] In the mid-1630s the problem had
become so serious that the judge of the Admiralty Court of Leinster sent over to
London a schedule containing a list of prohibitions issued in Ireland against the
Irish admiralty courts.[211]

The English Admiralty's counter-arguments were principally based on the *non
obstante* clause in the patent granted to the lord high admiral. The patent entrusted
him with jurisdiction over maritime causes '*aliquo statuto … non obstante*'. The lord
admiral asserted that the *non obstante* clause in the patent had superseded the
legislation of Richard II. A second argument was based on the implicit finality of
admiralty decisions which could be evinced from the Judgment of Delegates Act
1566.[212] That Act provided for an appeal in marine cases to a Court of Delegates
'and no further appeal to be had or made'. This exhaustive code of appeal, it was
argued, implicitly excluded review by prohibition. Sir Julius Caesar argued that
appeal to the Court of Delegates was to be 'taken as final in all civil and marine
causes, and no further appeal or complaint to any other court was allowed'.[213]

The Admiralty initiated four efforts to restrain the interference of the courts of
common law. In the first, in 1575, the Admiralty Court judge, Dr David Lewes,
submitted a formal letter of protest to the King's Bench about its practice in
issuing admiralty prohibitions.[214] Four principal causes of complaint were
identified: (i) the practice of issuing writs of prohibition *ex parte* and 'upon bare
suggestions or surmises'; (ii) the practice of issuing writs of prohibition after
sentence by the Court of Admiralty; (iii) the refusal of the King's Bench to
recognize the customary jurisdiction of the Court of Admiralty to adjudicate
breaches of contracts where the contract had been negotiated on land outside the
kingdom; (iv) the refusal of the King's Bench to concede the right of the Court of
Admiralty to adjudicate alleged breaches of charter parties made on land within
the realm. The King's Bench subsequently denied that it had ever agreed to act on
these complaints and continued with its attacks on the Admiralty Court.[215] In 1600
the Privy Council tried again.[216] The council recited complaints made by foreign
ambassadors about the disruption to proceedings in the Court of Admiralty caused
by the issuing of writs of prohibition, and directed the attorney and solicitor
generals, together with serjeants Christopher Yelverton and Francis Bacon, to

210   4 Feb. 1600, *Acts of the Privy Council 1599–1600*, vol. 30, pp 43–4.
211   A. Cooke to the earl of Northumberland, 23 Aug. 1638 (Alnwick Castle, Northumberland MS,
      vol. 14, f. 170).
212   8 Eliz., c. 5 (Eng.), 1566.
213   G.I. Duncan, *The High Court of Delegates* (Cambridge, 1971), pp 65–7.
214   The document, dated 12 May 1575, is set out in full in *Hale and Fleetwood*, pp xcii–xciii.
215   *4 Co Inst*, p. 136.
216   4 Feb. 1600, *Acts of the Privy Council 1599–1600*, vol. 30, pp 43–4.

consider 'both out of what courts duly and orderly such prohibitions ought to be awarded, and anciently have been used, and also in what causes, and in what sort'. In 1611 a further complaint was submitted by Sir Daniel Dun, judge of the Court of Admiralty, to the Privy Council.[217] Dun's letter complained that prohibitions were granted in respect of transmarine contracts 'wherein the common law cannot administer justice'; that 'charter parties made only to be performed upon the seas are daily withdrawn from the court by prohibitions'; that the *non obstante* clauses in the lord admiral's patent superseding the statutes of Richard II were being ignored; and, that the agreement of 1575 was not being observed. Finally, in 1633, Charles I, on the petition of Sir Henry Marten, convened a conference of senior judges and law officers to settle the claims for immunity from prohibition claimed by the Court of Admiralty over four categories of litigation: contracts of freight; contracts for the building, equipping and victualling of ships; foreign contracts; and disputes arising from incidents occurring in rivers below the first bridge. Exchanges between the two sides were more constructive than they had been earlier in the century. On behalf of the admiralty, Henry Marten argued for the efficiency of the *in rem* jurisdiction as a means of protecting the interests of unpaid mariners and suppliers. William Noy, the attorney general, conceded that 'if the subject matter be maritime, then the Admiralty have cognizance albeit the contract be made on shore'. This was a significant victory for the Admiralty. It was settled that the Admiralty Court was to have jurisdiction over claims involving charter parties, freight, and the provisioning of vessels. The negotiations between the two sides were settled in a protocol dated 18 February 1633:

1. If suits shall be commenced in the Court of Admiralty upon contracts made, or other things personally done beyond the sea, or upon the sea, no prohibition is to be awarded.

2. If suit be before the admiral for freight, or mariners' wages, or for the breach of charter parties for voyages to be made beyond the sea, though the charter parties happen to be made within the realm ... a prohibition is not to be granted; but if suit be for penalty, or if the question be made, whether the charter party be made or not?, or whether the plaintiff did release, or otherwise discharge and same within the realm?, that is to be tried in the king's courts at Westminster, and not in the king's Court of the Admiralty ...

3. If suit shall be in the Court of Admiralty for building, amending, saving or necessary victualling of a ship against the ship itself, and not against any party by name ... no prohibition is to be granted, though this be done within the realm.

4. Likewise the admiral may enquire of, and to redress, all annoyances and obstructions in navigable rivers beneath the first bridges that are any impediments to navigation, or passage to, or from the sea; and also to try

217 The full text of the objections and answers is set out in *4 Co Inst*, pp 134–6.

personal contracts and injuries done there, which concern navigation upon the sea, and no prohibition is to be granted in such cases ...[218]

*The reception of the Privy Council order of 1633 in Ireland*

Demands soon followed for the extension to Ireland of the English Privy Council's protocol of February 1633. In 1635 the marshal of the Irish court, in a memorandum on reform of the Court of Admiralty, recommended the extension to Ireland of the 1633 articles.[219] In 1637, a query from Sir Adam Loftus on the 'common law holding pleas of such causes as are properly maritime, and prohibiting the admiralty to proceed in such causes as are properly maritime' was referred to the judge of the English Court of Admiralty, Sir Henry Marten. Marten advised that:

> the best course I can think of for settling of the power and right of the admiralty in Ireland will be that a copy be taken out of the council book of the articles dated 18 Feb. 163[3] agreed before his majesty by the judges of the common law of this kingdom expressing in what cases prohibitions ought not be sent to the admiralty and that some mandatory [?] be sent from his majesty, either immediately to the judges of the common law, or to be signified to them by the lord deputy, requiring the observance of these articles in that kingdom.[220]

Sir Edward Nicholas 'by command from the commissioners of the Admiralty' communicated the 1633 articles to the lord deputy.[221] In order to put matters beyond any doubt, the king issued an instruction directed to the lord deputy and Privy Council[222] requiring that the protocol be observed in Ireland.

However, the instructions from London met with intense hostility amongst the judges of the courts of common law. Dr Alan Cooke referred to the 'opposition which is of late occasioned by a letter which Mr Smith brought over from his majesty which restrains the power of the judges in granting prohibitions, who are thereby so incensed as that there is no act that I have done, or can do, but is questioned at the council board'.[223] Cooke was so apprehensive about the vindictive attitude of the judges who sat on the Irish Privy Council that he warned the Admiralty to expect retaliation. Cooke's apprehensions were accurate. Early in 1638, Cooke, together with a deputy admiralty marshal, Richard Hatton, was

---

218  The text of the resolutions has been reproduced frequently: *A compendious view*, ii, pp 162–3; *Hale and Fleetwood*, pp cii–ciii; TNA (PRO), SP 16/228, f. 28.

219  Memorandum by Robert Smith, 26 Sept. 1635 (TNA (PRO), SP 63/255, f. 111).

220  H. Marten to the commissioners of Admiralty, 8 July 1637 (TNA (PRO), SP 63/256, f. 116).

221  E. Nicholas to T. Wentworth, 16 Aug. 1637 (TNA (PRO), SP 14/215, f. 79).

222  A. Cooke to the earl of Northumberland, 23 Aug. 1638 (Alnwick Castle, Northumberland MS, vol. 14, f. 170).

223  A. Cooke to the commissioners of Admiralty, 22 Jan. 1638 (TNA (PRO), SP 63/256, f. 185).

summoned by the council in connection with some irregularity in the seizure of the goods from a shipwreck near Dublin. Cooke was fined and Hatton imprisoned for ten weeks. The real cause, Robert Smith believed, was the 1633 protocol banning prohibitions:[224] 'certain it is the judges were bitter against the Admiralty, and no wonder for they had about the same time seen the king's letter concerning prohibitions'.[225]

ADMIRALTY DROITS

*Admiralty wreck*

The common law position was that the right to maritime wreck was a royal perquisite which had been delegated by the Crown to the lord admiral.[226] The extent of the delegation to the lord admiral of this prerogative was far from complete. The admiralty entitlement was limited by a distinction between wreck found at sea and wreck washed ashore. The Admiralty was merely entitled to wreckage picked up on the sea – so-called 'findalls.' Excluded from the lord admiral's grant was the more common wreck or cargo washed up on the shore; wreck found on land vested in the Crown. The Admiralty Act 1391,[227] which had provided that 'wreck of the sea shall be tried, determined, discussed and remedied by the laws of the land, and not before or by the admiral, nor his lieutenant in any wise', was interpreted as excluding the Admiralty's entitlement when wreck reached land. In *Constable's Case*[228] the English Court of King's Bench confirmed the distinction between wreck washed ashore (which belonged to the Crown) and flotsam, jetsam and lagan (which alone vested in the admiral):

> Where it is provided by the statute of 15 Ric. II, c.3 that the Court of Admiralty shall not have cognizance or jurisdiction of wreck of the sea, yet it shall have conusance or jurisdiction of flotsam, jetsam or lagan; for wreck of the sea is when the goods are by the sea cast on land, and so *infra comitatatus*, whereof the common law takes conusance and jurisdiction, but the other three are all on the sea, and therefore of them the admiral has jurisdiction.

The Irish law officers considered the law of wreck in 1589 following the destruction of the Spanish Armada upon the coast of Munster.[229] The opinion,

---

224  R. Smith to E. Nicholas, 1 Feb. 1638 (TNA (PRO), SP 63/256, f. 187).

225  The concession in the 1633 protocol that the admiral's competence extended as far as the 'first bridges' was also being disregarded in Ireland in the 1630s. 'An answer to Judge Gosnold' (n.d.) (Camb, Magadalene, Pepys Library, MS 2872, f. 212).

226  *Constable's Case* (1601) 5 Co Rep 106a; 77 ER 218; *Case of the Royal Fishery of the Bann* (1611) Davies Rep 149.

227  15 Ric. II, c. 3 (Eng.), 1391.                  228  (1601) 5 Co Rep 106a; 77 ER 218.

229  TNA (PRO), SP 63/144, ff 184–5 (25 May 1589).

drafted in response to a claim made by the local manorial lord, Sir Edward Denny, to the benefit of the goods carried on Armada vessels which had been washed ashore on his lands in Kerry, rehearsed the effect of the 1391 Act: 'because the goods, meant by the former law both to the queen and to the subject, was interrupted by the admiral's officers … to redress these inconveniences the statute of decimoquinto Rich 2 [was enacted]'. The result 'as touching the vice-admiral's jurisdiction' was that the Act of 1391 had extinguished his authority over wreck found on land.

The Admiralty's right to wreck depended on the fulfilment of two conditions: the first was the goods having been found at sea; the second was the goods having been abandoned. A dispute concerning the application of the definition of 'abandonment' engaged senior English and Irish civilians in 1626. A French vessel, freighted by some Galway merchants, had been chased into Berehaven by pirates. The crew fled ashore, and the vessel was then rifled by the French and Spanish pirates. The following morning the vessel was recovered by a posse from Berehaven and handed over to the deputy vice-admiral, Robert Skerret. The vessel was claimed for the admiral on the basis that having been abandoned by the crew, the vessel was derelict and liable to seizure for the benefit of the lord admiral. Advice[230] received from the Dublin-based, English civilian, William Clerke,[231] confirmed this. Clerke's opinion was shown to Sir Henry Marten who, writing from his home in Kensington, dismissed Clerke's extreme pro-Admiralty position. Marten concluded that the vessel had not been abandoned and that, therefore, the admiralty had no claim. The vessel, he reasoned, was not claimable as derelict on the ground that there had been no abandonment:

> as for the dereliction or abandoning the ship, whereupon Mr Clerke insists to entitle the Admiralty, it deserves no answer since it is apparent that these men, though they had withdrawn their bodies out of the said ship for fear, yet did with their minds and eyes from the shore follow and retain still the possession and continue the hope and expectation to recover the ship and some goods …[232]

Clerke's confidence was not at all disturbed by Marten's opinion. Describing it as 'curiously delivered', Clerke self-piteously suggested that Marten 'would be unwilling to acknowledge a mistake, and much less to subscribe to, the humble opinion of so obscure a person as Mr Clerke'.[233] Proceedings were then commenced by the Galway merchants, and the case was heard at St Finbarr's Cathedral, before Robert Travers (surrogate to the judge of the Munster court,

230   17 Aug. 1626 (TNA (PRO), SP 63/243, f. 81).
231   See the biographical note in B. Lavack, *The civil lawyers in England* (Oxford, 1973), p. 219.
232   19 Sept. 1626 (TNA (PRO), SP 16/36, f. 31).
233   Viscount Falkland to E. Nicholas, 7 Oct. 1626 (TNA (PRO), SP 63/243, f. 167).

Lawrence Parsons). Judgment was given for the Galway merchants.[234] Travers, finding in favour of the owners, held that the vessel had not been legally abandoned when it was temporarily deserted by the crew merely for 'safety of their lives'. An appeal was initiated.[235] The lord deputy, Viscount Falkland, sent Clerke's opinion to the English civilian (and future judge of the Court of Admiralty) Richard Zouche, who also disagreed with Clerke, and recommended that the Admiralty withdraw its claim.[236] Meanwhile Viscount Falkland, a little bewildered by the intensity of the legal argument, commented that 'there is no end of writing of books nor, for ought I see, of contradictory opinions in admiralty causes'.[237]

The extent to which the processing of admiralty derelict made up a significant component of the work undertaken by courts of admiralty in Ireland was reduced by three factors. The first was the practice of vice-admirals discreetly seizing and disposing of admiralty droits without having the seizure confirmed by a judicial process.[238] A second factor was the small quantity of admiralty derelicts discovered by the Admiralty. The accounts returned to London indicate that the quantum of admiralty derelict recovered in Ireland was minimal. In 1628 the vice-admiral of Leinster, could report nothing by way of derelict 'except perhaps an anchor, a cable or an old boat, which by reason of the smallness of their value (after the deducting of his part who finds them) are not worthy to be presented in account'.[239] In 1635 the Vice-Admiralty of Munster had 'little to accompt for but parcels of wreck'. The 'harbours [being] far, the one from another, the people purloin them upon their first coming to shore'.[240] Thirdly, landlords adjoining the sea were resisting the Admiralty's claims to wreck by reference to their own patent grants of wreck.[241]

*Pirates' goods*

The admiral's patent included a grant of *bona piratarum*.[242] A 1573 memorandum instructed the admiral of Ireland to recover pirates' goods and to ensure that disputes about pirates' goods were 'tried by law here in Ireland'.[243] The establishment of admiralty courts in 1575 enabled that judicial function – determining

234 'W. Clerke his contradictory to Sir Robert Travers upon the Berehaven business', 8 Dec. 1626 (TNA (PRO), SP 63/243, f. 276).

235 *Cal. S.P. Ire. 1625–1632*, p. 166.

236 Viscount Falkland to E. Nicholas, 28 Dec. 1626 (TNA (PRO), SP 63/243, f. 297).

237 Viscount Falkland to E. Nicholas, 6 Jan. 1627 (TNA (PRO), SP 63/244, f. 1).

238 For instance, an account drawn up in 1632 by the vice-admiral of Connacht, George St George, of the disposal of beached whales found in county Mayo made no reference to any process in the Court of Admiralty (TNA (PRO), HCA 30/158, f. 271).

239 A. Loftus to E. Nicholas, 22 Nov. 1628 (TNA (PRO), SP 63/247, f. 262).

240 T. Wentworth to the commissioners of Admiralty, 2 Oct. 1635 (TNA (PRO), SP 63/255, f. 117).

241 W. Hull to E. Nicholas, 18 Apr. 1628 (TNA (PRO), SP 63/246, f. 89). See p. 25 above.

242 *Prinston v. The Court of Admiralty* (1615) 3 Bulst 147; 81 ER 126.

243 TNA (PRO), HCA 14/13, f. 141.

whether the goods be forfeited or restored – to be carried out. Sir Adam Loftus intervened in a dispute between the admiral of Ulster and Lord Kilburry over the right to pirates' goods cast ashore at Coleraine, summoning the landowner to the Court of Admiralty and issuing a commission for an enquiry into the provenance of the goods.[244] In 1672 the vessel and goods belonging to an enterprise operated by a French pirate were arrested as *bona piratarum* in Kinsale.[245]

An advantage of having property condemned as pirates' goods was that the proceeds belonged to the Admiralty. This provided a means of keeping the property out of the hands of rivals such as the Crown or the revenue commissioners. In 1627 Edward Nicholas informed the vice-admiral of Connacht that he had managed to have a French vessel which had been taken into Galway condemned as a piracy seizure:

> There are divers officers here that would have the prize adjudged to the king had I not laboured very earnestly in it and gotten it sentenced as piratically taken and so forfeited to my lord [admiral]; and if it had been adjudged to the king neither my lord nor his officers would have been the better for it.[246]

In 1634 Lord Deputy Wentworth initiated proceedings for the recovery of pirates' goods in the Irish Admiralty Court in order to secure the property from the revenue commissioners. A Spanish vessel had been seized in Galway and proceedings had been initiated by the revenue commissioners in the Court of Exchequer under the False Entries Acts 1569–71.[247] An Irish merchant had met the captain of the Spanish vessel by chance and recognized him as having been involved in piracy. Acting on this report, Wentworth 'caused a second seizure to be made of the ship under the seal of the Admiralty court'. Wentworth argued that recovery under the pirates' goods process in the Admiralty court was the preferred outcome: if the goods were forfeited under the False Entries Acts 1569–71 the profits would fall into the hands of the revenue farmers.[248]

The intervention of the Court of Admiralty in the pirates' goods recovery process was sometimes resisted by local officials who would, of course, have preferred to have the matter dealt with informally. In 1634 a dispute arose between the judge of the Munster court, Henry Gosnold, and the deputy vice-admiral for Munster, Henry de Laune, who complained about the insistence of the admiralty judge in requiring that seizures of pirates' goods be judicially processed. De

244  A. Chichester to the commissioners of Admiralty, 8 Oct. 1634 (TNA (PRO), SP 63/254, f. 458).
245  L. Jenkins to Charles II, 21 Apr. 1673, *Life of Jenkins*, ii, p. 772.
246  E. Nicholas to G. St George, 9 Oct. 1627 (TNA (PRO), HCA 14/215, f. 53).
247  11 Eliz. c. 10 (Ire.), 1569 & 13 Eliz., c. 2 (Ire.), 1571.
248  In 1635 Falkland reported that a ship had been arrested for piracy by the Admiralty Court of Munster. However, 'the farmers obtained a judgment in the Exchequer for the goods, before any sentence could be obtained in the Admiralty'. T. Wentworth to the commissioners of Admiralty, 2 Oct. 1635 (TNA (PRO), SP 63/255, f. 116).

Laune, who had seized pirates' goods from two Devon merchants, was reluctant to submit to the determination of the Munster Court, complaining about the meanness of Gosnold's salvage awards:

> for otherwise if it be left to the determination of Mr Justice Gosnold, or judge surrogate for the Admiralty of this province of Munster, there must little or no benefit be expected to accrue to his majesty out of them … for his tenet is that nothing is due or ought to be required by the officers out of the same, an opinion as contrary to practice as it is (I think) to law and reason.[249]

Gosnold had, De Laune complained, 'so affront[ed] me as to send his marshal'. In response Gosnold laid bare the culture of corruption and law avoidance which was commonplace amongst Munster admiralty officials:

> There is a certain French man, one Henry de Laune, who had formerly been employed by the late Lord Falkland, as his agent for sea casualties within this province. He in his master's time, when he had some authority, offered me many wrongs and since his lord's decease, having none at all, persists therein, taking upon him to dispose of all ships and goods of his own authority without relation to me or his majesty's Court of Admiralty where all things ought to be certified and remain of record for the benefit of all parties interested … I was enforced to complain to the lord chancellor, whose surrogate I am, and obtained from him a sharp reprehension directed to him and his fellows in the several parts of the province …[250]

*Supervision of the collection of admiralty droits*

Under the duke of Buckingham and his secretary, Sir Edward Nicholas, the supervision by London of the collection of admiralty droits in Ireland came under much stricter scrutiny. In 1625 Buckingham circularized all vice-admirals with strict instructions to return quarterly accounts. Vice-admirals were to give 'speedy account of all passages, seizures, forfeitures, or other droits whatsoever occurring';[251] a precise inventory of goods (expressed in weight, measure, quantity and quality) was to be prepared; care was to be taken that no sale of value be made without an appraisement undertaken with the assistance of 'two or three of the chief officers or men of wealth'; goods seized by pirates were not be restored to the owners without 'just payment made of such charges and salvage as shall be due and fit'; and a true account of admiralty seizures was required to be lodged in the High Court of Admiralty every Michaelmas term. These accounts were to be audited by

---

249  H. De Laune to the lord admiral, 20 Jan. 1634 (TNA (PRO), SP 63/254, f. 214).
250  H. Gosnold to the lord deputy, 23 Jan. 1634 (TNA (PRO), SP 63/254, f. 224).
251  Buckingham's instructions to the Irish vice-admirals, 9 Sept. 1625 (TNA (PRO), SP 63/241, f. 240).

the judge of the English Court, and Irish defaulters noted.[252] The power of local vice-admiralties to condemn admiralty droits was withdrawn in the case of 'considerable droits and admiralty casualties'; these were required to be returned to the High Court of Admiralty and adjudged there.[253]

*Profits and allowances*

Detailed annual accounts were returned from the provincial admiralties to the High Court of Admiralty from the late 1620s to the late 1630s. The annual returns show that the value of the admiralty droits collected by local provincial admiralties was small, and in some years nothing was returned. Where the value of the droits recovered by the admiral was less than £20, the vice-admiral was allowed the whole amount – a rule which, it was suggested, led local admirals to deliberately devalue.[254] Where the amount realized through the sale of admiralty droits exceeded £20, the vice-admiral was permitted to retain just a moiety.

ADMIRALTY CUSTOMS AND LICENCES

In addition to a small income from court fees, the seventeenth-century court principally financed itself through a series of exceptional revenues. It extracted the customs of anchorage and beaconage. It derived fees from issuing fishing licenses, and from granting licences to operate ferries (ferriage).

*Anchorage and beaconage*

The admiral marshal (in his capacity as waterbailiff) levied anchorage and beaconage (customs duties extracted from vessels using ports in return for works carried out by the admiralty for the safety of the port). These customs made the marshal (or waterbailiff) the most remunerative of the court's offices: 'the waterbailiff is the man that receives anchorage, beaconage and portage and doth maintain all the beacons, poles [?] and perches at his own charges and receives small fees from such boats as fish for herrings'.[255] The custom of anchorage was unpopular and sometimes resisted by foreign traders: in 1613, in the course of proceedings in the Irish Court of Exchequer for non-payment of customs in Dublin port, two Dutch merchants, Peter Wyhan and Christian Barr, complained

252  Loftus was recorded as not having returned any accounts of the proceeds of the Leinster Court of Admiralty for 1633 (TNA (PRO), SP 16/271, f.45). A minute drawn up in 1638 noted that no accounts had been received from Viscount Chichester for Ulster since 10 Oct. 1635, or from Sir Robert Loftus from the date of his patent. 'Note of Vice-Admirals who have not accounted in the Admiralty', 13 Apr. 1638, *Cal. S.P. Dom. 1637–8*, pp 362–3.
253  Rules and Orders, 2 May 1635 (TNA (PRO), SP 16/264, f. 123).
254  W. Hull to E. Nicholas, 22 Mar. 1628 (TNA (PRO), SP 63/246, f. 89).
255  R. Smith to E. Nicholas, 22 Aug. 1634 (TNA (PRO), SP 63/254, f. 359).

of the amount of duties they were forced to hand over in Dublin, including 'a distinct custom for anchorage and beaconage to the vice-admiral who had care of the said port for preserving perches'.[256]

Originally it was the Corporation of Dublin which had extracted this duty. However, the admiralty's right to extract beaconage and anchorage in Dublin was conclusively established by the decision of the King's Bench in the *quo warranto* proceedings, *AG v. Corporation of Dublin*[257] which held that the corporation had no right to exercise the right of extracting beaconage and anchorage. Following the decision in the *quo warranto* proceedings, the office of waterbailiff was granted by the earl of Nottingham jointly to the marshal, William Ellesworth, and to Andrew Ward.[258] Ward died in the middle of the second decade of the seventeenth century, and this remunerative office passed to Ellesworth. On Ellesworth's death in 1632, the office was granted to the energetic English Admiralty official, Robert Smith.[259] These customs provided a useful revenue stream for the judge of the court: by the early seventeenth century an arrangement had become established under which the judge was allowed a moiety of these revenues.[260] It was probably for fear of losing this revenue that Loftus fiercely resisted the attempts by Smith to implement the grant made by the Admiralty, refusing even to allow Smith to have sight of Ellesworth's patent. After a long dispute between Smith, assisted by Sir Edward Nicholas on the one side, and Loftus, backed, for a period, by the lord deputy, the office was eventually ceded to Smith. A further internal conflict over entitlement to the revenues of anchorage was carried on between the waterbailiff of the central Court of Admiralty and the local vice-admirals. The bailiff's attempts to convert anchorage collection into a national operation were frustrated by provincial vice-admirals who viewed the customs of anchorage and beaconage as annexed to their grants. Robert Smith, noting that anchorage was the 'greatest benefit appertaining to the place', requested that 'for the prevention of future trouble ... to exempt anchorage out of such patents as shall be passed unto vice-admirals in these parts, its ... properly appertaining to your petitioner's place'.[261]

*Fishing licensing*

By the early seventeenth century the Admiralty Court of Ireland had assumed the function of regulating sea fishing. In 1640 Dr Alan Cooke reported that he had settled a demarcation dispute 'between the Scottish men living in the north part of Ireland and the Irish fishermen' which had resulted from the 'great fishing of

256 RIA, Haliday MS 12/E/2, f. 306.  257 Ibid., f. 450. See p. 24 above.
258 R. Smith to E. Nicholas, 22 Aug. 1634 (TNA (PRO), SP 63/254, f. 359).
259 'Petition of Robert Smith', 29 July 1633 (TNA (PRO), SP 63/254, f. 90).
260 R. Smith to the commissioners of Admiralty, 22 Aug. 1634 (TNA (PRO), SP 63/254, f. 359).
261 R. Smith to the commissioners of Admiralty, 18 Sept. 1635 (TNA (PRO), SP 63/255, f. 108).

herrings this year'.[262] Both sides were affected by 'deadly hate and [could not] agree among themselves' and Cooke had established a system for dividing the fishing grounds. The Irish court used this general regulatory power as the justification for a taxation imposition. Fishermen using fishing vessels were required to obtain an annual admiralty licence, and the court charged a lucrative fee for issuing that licence. By the 1630s fees from fishing licences were producing a steady income for the court's officers.[263] The licence fee was, however, resented, and in 1651 it was proscribed by the Commonwealth government: the Parliamentary commissioners decreed that the sum formerly 'demanded of the said fisher boats as fees, salaries or duties belonging to the admirals or judges of any court or any officers of the Admiralty' be abolished. Instead a fee of 10s. per vessel was to be used to fund 'the payment of one ship of war to attend the said fishery for the guard of the said fishing'.[264]

## Ferriage

In the mid-1630s the Admiralty lost a constitutional dispute with the lord lieutenant, Sir Thomas Wentworth, over the right to license ferries operating over navigable rivers in Ireland. In 1637 Sir Henry Marten, judge of the Court of Admiralty of England, was asked to confirm whether it lay within the power of the lord admiral to grant the franchise of ferriage in Ireland. Marten confirmed that maritime ferriage fell within the prerogatives attached to 'the King's Admiralty of England'. The 'sea is not only under his majesty's dominion, but is his proper inheritance, in so much as some think that before the statue of 18 Ed III[265] no subject could have passed the seas without his licence'.[266] Further, Sir John Davies in the *Case of the Royal Fishery of the Bann*[267] 'saith it is manifest by many authorities and records within the kingdom of Ireland that the king had the same prerogative and interest in the arms of the sea, and navigable rivers where the sea doth ebb and flow, as he hath as to *mari*'. It followed that if 'the sea be his majesty's proper inheritance, his majesty has sole interest in the soil and water of such rivers, and consequently the profit incident thereunto'. 'As for the use and practice', he reported that he had seen an exemplification of a patent, issued in 1610 by the earl of Nottingham, granting ferriage rights.

With its legality confirmed by Marten's opinion, in 1637 Sir Edward Nicholas was entrusted with a grant of ferriage in Ireland. Nicholas' patent authorized him to license ferries operating 'from shore to shore over all navigable rivers and arms of the sea below the first bridges towards the sea' in Ireland.[268] The administration

---

262  A. Cooke to the commissioners of Admiralty, 19 Oct. 1640 (TNA (PRO), HCA 25/215).
263  R. Smith to the commissioners of Admiralty, 22 Aug. 1634 (TNA (PRO), SP 63/254, f. 359).
264  20 Sept. 1651 (NLI, MS 11,959, f. 13).
265  18 Edw. III, st 2, c. 3 (Eng.), 1344. This measure had provided that the sea 'be open to all manner of merchants to pass with their merchandize [where it shall please them]'.
266  H. Marten to the commissioners of Admiralty, 14 Feb. 1637 (TNA (PRO), SP 63/256, f. 40).
267  (1611) Davies Rep 149.
268  Draft patent of ferriage in Ireland, 23 Aug. 1637 (TNA (PRO), HCA 14/49).

of the grant was handed over to his emissary in Ireland, Robert Smith, who was under strict instructions not to operate in any districts where ferriage licences had already been granted by Lord Deputy Wentworth. With great diffidence Nicholas wrote to Wentworth, explaining this new arrangement: he had requested Robert Smith to execute the office but with a strict proviso 'not to interfere with any ferriage your lordship had disposed of'.[269] Nervously he assured the lord deputy that if he considered 'the place not be proper for me I will readily lay any grant thereof at your lordships foot'. Nicholas also took the precaution of writing to the judge of the Admiralty Court, Sir Adam Loftus, requesting his assistance in supporting the grant, and tempting him with rewards for any assistance: 'if by your lordship's grant to me I shall make any benefit ... I shall ... thankfully acknowledge your favour by any service that I may in any way render your lordship, or any friend of yours, on this side'.[270]

The right to regulate ferriage and to make grants of local ferriage jurisdiction was already being exercised by the lord deputy, who considered that the right belonged to him under his commission. Wentworth received Smith in his bedchamber in Dublin Castle. The interview opened badly with the lord deputy (irritated by Nicholas' letter) challenging Smith with an intimidating 'so this is your doing?'[271] Important ferriage grants in Dublin, Coleraine and Londonderry had already been divested by the lord deputy. The lord deputy was prepared to allow Nicholas the profits from ferry licences so long as it was understood that this was gift from the deputy and that the admiralty grant had no legal effect. Nicholas appears to have given up the effort to establish an admiralty ferriage operation independent of the lord deputy.[272]

269  E. Nicholas to T. Wentworth, 16 Aug. 1637 (TNA (PRO), SP 14/215, f. 156).
270  E. Nicholas to A. Loftus, 16 Aug. 1637 (TNA (PRO), SP 14/215, f. 157).
271  R. Smith to E. Nicholas, 4 Oct. 1637 (TNA (PRO), SP 63/256, f. 145).
272  R. Smith to E. Nicholas, 1 Feb. 1638 (TNA (PRO), SP 63/256, f. 187).

# CHAPTER TWO

# The Court of Admiralty of Ireland in the later Stuart period, 1660–1710

THE COURT OF ADMIRALTY OF IRELAND had been in abeyance since the removal of Adam Loftus in 1638. The court remained in suspension for the next thirty-two years. As late as a decade after the Restoration in 1660, long after the rest of the Irish judicature had been re-established, the Court of Admiralty of Ireland remained out of commission, with admiralty work being conducted through the minor vice-admiralty courts instead.

The process of re-establishment began hesitantly in the early 1660s. In 1663 the new lord admiral, the duke of York, intimated that he was willing to consider restoring the national admiralty court. But he delayed before doing so in case 'some inconveniences shall appear which may have induced the discontinuance of it'.[1] While he prevaricated, representations urging him to re-commission the court were being made by Irish mercantile interests and by the Irish Privy Council.[2] By 1670 the duke of York had finally resolved to re-establish the court, and petitioned his brother, Charles II, 'about setting of a court of admiralty for the whole kingdom of Ireland'.[3] The king referred the petition to a special sub-committee of the Privy Council (on which the judge of the English Court of Admiralty, Sir Leoline Jenkins, played an active role).[4] On 10 June 1670 that committee reported that there was a sound case for reviving the Irish court. The Privy Council then delegated the function of implementing the decision to the duke of York:

> Upon consideration of the papers and other matters, this day offered, concerning the settlement of a court of admiralty in Ireland to sit at Dublin, as had been done in former time; in regard the board were satisfied that the lord high admiral of England hath in him power and authority to settle there one or more courts of admiralty as he shall see cause for that kingdom, as hath been done in former times, the council do not think fit to give any other direction therein, but to leave it to his royal highness lord high admiral of England to settle with speed one or more courts of admiralty as he shall judge most convenient, that there be no failure of justice there.[5]

1 James, duke of York, to the duke of Ormond, 11 July 1663 (TNA (PRO), ADM 2/1,745, f. 94).
2 23 Aug. 1670 (TNA (PRO), ADM 2/1,755, f. 27).
3 13 May 1670 (TNA (PRO), PC 2/62, f. 86).
4 TNA (PRO), PC 2/62, f. 97.      5 TNA (PRO), PC 2/62, f. 100.

In August 1670 the duke of York re-established the court. An accompanying statement justified the decision on grounds of 'the good of commerce and the dispatch of justice':

> frequent instances have been made unto me, partly from his majesty's Privy Council for his kingdom of Ireland and partly from … his majesty's subjects concerned in the maritime affairs and concerns of that kingdom, that I would establish and settle the jurisdiction of the admiralty in that kingdom in the like manner as it stood established and settled before the late unhappy confusions; and whereas a committee of his majesty's Privy Council for his kingdom of England, to whom this whole matter had been referred, did report it to the council, and they thereupon judged it necessary for the good of commerce and the dispatch of justice in that kingdom of Ireland, that the judicature for maritime affairs formerly settled at Dublin should be revived again as it stood in the year 1640.[6]

It would turn out that the commercial argument for re-establishing the Court of Admiralty in Ireland had been over-stated. During the later Stuart period the court struggled to justify itself. It transacted very little instance work. Prize jurisdiction was effectively withdrawn from it. It could not support itself through fees generated by litigation, and it was forced to rely instead on low-grade administrative work, principally the revenue generated by the sale of fishing licences.

## THE JUDGES OF THE COURT OF ADMIRALTY OF IRELAND, 1670–1708

### *William Glascock, 1670–6*

In August 1670 William Glascock was appointed judge of the newly restored central Court of Admiralty of Ireland.[7] James, duke of York, directed that the warrant of appointment follow the form of the 'commission formerly granted to Sir Adam Loftus'. Glascock had been a member of Parliament for Newport on the Isle of Wight since 1661[8] and was attached to the faction based around the duke of York, an association to which he owed his appointment to the Admiralty Court. For undertaking the job of judge of the Admiralty Court Glascock was rewarded with a salary of £100 *per annum*[9] paid for by the lord admiral. He was academically well

6   23 Aug. 1670 (TNA (PRO), ADM 2/1,755, f. 27).
7   TNA (PRO), ADM 2/1755, f. 27; warrant of appointment, 29 Aug. 1670 (TNA (PRO), HCA 30/821, no. 191).
8   B.D. Henning (ed.), *The history of Parliament; the Commons, 1660–1690, Members C–L* (London, 1983), pp 396–7.
9   *The autobiography of Sir John Bramston, K.B.* (Camden Society, London, 1845), p. 313.

enough equipped for civilian office, having studied civil law, first at Cambridge, and then at Leiden. But his tenure at the Irish court was not distinguished. There were long periods of absenteeism while he attended to his London duties, and during these periods Dr John Topham (who also served as a master in chancery) acted as his surrogate.[10] Eventually, the lord lieutenant, the earl of Essex, lost patience with Glascock's pluralism. In 1676 Essex, according to Sir John Bramston's *Autobiography*,[11] engineered Glascock's dismissal:

> [Glascock] … served the king industriously. His majesty made him judge of the Admiralty in Ireland, and granted him a salary of £100 per annum; but his employment in the parliament not suffering him attend there, the earl of Essex, lieutenant of Ireland, put another into that office, and his salary by that means was lost.[12]

### Sir William Petty, 1676–83

In July 1676 William Glascock 'who had voluntarily surrendered the same' was superseded as judge of the Irish Court of Admiralty by the political economist and polymath Sir William Petty.[13] The appointment was not an obvious one. Petty was not, after all, even a lawyer. But Petty lobbied hard for the position. The office was, Petty naively imagined, a position of prestige. Somewhat embarrassingly, after his elevation, he wrote enquiring as to the diplomatic precedence of the judge of the Court of Admiralty, and as to whether the judge was entitled to a place on the Privy Council.[14] His relationship with the lord lieutenant (the duke of Ormond) had become strained during the 1660s, but his position as judge would provide him, or so he thought, with an opportunity to restore good relations. He made his first attempt with a sycophantic verse which (having sought advice from Samuel Pepys

---

10  In 1673 Topham, a Trinity College Dublin graduate in civil law, replaced Dr Dudley Loftus as master in chancery, following Loftus' imprisonment for defiance of the new rules for the regulation of the Corporation of Dublin (*Cal. S.P. Dom. 1673*, p. 592; *A catalogue of the graduates of Trinity College Dublin* (Dublin, 1869), p. 565). During the 1670s Topham also served as advocate general of the army (*Cal. S.P. Dom. 1673*, p. 186).

11  *The autobiography of Sir John Bramston* (Camden Society, London, 1845), p. 313.

12  Bramston's account could not be entirely accurate. The lord lieutenant was not constitutionally competent to dismiss the judge of the Irish Court of Admiralty. The judge owed his appointment to the lord admiral, the duke of York, and it was he alone who was competent to dismiss the judge. Whatever the source of Glascock's dismissal, the termination of Glascock's two Irish judicial offices did not go uncompensated. When one of the judges of the Provincial Court of Connacht, Sir Ellis Leighton, was found to have misbehaved in dealings he had conducted in the court at France, Charles II instructed the earl of Essex to transfer the pension from Leighton 'to our trusty and well beloved Sir William Glascock, late one of the commissioners of appeals in our said kingdom of Ireland, from which place he hath been removed in respect of his necessary attendance upon us in our court here' (BL, Stowe MS 210, f. 343).

13  11 July 1676 (TNA (PRO), ADM 1/3,883, f. 26).

14  1 Aug. 1676 (McGill, Osler MS 7614).

as to whether he should proceed with the gesture)[15] he presented upon Ormond's arrival at Skerries in 1677.[16]

But there were also less self-promoting concerns. Petty was genuinely interested in maritime affairs. In 1663 he had made his first disastrous attempt at a catamaran design, and he may also have imagined a connection between the 'speedy, cheap, and satisfactory'[17] justice of the Admiralty Court, and the advancement of commercial activity in Ireland. While he did not prove a success as judge, his principal interest in maritime administration continued after he left the court. In 1685, after his resignation from the court, he was at work preparing a projected 'Treatise of navigation' and investigating inventions for de-salinating seawater.[18]

It is unclear who prevailed upon the duke of York to appoint Petty. Petty enjoyed an extensive range of contacts both within the Admiralty and amongst the duke of York's inner circle. He could count amongst this set of contacts: Sir William Glascock, Sir Robert Southwell, Sir Peter Pett (the king's advocate in Ireland), Sir John Werden (secretary to the duke of York), Sir Allen Apsley, Samuel Pepys (secretary to the Admiralty), Sir George Carteret (treasurer to the Admiralty), as well as the duke of York himself. Relations with Carteret had deteriorated; the two men had fallen out in a land dispute. In a fit of neurosis, Petty re-assessed his judicial appointment as an elaborate scheme engineered by Carteret to humiliate him: 'Sir George Carteret and others promoted this business and made [William] Glascock the instrument of their revenge'.[19]

The same constitutional difficulties which had retarded the development of the court in the early seventeenth century persisted. Petty had been very early apprised of encroachments upon the court by two rival sources: intrusions upon its revenue perquisites by manorial lords with admiralty grants, and encroachments upon its judicial role by corporations. In a memorandum on the state of admiralty jurisdiction in Ireland, Petty identified the four institutional difficulties whose elimination was necessary for the development of the Court of Admiralty:

> First: there are many controversies between admiral and admiral (viz.) between the lord high admiral and mayors, corporations and lords of manors who pretend to be local admirals in their several precincts. Second: between the Admiralty Court and other courts who begin to wax wanton in sending prohibitions to ours – perhaps because we do more speedy, cheap and satisfactory justice than they. Third: between the admiralty of England and the admiralty of Ireland, for that of England acts here from appeals made unto them from hence thither ... Fourth: care has been taken to settle

15 W. Petty to R. Southwell, 22 Aug. 1677, *Petty–Southwell Corr.*, p. 33.
16 'A Naval Allegory; by the registrar of the Admiralty of Ireland; To his grace James, duke of York, as grand pilot of the good ship *Ireland*, upon his fourth expedition on that bottom'. *The Petty Papers*, ed. marquis of Lansdowne, 2 vols (London, 1927), ii, p. 248.
17 Undated memorandum by Petty on admiralty law (BL, Lansdowne MS 1,228, f. 8).
18 BL, Add. MS 72893, ff 30–1.
19 W. Petty to P. Pett, 26 Aug. 1676 (McGill, Osler MS 7,614, f. 12).

> matters between the vice-admiral and the judges of vice-admiralties, but all
> is not so clear between the vice-admirals of particular provinces and the
> judge of the High Court [of Admiralty of Ireland].[20]

The authority of the court was being undercut by writs of prohibition issuing from
the King's Bench; in 1679 Petty recorded the existence of five such writs currently
hanging over him.[21] A further source of disruption were replevins issued by local
municipal courts. But the real cause of the depression in the business of the court
was not these external interferences, but the very low level of its caseload. In his
address to the Admiralty sessions in October 1676, Petty noted that there were only
five items of business currently before the court.[22] There is no indication that Petty
managed to reverse this decline, and the reforming optimism of the first few
months following his appointment was superseded by a period of despair and
lethargy. When, in 1683, Petty tendered his resignation, he cited as his principal
ground the fact that the office 'gives me no such work as I expected'.[23]

   Despite these institutional obstacles, and a demoralizingly low caseload, Petty,
particularly during the first three years of his tenure, busied himself in attempting
to consolidate the authority of the court. But while the court did not flourish, and
while Petty found being a lawyer more difficult than he originally imagined, he was,
at least, active and inventive. Petty's weaknesses were a poor legal knowledge
(instanced by his disastrous handling of a series of prize cases in the late 1670s) and
a tendency to use the court to his own ends (as in the *Elliston* case in 1679 where
Petty used its processes in order to pursue one of his own debtors).[24]

### Dr Dudley Loftus, 1680–3; Petty resigns

By 1680 Petty had begun to withdraw from active involvement in the court.
During the following three years he directed his talents to other concerns: the
reform of revenue administration, his Kerry estates, the Royal Society, and his
experiments with the double-bottomed ship.[25] After Petty had withdrawn to his
residence in Picadilly, the court was delegated to surrogates,[26] Dr Henry Styles[27]
and Dr Dudley Loftus. Loftus (the son of the late judge, Adam) had been
associated with the court since as far back as 1654, when he had been appointed

---

20   Undated memorandum by Petty on admiralty law (BL, Lansdowne MS 1,228, f. 8).
21   W. Petty to R. Southwell, 4 Jan. 1679; *Petty–Southwell Corr.*, pp 63, 66.
22   1 Oct. 1676 (BL, Lansdowne MS 1228, f. 46).
23   W. Petty to J. Werden, 6 [?] Aug. 1683 (McGill, Osler MS 7,612).
24   See p. 96 below.
25   E. Fitzmaurice, *The life of Sir William Petty* (London, 1895), pp 250–8.
26   In the appeal in the mariners' wages case, *Pippard v. Furlong*, the ground of appeal was that his
     surrogate Loftus had been irregularly appointed, and had acted without 'any legitimate
     deputation having been made signed and signified'.
27   In 1679, acting as Petty's surrogate, Styles condemned a prize called the *Prince of Bristol* (TNA
     (PRO), ADM 1/3,882).

judge of the Commonwealth Court of Admiralty.[28] Following the Restoration he had served as deputy to Carey Dillon in the Admiralty Court of Leinster,[29] and then as surrogate to Sir Paul Rycaut right up to the mid-1690s.[30] While Loftus was, unlike Petty, a trained civilian, his principal failing was a confrontational and troublesome personality; in the 1660s he had been dismissed from his office as judge of the Court of Prerogative; in 1673 he had been incarcerated in Dublin Castle[31] and stripped of his office as master in chancery for agitating against government-instigated reforms of the municipal corporations. His appointment as Petty's surrogate was a partial rehabilitation following the virtual termination of his public career six years earlier. But Loftus' trouble-making disposition was incorrigible. It was this side to his personality which underlay the most dramatic incident during his period as Petty's surrogate, the imprisonment for contempt of the officials of the mayor of Dublin in the *Jacob of Dublin* case.[32] This incident may have confirmed the feeling that Loftus was unsuited for office, and although possibly the most experienced admiralty lawyer in late seventeenth-century Dublin, his contribution was never formally acknowledged by his appointment to the position of judge. Dudley Loftus, acting merely as surrogate judge, remained in the shadows of the court for forty years.

William Petty resigned office in 1683. In the end, it was university politics which appears to have determined both the timing of William Petty's departure, and the choice of his successor. Dr Henry Styles was a senior fellow at Trinity College Dublin and regius professor of civil law. In addition to holding the regius professorship he had served as vice-provost of Trinity; when the position of provost fell vacant in 1683, Styles was considered to be the leading candidate. The lord deputy, the earl of Arran, reported that, while everyone 'both of the clergy and laity' with whom he had discussed the matter 'thought [Styles] to be the fittest man', the primate, who rated him as morally deficient, was determined that he not succeed.[33] Arran (correctly as it turned out) calculated that, unless Styles made his peace with the archbishop of Armagh, Michael Boyle, an appointee would have to be translated from one of the English universities. This is what happened: in July

28  A. Clarke, *Prelude to restoration in Ireland* (Cambridge, 1999), p. 228; *Cal. anc. rec. Dub.*, i, pp 39–41.

29  Loftus was referred to as surrogate to Carey Dillon in the appeal to England in the *Assistance of Liverpool* (TNA (PRO), HCA 3/51, f. 596 (24 Apr. 1673)).

30  Loftus served as surrogate to Sir Paul Rycaut (who acted as as absentee judge from 1689 to 1698 while simultaneously serving as resident to Hamburg). Rycaut considered Loftus 'a very unfit man for that place, but I know no other to employ'. P. Rycaut to Maudit, 16 June 1691 (BL, Add. MS 1,153 C, f. 199).

31  The earl of Essex reported that 'after having heard him what he could say for himself, we committed him to prison' for 'fermenting the differences now in the city'. The warrant of committal of the Privy Council was dated 1 Sept. 1673 (TNA (PRO), SP 63/334, ff 103, 107).

32  D. Loftus to W. Petty, 30 Sept. 1682 (BL, Add. MS 7, 2893, f. 87); Bodl., Carte MS 39, f. 614 & Carte MS 144, f. 406.

33  Earl of Arran to the duke of Ormond, 29 Jan. 1683 (Bodl., Carte MS 168, f. 79). See also R.B. McDowell and D.A. Webb, *Trinity College Dublin, 1592–1952* (Cambridge, 1982), pp 25–7.

1683 the Oxford divine Dr Robert Huntington was appointed in preference to Styles. In the meantime Petty, who was now dividing his time between Ireland and England, had become preoccupied with another project: obtaining the commission for the administration of licences for wine, beer and strengthened wines.[34] The timing of Petty's resignation, occurring just after Styles' failure to be appointed Provost,[35] suggests that Petty was obliging Styles with an escape route from Trinity, while providing himself with cover with which to disengage. In August 1683 Petty wrote to John Werden (the secretary of the duke of York) a dispirited letter, identifying the lack of judicial business as his ground of resignation:

> I troubled you lately with a letter of the 4th inst. about the passes and ballastage. This is to desire your assistance for the bearer, Dr Styles, to succeed me in the place of judge of the admiralty, which I do not quit because it affords me no wages, but because it gives me no such work as I expected, and should have been glad to have bestowed my time upon, even without recompense or reward, than the satisfaction to have done well. This gentleman would better perform what is now to be done than I can do.[36]

### Dr Henry Styles, 1683–6

In August 1683 Dr Henry Styles, the distinguished academic civilian,[37] and university administrator, who had served as Petty's surrogate, was appointed judge.[38] Styles was, like Petty, over-qualified for the rather modest, if impressive-sounding, office of judge of the Irish Court of Admiralty. On his appointment, Styles, perhaps over-estimating the extent of his judicial commitment, took full leave of absence from Trinity.[39] He served as judge for a period of just under three years. The fragments which survive from his short tenure suggest that he was encountering the same problems as Petty. As with Petty there were fights with Dublin Corporation.[40] As in Petty's time the income generated by fishing licences remained the court's principal revenue, and Styles was reduced to undignified squabbling over licences, involving himself in a dispute with the vice-admiral of Leinster, Carey Dillon.[41]

---

34  Earl of Arran to Rochester, 18 Oct. 1683 (Bodl., Carte MS 169, f. 14).
35  Robert Huntington, a fellow of Merton College, Oxford, was appointed provost in September 1683; C. Maxwell, *A history of Trinity College Dublin, 1592–1892* (Dublin, 1946), p. 76.
36  W. Petty to J. Werden, 6[?] Aug. 1683 (McGill, Osler MS 7,612).
37  In 1668 Styles, on his election of professor of law, had petitioned the king for a salary, complaining that the absence of such a salary 'doth much obstruct the advancement of that study there'. The matter was referred to Ormond, as lord lieutenant and chancellor of the university. Ormond directed that a sum of not less than £40 *per annum* be attached to the office of professor of civil law at Trinity College Dublin, to be paid out of 'the revenue lately settled upon the college'; *Cal. S.P. Ire. 1666–1669*, pp 654–5.
38  Warrant of appointment, 28 Aug. 1683 (TNA (PRO), ADM 1/3883, f. 27).
39  *Ormond Calendar*, v, p. 634.                    40  *Cal. anc. rec. Dub.*, v, p. 301.
41  P. Rycaut to S. Maudit, 13 Dec. 1692 (BL, Add. MS 37,663, f. 39).

*Sir Paul Rycaut, 1686–98*

In July 1686 Samuel Pepys, the secretary to the Admiralty, sitting at his office in York Buildings, opened a petition from Sir Paul Rycaut, secretary to the earl of Clarendon, the lord lieutenant of Ireland. Rycaut sought an appointment to the vacant position of judge of the Court of Admiralty and enclosed a testimonial (what he described as 'the powerful recommendation of his excellence the lord lieutenant') from Clarendon:

> the office of judge of your majesty's Court of Admiralty in this kingdom is vacant by the death of Dr Styles. The petitioner therefore humbly beseeches your majesty would be graciously pleased to confer the office of judge of the said Court of Admiralty upon your petitioner to hold the same together with his office of secretary.[42]

Sir Paul Rycaut had no expertise in admiralty law and was quite open in letting it be known that his sole interest was the money derived from the position. He considered himself entitled to the position in return for the public services which he was discharging in the lord lieutenant's office. He sought the office of judge (a 'lean place') on the basis that he would be granted a salary of £50.[43] He concluded with a hint to Samuel Pepys (who shared Rycaut's interest in money) that he would be amenable to handing over a small bribe, suggesting that 'in case anything should offer here wherein I might be useful to you, you may be confident that none shall be more ready than myself'. Within a few weeks Rycaut was able to report that news had arrived, *via* Samuel Pepys, that the office had been granted to him:

> By the last post I received a letter from Mr Pepys wherein he acquaints me that his majesty was graciously pleased, with all readiness, to bestow upon me the office of judge of the Admiralty Court in Ireland, and that my commission was sealed and lay at his office and should be delivered to the person whom I should appoint, and I have accordingly ordered a friend of mine to call for it and pay the fees. And though the benefit of the office is very inconsiderable, yet I am proud thereof, considering the circumstances with which his majesty was pleased to bestow it upon me.[44]

In September 1686 he wrote with a touch of urgency to his agent in London requesting him to collect his judicial commission from Samuel Pepys, since he was keen to begin collecting money for issuing the fishing licences which were due for renewal that month:

---

42  W. Rycaut to S. Pepys, 26 July 1686, *Rycaut's memoranda*, p. 125.
43  Ibid., p. 161.
44  P. Rycaut to J. Cooke, 17 Aug. 1686, ibid., pp 164–5.

I did desire you to take out the commission (for admiralty judge) paying the
fees for it, which I suppose will be six or seven pounds, and indeed I would not
presume to trespass so far upon you, were I not at present pressed to have it in
my possession, for till that time I cannot act and the term draws on when some
causes will be tried, and this now is the season for giving out licences for the
fishing, which will be a loss to me if my commission comes not speedily.[45]

However, the absence of a proper warrant of appointment did not bother him
unduly, for on the same date he recorded: 'I signed forty fishing licences being
judge of the Admiralty'.[46] Rycaut served as judge in Ireland for, at the most, five
months, at which point he permanently departed Ireland.

Rycaut, however, did not resign his judicial position when he permanently
emigrated. Business, instead, was delegated during the years 1687 and 1688, to his
cousin Thomas Rycaut, a Dublin attorney. Sir Paul claimed that the arrangement
was officially sanctioned, and that he had been allowed to 'act by surrogate during
my attendance on his majesty's affairs in those parts'.[47] This absenteeism was
maintained even when, in July 1689, Rycaut was appointed resident in Hamburg
and the Hanse Towns.

During the civil war between 1689 and 1690 most Irish courts were packed with
Jacobite appointees. However, there was no Jacobite takeover of the Court of
Admiralty.[48] Instead it is likely that the court temporarily ceased to operate; in 1692
Rycaut referred to the 'suspension of my office' which had occurred during the
'late troubles'.[49] In November 1690, when stability was restored, Rycaut instructed
the registrar, Thomas Wilkinson, to draw up a commission appointing Dr Dudley
Loftus as surrogate. Under the profit-sharing arrangement with Loftus, the latter
was entitled to a moiety of the fee income generated by the court.[50] A temporary
commission of surrogacy was also granted to the ecclesiastical lawyer Sir John
Coghill.[51] After eighteen months had elapsed 'without a syllable' from Loftus,
Rycaut decided to withdraw the office from him. His real preference was to sell the
position outright but he had 'since understood by my advices that there is a strict
prohibition against selling offices in Ireland'.[52] He offered the position, first, to Sir

45   P. Rycaut to J. Turner, 4 Sept. 1686, ibid., p. 167.
46   7 Sept. 1686, *Rycaut's memoranda*, p. 131.
47   P. Rycaut to earl of Bath, 21 Mar. 1693 (BL, Add. MS 37,663, f. 126).
48   In 1689 the Jacobite administration packed the Courts of Chancery, Common Pleas, Exchequer
     and King's Bench with its own supporters. However, there is no record of a Jacobite appointee to
     the Court of Admiralty. W. King, *The state of the Protestants of Ireland under the late King James'
     government* (London, 1691), pp 335–6.
49   P. Rycaut to W. Mayne, 22 Apr. 1692 (BL, Lansdowne MS 1,153D, f. 209).
50   P. Rycaut to Maudit, 16 June 1691 (BL, Lansdowne MS 1,153C, f. 199).
51   The Munster vice-admiralty correspondence book of Southwell included an opinion dated 26
     July 1691 'of Sir John Coghill judge of the admiralty there in the case of a retaken ship' (BL, Add.
     MS 38,147, f. 10). This entry indicates that Coghill may also have been acting as an occasional
     surrogate.
52   P. Rycaut to W. Mayne, 22 Apr. 1692 (BL, Lansdowne MS 1,153D, f. 209). Rycaut was thinking

John Coghill,[53] who declined, and next to his English-based nephew, Walter Mayne.[54] Mayne, eventually, made his way to Dublin. Though 'ingenious and industrious' Mayne was not a lawyer and not capable of independently functioning as judge.[55] Mayne had a civilian contact in Dublin, Dr Charles Ireton, who, Mayne suggested, would be able to provide him with technical assistance. However, this arrangement fell through. Next Rycaut opened negotiations with Sir John Eustace,[56] who had offered to purchase the office for the agreed price of £100.[57] That deal also collapsed when the financially disorganized Eustace failed to realize the purchase price. However, by 1693, another candidate, Thomas Lamplugh,[58] had arrived on the scene. Concerned, perhaps, to avoid the penalties for selling judicial offices, this arrangement envisaged that Lamplugh would rent, rather than buy, the office, paying a £30 fine, and £30 thereafter by way of annual rent.[59] Throughout these fruitless negotiations, Loftus carried on as surrogate.

While Rycaut in Hamburg was fretting over the return from his investment, the court in Dublin was in disarray. Dudley Loftus, who was now seventy-five, had just one year to live. The Court of Admiralty, which two years earlier had produced a healthy fee return from both fishing licences and from prize condemnations, now produced nothing, and may have become inactive:[60] 'I fear we shall have a bad account of the judges' fees belonging to the admiralty in Ireland, because Sir John Coghill writes me that Mr Wilkinson told him that there was no money arising from the office, nor from the fishing licences'.

Rycaut died in 1698. Even by the not very professional standards of the seventeenth-century Irish Admiralty Court, Rycaut's tenure was regarded as a disaster. Writing sixty years later, one of Rycaut's successors, Robert FitzGerald, made the assessment that 'Sir Paul Rycaut left the office in a very different state from that in which he found it'.[61]

of the Sale of Offices Act 1551 (5 & 6 Edw. VI, c. 16 (Eng.)) which prohibited the sale of offices which concerned the 'administration or execution of justice'.
53 P. Rycaut to J. Coghill, 11 Nov. 1691 (BL, Lansdowne MS 1,153D, f. 11).
54 P. Rycaut to W. Mayne, 22 Apr. 1692 (BL, Lansdowne MS 1,153D, f. 209).
55 P. Rycaut to J. Coghill, 2 Sept. 1692 (BL, Lansdowne MS 1,153D, f. 338).
56 P. Rycaut to J. Eustace, 4 Mar. 1692 (BL, Lansdowne MS 1,153D, f. 137). A nephew of Sir Maurice Eustace, lord chancellor, John Eustace was admitted to Lincoln's Inn in 1658, and knighted in 1663. *The records of the Honourable Society of Lincoln's Inn: admissions from A.D. 1420 to A.D. 1893, and chapel registers*, ed. W.P. Baildon, 2 vols (London, 1896), p. 279; F.W.X. Fincham, 'Letters concerning Sir Maurice Eustace, lord chancellor of Ireland', *English Historical Review*, 35 (1920), 251; E. Tickell, 'The Eustace Family and their lands in County Kildare', *Jnl of the Kildare Archaeological Society*, 13 (1958), 321, 322.
57 P. Rycaut to Maudit, 13 Dec. 1692 (BL, Add. MS 37,663, f. 39).
58 Admitted to Gray's Inn, 1676 (*Gray's Inn Admission Register 1521–1887*, p. 323).
59 P. Rycaut to Maudit, 20 Jan. 1693 (BL, Add. MS 37,663, f. 69).
60 P. Rycaut to Maudit, 13 Feb. 1694 (BL, Add. MS 37,663, f. 380).
61 R. FitzGerald to the commissioners of Admiralty, 29 June 1758 (TNA (PRO), ADM 1/3,883, f. 13).

*Dr William King, 1701–8*

By the late 1690s the collapse of the Irish Court of Admiralty had become a matter of real concern in London. In November 1699, Thomas Knox, the deputy vice-admiral of Leinster, submitted a policy paper to the Board of Admiralty proposing a revival of the provincial admiralty courts in Ireland, with Thomas Farren, the active judge of the Admiralty Court of Munster,[62] becoming judge of all four of these courts. The paper was referred to the judge of the Court of Admiralty in London, Sir Charles Hedges.[63] Hedges, whose pamphlet, *Reasons for settling admiralty jurisdiction*,[64] had made the case for a revived vice-admiralty system in England, endorsed the proposal for a resuscitation of the vice-admiralty system in Ireland. Knox's scheme proposed that the same three officers be appointed to each of the four provincial courts:

> Mr Thomas Farren who has acted as judge of the Vice-Admiralty Court of Munster, who has a good character, and I know in some particulars, has behaved himself very well in his office, may be constituted judge of each of the vice-admiralties. That Mr Thomas Wilkinson who has acted as an admiralty registrar at Dublin be made registrar of every one of the four vice-admiralties. That Mr Knox be marshal of all the courts with power to make deputy or deputies. That Mr Knox have also a deputation from Mr Corbet, who is your lordships' collector and receiver general, to look after and manage the perquisites of the admiralty in Ireland.[65]

The Knox scheme addressed the problem of the inactive vice-admiralties. However, the problem of the collapse of the national Court of Admiralty still required to be solved. In November 1700 Sir Charles Hedges wrote to the Admiralty noting that the place of judge of the Irish Court of Admiralty had been vacant since 1698, and recommending Dr William King who was, he said, 'qualified by his knowledge and experience in civil law'.[66] King, having graduated with an LLD from Oxford, had been admitted to practise at Doctors' Commons in 1692.[67] He had been nominated to serve on the Court of Delegates where his judicial performance was praised.[68] However, although talented, he was lazy and was bored by law. He never established a viable practice in London, and the

62  Admiralty Board minutes, 8 Nov. 1699 (TNA (PRO), ADM 3/15).
63  Ibid.
64  *Reasons for settling admiralty-jurisdiction, and giving encouragement to merchants, owners, commanders, masters of ships, material-men and mariners, humbly offered to the consideration of his majesty, and the two Houses of Parliament* (London, 1690).
65  C. Hedges to the commissioners of Admiralty, 23 Nov. 1699 (BL, Add. MS 24,107, f. 177). The board, on 8 Dec. 1699, agreed to adopt the proposals (TNA (PRO), ADM 3/15).
66  C. Hedges to the commissioners of Admiralty, 27 Nov. 1700, *Cal. S.P. Dom. 1700–1702*, p. 153.
67  G.D. Squibb, *Doctors' Commons* (Oxford, 1977), p. 185.
68  *Original works of William King LLD*, ed. J. Nichols, 3 vols (London, 1776), i, p. xiv.

Hedges' nomination to the Irish court may have been designed as an act of patronage. King arrived in Dublin late in 1701. Under the terms of the English Test Act 1691[69] he was required to postpone the commencement of duties until he had first taken the statutory oaths before the King's Bench. Having taken the test, he then briefed himself on the difficulties currently affecting the court. This confirmed the pessimistic reports – 'full of all manner of discouragements' – which he had received in London.[70] In November 1701 he furnished a terse memorandum on the depressing state of the Irish Admiralty Court at the turn of the eighteenth century:

> All things have been in great confusion as to the admiralty affairs for these last ten years past. There has been a surrogate named but little done unless some licences granted for fishing. There is a registrar, who is Mr Wilkinson, that is an experienced practitioner and well respected both here and in England. There is a marshal that was formerly a sea captain ... There is a seal of the admiralty. But neither oar nor any certain place to which any person may be cited. The mariners for their wages, the masters for damages and such like affairs apply to the sheriffs' courts who know nothing of the matter. There has lately been two wrecks ... one ... in Wicklow of lead to a considerable value. The fishermen are insulted in the sea by persons that have no rights to the pretence of admiralty jurisdiction. There was a whale lately thrown upon the coast which a youth has converted to his own use.[71]

King concluded by suggesting the 'necessity of a general inquiry round the whole coast of Ireland, if your Lordships will not let it suffer under pretence of grants both of admiralty jurisdiction and perquisites'.

Under Dr King the Dublin court had begun, once again, to exercise ordinary instance jurisdiction.[72] However, work was (as it was in the English Court of Admiralty in the early eighteenth century) slack, and King was granted, as another outlet for his civilian training, the office of vicar general of Armagh. He was particularly associated with the campaign to regain those admiralty jurisdictions which were being withheld from the court by municipal corporations. In 1702 he sought the intervention of the Admiralty against the claims of the city of Dublin, and in 1706 he brought to the attention of the Admiralty the jurisdictional claims of Cork. In 1707 King was charged with the management of the *quo warranto* action challenging the municipal admiralty jurisdiction asserted by the Corporation of Galway.[73] After six years' exile in Dublin, King returned to London late in 1707. An eighteenth-century biographer adopted the severe assessment that

69  3 Will. & Mar., c.2 (Eng.), 1691.
70  W. King to J. Ellis, 13 Nov. 1701 (BL, Add. MS 28,887, f. 369).
71  Ibid.
72  See the 1705 appeal from Ireland to the English Court of Admiralty, the *Mary Flyboat of Dublin* (1705) (TNA (PRO), HCA 3/63, f. 408).
73  See p. 77 below.

King had 'neglected all his business' while judge of the Irish Court of Admiralty.[74] But King had, at least, begun the process of attempting to revive the authority of a court which had been virtually extinct by the time he had arrived. Under Dr King the court appears to have been restored to its usual, if modest, level of activity.

## THE PERSONNEL AND ADMINISTRATION OF THE COURT OF ADMIRALTY OF IRELAND IN THE LATE SEVENTEENTH CENTURY

### The registrar of the court

In 1676 James Waller was appointed registrar to William Glascock.[75] Waller, a brother-in-law of Petty, was continued under Petty's regime. Waller's functions appear, in practice, to have been undertaken by a deputy:[76] the Dublin notary Thomas Wilkinson (described by Petty as 'a man well versed in these affairs').[77] On his resignation, Petty proposed Wilkinson as Waller's successor, and Wilkinson continued to serve until his death in 1718. Sir Paul Rycaut detected a disingenuousness in Wilkinson's personality, observing that 'he is a cunning man and loves his own interest'.[78] He stood his ground when, in 1699, the proposal to remedy the collapse of national admiralty jurisdiction through the revival of the four provincial courts was being put in place. Wilkinson, who had been proposed as registrar, refused to join Thomas Farren's peripatetic court.[79]

### The marshal

Petty's job description of the office of marshal was that it was a position suitable for 'some stout, active fellow'.[80] The duke of York handed out offices in the Irish court as favours to members of his entourage: in 1661 the office of marshal and waterbailiff was officially divided between Robert Smith, a messenger in the chamber of King Charles II, and Smith's son-in-law, Richard Sturt.[81] Later,

---

74  *Original works of William King*, ed. J. Nichols, 3 vols (London, 1776), i, p. xviii.
75  Appointed, 6 July 1676 (TNA (PRO), ADM 1/3,883, f. 25).
76  See, for instance, an affidavit of 14 December 1678 attested by Thomas Wilkinson who is described as deputy registrar (TNA (PRO), HCA 15/9, f.41).
77  W. Petty to J. Werden, 6[?] Aug. 1683 (McGill, Osler MS 7,612).
78  P. Rycaut to Maudit, 16 June 1691 (BL, Lansdowne MS 11,53C, f. 199).
79  C. Hedges to the Admiralty, 23 Nov. 1699 (BL, Add. MS 24,107, f.177). In place of Wilkinson, Walter Bunbury was appointed registrar of the Courts of Vice-Admiralty of Leinster, Munster, Connacht and Ulster in February 1700, *Court of Admiralty Commission Report, 1864*, Appendix G., p. 76. On the re-establishment of the central Court of Admiralty under Dr William King, Bunberry petitioned to be appointed registrar; Wilkinson, however, was preferred (TNA (PRO), ADM 3/16).
80  W. Petty to T. Palmer, 3 Mar. 1677 (McGill, Osler MS 7612).
81  Duke of York to H. Hyde, 6 May 1661 (TNA (PRO), ADM 2/1725, f. 48).

Charles Sturt (presumably a relative of Richard Sturt) and George Pigott succeeded to the office of marshal in 1676.[82] Charles Sturt, who was active between the 1660s and the early 1680s,[83] was Munster-based and in Dublin the functions of the admiralty marshal were discharged by an array of deputies.[84] When, Sturt died, in July 1682, the office of marshal was filled by Captain Francis Robinson, a military man who had fallen on hard times. There were doubts over Robinson's judgment, and when a few months later the fight over the replevin proceedings in the *Jacob of Dublin* broke out, the lord deputy, the earl of Arran, who had served in the army with Robinson,[85] held the new admiralty marshal partly responsible for the mess. 'The person employed by the Duke', he wrote to his father 'is liable to mistakes and to do extravagant things. I found him so when he was in the army, and it may be doubted whether his civil employment will reform him. I believe so it will be when poverty is the best qualification a man has for an office'.[86]

Throughout the 1690s the office of marshal was filled by Austin Burch.[87] Thomas Knox reported to London that Burch was 'almost blind, nay ignorant'; Burch, he wrote, lived 'on the seashore, where he is near, receiving his fees; but never makes any enquiries either into encroachments on the jurisdiction of the admiralty or any other thing relating to his office of admiralty; but says that it is to the water bayley's place he must rely on'.[88] The powers entrusted to Burch were unorthodox:[89] 'he is appointed not only marshal but water bayley of this kingdom and it stuffed with such powers as I am sure are in no way suitable with the office of marshal as they are appointed in England, nor I presume will the lords of the Admiralty ever allow of a High Court of Admiralty distant from Doctors' Commons'.

The Court of Admiralty of Ireland did not have a settled, official place of business during the reign of Charles II. It discharged its annual criminal 'court of inquiry' at the Dublin port district of Ringsend. The greater part of its business appears to have been conducted from the judge's home. During Petty's tenure the

---

82  The book of admiralty civil commissions and warrants 1663–84 contains the entry: 'Note there was a warrant granted for Charles Sturt and George Pigott to be marshal of the admiralty in Ireland entered in the Book of Household Affairs, folio 225' (TNA (PRO), ADM 2/1,755, f. 34). On 12 July 1676 Sir Peter Pett informed Sir Robert Southwell that he 'sent the warrant about George Pigott and Charles Sturt to Sir William Glascock' (BL, Add. MS 72,852, f. 119). The appointment of Sturt and Pigott is omitted from the list of marshals appendixed to the *Court of Admiralty Commission Report, 1864*.

83  W. Petty to Lady Helena Southwell, 9 Feb. 1678 (BL, Add. MS 72,852, f. 148).

84  The names of some of those operating as deputy marshals in Dublin in the late 1670s include Patrick Little and John Murphy; affidavits dated 8 Jan. 1679 & 3 July 1679 (TNA (PRO), HCA 15/9 & HCA 15/11).

85  The earl of Arran had been colonel of the King's Regiment of Guards of Ireland.

86  Earl of Arran to the duke of Ormond, 5 Dec. 1682 (Bodl., Carte MS, vol. 219, f. 406).

87  Appointed 2 Mar. 1690 (TNA (PRO), ADM 1/3,883, f. 71).

88  T. Knox to C. Hedges, 25 Feb. 1700 (BL, Add. MS 24,107, f. 195).

89  Ibid.

address of the Court of Admiralty was George's Lane[90] (Petty's Dublin address). In 1688 the court was referred to as sitting at the home of Dudley Loftus on Cork Hill.[91] Nor did it possess that traditional symbol of admiralty authority, a ceremonial silver oar. In 1662 the duke of York waived the income generated by the sale of oil from a whale condemned by the Leinster Admiralty Court in order to allow the court acquire a silver mace. But by the first decade of the eighteenth century no mace had yet been manufactured.[92]

More serious than its lack of a physical apparatus was the court's deficiency of intellectual resources. This absence was particularly felt when non-lawyers like Petty presided. The registrar of the English court, Thomas Bedford, noting that 'Sir William Petty grows weary under his difficulties in proceedings, and that it is improbable to discharge his office without others frequently arising'[93] suggested that he hire 'some understanding proctor or clerk from here'. On the other hand, he did concede that that 'would be difficult to do unless about £100 be secured, which is improbable the profits ever will afford'. There were certainly civilians practising in Dublin. In his *Anatomy of Ireland*, published in 1691, William Petty estimated 'there are belonging to the prerogative, archdeacons' courts, courts martial and admiralty courts, not above ten advocates, and thirty proctors'.[94] The small group of lawyers who practised as advocates in late-seventeenth-century Ireland included men such as Dr Dudley Loftus, Dr Henry Styles, Dr John Topham,[95] the Munster-based Dr Joshua Boyle,[96] and one of Rycaut's proposed surrogates, the civilian Dr Charles Ireton.[97]

Petty found it difficult even to assemble an elementary admiralty law library in Dublin.[98] Soon after his appointment, Petty was reminding his predecessor, William Glascock, to provide him with admiralty texts:[99] 'Pray Sir William Glascock to send me ye books and papers he promised and particularly *Les Uses et Coutumes de la Mer*'.[100] Petty owned a copy of Francis Clerke's well-organized, sixteenth-century treatise on admiralty practice, *Praxis Curiae Admiralitatis Angliae*. Clerke's *vade mecum* was a boon to the 'part-time, sometimes honorary, and rather amateurish judiciary'[101] of the courts of vice-admiralty in the late

90  Georges Lane (Georges Street) was described as the address of the Court of Admiralty in Petty's 1677 grand jury speech (BL, Lansdowne MS 1,228, ff 46, 52).
91  TNA (PRO), HCA 15/14.
92  W. King to J. Ellis, 13 Nov. 1701 (BL, Add. MS 28,887, f. 369).
93  Bedford's opinion, Doctors' Commons, 11 Apr. 1678 (BL, Add. MS 72,852, f. 152).
94  *The Political Anatomy of Ireland* (London, 1691), p. 41.
95  See above p. 50.                    96  See p. 63 below.
97  See p. 57 above.
98  Remnants of Dudley Loftus' law library, including some admiralty materials, survive: Marsh's Library MS Z3.2.1.
99  W. Petty to P. Pett, 1 Aug. 1676 (McGill, Osler MS 7,612).
100 E. Cleirac, *Us et coutumes de la mer* (Rouen, 1661).
101 D.M. Derrett, 'The Works of Francis Clerke, Proctor', *Studia et Documenta Historiae et Juris*, 40 (1973), 52.

seventeenth century, and Petty highly recommended it.[102] In addition to this lack of textbooks, Petty also required copies of official treaties and proclamations. In 1676 Petty requested 'from the lords commissioners of Admiralty, or Mr Pepys, a collection of all proclamations and other acts of state which they act by in England, as well as a supply of precedents and forms of instruments'.[103]

## THE PROVINCIAL COURTS OF ADMIRALTY OF IRELAND IN THE LATE SEVENTEENTH CENTURY

### Vice-admiralty judicial appointments

Immediately after the Restoration, the duke of York, as lord high admiral, made appointments to three of the provincial admiralty courts of Ireland: Edward Cooke was appointed judge of the Vice-Admiralty of Leinster in 1660.[104] The office of judge of the court of the vice-admiralty of Ulster (the quietest of the provincial vice-admiralties), was filled in 1661 by John Dolway 'student in laws'.[105] In 1666 Nicholas Turke succeeded Dolway as judge of the Ulster Admiralty Court. The position remained in family hands when, in 1684, Nicholas Turke's son, Richard Turke, was appointed judge of the Ulster court.[106] In 1663 the duke of York attended 'to the want of a judge of the Vice-Admiralty of Munster'[107] by appointing Dr Joshua Boyle.[108] Cooke and Boyle continued to serve for the next twenty years; a memorandum prepared for Samuel Pepys in 1687 listed Joshua Boyle as still serving as judge of the Munster court and Edward Cooke as judge of the Leinster court.[109]

Where there was no vice-admiralty judge, the judicial side of provincial vice-admiralty work could, in default, be discharged by the provincial vice-admiral. The entitlement of the vice-admiral, or his deputy, to act judicially in the absence of the judge was confirmed in an opinion on the Irish vice-admiralty prepared in 1663.[110]

---

102 'Now as to the admiralty proceedings, these rules are comprehended in a small book called Clerke['s] *Practice* which is not unlike the little books both in England and Ireland, wherein the rules of their respective chanceries are contained' (BL, Lansdowne MS 1,228).
103 29 July 1676 (McGill, Osler MS 7,612).
104 19 Dec. 1660, *Court of Admiralty Commission Report, 1864*, Appendix G., p. 75.
105 19 Mar. 1661 (TNA (PRO), HCA 30/820, no. 185).
106 14 Aug. 1684 (TNA (PRO), ADM 7/298, f. 509). This appointment was omitted from the list of patentee officers appendixed to the *Court of Admiralty Commission Report, 1864*.
107 11 July 1663 (TNA (PRO), ADM 2/1,745, f. 94).
108 *Court of Admiralty Commission Report, 1864*, Appendix G, p. 75. Boyle had been recorder of Youghal in 1641: R. Caulfield (ed.), *The Council Book of the Corporation of Youghal* (Guildford, 1878), p. 217, and registrar to the dean and chapter of Waterford and Lismore in 1663: H. Cotton, *Fasti Ecclesiae Hibernicae* (Dublin, 1857), i, p. 122. He was a cousin of Richard Boyle, earl of Cork (ibid., p. 184).
109 Cambridge, Magdalene, Pepys MS 2,762, f. 2.
110 Declaration of duke of York, 10 Dec. 1663 (TNA (PRO), ADM 2/1,755).

Two English civil lawyers, William Turner and David Budd, wrote that if 'the judge do not keep courts and do those things fitting to be done by his place that then the vice-admiral, or his deputy, may keep courts as judges and receive the judges' accustomed fees'. Some of these officers were regarded as reasonably legally competent. Colonel Spencer, the deputy vice-admiral of Connacht, was praised by Sir Peter Pett as knowing 'more law' than any admiralty judge in Ireland 'except one'.[111] Spencer presided as vice-admiralty judge in Connacht, in two important prize-related cases, the *Sacrifice of Abraham* in 1666, and *Fleming v. Lynch* in 1667, while the *Unity of Amsterdam* case in 1701 was heard at Galway before the vice-admiral of Connacht.[112] Similarly, in the early 1670s, Carey Dillon, the vice-admiral of Leinster from 1668,[113] appears to have occupied both the administrative function of vice-admiral and the judicial function of judge.[114]

From the late 1670s a third level of admiralty judicature appeared: alongside the central court, and the judges of the vice-admiralties, local judges began to be appointed by the Court of Admiralty in Dublin. These were agents of the national Irish court rather than appointees of the Admiralty in London. The practice of establishing deputies appears to have been an innovation of Sir William Petty who, upon his appointment, began establishing a network of local admiralty judges with jurisdiction to try cases worth under £50.[115] Petty informed the vice-admiral of Munster that he was trying 'several ways how to divide the judicatures, and am loath to fix any thing without some experience'.[116] A deputation dated 29 September 1677 appointed Thomas Palmer to execute the office of deputy judge of the Admiralty, with authority to act in cases worth less than £50, from the town of Bantry to the town of Tarbert:[117]

> … as I myself were present, always excepting the judgment of wrecks, prizes and piracy, and all other causes when the matter in question exceedeth not fifty pounds, of all which causes I do hereby appoint a true statement and report to be sent to me that I may give him future orders therein, empowering him to receive all manner of fees, perquisites and dues and other profits of right belonging to me.[118]

---

111  P. Pett to the earl of Clarendon, 9 June 1666 (Bodl., Clarendon MS 84, f. 190).

112  G. St George to the commissioners of Admiralty, 10 Apr. 1701 (TNA (PRO), ADM 1/3,666, f. 238).

113  Warrant dated 13 Mar. 1668, *Court of Admiralty Commission Report, 1864*, Appendix G., p. 75.

114  Dillon is referred to as presiding over the court in the appeal *Peake v. Armitage* 3 Feb. 1669 (TNA (PRO), HCA 3/51,f. 247); *Therogood v. Boyce* (TNA (PRO), HCA 15/15).

115  'We are at present setting our judges and officers in many places, but have finished nothing as yet'. W. Petty to R. Southwell, 29 Sept. 1677, *Petty–Southwell Corr.*, p. 36.

116  W. Petty to R. Southwell, 18 Nov. 1677, *Petty–Southwell Corr.*, p. 40.

117  TNA (PRO), ADM 7/298, f. 509.

118  Petty also granted a deputation (1 Oct. 1677) to Charles Ireton (for counties Down, Armagh, Sligo, Antrim, Donegal & Derry) (TNA (PRO), ADM 1/3,883, f. 34).

An officer called Brown was appointed local judge for the area from Valencia to Smerwick.[119] Thomas Meade, the Kinsale lawyer who represented the interests of the Perceval family, was appointed deputy judge with a commission entitling him to act in Kinsale and 'all the coast of Cork to the west thereof'.[120] Edward Eyres was appointed judge in Galway.[121] These were small claims' judges only – their competence was restricted to suits worth less than £50. Petty refused to expand the jurisdiction of these local appointees, reluctant to 'expose the greater cases happening in the out ports' to local courts 'where there is little help of experienced advocates, and proctors'.[122]

The practice of appointing local deputies was continued by Petty's successors. In 1686 Sir Paul Rycaut reassured the bishop of Killala that he intended to re-appoint Dr Michael Jones 'to be my deputy or surrogate in your country, as he was to my predecessor, Dr Styles',[123] and later in the year Rycaut appointed John Bodkin to be the deputy admiralty judge at Galway.[124] These deputations lapsed with the demise of the judge from whose authority the office derived. In 1692, following the termination and re-appointment of Sir Paul Rycaut, John Coghill (whom Rycaut was using as his overseer in Dublin) wrote to Rycaut, advising him that the warrants constituting local deputies required to be resuscitated. Rycaut replied directing that the appointments be renewed:[125] 'I take notice, as you write to me, for me send special authorities to constitute deputies in every province. I desire you to send me a draft of such a deputation, with the name of the persons who you think fit to be constituted in such matters'.

The Irish provincial admiralty judicature fell into abeyance in the late seventeenth century. Only the Munster Admiralty Court continued to operate into the early eighteenth century. In 1689, Richard O'Donovan was appointed admiralty judge in the province of Munster by James II.[126] Nothing is heard of this Jacobite appointee thereafter, and he is likely to have been a casualty of political régime change.[127] He was succeeded by Thomas Farren who served as judge in Munster during the 1690s. In 1698 Farren deposed that he had 'been judge of the said [Munster] Court of Admiralty ever since the late troubles in this kingdom, and for some years before'.[128]

119  W. Petty to Crookshank, 12 Sept. 1677 (McGill, Osler MS 7,612).
120  'I doubt T. Meade grumbles inwardly that he is not judge of all Munster, whereas I design him but for Kinsale and all the coast of Cork westward thereof', W. Petty to R. Southwell, 18 Nov. 1677, *Petty–Southwell Corr.*, p. 40.
121  TNA (PRO), ADM 1/3,883, f. 36.
122  W. Petty to E. Eyres, 29 Dec. 1677 (TNA (PRO), ADM 1/3,883, f. 36).
123  P. Rycaut to R. Tennison, 31 Aug. 1686, *Rycaut's Memoranda*, p. 166.
124  P. Rycaut to J. Bodkin, 18 Nov. 1686, *Rycaut's Memoranda*, p. 177.
125  P. Rycaut to J. Coghill, 2 Sept. 1692 (BL, Add. MS 1,153 D, f. 337).
126  Appointed 23 July 1689; *Court of Admiralty Commission Report, 1864*, Appendix G., p. 80.
127  A Richard O'Donovan is identified as serving in Daniel O'Donovan's infantry: *King James' Irish army list*, ed. J. Dalton (reprinted, Missouri, 1997), p. 885.
128  TNA (PRO), HCA 15/18.

*Intra-jurisdictional issues; the demarcation of functions between the provincial judge and the provincial vice-admiral*

In the early 1660s an internal dispute occurred within the Vice-Admiralty of Leinster, between the judge of the Leinster court, Edward Cooke, and the Leinster vice-admiral, Sir George Wentworth, over the proper division of jurisdiction between the vice-admiral and the judge of vice-admiralty. The matter was referred to the lord admiral, James, duke of York, who, in turn, obtained an opinion from two leading civilians, Dr William Turner and Dr David Budd. These opinions provided a comprehensive analysis of the constitution of the Irish provincial vice-admiralties, and delineated the lines of demarcation between judge and vice-admiral. The judge's functions were to

> proceed alone in all matters of instance whatsoever between party and party
> … to decree compulsories against such as refuse to appear; to grant
> commissions for examination of parties' principals and witnesses; to take all
> manner of recognizances before him and, as need shall require, so declare the
> same to be forfeited; and to order all such things as are requisite to be
> decreed and done concerning any suit or matter depending in court before
> him for the concluding and, at last, to give and pronounce sentence definitive
> as the merits of the case shall require. The judge, by deputation from the
> vice-admiral, is alone to take cognizance of, and determine, all contracts
> made beyond the seas to be performed here, and of those which are here
> made and are to be expedited beyond the seas (although the power thereof is
> particularly mentioned in the vice-admiral's patent) … the judge has power
> to impose fines upon offenders, to commit them to prison for non-payment
> of these fines, to examine and commit any person to prison taken and
> apprehended upon suspicion of piracy, and [to] proceed to the adjudication
> of goods forfeited and confiscable (saving to the High Court of Admiralty the
> right of proceeding against all such ships and goods for which any shall there
> put in their claim and such as being of very great value … as it hath always
> been accustomed) … and after condemnation thereof to dispose of the same
> upon accompt to be made thereof unto me, as his patent directs.[129]

The vice-admiral was to be permitted, at the discretion of the judge, to sit in the court with the judge. He was also entitled to act judicially where the judge failed to keep a court:

> And that there be right understanding between the vice-admiral and the
> judge (admitting the exercise of judicial proceedings in, and sentencing of,
> all causes depending in court to belong only to the judge as aforesaid) the
> vice-admiral may, at his pleasure at any time sit with the judge in court, in

129  TNA (PRO), ADM 2/1,755.

regard he may often times be specially concerned in some matters of office depending in the said court; and that the appointments of the courts successively be with his knowledge and approbation; and if the judge do not keep courts and do those things fitting to be done by his place that then the admiral or his deputy may keep courts as judge and receive the judges' accustomed fees.

However, judges and vice-admirals continued to skirmish, especially over money matters. In the late 1660s a dispute over fishing licences had broken out between the vice-admiral of Leinster, and the judge of the Leinster court, with the vice-admiral claiming entitlement, by virtue of his commission, to the perquisite. In 1667 Dr John Topham, judge of the Leinster court, protested that the appropriation of the entire fishing licence revenue by the vice-admiral threatened the viability of the court:

> The case is this: the money which is given for licence to fish is certainly a perquisite always belonging to the judge and officers of the court. Of late, the vice-admiral, pretending right in behalf of the admiral, has made great contest and (as he says) obtained his highness' grant. The whole sum does not exceed £80 a year amongst all the officers, judge, registrar and marshal, and this is the only perquisite belonging to the office. If you find it disposed of, and not to be granted to the next judge, the grant of the judgeship itself will be worthless.[130]

Although the Turner/Budd directions of 1663 expressly assigned all admiralty droits and perquisites (including, it would follow, the revenue generated by fishing licensing) to the vice-admiral, the admiralty judges continued to claim entitlement to fishing licence fees. The fight continued into the 1670s with the vice-admiral of Leinster, Carey Dillon, disputing Petty's keeping the revenue, and Petty claiming an entitlement by virtue of the reference in his patent to his being 'the commissary' of the lord high admiral.[131] A truce was reached between Dr Styles, the judge of the Admiralty Court, and Carey Dillon, the Leinster vice-admiral, in 1686, under which the judge and vice-admiral agreed to evenly divide the licence revenue. That agreement was re-established between Sir Paul Rycaut and Carey Dillon (Lord Roscommon).[132] However, the accord broke down when the earl of Bath replaced Carey Dillon as vice-admiral of Leinster. Warning his deputy about Bath's 'pretensions in the fees', Rycaut advised that the revenues should be split in the same way as 'agreed between Dr Styles, my predecessor, and the Lord Roscommon'.[133]

130  J. Topham to E. Conway, 14 May 1667, *Cal. S.P. Ire. 1666–1669*, p. 362.
131  W. Petty to A. Apsley, 9 Sept. 1676 (McGill, Osler MS 7,612).
132  P. Rycaut to J. Coghill, 2 Sept. 1692 (BL, Lansdowne MS 1,153D, f. 338).
133  P. Rycaut to S. Maudit, 13 Dec. 1692 (BL, Add. MS 37,663, f. 39).

ADMIRALTY JURISDICTION AND THE REVOLT OF THE MUNICIPAL
CORPORATIONS

Soon after assuming duties as judge of the Court of Admiralty of Ireland, Sir
William Petty wrote to George Gamble:[134] 'I find that many corporations in Ireland
do so far pretend to admiralty jurisdiction [that they may] eat up the main body.
Pray see what is done in England, and whether the vice-admiral here ought to do
the same'. During the late-seventeenth century most seaside corporations had
established their own parallel systems of admiralty jurisdiction, which they
justified by reference either to charter or to custom. As the authority of the Court
of Admiralty weakened in the 1690s, the extent of this rebellion intensified. It was
at this point that the Admiralty in London began to make serious efforts to retake
control. Beginning in the late 1690s, a series of *quo warranto* proceedings were
initiated, targeting successively the towns of Wexford, Waterford and Galway.[135]

*Dublin*

Dublin's Elizabethan charter of January 1582[136] entrusted the office of admiral to
the mayor of Dublin. The claims of the Corporation of Dublin to admiralty
jurisdiction were – in light of the express grant of admiralty jurisdiction given by
the charter of 1582 – legally plausible. Dublin Corporation resented the activities
of the Admiralty Court, and the two remained in constant conflict during the
1670s and 1680s. One of the corporation's chief grievances was the pretensions of
the Court of Admiralty to license, and to regulate, fishing. In 1677 the corporation
complained[137] that 'the fishing of Salmon Pool, and within the city liberty, anciently
belonged to the sheriffs of this city, and that the Court of Admiralty of late
pretended a right thereunto'.

   However, the subject of the most violent dispute between the Admiralty Court
and the mayor of Dublin was over the right to ballastage (the duty paid in return
for taking ballast from Dublin port). The master of the *Jacob of Dublin*[138] had
refused to pay the ballastage duty claimed by the Court of Admiralty, and the *Jacob*
was arrested by the deputies of the marshal. In 1682 the vessel was then re-taken
under process of replevin issued out of the Recorder's Court in Dublin.
The headstrong marshal of the Court of Admiralty, Captain Francis Robinson,
over-reacted: the *Jacob* was re-seized from the officers of the mayor of Dublin. The

---

134  W. Petty to G. Gamble, 1 Aug. 1676 (McGill, Osler MS 7,612).
135  The problem of interference with admiralty jurisdiction by municipal corporations had largely
     ceased by the middle of the eighteenth century. In 1841 all of the admiralty jurisdictions given
     by charter to municipal corporations in Ireland and England were abolished: s. 174 of the
     Municipal Corporations Act 1841 (3 & 4 Vict., c. 108, 1841).
136  *Cal. anc. rec. Dub.*, i, pp 36–7.                    137  *Cal. anc. rec. Dub.*, v, p. 147.
138  There are accounts of this in both the Petty papers (BL, Add. MS 7,2893, f. 87) and in the
     Ormond papers (Bodl., Carte MS 39, f. 614 & Carte MS 144, f. 406).

tension intensified when a rule was issued by the trouble-making Dr Dudley Loftus, surrogate judge of the Court of Admiralty, for the committal of the Dublin under-sheriffs to prison for contempt. The use of the attachment power by the Court of Admiralty against officers of another court was highly provocative, and the violence of the dispute escalated into a matter of high-level political concern. The duke of York requested the lord deputy to investigate the 'pretensions of the mayor of Dublin'.[139] The earl of Arran advised that the resolution of the dispute should be left to legal proceedings in some superior court and that, in the meantime, steps should be taken to calm the parties:

> Sir John Werden, the duke's secretary gave me notice of some disorder in something belonging to the admiralty between the officer of the court and the lord mayor who, by virtue of a charter, lays claim to a jurisdiction. The right must, no doubt, be judged according to law if the parties have a mind to it, but care ought in the meantime to be taken to prevent violence.[140]

The dispute over ballastage continued throughout the 1680s; in 1688 Dublin Corporation initiated legal action against Francis Robinson, the marshal of the Court of Admiralty, for requiring ship owners, who refused to pay ballastage duty to him, to throw their ballast into the River Liffey.[141]

Another aspect of the court's work, about which Dublin decided to make an issue, was admiralty inquests. In February 1683, the admiralty judge, Dr Henry Styles, was censured for holding an inquest into the deaths of persons who had drowned off Merrion Strand, 'where he impaneled and swore a jury, and examined witnesses upon oath, and recorded that inquest ... the said person being drowned and the whole matter transacted within the county of the said city'. The corporation resolved to initiate a criminal prosecution against Styles for violation of the city's prerogatives.[142] Five years later there was another tussle over the right to exercise the office of admiralty coroner: early in 1688, one of the corporation's coroners alleged that he had been 'interrupted in the execution of his office by the judge of the admiralty' as he presided over an inquest in Ringsend. The City Assembly endorsed the coroner's assertion 'that the coroners of the city' and 'not the Admiralty [Court] have jurisdiction of taking inquests of bodies found dead within the county of the said city'.[143]

The corporation also threatened litigation when the court attempted to seize wreck washed up in Dublin bay. In 1683 Carey Dillon (the vice-admiral of Leinster) was reported as having seized 'under the pretence or colour of his office of vice-admiral'[144] a 'parcel of silver coin covered with sand at the strand near Ringsend,

139 Duke of York to the earl of Arran, 25 Nov. 1682 (Bodl., Carte MS, vol. 39, f. 614).
140 Earl of Arran to the duke of Ormond, 5 Dec. 1682 (Bodl., Carte MS, vol. 219, f. 406).
141 RIA, Haliday MS 12/E/2, f. 432.        142 *Cal. anc. rec. Dub.*, v, pp 301–2.
143 *Cal. anc. rec. Dub.*, v, p. 461.        144 *Cal. anc. rec. Dub.*, v, p. 294.

which by the charters of this city were granted by his majesty's royal predecessors unto this city'. Legal proceedings were taken for the recovery of the money. In 1684 Henry Forrest petitioned the corporation that he had been threatened by Judge Styles for having 'taken away from some persons near Ringsend a cable, found upon the strand of Merrion, within the franchises of the city'.[145]

### New Ross, Wexford and Waterford

By the late seventeenth century even the minor town of New Ross claimed the right to regulate and license fishing by virtue of what it claimed was its own admiralty jurisdiction. In 1688 its council promulgated an ordinance that[146] 'none shall fish on the waters of the rivers belonging to the small admiralty within the jurisdiction of our corporation but by licence yearly from the mayor'. Further down the coast, Wexford was also defiant. In 1692 Sir Paul Rycaut warned his surrogate that 'you must scuffle hard with some mayors of towns especially Wexford'.[147] In fact, the conflict with Wexford had a long history. In 1663 the admiralty commissioner William Coventry requested that the judges should confer on taking *quo warranto* proceedings against Wexford, and hinted that the duke of York would be amenable to making a contribution to the costs of the litigation 'out of the profits what should be fit'.[148] However, Wexford continued to resist: in 1666 the mayor of Wexford (in what was, presumably, a reference to fishing licensing) complained that 'the admiralty, being the chiefest branch, or support, of the corporation being allowed in their ancient charter, is kept from them'.[149] In 1687 proceedings were initiated in the Court of Admiralty against the mayor of Wexford for obstructing the admiralty fishing licence collection. When the court found that the mayor was guilty of contempt the corporation initiated an appeal to the English Court of Admiralty.[150] Before the appeal was heard 'the parties came to a composition to avoid law suits'.[151] However, the proceedings in the Admiralty Court had not curbed the town's defiance. In 1694 the agent of the earl of Bath (the vice-admiral of Leinster) complained that 'the town of Wexford in that Province … pretend[s] to an admiralty within the port and harbour, and the keeping of courts accordingly'.[152] The judge of the English Court of Admiralty, Sir Charles Hedges, advised that *quo warranto* proceedings be initiated, and, on 11 October 1694, an instruction issued from the Privy Council in Whitehall that a royal letter be directed to 'the lords justices of Ireland to cause a *quo warranto* to be forthwith brought against the town of Wexford in Ireland for trying the title which

145   *Cal. anc rec. Dub.*, v, p. 318.
146   NLI, Report on private collections no. 226, p. 2.
147   P. Rycaut to W. Mayne, 22 Apr. 1692 (BL, Add. MS 1,153D, f. 208).
148   10 Dec. 1663 (TNA (PRO), ADM 1/1,755).
149   Thomas Barrington to the duke of Ormond, 30 Mar. 1666, *Ormond Calendar*, iii, p. 214.
150   *Garrett Coursy v. Edmund Sale & Talbot Keane*, 1687 (TNA (PRO), HCA 3/58, f. 19).
151   P. Rycaut to the earl of Bath, 21 Mar. 1693 (BL, Add. MS 37,663, f. 126).
152   Commissioners of Admiralty to C. Hedges, 3 Apr. 1694 (TNA (PRO), ADM 2/1046, f. 146).

they claim to admiralty jurisdiction within that town independent from the said commissioners of Admiralty'.[153]

Wexford, in its defence to the *quo warranto* proceedings, asserted that an admiralty jurisdiction had been acquired by prescription. At the same time (nervous that its legal defence was not likely to succeed) the town sought a compromise. The deal which it proposed involved it recognizing the rights of the lord admiral, and abandoning all claims to local admiralty jurisdiction; in return, the Admiralty would entrust it with a special grant entitling it to levy fishing licence fees. The corporation pleaded that the fishing licence revenue was essential to its financial independence:

> the greatest trade of the town consists of the fishery, and the profits of licensing the same within the limits of the corporation, tho' but very small, is what has been the constant revenue of the same to maintain the government thereof. The said corporation do humbly propose to your lordships that they wholly disclaim the exercise of admiralty jurisdiction and submit it to your lordships whether you will please to give the mayor the commission to exercise the same under your lordships' direction or wholly to exercise them.[154]

The Irish Privy Council, impressed by Wexford's readiness to submit, and by the reasonableness of its demand, directed that a *nolle prosequi* be entered suspending the *quo warranto* proceedings.[155] The problem was that this was done entirely without reference to London. The Irish move provoked a furious response from the Admiralty who secured a royal letter addressed to the Irish Council countermanding the *nolle prosequi*.[156] That letter appears to have gone mysteriously astray and the *nolle prosequi* remained effective.[157] The Admiralty continued to press for 'taking off that stop put upon the court'.

The Corporation of Waterford, too, was continuing to assert an independent admiralty jurisdiction, with the full apparatus of admiralty courts and admiralty taxes. In 1697 the commander of the military fort at Duncannon complained of the 'insolency and obstinacy' of the Corporation of Waterford which was extracting admiralty revenues and holding formal admiralty courts. The town, it was alleged:

> exercise[s] admiralty jurisdiction in all its power, not only on the river, as the sea coasts adjacent, but make[s] all fishing boats take licences from them for

---

153 Privy Council Register, 11 Oct. 1694 (TNA (PRO), PC 2/75, f. 490).
154 Petition of Philip Savage on behalf of the Corporation of Wexford, 1698 (TNA (PRO), ADM 1/3,665, f. 116).
155 Edward Whittaker's report to the commissioners of Admiralty, 8 Apr. 1697 (TNA (PRO), ADM 1/3665, f. 115). Edward Whittaker was admiralty solicitor, 1692–9.
156 24 Jan. 1696; *Cal. S.P. Dom., 1696*, p. 26.
157 TNA (PRO), ADM 1/3,665, f. 115.

fishing, and anchorage from all ships riding in the harbour, and all this by virtue (as they pretend) of an admiralty jurisdiction vested in the mayor and corporation. ... they come down when they please, and hold courts of admiralty with such great form and pomp, under the very nose of the king's fort, and to show their power more, they bring down lighters and takes ballast under the walls by force.[158]

Waterford's contempt of the Admiralty was attributed to a co-ordinated effort amongst south-eastern seaports; Waterford 'would never have ventured, nor have been at the expense of carrying so high, if they had not been backed by other sea ports, amongst which, the town of Wexford, I believe, is the chief'. The report was sent to Sir Charles Hedges (who acted, in effect, as attorney general to the Admiralty). Hedges advised that 'the like method be used against Waterford as against Wexford, unless the lords shall rather think fit to expect and see what will be the issue of that case'. Hedges was confident that Waterford would lose: 'the determination' of the proceedings, he predicted, 'will ... either put an end to the claim of Waterford, or else your lordship's solicitor may be better instructed how to proceed'.[159] It was not until 1700 that the Admiralty resolved that *quo warranto* proceedings be issued against Waterford.[160] However, as with Wexford, it is not clear whether these proceedings were ever concluded. The marshal of the Irish Court of Admiralty, in a memorial written in 1711, recollected that 'a *quo warranto* was ordered to be issued against the Corporation of Waterford, but by the much lamented death of his royal highness there has been no progress made in those proceedings'.[161] In the meantime, the corporation prosecuted aggressive legal proceedings against officers of the Court of Admiralty. It was reported that 'when the said marshal by his deputies has demanded his dues of anchorage at Waterford (where they have heretofore been constantly paid) his deputies have been imprisoned and several actions have been brought against him and them both at Waterford and Cork for the execution of their office'.[162]

*Cork, Kinsale, and Limerick*

The Corporation of Cork justified its claim to operate an admiralty court by reference to the charter granted by Henry VII to the city in 1500.[163] That grant had been made in return for an annual rent. The corporation was careful to honour this rent, and when the exercise by the Corporation of Cork of admiralty functions was

158 J. Jefferies to C. Hedges, 19 Jan. 1697 (BL, Add. MS 24,107, f. 105).

159 C. Hedges to the commissioners of Admiralty, 13 Feb. 1697 (BL, Add. MS 24,107, f. 105).

160 The Admiralty minutes for 2 Jan. 1700 contain the following entry: 'Upon reading a letter from Mr Tho. Knox touching the pretended admiralty jurisdiction of the town of Waterford in Ireland, resolved that the same method may be taken for bringing a *quo warranto* against this town as was sometime since for the town of Wexford' (TNA (PRO), ADM 3/15).

161 Memorial of William Bodens, May 1711 (TNA (PRO), ADM 1/3,668, f. 61).

162 Ibid.       163 See p. 23 above.

questioned in the early 1660s the corporation directed[164] 'that a copy of the record out of the Exchequer on which the rent paid by the corporation for the admiralty of the city is grounded, be taken out, and produced to the next judge of assize'.

Conflict with the Admiralty Court of Munster intensified during the period that the energetic Thomas Farren (who, awkwardly, also served as town clerk of the Corporation of Cork) acted as judge. In February 1694 the corporation resolved to prosecute officers of the court if they continued to exercise admiralty jurisdiction within the city.[165] Farren, however, continued to provoke the corporation, arresting, in the course of an instance suit, a corporation freeman, John Spread. When ordered by the mayor of Cork to release John Spread, Farren informed the judge of the national Court of Admiralty in Dublin. The mayor of Cork was directed to appear before the court in Dublin.[166] The corporation reacted to this by threatening to dismiss Farren from his office as town clerk. Farren appeared, made obeisance and promised not to make further encroachments. It was decided to let the matter lie 'and the said Farren to stand in *statu quo*'.[167] However, five years later the corporation was once again complaining about the activities of Judge Farren and the Munster court (when he attempted to exercise jurisdiction in a collision case which had occurred in Cork harbour).[168] Astutely, the corporation invoked the locality rule of admiralty jurisdiction,[169] arguing that the Munster Admiralty Court had no competence since the collision had arisen 'in the body of the county'; therefore it was 'not at all maritime, or conusable in the admiralty court'.[170]

The Sheriff's Court of Cork also assisted the campaign against the Court of Admiralty, issuing replevins for the re-seizure of the goods which had been arrested by the Admiralty Court. In an affidavit sworn in 1698, David Martell and Michael Morland, two bailiffs to the sheriff of Cork, deposed that they had 'known it customary and usual to replevy ships and goods which have been under the arrest of the Admiralty Court'.[171] But when, in June 1698, the sheriff of Cork issued a replevin in order to retake possession of the *White Horse*, Cork

164 C.S. Smith, *The ancient and present state of the county and city of Cork*, 2 vols (Dublin, 1774), ii, p. 416.

165 'Whereas several infringements on the privileges of this corporation anciently granted by charter to be used on the water have been made by Mr Thomas Farren, judge of the admiralty, and his under-officers, it is agreed for the future, that if any such practices shall be used to debar us of our ancient right on the water within this harbour, that it be opposed at the public expense of this corporation, and the admiralty officers so encroaching our liberties to be *toties quoties* committed for their offence, until they enter sufficient security to answer same according to law'. 8 Feb. 1694, *The Council Book of Cork Corporation*, pp 231–2.

166 8 May 1694, *The Council Book of Cork Corporation*, p. 233.

167 11 May 1694, ibid., p. 234.              168 1 June 1699, ibid., p. 274.

169 See p. 33 above.

170 The problem persisted into the early eighteenth century. In 1703 the corporation resolved that the mayor should write to the solicitor general complaining about the arrest in the city of a Mr Hancock in an admiralty matter. *The Council Book of Cork Corporation*, p. 305.

171 20 Sept. 1698 (TNA (PRO), HCA 15/18).

Corporation found itself confronting an opponent more formidable than the mere Munster Court of Admiralty. A warrant had been issued by the Court of Admiralty of England, at the suit of three bankruptcy commissioners, for the arrest of a vessel called the *White Horse* lying in Cork. Following the arrest of the ship under the English warrant, a replevin was issued by the Sheriff's Court for its restitution (at the suit of Charles Riviere who claimed to be owner of the *White Horse*). The interference with the Admiralty process was brought to the notice of the English court, and in July 1698 the under-sheriffs of Cork, James Weeks and David Gould, were summoned to the English court to answer charges of contempt.[172]

Other corporations were making life difficult for the Munster Court. In 1663 the Corporation of Kinsale committed itself to expelling the Munster Admiralty Court from the town:

> Doctor Joshua Boyle having lately employed Richard Sturt, his marshal, to impanel a jury and proclaim a court of admiralty within the jurisdiction of this town and liberties, it was resolved, by consent of the sovereign, burgesses and freemen, that the sovereign shall oppose and hinder said Dr Boyle and his officers in their progress to the keeping said court within the jurisdiction; and if any suit of law arise thereupon the cost shall be borne by the corporation.[173]

The conflict was brought to the attention of the Irish Privy Council which, in 1665, directed the corporation to justify its resistance to the Admiralty.[174] Kinsale continued to insist upon its claim to an admiralty franchise. In 1681 the corporation petitioned the Privy Council and the lord lieutenant, complaining of a violation of 'the privilege of the corporation in right of the admiralty'[175] said to have been committed by Thomas Meade (one of Petty's deputy admiralty judges). In the first decade of the eighteenth century the judge of the English Court of Admiralty, Sir Charles Hedges, and the Irish attorney and solicitor generals were directed to examine the legality of the claims made by Cork and Kinsale.[176]

The Corporation of Limerick – justifying its position by reference to the grant in its charter of 1609 of the powers of the Courts of Admiralty of Ireland and England – continued to administer a local admiralty jurisdiction throughout the latter half of the seventeenth century.[177] Daniel Hignet, a surveyor employed on William Molyneux's geography of Ireland project, reported about Limerick that 'they have an admiralty jurisdiction, and the mayor is admiral (to whom all royal

---

172  The proceedings were entitled *Roe v Weeks & Gould* (TNA (PRO), HCA 15/18).
173  4 July 1663, R. Caulfield (ed.), *The Council Book of the Corporation of Kinsale, 1652–1800* (London, 1879), p. 81.
174  Ibid., p. 89.                          175  Ibid., p. 158.
176  The report does not survive; it is referred to in the minutes of the Admiralty commissioners, 22 Jan. 1707 (TNA (PRO), ADM 3/22).
177  *Appendix to the report of the commissioners appointed to inquire into municipal corporations in Ireland* (HC 1835 (25) xxvii 1, 349).

fishes do belong)'.[178] In 1698 the Corporation of Limerick claimed that it was entitled to a Dutch wreck, the *Guinea Galley of Middleburgh*, which had been taken into the Shannon. The corporation justified its intervention by reference to its charter; it had been necessary 'to secure her for some time 'til by a trial in that admiralty court here (which by our charter we have power to hold)'.[179] A report was commissioned from Sir Charles Hedges, the judge of the English Court of Admiralty. Predictably, Hedges (who may not have been made aware of the terms of Limerick's charter) dismissed the claim of the corporation, denying that any 'could pretend [an interest] unto except his majesty and the proprietors'.[180]

## Galway

In 1701, the *Unity of Amsterdam*, having just set out from Galway on the second leg of a voyage from Amsterdam to America, got into trouble; the crew were forced to disembark at Achill Head (where they found 'neither habitation nor any person but a shepherd').[181] The men had lost confidence in the safety of the vessel, and as soon as it put back into Galway, proceeded to seek the intervention of the deputy vice-admiral of Connacht. A deal was struck between the crew and the master of the *Unity*: 'that if the ship should be viewed by three of the ablest shipwrights of the town of Galway', and found to be seaworthy, the men were to proceed; otherwise the master was to pay their wages, and discharge them.

However, the master refused to stand by the arbitration agreement, and the crew was obliged to pursue its wages claims by way of litigation. Accordingly, proceedings for mariners' wages were initiated before an admiralty court. Those proceedings were broken up by the town clerk of Galway who 'came into open court … and protested against the proceedings and jurisdiction of that court as not in them but in the mayor of the town of Galway' by virtue of their charter'.[182] In order to derail the admiralty proceedings a replevin, returnable into the King's Bench, was obtained by the corporation. The vessel was then re-seized from the custody of the court with all of the aggression characteristic of the replevin process:

> the sheriffs went down to the ship, and seized her, and commanded the officer placed on board her by the admiralty immediately to leave her, but he seeming to refuse, they not having any authority from the Admiralty, they offered with all violence imaginable to threw him over board, and with great many scoffing words to the Admiralty jurisdiction, harried him out of the ship.[183]

178  Commonplace book of papers relating to natural history of Ireland (TCD, MS 883/1 [1.1.2]).
179  J. Young to the lords justices of Ireland, 24 Apr. 1698 (BL, Add. MS 24,107, f. 145).
180  C. Hedges to the commissioners of Admiralty, 9 May 1698 (BL, Add. MS 24,107, f. 162).
181  G. St George to the commissioners of Admiralty, 10 Apr. 1701 (TNA (PRO), ADM 1/3,666, f. 238).
182  Ibid.
183  G. St George to the commissioners of Admiralty, 22 Sept. 1701, ibid.

The dispute was referred to the English civilian, Dr George Oxenden, who suggested two courses of action: his first suggestion was that the Admiralty Court issue proceedings for contempt. Oxenden mentioned the contempt proceedings taken by the English Court of Admiralty against the Corporation of Cork in 1698 during the *White Horse* litigation when the corporation had attempted to frustrate the court's process by replevin.[184] Somewhat overestimating the capacity of the weak Irish Court of Admiralty, Oxenden advised that the court should adopt a similar strategy:[185]

> our proceedings in the High Court of Admiralty are thus: we send out a warrant to all those persons who executed the writ of replevin and violated the arrest of the admiralty, to answer by articles of contempt. Thereupon we can fine them and thereby compel them to restore the ship …[186]

Alternatively, and more sensibly, Oxenden advised that the court contest the replevin proceedings, 'or if [the Admiralty judge] will not proceed this way, or if he be too late to do it, then he must join issue to their declaration, as I suppose he has done, and show by the pleadings that this matter does not of right belong to the jurisdiction of the corporation'.

The Irish law officers were called in to advise on the feasibility of *quo warranto* proceedings against the town. By its Elizabethan charter of 1578,[187] the town of Galway had been granted exclusive admiralty jurisdiction over all transactions occurring within Galway Bay. Following the Restoration, letters patent were issued confirming the entitlement of the town to exercise such privileges as it had exercised on 22 October 1641. Only such functions as were active in 1641 were perpetuated by the 1660 charter. The critical legal question then was what, if any, admiralty privileges had been exercised by the Corporation of Galway in October 1641: 'although the charter of Queen Elizabeth had granted the jurisdiction of the town of Galway, exclusive of the authority of the lord high admiral, within the limits contained in the charter, yet if they were not in possession of that jurisdiction in the year 1641 … then it seems to us they were not restored to the exercise of it by the patent of Charles II'. The attorney general was confident that the corporation did not exercise admiralty functions in 1641 and therefore recommended that 'a writ of *scire facias* in nature of a *quo warranto* do issue against the mayor and Corporation of Galway to oblige them to show by what authority they exercise admiralty jurisdiction'.[188]

184   *Roe v. Weeks & Gould* (TNA (PRO), HCA 15/18). See p. 74 above.
185   G. Oxenden to the commissioners of Admiralty, 23 June 1701 (TNA (PRO), ADM 1/3,666, f. 188).
186   Oxenden recalled that this was the strategy adopted with the Sheriff's Court of Cork in the *White Horse* case in 1698: 'this has been done lately by Sir Charles Hedges upon our arrest of a ship in a port in Ireland, and sentence given thereupon by him, and a replevin made by the courts at common law in Ireland, upon which proceedings the persons restored the ship …', ibid.
187   J. Hardiman, *The history of the town of Galway* (Dublin, 1820), Appendix, p. xvii.
188   Opinion of R. Rochfort and R. Levinge, 17 Mar. 1706 (PC 1/2/53).

In February 1707 the commissioners of Admiralty resolved that a memorial be laid before Queen Anne inviting her to direct the attorney and solicitor generals of Ireland to prosecute a *quo warranto* against the town of Galway.[189] The case against the Corporation of Galway was initiated in the Court of Exchequer in Ireland. It dragged on until 1725 when, in a significant embarrassment for the Admiralty, it was held that the corporation did, in fact, exercise admiralty jurisdiction in the year 1641 and that this franchise had been perpetuated by the town's post-Restoration charter.[190]

PRIZE IN IRELAND DURING THE LATE SEVENTEENTH CENTURY

*The Second Anglo–Dutch War (1665–7)*

The highest level of prize activity transacted in seventeenth-century Ireland occurred during the Second Anglo–Dutch War (1665–67). An account prepared by Sir Peter Pett, the king's advocate in Ireland,[191] recorded that in 1667 seventeen vessels had been condemned by the Munster Court of Admiralty, and eleven condemned by the Connacht Court of Admiralty.[192] The income generated by these condemnations was considerable.[193]

The constitutional basis of Irish prize jurisdiction during the Second Anglo-Dutch War derived from an express grant from the king. In June 1665, Charles II, acting upon the advice of the commissioners for prizes, promulgated a sophisticated scheme for the administration of prizes in Ireland equivalent to that which operated in England. It was decreed that Irish courts of vice-admiralty would be invested with prize jurisdiction, and that the law, procedure and evidence regulating these proceedings would be subject to the same code (the 1665 'rules for the Admiralty Court in the adjudication of prizes')[194] that regulated prize proceedings in the High Court of Admiralty in England.[195] It was also decreed that decisions of Irish prize courts would be subject to review by a special Irish court of prize appeals (with further appeal to the Court of Admiralty in England):

> and that you cause in like manner, a commission of appeals to issue unto such persons of the Privy Council whom you judge most proper for the same; still preserving the jurisdiction of the High Court of Admiralty here in England, unto which any person aggrieved may, if they please bring their appeal, notwithstanding the said commission.

189  12 Feb. 1707 (TNA (PRO), ADM 3/22).
190  See p. 76 above.
191  Pett defined his function as providing 'advice and drawing the judicial proceedings about the prizes in the vice-admiral courts'. 26 Dec. 1667 (Bodl., Carte MS 35, f. 766).
192  Ibid. Pett reported that, of the vessels condemned in Munster, four were legally contested before the Munster Court and three before the Connacht court.
193  Order of 14 Aug. 1667 (Bodl., Carte MS 52, f. 155).
194  'Rules for the Admiralty Court in the adjudication of prizes, 1665', *Law and Custom of the Sea*, ii, pp 53–7.
195  Instructions to the lord lieutenant, 26 June 1665 (TNA (PRO), PC 2/58, f. 96).

Within days of the royal letter a set of detailed instructions for the disposal of prizes along the lines of the English model was drawn up by the Irish Privy Council and circulated to each of the vice-admiralties.[196]

The Irish court also obtained a limited role in issuing letters of marque. Originally, the English High Court of Admiralty had exclusive jurisdiction over the issue of letters of marque to privateers; prior to 1666 a letter of marque was not obtainable from any of the admiralty courts operating in Ireland. The issue of whether a right to grant letters of marque might be conceded to the Irish court had been raised with the English advocate, Thomas Exton. Exton was 'positive against sending blank commissions'.[197] However, the encouragement of Irish privateering was necessary to the war effort, and it was important that privateers be able to obtain licences without bureaucratic inconvenience. William Coventry, the English Admiralty commissioner, described how, following Exton's veto he 'had cast about for some expedient'. The proposal put to Ormond was that an admiralty judge in Ireland would take the necessary oaths and security 'for observing the rules and paying tenths', and the bonds and documentation would be sent over to London; the English court would then return a letter of marque. This arrangement would save the privateer from the bother of having to travel to London, while the English court would still formally issue the letters and retain its fees.

*Prize procedure during the Second Anglo–Dutch War*

Problems involving the treatment of prisoners of war taken on captured enemy vessels exercised the Irish administration soon after the outbreak of the Second Anglo–Dutch War. When, in April 1665, the first prizes began to be taken in, Sir Oliver St George, vice-admiral of Connacht, sought advice[198] from the Privy Council about the humanitarian problems caused by the detention of the crew of two Dutch vessels which had been brought into Galway. There were about sixty-four Dutch prisoners.[199] The sheriffs had refused to allow the use of the common gaol, and St George had been forced to keep the crew in private houses. In order to prevent them starving he had granted an allowance of six pence per prisoner *per diem*. A similar issue had arisen in Munster where Robert Southwell, the deputy vice-admiral, had quartered forty-six Dutch sailors captured on the prize, the *Bonnaventure*, in private houses in Kinsale.[200] The Privy Council instructed St George that the wounded should be provided for, and that the 'prisoners should be all civilly used, and if there were amongst them any persons of quality above the rest, that they should have all the civility and respect befitting their qualities'.[201] In

196   The earl of Ossory to G. Wentworth, 9 June 1665 (Bodl., Carte MS 34, ff 248–9).
197   W. Coventry to the duke of Ormond, 8 May 1666 (Bodl., Carte MS 47, f. 450).
198   O. St George to the earl of Ossory, 28 Apr. & 2 May 1665 (Bodl., Carte MS 34, ff 199 & 201).
199   O. St George to the lords justices, 26 May 1665 (Bodl., Carte MS 34, f. 246).
200   R. Southwell to P. Davis, 1 May 1665 (Bodl., Carte MS 34, f. 192).
201   Lords justices to the duke of Ormond (25 May 1665) (Bodl., Carte MS 34, f. 222). On 29 Nov. 1665 the English Privy Council, confident that the 'success of prizes will far exceed all such

May 1665 authoritative instructions 'concerning the sick and wounded soldiers and mariners which have been on shore at Galway' were transmitted from the Privy Council in London. These authorized a payment of five pence *per diem* for ordinary sailors, and 'for those of superior rank, a higher maintenance payment, but not exceeding 12*d. per diem* (the money to be defrayed out of the sale of the prize)'.[202] The order did not (St George later complained) provide compensation for the medical expenses which he had incurred in treating sick and wounded prisoners.[203]

Article 8 of the 1665 'rules for the Admiralty Court in the adjudication of prizes'[204] directed, as a preliminary to the initiation of prize proceedings, that a monition advertising the impending prize proceedings be publicly displayed. The court was required to 'send forth a process to be hanged up on the Exchange, or other most public place, whereby all that pretend to have any right to claims may come in and enter their claims in court'. The rules stipulated fourteen days as the period within which a notice of claim was to be entered. Where no notice was entered within fourteen days, the court was required to proceed towards adjudication. Sir Peter Pett, the king's advocate in Ireland, described the operation of the process of monition in Galway in 1666,[205] 'I drew up an original monition and warrant to be publicly fixed in Galway … and the time therein allowed that is usual for any to claim the said ship and goods; at the expiration of which, the warrant and monition being returned in the Court of Vice-Admiralty in Connacht, none appeared in court to claim'. In emergencies captured goods could be condemned even before the judicial process had begun. In 1665 the vice-admiral of Connacht, Sir Oliver St George, sought guidance on how to deal with the cargo of two Dutch vessels which had been taken into Galway.[206] Wine and brandies had become 'leakish' and permission was sought to dispose of them before the prize proceedings had opened. The right to take preventive action was confirmed by the general instructions of June 1665[207] which directed that, where goods were 'in a perishing condition', they could be sold prior to trial, and the proceeds 'put into the hands of the vice-treasurer until the property in the same be made appear to belong, either to his majesty or the claimers'.

The principal source of prize doctrine during the Second and Third Anglo–Dutch Wars was the 1665 'rules for the Admiralty Court in the adjudication of

charges' directed that the Irish vice-admirals were to be reimbursed for looking after the Dutch prisoners of war, and that the prisoners were not to be transported to England (TNA (PRO), SP 63/319, f. 406).

202 Ibid.
203 Lords justices to the duke of Ormond, 24 May 1665 (Bodl., Carte MS 34, f. 221).
204 Rules for the adjudication of prizes 1665, pp 53–7; E.S. Roscoe, *A history of the English Prize Court* (London, 1924), pp 35–8.
205 P. Pett to the earl of Clarendon, 9 June 1666 (Bodl., Clarendon MS 84, f. 190).
206 O. St George to the earl of Orrery, 28 Apr. 1665 (Bodl., Carte MS 34, f. 199).
207 Bodl., Carte MS 34, f. 248.

prizes'.[208] Amenability to classification as prize was expanded by two principles of infection; firstly, Article 1 provided that where a vessel was judged to belong to the United Provinces, neutral goods on board were automatically tainted and deemed enemy's goods. Secondly, where a vessel belonged to British subjects, or nationals of allies of the British Crown, but was carrying goods of the United Provinces, both the ship and the goods were liable to condemnation. The second of these principles was applied by the Admiralty Court of Connacht in the *Sacrifice of Abraham*. The vessel was owned by nationals of the Republic of Genoa, an ally of the Crown; however, the cargo was Dutch, and this, the court held, tainted the vessel as well.[209] Article 4 of the 1665 rules deemed as conclusive proof of enemy status: 'resistance to a naval vessel, or a commissioned privateer; burning or tearing or concealing the ship's documents; having no ships documents; or offering false evidence'. The principle that burning ships' documents proved hostile origin was applied in the *St Catherine*:[210] where the captain was proven to have given orders for the burning of 'several of the ship's papers, a little before the ship was seized and that the papers were accordingly burnt while endeavours were made to seize it'.

The crew was a primary source of evidence of origin. In 1666, when the *Catherine* was driven into Inishbofin, an instruction was issued that the crew be made available for examination in preparation for the prize suit to be held before the Connacht Admiralty Court.[211] Interpreters assisted in the examination of foreign crews; in Galway in 1666 'every examination was taken upon oath and attested by ... the sworn interpreter'.[212] Dr Joshua Boyle, judge of the Court of Admiralty of Munster described how he 'swore an able interpreter'[213] to assist in the translation of Dutch documents in Waterford in December 1665. Findings as to the quality or value of merchandise were commonly made by commissioners of appraisement – expert valuers appointed by the court. Sir Oliver St George, presiding over the Court of Admiralty of Connacht, appointed an eleven-man commission to determine whether the wine rescued from a Dutch vessel was in such perishable condition that it required to be sold prior to condemnation. The

208  'Rules for the Admiralty Court in the adjudication of prizes, 1665', *Law and Custom of the Sea*, ii, pp 53–7; Roscoe, *A history of the English Prize Court*, pp 35–8.
209  The Court of Admiralty of Connacht had justified its decree on infection grounds: '1. First that she had been laden in a port belonging to his majesty's enemies; 2. That the whole cargo was laden not only in such a port then in amity, but even by a broker and inhabitant of Amsterdam then in hostility with his majesty; 3. That a part of the lading and goods, as was confessed, belonged to his majesty's enemies; 4. That divers of the mariners that sailed the said ship were unfree persons and subjects of his majesty's enemies'. Report of L. Jenkins, R.Wiseman, W. Turner and W. Walker, 1668 (TNA (PRO), SP 79/1, f. 333).
210  P. Pett to the earl of Clarendon, 9 June 1666 (Bodl., Clarendon MS 84, f. 190).
211  9 Mar. 1665/6 (Bodl., Carte MS 144, f. 68).
212  P. Pett to the earl of Clarendon, 9 June 1666 (Bodl., Clarendon MS 84, f. 190).
213  J. Boyle to T. Page, 12 Dec. 1665 (Bodl., Carte MS 34, f. 508).

commissioners (who included the collector of customs, local merchants, a vintner and a wine cooper) tasted the wine and reported to the court that it would decay unless immediately sold.[214]

The 'general instructions re the disposal of prizes' of June 1665[215] included measures designed to prevent corruption, and collusive under-sale in the auction of vessels condemned as prize. The instructions required that vessels, wares and merchandises be judicially inventoried and appraised after condemnation. Notice of the sale of the goods was to be given by 'beat of drum and public writing'. The sale was to take place not less than ten days after such notice. The auction was to be administered by the magistrate of the town and by the vice-admiral 'unto such as will give most either upon contract or by inch of candle'.[216] At every first bidding 'a competent sum [was to] be advanced above the appraisement'. At 'sales by the candle, whosoever at the going out of the candle shall bid the highest price above the appraisement, [was] to have the said prize ship and goods delivered to him'. Admiralty officials were instructed to 'do their utmost to prevent combinations upon any sale'. The vice-admiral, his deputy and the magistrate appointed to conduct the sale, were forbidden 'to buy or otherwise interest themselves in any prize, ship, or goods'. An account of the sale was to be prepared by the vice-admiral and sent to the Irish Privy Council and the Irish prize commissioners. There could be a social dimension to the day. A prize sale in Kinsale in 1665 was followed by dinner for the merchants and appraisers in William Swan's inn.[217]

Notwithstanding the strict instructions of June 1665, Irish prizes were prey to theft and fraud. The most serious cases occurred in Galway. In 1666 sixteen persons, including a number of customs officials, were charged with embezzlement of goods on board the prize the *St Catherine*. The king's advocate estimated that between £600 and £700 worth of the ship's cargo (which included musk, amber, oriental pearls, diamonds, rubies, gold, silver lace and Flanders lace) was unaccounted for.[218] The *Sacrifice of Abraham*, a Genoese vessel owned by the baron d'Isola, was the subject of the most serious seventeenth-century Irish prize scandal.[219] The *Sacrifice* was seized off the west coast of Ireland in June 1667, and taken into Galway by the *Guinea* frigate. Very damning accusations, alleging open theft, were made about the conduct of the vice-admiral of Connacht, Sir Oliver St George. St George, it was said:

> came on board the vessel and took what he pleased out of the captain's cabin, and that his servants did the like … The boatswain and steward, with large

214  12 May 1665 (Bodl., Carte MS 34, f. 248). In Waterford commissions were appointed by the Court of Admiralty of Munster to appraise and value the cargo of the *St Jean of Dieppe*, which had just been condemned by the court (Bodl., Carte MS 34, ff 661, 667, 669).
215  9 June 1665 (Bodl., Carte MS 34, f. 249).
216  The duke of Ormond to H. Arlington, 15 Nov. 1665, *Cal. S.P. Ire. 1663–1665*, p. 663.
217  Robert Southwell's s accounts 1665, 24 Aug. 1665, *Cal. S.P. Ire. 1663–1665*, p. 665.
218  P. Pett to the earl of Clarendon, 9 June 1666 (Bodl., Clarendon MS 84, ff 190–1).
219  Report of L. Jenkins, R.Wiseman, W. Turner and W.Walker, 1668 (TNA (PRO), SP 79/1).

promises of reward in money ... were tampered with to swear there were Hollanders or enemy's goods on board ... Before, and after, the sale of the said ship the officers on shore took away the best of the lading of the said ship and ... the said Sir Oliver St George caused several cart loads thereof to be sent to his country house.[220]

    Two additional allegations were made about the administration of the sale of the prize. The first was that the vessel was sold at an under-value. At the auction in Galway, one bidder, Thomas Martin, allegedly bid £25,000 for the vessel. Although this was the highest bid, the vessel was not sold to Martin. Instead, in disregard of the requirement in the 1665 instructions that the prize be sold to the highest bidder, the ship and its cargo was sold to the Dublin Alderman, Louis des Mynieres, who had bid only £9,000. This gave rise to excited gossip of a collusive under-sale between Louis des Mynieres and John Stepney, one of St George's officers.[221] The Connacht Vice-Admiralty defended the sale to the second highest bidder on the ground that Martin's offer was disingenuous. Thomas Martin, they alleged, was 'a great friend of the Genoese' who had used 'all artifices imaginable to obstruct and retard our proceedings'.[222] The officers of the Connacht vice-admiralty claimed that Martin had 'declared he would bid ten thousand pounds more for the ship and goods than anyone else, though it is well known ... he could [not] procure the payment of the tenth part of that sum'.
    Inquiries were conducted before the Privy Councils of both Ireland and England. Two measures were adopted by the Irish council. Firstly, the cargo purchased by des Mynieres was ordered to be independently re-appraised.[223] The goods were found to have been under-valued, and in October 1667 des Mynieres was ordered to repay £1,615.[224] Secondly, because, in violation of the instructions of June 1665, revenue and customs dues had not been levied, the attorney general recommended that an information for unpaid customs dues be exhibited against the defaulters in the Court of Exchequer in Dublin.[225]
    The Irish response was much too tame for the English Privy Council, which was pressing for a thorough inquiry into the corruption in Galway. The Privy Council complained that the proceedings in the Irish Court of Exchequer had been 'purposely' brought 'to evade the fraud by small penalties'.[226] In March 1668 a separate enquiry was established in London. The accused conspirators aggravated the anger mounting in the English Privy Council by dragging their heels in

220  Bodl., Carte MS 35, f. 605.
221  L. Des Mynieres to the duke of Ormond, 28 Sept. 1667 (Bodl., Carte MS 35, f. 738).
222  O. St George, J. Stepney and J. Spencer to the Irish prize commissioners, 23 Aug. 1667 (Bodl., Carte MS 35, f. 675).
223  Bodl., MS Carte 144, f. 112.
224  R. Leigh to J. Williamson, 8 Oct. 1667 (TNA (PRO), SP 63/323, f. 130).
225  The duke of Ormond and Irish Privy Council to the English Privy Council, 24 Mar. 1668 (Bodl., Carte MS 36, f. 245).
226  Privy Council to the duke of Ormond, 28 Mar. 1668 (Bodl., Carte MS 52, f. 195).

attending. Colonel Spencer offered the lame excuse that he feared arrest on foot of two civil actions currently in train against him in England.[227] Des Mynieres provocatively pleaded that the council had not complied with the security conditions required by the Privy Seal Out of England Act 1517.[228] In July 1668 a warning was issued by the Privy Council to Sir Oliver St George, Colonel John Spencer, Louis des Mynieres and John Stepney that 'setting apart all delays and excuses they give their personal attendance on his majesty before the 17 of August next, or they will answer the contrary to their peril'.[229] Opinion in the English Privy Council was exceptionally hostile. The duke of Ormond reported after the July meeting: 'I saw the unanimous sense of the board so bent against them, and the king so prepossessed, that I let the torrent pass for that time, but yesterday morning I showed the king that he was artificially, but yet hugely, misinformed in many of the particulars'.[230] The Privy Council inquiry concluded in November with a direction that the *Sacrifice* be permitted to enter a late appeal in the English court against the Connacht sentence, with the punitive rider that Sir Oliver St George pay the costs of defending the appeal: since 'the carrying on of the said service will necessarily occasion an expense, which it was not thought reasonable Sir Peter Pett should defray at his own charge'.[231]

*Vessels seized in ports; the order-in-council of 6 March 1666*

A dispute about the proceeds of five prize sentences decreed in 1665 by Dr Joshua Boyle, the judge of the Admiralty Court of Munster, resulted in what would remain, up to the twentieth century, one of the central documents on the English law of prize, the order-in-council of 1666. According to early seventeenth-century constitutional doctrine the right to the proceeds of prize seized by privateers or men-of-war vested (subject to the clams of privateers acting under a letter of marque) in the Crown. But to whom did enemies' vessels, which had not been seized at sea by a naval man-of-war or a privateer – taken in port by, for instance, customs officers or admiralty officials – belong? Did they belong to the Crown? Or had they, as the Admiralty contended, been ceded by the Crown to the lord

---

227  A. Broderick to the duke of Ormond, 4 June 1668 (Bodl., Carte MS 36, f.359).

228  7 Hen. VIII (Ire.), 1517. Under the Act no Irish subject could be required to travel to England to answer any complaint unless sufficient security had been lodged in the Court of Chancery.

229  17 July 1668 (TNA (PRO), PC 2/60, f. 196).

230  Duke of Ormond to earl of Ossory, 18 July 1668 (Bodl., Carte MS 48, f. 276).

231  17 Nov. 1668 (TNA (PRO), PC 2/61, f. 60). The appeal by the owners of the *Sacrifice* against the Galway sentence dragged on inconclusively for over a decade. By 1680 Sir Leoline Jenkins reported that the appeal had, once again, been abandoned: 'There has been no citation about three years last put by the claimants, or any of them, nor any instance made for proceedings in order to a sentence on his majesty's behalf', and concluded that it was 'very probable that the Genoese have wholly given over their pretensions'. 'Sir Peter Pett's account of the *Abraham Sacrifice*, a Genoese' (n.d.) (BL, Add. MS 18,206, f. 20).

admiral, by virtue of the right in his patent to *casualia maris*? That legal question had, by the time of the Restoration, 'grown into obscurity'.[232]

The issue, prompted by a series of seizures made in Munster, was settled in 1666. Five vessels, of French and Dutch origin, had been detained by officers in ports in Munster on the outbreak of war. The *Peter of Shellavit*, the *Isabel of Nantz*, and the *Susanah of Nornac* were taken by officials of the Munster Vice-Admiralty after the declaration of war with France; the *Prince of Denmark* and the *Orange Tree* had been seized after the outbreak of war with the United Provinces. In all of these cases Dr Joshua Boyle, judge of the Munster Court, condemned the vessels to the Crown. The vessels had been sold and the proceeds paid into the Exchequer in Ireland. The Admiralty, however, claimed that the court's order, that the prizes be disposed of to the Crown, infringed the residual rights of the lord admiral. These were not, it was argued, conventional prize since they had not been captured by a naval vessel or privateer. They were *casualia maris* and were included in the admiral's patent.

Sir Peter Pett, the king's advocate in Ireland, requested an authoritative resolution of the dispute by the English Privy Council. The Privy Council re-directed Pett's queries to a panel composed of the judge of the Court of Admiralty (Sir Leoline Jenkins), the king's advocate (Robert Wiseman) and the admiralty advocate (William Turner), and the matter was debated at a conference before the king, at Worcester House in Oxford. It was resolved that Joshua Boyle had erred in law: the Crown prerogative of prize did not extend to enemy vessels seized by customs or admiralty officers in port. Instead, the vessel belonged to the Admiralty:[233] 'enemy's ships that come in voluntarily to his majesty's ports, or are driven in thither by stress of weather, or other accidents, do belong to the lord high admiral, if his officers, or those of the custom house, (or indeed any other) do seize them'.

Following the Oxford conference, in 1667 the English Privy Council advised the Irish lord lieutenant that an error had been committed by the 'judge of the Admiralty in the province of Munster, not knowing the rules prescribed here'. Boyle, he was informed, had incorrectly 'adjudged the vessels for his majesty's benefit'. The lord lieutenant was directed to 'give command to the judges of the Courts of Admiralty in the several provinces in Ireland, upon all adjudications of prizes … diligently and circumspectly to pursue and be guided in all matters comprised in the said order according to the Rules [of 1666]'.[234] The application of the principles laid down in the order of 1666 would again become a highly contentious issue in Ireland during the 1690s.[235]

---

232  Per Sir W. Scott in the *Marie Francoise* (1806) 6 C Rob 282, 293; 165 ER 933, 936.
233  L. Jenkins to the earl of Arlington, 3 Mar. 1666, W. Wynne, *The life of Sir Leoline Jenkins*, p. 767.
234  Privy Council to the lord lieutenant and Privy Council in Ireland, 4 Jan. 1667 (TNA (PRO), PC 2/59, f. 131).
235  See p. 92 below.

*Prize in Ireland during the Third Anglo–Dutch War, 1672–4*

No prize commission was issued to any of the courts of admiralty of Ireland during the Third Anglo–Dutch War, 1672–4 – a consequence, possibly, of loss of trust following the *Sacrifice of Abraham* scandal of the 1660s. Instead of creating a local prize judicature in Ireland, the adjudication of prize captures was centralized in London.[236] However, sub-commissioners, acting on behalf of the English commissioners of prizes, were established at Kinsale with the function of providing ancillary support for prize proceedings in England. These commissioners assisted the London court by detaining and preserving the vessel, administering standard-form interrogatories to the crew, and preserving the ships' papers. They were instructed to:

> Take and receive into your custody all ships and goods brought in as prize into the port of Kinsale, or any other port, creek or river in his majesty's kingdom of Ireland. To take a fair accompt of ships, tackle, apparel, furniture, stores of ammunition, and provisions and the goods, wares and merchandise seized without breaking of bulk or unloading of same, a duplicate of which you are to return to us by the first post.[237]

Their orders required them to 'make due search, and enquiry for, and demand and take, all bills of lading, charter parties, letters, sea briefs, and all other writings and papers whatsoever' and 'to examine as well the master and officers of the prize ship, or any two or three of the most knowing amongst them, to each point in the said commission and interrogatories'. They were to 'seal up and send over unto us [the cargo] in the said prize ship ... to the end proceedings in the Admiralty here may be had thereupon in order to the condemnation of such ship or goods'. Finally, they were instructed to 'prevent and hinder ... all embezzlements that may by fraud ... by making tight and sound any cask that you can come at without breaking bulk, or stopping any leakage, and placing sufficient honest sailors on board'.

*Prize law in Ireland, 1677–80: the Christian Albert, Golden Salmon and Fleming cases*

Although no prize commission had been issued to Ireland since 1665, the Irish Admiralty Court, under Sir William Petty, exercised jurisdiction on at least three occasions between 1676 and 1679. There were a number of peculiarities about two, in particular – the *Christian Albert* and the *Golden Salmon* – of these cases. Firstly, jurisdiction was exercised although the Irish court had not been entrusted with any

---

236  There is, however, a record of one condemnation by an Irish admiralty court during the Third Anglo–Dutch War: in 1673 the *Bachelor*, a Dutch trading ship, loaded with 160 bales of silk, and gold and plate, was condemned by what may have come to be regarded as the notorious Admiralty Court of Connacht. *Cal. S.P. Dom. 1672–1673*, p. 454.

237  Instructions to the prize sub-commissioners at Kinsale (BL, Harleian MS 1,511, f. 341).

authority to exercise prize jurisdiction; indeed, the Crown was not even at war; the Third Anglo–Dutch War had ended two years earlier. Secondly, the privateers to whom vessels were condemned did not act under letters of marque granted by the English government, but operated under commissions granted by France and Sweden. Petty, was, in effect, setting up a sort of international prize court. Inevitably this exorbitant assertion of jurisdiction resulted in embarrassing diplomatic complaints and official censure.

In the spring of 1676 the Swedish envoy to England, Baron Sparr, issued a letter of marque to an Irish privateer, Terence Byrne. The Swedish government subsequently became concerned to secure observance of a proclamation issued by the English Crown forbidding English privateers from taking letters of marque granted by other states. The Swedish envoy tried to revoke the commission which it had issued to Byrne. Meanwhile, Charles V of Denmark had occupied the territories of Sweden's ally, the duke of Holstein-Gottorp. Byrne, who had ignored the instruction to return his commission, then captured the *Christian Albert*, a vessel belonging to subjects of the town of Eckenförde in Holstein-Gottorp. In December 1676 Byrne sailed his capture into Kinsale, where he had the ship arrested by virtue of a warrant from the Irish Court of Admiralty. A 'tedious and chargeable lawsuit at the Court of Admiralty', in the words of the Swedish envoy, was instigated.[238] The claimant, Peter Tamm, master of the *Christian Albert*, argued that the people of Holstein-Gottorp continued to be allies of the King of Sweden; accordingly, the capture was outside the terms of the letter of marque issued by the Swedish government. This was supported by the Swedish government who contended that occupation by the Danes had not made the inhabitants of Holstein subjects of Denmark: 'yet can such an inroad and usurpation by no legal means assert and make the duke [of Holstein-Gottorp's] subjects to be the king [of Denmark's] subjects'. The captor Byrne, on the other hand, sought to prove, calling witnesses and presenting documentary evidence, that the people of Holstein had submitted to allegiance with the kingdom of Denmark, and that by committing their allegiance to Denmark, the seizure was justified by his Swedish commission. Petty never finally determined this question. A memorial strongly critical of the Irish court's handling of Byrne's prize claim was submitted by the Swedish envoy in England. In November 1677, Petty reported that he 'had heard that Tamm hath caused Monsr Leyinburg to write something to my lord lieutenant reflecting upon my justice, which is totally untrue in matter of fact'.[239] The Irish court was seriously overreaching itself. It was not an international court. It had no jurisdiction to process captures under Swedish letters of marque, or to determine complex disputes of north European politics. The matter was transferred from the Court of Admiralty to the Irish Privy Council, which also found it impossible to

---

238  'Memorial of the envoy of Sweden touching a ship of Holstein, Peter Tamm master', 15 Apr. 1678 (TNA (PRO), SP 95/11, f. 31).
239  W. Petty to R. Southwell, 10 Nov. 1677, *Petty–Southwell Corr.*, p. 38.

determine the issue of the allegiance of the people of Eckenförde. By 1678 the matter had not yet been resolved, and Peter Tamm's vessel remained under arrest.[240]

In the *Golden Salmon* litigation in 1677 the Irish court again wildly exceeded its powers. The *Golden Salmon* was a Dutch whaling vessel returning from Greenland. By the time that she was seized by her French captor 'all her crew had forsaken her and escaped on long boats'.[241] The captor then took the vessel into Youghal where prize condemnation proceedings were opened. These resulted in a sentence in favour of the captor:

> There came into Youghal, a French man in a Dutch ssuit (sic.) without a commission, and without bringing with him any of the taken ship's company. Hereupon we accuse him of a piratical act. He (as the readiest way to clear himself) claims from us the adjudication of his prize. We, upon discussion of the matter, clear him of piracy and adjudge the said suit unto him as lawful prize, and demand of him the tenths, in right of the admiral of Ireland.

Following condemnation, the *Golden Salmon* was purchased by a Youghal merchant, Walter Galway. However, there were two problems; first, what jurisdiction did the Irish court have to condemn a prize to a captor who acted under a letter of marque granted by a foreign state (France), and not by the English government? Second, how could the court exercise prize jurisdiction now that hostilities between France and the Dutch had ceased? Showing signs of panic, Petty urged his friend, Sir Robert Southwell,[242] the secretary to the commissioners of prizes, to 'acquaint his royal highness, or Sir John Werden herewith. We here are the blind leading the blind'.

Dutch interests were beginning to protest. The proprietor, Cornelius Thenispeck, sought the intervention of the commissioners of Admiralty. As an interim measure, the lord lieutenant, the duke of Ormond, by order in council, directed the mayor of Youghal to prevent the purchaser, Galway, disposing of her. Sir Leoline Jenkins was called upon to sort out the constitutional and diplomatic imbroglio, particularly delicate given the rapprochement currently being negotiated between England and the Dutch.[243] Article 21 of the treaty of Breda of 1667 forbade England from providing assistance to privateers from third-party states attacking Dutch vessels. Jenkins was particularly worried that the clumsy activities of the Irish court had precipitated an infringement of the duty in Article 21. Was

240 Order in Council, 27 Mar. 1678 (*Cal. S.P. Dom. 1678*, pp 74–5).

241 'Report about the Dutch ship being called the *Salmon* carried by a French privateer to Youghal in Ireland and there condemned by the captor' (BL, Add. MS 18,206, f. 127); L. Jenkins to the king, 5 Jan. 1680, *Life of Jenkins*, ii, p. 733.

242 W. Petty to R. Southwell, 10 Nov. 1677, *Petty–Southwell Corr.*, p. 38.

243 C. Grose, 'The Anglo–Dutch alliance of 1678', *English Historical Review*, 39 (1924), 349–72, 526–51. K.H.D. Haley, 'The Anglo–Dutch rapprochement of 1677', *English Historical Review*, 73 (1958), 614.

the Irish court, by the condemnation of a Dutch prize taken by the French, not guilty of constructive aggression against the Dutch?

> All of your majesty's subjects are bound by [the Treaty of Breda] and are bound to take notice of it, and are concluded by it; and it was, therefore, an error to lend or interpose your majesty's authority in a judicial way by condemning of this ship ... Besides such proceedings are contrary to a fundamental maxim of neutrality: ... a neutral ship being in peace when his neighbours are at war, ought not to make the condition of one neighbour better than that of another; as here the French man has the help and benefit of a court of law and an open free market for his prize ...[244]

In London Sir Robert Southwell circulated Petty's letter to two leading English civilians, Thomas Bedford and William Trumbull. Their responses can only have further aggravated Petty's embarrassment. Bedford expressed amazement at Petty's assertion of international prize jurisdiction: what business did an Irish court have to administer French prize proceedings?:

> As to Sir William's letter, I cannot but wonder that he should take upon himself to adjudge a prize to the French, which no one can do but such as are empowered by the French King to reside within our king's territories, and with her leave, as our commissioners did in Galicia in the late war against the Dutch ...[245]

Bedford was brutal in his assessment of Petty's incompetence:

> I see the good gentleman means well, but had not been well versed in the practical part of admiralty proceedings. I fear this matter will be complained of both by the French and the Dutch. The latter may expect that we should not arrest their ships in point of property (when brought into his majesty's ports) ... French captors ought to have the liberty to carry their own prizes from any of his majesty's ports (into which they may happen to come), to the end to bring them to trial in the proper Admiralty ... the French doubly will not like it well if we should pretend to the 10ths of their prizes ...

Leoline Jenkins insisted upon the necessity of reversing both the Petty sentence and the sale of the vessel. There was a risk that the Dutch would retaliate against this breach of the treaty of Breda; it 'may, for ought I know, run up as high as to reprisals against us'.[246] The vessel should be returned to the original Dutch proprietor.[247] There were, however, problems as to who could undo the order of the

244  *Life of Jenkins*, p. 734.
245  T. Bedford to R. Southwell, 11 Apr. 1678 (BL, Add. MS 72,852, f. 152).
246  5 Jan. 1680 (BL, Add. MS 18,206, f. 127).
247  Bedford, on the other hand, thought that the vessel belonged to the French captor. His analysis

Irish Court of Admiralty disposing of the property to Walter Galway. The obvious option was by way of appeal to the English Court of Admiralty. The problem here was that the sale had been made on land; however (by reason of the locality rule)[248] the English Court of Admiralty had no jurisdiction over transactions made *infra corpus comitatus*. Therefore, an appeal to the English court could not rescind the sale to Galway: 'tis more than probable the bargain was made between the buyer and privateer on land, and consequently the cognisance of the validity of it, will be prohibited to the admiralty [court]'. In the absence of any competent tribunal, Jenkins advised that the sentence be rescinded by an executive order.

Having had his lack of technical competence so publicly exposed in the *Golden Salmon* debacle, Petty's lack of self confidence must have been reduced even further in the next prize-related case to come his way: *Fleming v. MacDonnell*. *Fleming v. MacDonnell* was one of the most intricate cases heard before the Irish Court of Admiralty in the late seventeenth century; Petty confessed to having been 'almost frightened' with 'the trouble and perplexity of [the] business'.[249] A sizeable privateering business had been generated by prize commissions granted by the marquess of Ormond in the late 1640s against the vessels of the Parliamentary army.[250] In 1649, acting under one of these commissions, Randal MacDonnell, the marquess of Antrim, seized a ship, laden with wines, belonging to a Scottish merchant, Thomas Fleming, en route from St Malo to the port of Leith in Edinburgh. The vessel was taken into Dunkirk where the prize was divided between the captors, Lynch, Antrim, and Vanderzypp. Fleming petitioned Charles II, then in exile, who, in turn, established an *ad hoc* admiralty court at Brussels. The sentence of the Royalist Brussels court directed the captors to make restitution of the vessel to Fleming. Fleming, however, spent nearly thirty years attempting to execute the order. He appears to have never succeeded. The first proceedings opened in Galway before the Connacht Court in August 1667.[251] Fleming lost and, in 1668, he submitted an appeal to the English Court of Admiralty.[252] However, that appeal appears to have been discontinued without being finally determined.[253] A decade later Fleming revived the matter before the

---

was premised upon the view that the proceedings by the Irish court were void (and that therefore the provisional title to the vessel had not passed from the French captor): the sentence 'was erroneously given by an incompetent judge and therefore void and the French should be permitted to carry away their prize unless the laws of Ireland are different from these here'. T. Bedford to R. Southwell, 11 Apr. 1678 (BL, Add. MS 72,852, f. 152).

248  See p. 33 above.
249  W. Petty to J. Williamson, 18 July 1678, *Cal. S.P. Dom. 1678*, p. 300.
250  J. Ohlmeyer, 'Irish Privateers during the Civil War, 1642–1650', *Mariner's Mirror*, 76 (1990), 119.
251  TNA (PRO), HCA 15/13. In 1666 the king had written to the duke of Ormond requiring that Fleming be provided with appropriate relief. In August 1666 Ormond referred the matter to the Connacht admiralty (Bodl., Carte MS 144, f. 87).
252  3 June 1668 (TNA (PRO), HCA 3/51, f. 109).
253  The final reference to *Fleming v. Lynch* in the Act Book of the High Court of Admiralty is 23 Oct. 1670 (TNA (PRO), HCA 3/51, f. 219).

Court of Admiralty in Dublin, 'the scope of the libel' again being to put the Brussels sentence into execution. This suit was tried before Petty by the Irish Court of Admiralty in 1678. At the trial, the proctor retained by the marquess of Antrim pleaded seven objections to the Brussels sentence. The three most important of these arguments were: (i) that the Brussels *ad hoc* admiralty court was a tribunal not known to the law; and did not 'conform to the solemnity of the law'; (ii) that the defendants had not been summoned to appear before the Brussels court; and (iii) that the defendants were entitled to the immunity provided by the Act of Free and General Pardon, Indemnity and Oblivion 1660.[254] However, these objections were overruled and a sentence ('after much contest and the ordinary delays of courts')[255] was pronounced in favour of Fleming.[256]

In response, MacDonnell initiated an appeal to the Court of Admiralty in London, which he let drop[257] in favour of the more effective strategy of requesting the Irish King's Bench for a writ of prohibition. The King's Bench obliged and the Irish Court of Admiralty was prohibited from proceeding further. In the suggestion grounding his application for prohibition, MacDonnell relied on the same grounds that he had argued at the proceedings before Petty: that the Brussels sentence was not by due course of law, and that the applicants were immunized by the Act of Oblivion 1660

> the lord marquess of Antrim, Ambrose Lynch, etc. had exhibited a sug-
> gestion in the Court of King's Bench, setting forth among other things, that
> by the law of the land, no judgment or sentence ought to be given against any
> person until they be, by due process of law, summoned to appear and answer,
> notwithstanding which Mr Fleming had impleaded the said lord marquess
> and the others in the Admiralty Court of Ireland upon a sentence given by
> certain delegates against one Cornelius Claizen Vanderzypp and his partners
> at Brussels the 11th day of August 1650; whereupon the said sentence is void
> in law and of no force against the said lord marquess or the others, and that
> they were never named nor are parties to the same, and that they did offer the
> same to the Court of Admiralty and prayed the benefit of the Act of
> Oblivion. But the said Court of Admiralty refused to admit of the said
> allegations, but proceeded to sentence against the said lord marquess ...[258]

Fleming's chance of a remedy had, once more, receded. Sir Leoline Jenkins was called in to advise Fleming. Jenkins' reaction was to complain that the Irish King's Bench had misunderstood the circumstances in which a writ of prohibition[259]

254  12 Car. II, c. 11 (Eng.), 1660.
255  W. Petty to J. Williamson, 18 July 1678, *Cal. S.P. Dom. 1678*, p. 300.
256  S. 10 of the Act of Oblivion exempted murder and piracy at sea from the application of the
     indemnity.
257  *Life of Jenkins*, ii, p. 788.                258  Ibid.
259  Fleming had requested that the king issue a letter directing the King's Bench to lift the
     prohibition. Jenkins advised that this was not the proper course of action: 'for a writ of

might properly be issued: this was confined to cases in which the Court of Admiralty had no jurisdiction over the subject matter of the proceedings, but was 'holding plea of things cognizable by the courts of common law'. However, the subject matter of this particular suit – a case of spoil and depredation at sea – was a matter cognizable only before a court of admiralty; accordingly, the Irish Court of Admiralty was not amenable to prohibition:

> the cause of action upon which delegates at Brussels gave their sentence was a cause of spoil and depredation upon the high and open seas, and consequently cognizable in the Court of Admiralty alone, and to be judged by the civil law; if so, the sentence cannot be pronounced void, but by a court of appeal proceeding according to the same law …[260]

Jenkins warned that 'if the prohibition be not taken off, Fleming is without remedy'. This was exactly how it turned out. The defendants' strategy of removing the threat of admiralty proceedings by a writ of prohibition seems to have worked perfectly. In 1681, with the Admiralty Court's order still frozen by the King's Bench, the king wrote to the lord lieutenant encouraging him to persuade the defendants to submit to 'arbitration of such of the judges as his grace shall appoint to determine the matters in difference'.[261]

### Prize law in Ireland during the Nine Years War, 1688–97

In 1690, the absentee judge of the Irish Admiralty Court, Sir Paul Rycaut, instructed his agent to enquire whether prize vessels taken into Dublin were to be condemned in Dublin, or in the court in London. If the Irish court were to have prize jurisdiction, Rycaut, without showing any embarrassment, instructed his agent to make a backhander (or 'present' as he termed it) to the secretary of the admiralty to speed his commission. But if there was to be no grant of prize jurisdiction his agent was not to furnish a tip 'but only pay the common fees'.[262] Indeed, he suggested, he was barely interested in the office of judge if there was to be no grant of prize, complaining that 'if the business of the patent sticks for want of a present I fear the thing will not bear it, in case that prizes brought into Ireland are not to be judged in my court, but in the admiralty [court] at London'. When it was confirmed that a prize commission had not been issued to the Irish court, an irritated Rycaut complained about the poor return on his investment: 'if I had been empowered thereby to have judged causes of prize in Ireland, it might have been worth the money paid for the patent, but without it, I fear, as my surrogate and other officers will contrive it, I will scarce see a return of my money again'.[263]

consultation upon the prohibition would be (as I humbly conceive) the only proper and legal remedy to the petitioner'. Ibid., p. 789.

260  Ibid.    261  Charles II to the duke of Ormond, 23 Apr. 1681, *Cal. S.P. Dom. 1680–81*, p. 248.
262  P. Rycaut to Delart, 9 Jan. 1690 (BL, Lansdowne MS 1,153C, f. 6).
263  P. Rycaut to Delart, 6 Mar. 1691 (BL, Lansdowne MS 1,153C, f. 77).

However, once prize captures began to be taken into Dublin, the lack of authority conferring prize jurisdiction did not appear to unduly bother the Irish court. Rycaut's surrogate, Dudley Loftus, condemned at least four (and possibly as many as eight or even nine) prizes in 1691.[264]

*Munster prize: Irish courts and the English High Court of Admiralty in dispute, 1690–1710*

The order in council promulgated following the Oxford conference of 1666[265] propounded the simple rule that enemy vessels seized in ports, on the outbreak of war, by admiralty or customs officers belonged to the lord admiral and his court. The order did not deal with the slightly different issue of enemies' goods seized from the vessels of Irish importers. The issue of who precisely owned enemy goods seized from Irish vessels was the subject of a series of bitter disputes during the 1690s, all of which involved French produce seized in ports in Munster. According to admiralty lawyers, French enemy goods seized from Irish vessels were an admiralty perquisite in the same way as French ships were an admiralty perquisite.[266] They were part of the admiral's general patent right to enemies' goods, and as with all admiralty perquisites, title was confirmed following a suit in a court of admiralty.

The customs commissioners, on the other hand, argued that the seizure of enemy imports from native vessels docked in port did not fall within any recognized category of admiralty perquisite: they were clearly not prize captures at sea; nor did they fall within the strict terms of the decision of 1666 (which dealt with enemy vessels, not produce). Accordingly, the Court of Admiralty had no jurisdiction. Instead the Court of Exchequer had jurisdiction under the Trade with France Acts 1689 and 1693.[267] The 1689 Act, reciting that 'the importing of French wines, vinegar, brandy, linen, silks, salt, paper and other commodities of the growth or manufacture of France hath such exhausted the treasure of this nation' provided that illegally imported French produce was to be liable to condemnation in the Court of Exchequer.

---

264 Hugh Baillie, in a 1748 report based on a search of the act books of the Irish court listed four prize condemnations during this period: the *Two Williams of Bordeaux*, the *St Lawrence of Bordeaux* (11 July 1691), the *Swallow of St Malo* (17 Nov. 1691), and the *St Michael of Dunkirk* (17 Dec. 1691); H. Baillie to the commissioners of Admiralty, 17 May 1748 (TNA (PRO), ADM 1/3990). In a later report he located four further instances: the *Golden Skipper (Norway)*, the *Fortune Prince of Gottenborg*, the *Mary of Dublin*, and the *Waterford Merchant of Biddeford*; Baillie's reply to Pinfold, 1755 (TNA (PRO), ADM 1/3882). Another list of 1691 prize condemnations compiled by John Hawkshaw listed the *Golden Skipper*, the *Two Williams*, the *Mary of Dublin*, the *Friends' Adventure* and the *Swallow of St. Malo*. J. Hawkshaw to T. Corbett, 6 Oct. 1744 (TNA (PRO), ADM 1/3990).

265 See p. 83 above.

266 Charles Hedges' opinion re the *John and Samuel* (BL, Add. MS 24,107, f. 164).

267 1 Will. & Mar., c. 34 (Eng.), 1689; 4 & 5 Will. & Mar., c. 25 (Eng.), 1693.

In 1693 a suspicious-looking vessel laden with salt and pitch, the *Postillion of Bristol,* landed in Cork. A vice-admiralty official was sent 'to drink with the men'. In the course of the drinking session the ship's mates 'did very frankly confess that they came directly from Rochelle in company with three other ships'.[268] Acting on this information, the vessel was seized by a deputy to the vice-admiral of Munster[269] and the standard-form interrogatories administered for the purpose of condemnation proceedings in the English Court of Admiralty. However, the Irish commissioners of customs disputed the assertion that the *Postillion* was properly a prize case. There had been no capture at sea: the vessel having 'been seized in port and not by a privateer does not come under the jurisdiction of the Admiralty of England'.[270] Before the ship could be transmitted to London, an order came from the Privy Council directing that the Munster Vice-Admiralty hand her over to the commissioners of customs, for the purpose of condemnation by the Irish Court of Exchequer. The Court of Exchequer dismissed the Admiralty's claim on the ground that the Admiralty Court had jurisdiction only over recognized forms of prize. There was no authority that goods in an Irish vessel in an Irish port were amenable to the law of prize. On the other hand the Court of Exchequer had jurisdiction under the Trade with France Acts 1689 and 1693. The chief baron of the Court of Exchequer, Sir John Hely, said that 'they are goods brought in by our own subjects and not by an enemy, for these goods and ships that are taken from an enemy will be judged prize, but the ship and goods of a subject which come into unload will not be looked on as prize'. There was no conflict; no admiralty rights were ever engaged. Hely assured the English Admiralty Court that he 'did not intend to clash with the Courts of Admiralty, but conceives that as the case is there will be no clashing'.[271] In March 1694 Sir Robert Southwell, the Munster vice-admiral produced an elaborate report chronicling the proceedings in Ireland and warning the Admiralty that unless responsive measures were taken 'the admiralty jurisdiction in Ireland will be condemned and slighted'.[272] Sir Charles Hedges also took a characteristically dramatic view, recommending that an executive direction be promulgated putting a stop to the proceedings in the Irish Exchequer. On 10 May 1694 an order suspending the rule of the Exchequer was issued by the English Privy Council.[273]

But, unexpectedly, the Irish Privy Council stood its ground against Whitehall. The Irish solicitor general, Richard Levinge, like the chief baron, argued that the seizure in port of illegally imported French goods carried in an Irish vessel did not correspond to any form of recognized prize seizure. Accordingly, the English Court of Admiralty had no original jurisdiction:

---

268  J. Waller to R . Southwall, 29 Aug. 1693 (BL, Add. MS 38 147, f. 42).
269  'The rights and jurisdiction of the lord high admiral of England asserted in Ireland by a process of the *Postillion* ketch, coming from France into Cork harbour in 1693; laid before the Admiralty by Sir Robert Southwell, vice-admiral of Munster' (BL, Egerton MS 744).
270  Ibid., f. 20.                           271  BL, Egerton MS 744, f. 27.
272  Ibid., f. 40.                           273  10 May 1694, *Cal. S.P. Dom. 1694–1695,* p. 130.

the ship being not seized at sea, by any of their majesty's ships, or any private men of war, but in port by an officer of the admiralty after entry, it might be doubtful whether the condemnation and sale thereof in the court would be effectual in law, whereas it could not be doubted but if judgment was given in the Court of Exchequer according to the acts, the proceedings and sale of the said ship and cargo would be good to all intents and purposes and could not be afterwards drawn in question by those who pretended to be owners of the said ship and cargo.[274]

In November 1694 the law officers of both kingdoms met in conference to resolve the dispute. Their ultimate decision was that both sides were correct. Enemy goods seized in port could both be an admiralty perquisite and also be subject to the trading with the enemy laws. The problem of competing claims was solved by the adoption of a pragmatic principle of first seizure: entitlement would be determined according to who first discovered the illegal imports. In the case of the *Postillion*, the first seizure had been made by the deputy vice-admiral of Munster, the right of determining the cause properly belonged to the Court of Admiralty: 'the first seizure being made by captain Waller's officers on behalf of your majesty's admiralty rights, and sentence of condemnation being thereupon obtained before any seizure or information upon the act of Parliament, that the right of seizure and of determining that cause did most properly lie before the Court of Admiralty'.[275]

Although French enemy cargo was usually both an admiralty perquisite and subject to the trading with the enemy acts, there were occasions when it did not fall within the statutory enemy trading régime. The *John and Samuel*[276] had been driven aground near Wexford, where her cargo was seized by customs officers, and proceedings under the Trade with France Act 1689 initiated against her in the Irish Court of Exchequer. Concurrently with the revenue proceedings, a case had been taken in the Court of Admiralty in London and the vessel had been condemned to the lord high admiral. The English civilian, Henry Newton, argued that the Trade with France Act 1689 did not apply. The 1689 Act was predicated on the 'importation' of the produce of France; however, Newton argued, 'being driven by stress of weather on the coast can, by no construction, be taken to be "importing" of goods (which supposes a voluntary act), on which account only the commissioners of the revenue in Ireland could proceed in the Exchequer there'.[277] A second opinion, written by the judge of the English Admiralty Court, Sir Charles Hedges, confirmed Newton's analysis of the word 'import':

274 'The rights and jurisdiction of the lord high admiral of England asserted in Ireland' (BL, Egerton MS 744, ff 28–30).
275 Ibid., ff 45, 46. Conflicts between the Admiralty and the customs over illegally imported French enemy goods continued notwithstanding the order of 1694: 'The case of the ship *St Stephen*', 1704 (PRO, ADM 1/3667, f.70); the *Venture of Dublin*, 1709 (PRO, ADM 1/3667, f. 435).
276 H. Newton to W. Bridgeman, 9 June 1698 (BL, Add. MS 24,107, f. 164).
277 Ibid.

It is true there appears to be some colour for the proceeding in the exchequer in Ireland, upon the statute of 4 & 5 Will. & Mar., but Dr Newton has fully cleared that point since the goods of this ship cannot be upon a fair construction be said to be 'imported' contrary to the true intent and meaning of the Act.[278]

## THE INSTANCE BUSINESS OF LATE SEVENTEENTH-CENTURY IRISH COURTS OF ADMIRALTY

The level of instance business processed by the court during the late seventeenth century remained desperately low. In his address to the admiralty sessions held at Ringsend in October 1677 Sir William Petty mentioned that there were only five items of business currently before the Irish court.[279] Of the three categories of litigation permitted by the English Privy Council protocol of February 1633[280] it was modest seamen's wages cases (along with salvage and collision)[281] which made up the principal business of the Court. In 1677, Petty observed that the work of the court 'chiefly concerns poor men'.[282] The entitlement of a sailor, unpaid or ill-treated, to walk into a court of admiralty was part of the sub-culture of the professional mariner in the late seventeenth century. In 1671 Nicholas Francis and the rest of the crew of the *Orange Tree of Rochelle* initiated a suit for unpaid wages before the Court of Admiralty of Munster (sitting in the 'dwelling house of Thomas Burrowes inn holder' in Kinsale).[283] In 1677 the Dutch ambassador lodged a protest when a group of English sailors aboard the Dutch man-of-war *Prince Casimir* had the vessel arrested by admiralty process for arrears of pay when it had docked at Waterford. The ambassador complained that the crew had 'endeavoured to compel [the master] by arrest to pay them their arrears, without finishing their voyage, which example had occasioned so great disorder in the ship', and requested the king to have the arrest annulled.[284] In 1704 sailors aboard the

---

278 Ibid.
279 1 Oct. 1677 (BL, Lansdowne MS 1,228, f. 46).  280 See p. 37 above.
281 In 1668 the Munster Court of Admiralty determined a salvage claim by Alexander Grey, the controller of customs at Youghal, arising from the rescue of the *St John Baptiste*, which had been driven on to rocks at Ballyfeard. The Munster court (13 Aug. 1668) found that it was due to the claimant's skill that the vessel had been rescued, and decreed to Grey 'the full and just sum of one hundred pounds sterling' together with costs and compensation for expenses spent on hiring boats and sailors (TNA (PRO), HCA 15/13). A salvage claim decided by Dr Rowland Davies in the Munster court in 1708, in a case involving the *Leopard of Bordeaux*, was the subject of an appeal to the High Court of Admiralty (TNA (PRO), HCA 15/13). The Munster court under Farren presided over a collision case in the late 1690s (*The Council Book of Cork Corporation*, p. 274).
282 W. Petty to R. Southwell, 10 Nov. 1677, *Petty–Southwell Corr.*, p. 39.
283 TNA (PRO), HCA 15/9.
284 21 Mar. 1677 (TNA (PRO), SP 63/338, f. 70).

transatlantic *Unity of Amsterdam* used the processes of the Admiralty Court of Connacht to obtain unpaid wages.[285] The Irish court was proud of its role as protector of exploited sailors. Sir William Petty commended its practice of waiving fees in wages cases: 'we can brag of justice and dispatch and forgiving of fees'.[286] On the other hand, the court's processes did not always work effectively, and masters managed to find ways of escaping them. In 1676 Thomas Oliver, unpaid for his service on the *Speedwell*, had the vessel arrested by the Connacht Admiralty Court. However, upon bail being offered, the vessel was released. When sentence was decreed in favour of Oliver he was left remediless: the vessel had departed and nothing could be recovered from the bailsman.[287] In 1688 Charles Hall, who had been hired to serve on a trip between the Canaries and Dublin, sued in the Irish Court of Admiralty for unpaid wages amounting to a sum of £14 15s.[288] Before Hall had even managed to procure a warrant of arrest, the vessel had escaped from Dublin to London. The Dublin court having proven ineffective, Hall was obliged to institute fresh proceedings before the Court of Admiralty in London.

Seventeenth-century courts of admiralty were allowed to exercise jurisdiction in suits for enforcement of bottomry bonds (a security under which a ship master, stranded in a foreign port, pledged the vessel in order to obtain credit to continue the journey). This was the only form of maritime security which an admiralty court was permitted to enforce.[289] However, in the *Orrery* in 1678 the Irish court, presided over by William Petty, sought to enforce a security of a type which was well outside the limits allowed to any admiralty court. It was also a suit in which Petty was disqualified by a substantial material interest. The story of the *Orrery* began in 1677 when Petty, one of the wealthiest men in Restoration Ireland, lent £1,100 to a London merchant, Mathew Elliston; in return for the loan Elliston pledged his share in the *Orrery*, a ship which he was in the course of building on the Kenmare river. Elliston's business failed and Petty's investment was wiped out. Petty, in order to enforce his security, had the *Orrery* arrested under a warrant issued by the Court of Admiralty. At night the defendants re-seized the *Orrery* as it lay under arrest on the Kenmare: sails were obtained and the rudder re-attached. There was a chaotic scene on the Kenmare river as the crew of the *Orrery*, led by a sailor called Battin, confronted the marshal and his assistants. Battin threw a court official named Mansfield overboard. As Mansfield struggled to regain his

---

285  TNA (PRO), ADM 1/3,666, ff 183, 238.

286  W. Petty to R. Southwell, 18 Nov. 1677, *Petty–Southwell Corr.*, p. 40.

287  TNA (PRO), HCA/15/14.

288  The respondents filed affidavits denying that Hall had ever served as master's mate, that he had been carried aboard as a passenger only, and furthermore, that he had been responsible for the loss of the vessel's cable. Affidavits of Thomas Bishop, Thomas Hart and John Roope, 19 June 1688 (TNA (PRO), HCA 15/14).

289  G.F. Steckley, 'Bottomry bonds in the seventeenth-century Admiralty Court', *American Journal of Legal History*, 45 (2001), 256.

grip, Battin threatened to strike Mansfield's hands with an axe, while shouting that 'he cared not a bird for the king's warrant, nor the king's office, bidding them take the king's warrant and wipe their arse with it'.[290]

The *Orrery* set sail for England, safely delivered from the hands of the Irish Court of Admiralty. Petty then sought to have his sentence enforced by the English Court of Admiralty. Far from maintaining discretion about presiding over litigation in which he was interested (and of a type over which an admiralty court did not have jurisdiction) he pestered the Admiralty with petitions, and pressurized Robert Southwell to intervene with Sir Leoline Jenkins: 'Sir William Temple, Sir William Godolphin, Mr Pepys and Mr Cooke, I think have all interests in Sir Leoline, and I hope you have likewise. For God's sake, use some means that we be not run down violently against the cries and clamours of our right'.[291] Petty's attempt to importune the English court was unavailing. In November 1679 the English Court of Admiralty in *Pilkington v. Orrery*[292] held that it had no power to enforce the sentence of the Irish Court of Admiralty.

*Admiralty droits*

The extent of the droit business processed by the Irish court in the seventeenth century fell well below its potential level. The jurisdiction was being undermined from three sources. The principal source of rivalry came from lords of manors adjoining the coastline who claimed title to droits found on their coastline as part of their manorial grants; a second source of interference was acts of pure theft by local people helping themselves to admiralty perquisites; a third source of interference came from the commissioners of customs in Ireland whose officers withheld admiralty perquisites from the admiralty courts.

At common law the right to royal fish formed one of Crown's prerogatives. That right had been delegated to the lord admiral, and formed one of the Admiralty's revenues.[293] The royal fish perquisite was regarded as a potentially valuable asset in seventeenth-century Ireland. In 1679 William Petty assured a correspondent that 'the admiralty jurisdiction and advantages in your parts are, or ought to be, more considerable than in others, among other things by the many porpoises and other royal fish taken there'.[294] In 1709 Sir Charles Hedges provided the Connacht Admiralty with a detailed account of the judicial procedure regulating the condemnation of royal fish:

> The best means ... for preserving my lord's right is by condemning them as perquisites of the Admiralty, which should be done without loss of time if St

290 Affidavit of the deputy marshal, Thomas Mansfield, 27 Sept. 1679 (TNA (PRO), HCA 15/8, f. 383).
291 W. Petty to R. Southwell, 18 Oct. 1679, *Petty–Southwell Corr.*, p. 79.
292 (1679) Burrell 253, 167 ER 560. (The vessel is spelt *Orrory* in the law report.)
293 *Case of the Royal Fishery of the Bann* (1611) Davies Rep 149.
294 W. Petty to H. Broaskoe, 31[?] July 1679 (McGill, Osler MS 7612).

George has a judge and other officers ready and proper for holding a court. And in case he has not such officers, he may sit himself as judge and assume a public notary instead of a registrar and proceed to the condemnation, first giving notice by monition to all persons who pretend any interest therein to appear before him and show cause, if they have any, why the said fishes should not be condemned as perquisites of the Admiralty, and if they not appear according to that monition he may proceed to condemnation by default; but if they do appear, or any pretensions are made they do belong to any lords of manors, he is to hear them, and in case they have good grants of royal fishes from the Crown, and these fishes are cast up by the sea upon their manors, he may declare for their right, or upon failure therein, give sentence for the lord admiral, and if the proceedings should take up any time he may order them to be sold as perishable at any time when the matter is depending, or before it.[295]

The principal rivals for this perquisite were landowners on whose coastline the fish had appeared, particularly those with grants which included admiralty rights.[296] In December 1678 a whale was washed up on the Wicklow coast. This novelty attracted 'many people [who] went out of curiosity many miles even to see the mangled carcass of this animal'. Petty travelled from Dublin to convene a court of admiralty. On arrival he found that pieces of the carcass had been cut off by servants of the local manorial lord (Richard Parsons) and as souvenirs by local people. The whale was now worthless 'by reason of her smallness, leanness, and the want of all utensils to make oil of her'. He proposed that those who had interfered with the whale were 'punishable for the injury … they have done the lord high admiral'.[297]

Landowners and corporations were also asserting entitlements to admiralty wreckage. In 1688 the Munster vice-admiral, Sir Robert Southwell, sent Samuel Pepys (the secretary for admiralty affairs) a 'book of accounts' kept by the deputy registrar of the Munster court.[298] This report noted that considerable quantities of wrecked wine remained un-appraised due to resistance by the court's usual rivals, the municipal corporations, and local manorial lords. The mayor of the town of Youghal, Richard Giles, it was alleged, was withholding wine from the court by virtue of his office as 'mayor and admiral'; two hogsheads and three half-hogsheads of wine remained in the possession of the countess of Castlehaven who, it was

---

295  C. Hedges to J. Warter, 24 Mar. 1709 (TNA(PRO) ADM 1/3667, f.349). John Warter was the solicitor to the Admiralty, 1703–18.

296  In 1700 Lord Inchiquin described how porpoises, yielding a considerable quantity of oil, had been beached at Ring, near Kinsale. A dispute had arisen between him and a local farmer as to who owned the fish, Inchiquin arguing 'I take them to be a royalty belonging to me, but he is resolved to dispute it at law'. Inchiquin to Sir Donat O'Brien, 16 July 1700, J. Ainsworth (ed.) *The Inchiquin manuscripts* (Dublin, 1961), pp 56–7.

297  W. Petty to R. Southwell, 4 Jan. 1679, *Petty–Southwell Corr.*, p. 63.

298  R. Banfield to R. Southwell, 11 June 1688 (Bodl., Rawlinson A 186, f. 49).

alleged, 'pretended unto' the goods by an admiralty patent;[299] wrecked casks of wine were being held in the possession of Henry Trent under a right 'granted by the lords' patent'; while the earl of Inchiquinn, was, again by virtue of a manorial grant, detaining two casks of wine. Early in the eighteenth century the Munster admiralty was involved in a dispute over the entitlement to a vessel which had been 'wrecked on the coast and claimed by the right Hon. Robert Boyle esq, lord of the manor'.[300] In 1709 the judge of the Munster court, Roland Davies, complained that he had been prevented from condemning a wreck found in Waterford by the interference of the earl of Burlington.[301] Even the Irish government was guilty of interference. In the mid-1660s the lord lieutenant, the duke of Ormond, was forced to countermand an order which he had made authorizing Lord Mayo to take charge of a vessel which had been wrecked at Broad Haven in County Mayo. The duke of Ormond apologized, saying that he did not intend 'to give cause of invasion upon the rights of [the Admiralty]'.[302]

The court's other principal rival was the commissioners of customs; both sides waged tedious battles over the right to wrecked goods, particularly in Munster. The commissioners, with their more expansive apparatus, were usually the first to seize abandoned cargoes, and would only release wrecked cargo to the Admiralty when customs duty had been paid. In 1682 Petty raised the problem of the customs commissioners retaining admiralty droits with Sir John Werden, the secretary to the duke of York. Robert Southwell reported to Petty that he had asked Werden to 'procure an instruction to the new commissioners for Ireland that the vice-admiral's officers, when they seize floating goods, may be allowed to retain them in their custody, whereas the late farmers' officers have still refused them for their duty, and I put that point to be now determined, whether such goods shall be liable to duty or not'.[303]

INTERFERENCE BY REPLEVIN, PROHIBITION AND APPEAL TO THE
HIGH COURT OF ADMIRALTY

*Replevin and prohibition*

'The other courts' complained Petty 'begin to wax wanton in sending prohibitions to ours'.[304] In an account written in 1679, Petty detailed five writs of prohibition which had recently been directed against the court[305] (a relatively high figure given

299  Ibid.
300  J. Warter to J. Burchett, 19 Mar. 1713 (TNA (PRO), ADM 1/3,688, f. 417).
301  R. Davis to E. Southwell, 25 Oct. 1709 (BL, Add. MS 38,152, f. 12).
302  9 Dec. 1665, *Ormond Calendar*, ix, p. 176.
303  R. Southwell to W. Petty, 19 Oct. 1682, *Petty–Southwell Corr.*, p. 109.
304  BL, Lansdowne MS 1,228, f. 7.
305  W. Petty to R. Southwell, 4 Jan. 1679, *Petty–Southwell Corr.*, pp 63–7.

its small case load).[306] Interference by prohibition was, of course, also a routine obstruction suffered by the English Admiralty Court. In 1678 the London civilian, William Trumbull, sympathized with Petty's complaint about prohibitions, remarking that 'we are fellow sufferers'.[307] The English admiralty registrar, Thomas Bedford, advised Petty that prohibitions must 'be patiently born until the vigilance of the Parliament provides for the settlement' of the jurisdictional intrusion.[308]

In addition to harassment by prohibitions, replevin enjoyed a particular popularity within Ireland as a means of frustrating admiralty process. It was even more accessible than the writ of prohibition since it could be obtained cheaply and on demand from local sheriffs' courts. The most publicized deployment of the process occurred in the *Jacob of Dublin* in 1682[309] when a replevin issued by the Dublin Sheriff's Court provoked the Irish Admiralty Court into an incendiary reaction, jailing the sheriff's officers. In 1698 the judge of the Munster Admiralty Court described how routine the use of the remedy had become:

> It has been … long before the said late troubles customary and usual throughout the kingdom for the sheriffs of the principal cities therein to grant replevins against ships and goods taken by virtue of warrants out of the several admiralty courts in the kingdom when the property of them have been claimed by others; and that the granting of these replevins is grounded on the common laws of this kingdom, and that no sheriff can deny such replevins upon good security offered them to return the said ships and goods if return of them shall be awarded; and if any sheriff should refuse granting them an action on the case would lie against them for their refusal.[310]

During the Nine Years War, replevin was used to disrupt the Admiralty's right to enemies' goods seized in ports.[311] On 1 January 1705 the *Thomas* of Dublin, *en route* from La Rochelle, laden with French wine, brandy and silks, put into Glendour, near Kinsale. She was arrested by an officer of the Vice-Admiralty of Munster,[312] and her cargo was condemned as prize by the English Court of

---

306  'A prohibition hath been brought, after an execution in the case of using unlawful ways of fishing; 3. The like prohibition in a suit for stopping and annoying a navigable river; 4. The like in the case of a pilot condemned to pay damages for casting away a ship in a gross manner', W. Petty to R. Southwell, 4 Jan. 1679, *Petty–Southwell Corr.*, p. 66. The two other prohibitions involved more significant commercial interests: a prohibition issued on behalf of Sir Humphrey Jervis in order to stop Petty's proceeding against the construction of Essex Bridge, and the prohibition issued to the marquis of Antrim to stop the proceedings for the recovery of Fleming's vessel (see p. 90 above).

307  8 Mar. 1678 (Bodl., Rawlinson A 191, f. 174).

308  11 Apr. 1678 (BL, Add. MS 72,852, f.152).

309  D. Loftus to W. Petty, 1682 (BL, Add. MS 72,893, f.87).

310  Affidavit of Thomas Farren, 21 Sept. 1698 (TNA (PRO), HCA 15/18).

311  See above p. 92.

312  'The case of the ship *Thomas* of Dublin' (TNA (PRO), ADM 1/3,667, f.92).

Admiralty. However, the importer managed to rescue the goods from the Munster Admiralty under 'the colour of a replevin … issued or pretended to be issued out of the chancery or of the exchequer of that kingdom'. In 1709 several hogsheads of French wines and vinegars were found floating on the sea 'within ten or twelve miles from Kinsale'.[313] The case was processed in the English Court of Admiralty and the wines condemned to the admiral under his right to enemies' goods. However, before the sale could be completed, a Wexford merchant named Archer, who claimed to be owner of the goods, obtained a replevin from the Court of Common Pleas.[314] Sir Charles Hedges (predictably) identified the use of replevins in Ireland as a grave threat to the rights of the Admiralty recognized by the 1666 Oxford conference,[315] and recommended that the attorney general and solicitor general be instructed to defend the original seizure:

> if some timely remedy be not applied it will be in vain to expect any relief for the future, and her majesty will have no advantage by constituting vice-admirals in that kingdom, or receive any profits from the perquisites of admiralty there. The wines and vinegars are legally condemned in the Admiralty Court here as enemy's goods and perquisites, after which a pretended claim is set up, and a replevin brought for part of the goods at common law, and the rest are detained contrary to law, whereas the claimer's relief, if he has any right, ought to have been prosecuted for by way of appeal to the lords of the council.[316]

In September 1709 the lord treasurer, Sidney Godolphin, wrote to Ormond requesting that the solicitor general and attorney general of Ireland be instructed to appear on behalf of the Admiralty in the *Archer* case – a request which seems to have gone unheeded.[317] Instead, the newly appointed judge of the Court of Admiralty in Ireland, Dr John Hawkshaw, was provided with over £50 for managing the litigation on behalf of the Admiralty. Hawkshaw, in turn, delegated this task to Dr Rowland Davies, the judge of the Munster Admiralty Court, who in late 1709 reported that the legality of the seizure would be tried at the next Munster assizes.[318] Davies sought to persuade the well-connected vice-admiral of Munster, Edward Southwell, to intervene personally with the chief justice of the Court of Common Pleas, Robert Doyne to side with the Admiralty over the replevin problem, for 'it is but vanity for us to hold any court when all decrees may

313   C. Hedges to the commissioners of Admiralty, 20 July 1709 (TNA (PRO), ADM 1/3,667, f. 424); E. Southwell to J. Burchett, 20 Dec. 1709 (TCD, MS 1,180, f. 241).

314   Archer also obtained a prohibition from the Common Pleas to prevent the Admiralty Court taking proceedings against persons who had disobeyed its orders. R. Davis to E. Southwell, 25 Oct. 1709 (BL, Add. MS 38,125, f. 12); J. Burchett to J. Lowndes, 20 Aug. 1709 (TCD, MS 1,180, f. 237).

315   See above p. 83.

316   C. Hedges to J. Burchett, 20 July 1709 (TNA (PRO), ADM 1/3,667, f. 424).

317   E. Southwell to J. Burchett, 20 Dec. 1709 (TCD, MS 1,180, f. 241).

318   R. Davies to E. Southwell, 27 Oct. 1709 (BL, Add. MS 38,152, f. 17).

thus be superseded'. While the result of the *Archer* case is unknown, the continued deployment of replevin against the Court of Admiralty throughout the eighteenth century suggests that the outcome was unlikely to have favoured the court.

*Appeal to the English Court of Admiralty*

The issue of whether any admiralty court in Ireland ought to be subject to appeal to London was one of the causes of the duke of York's long indecision during 1660s over the issue of whether the court should be re-established. On the one hand, if there was to be no supervision by the Court of Admiralty in England 'it may have very many objections against it'. On the other hand, if it was to be subject to the delays caused by appeal 'I do not know whether it will answer all the ends for which it may be desired'.[319] In the end, the decision was taken to re-establish the appeal to London. The exposure of Irish admiralty courts to correction by London was resented by some Irish judges, particularly William Petty. Although the grievance was somewhat overstated – there was less than one appeal per year – Petty expressed strong constitutional hostility to the English appeal. In Petty's view there was no jurisdiction to submit the Irish court to appellate review. Petty's argument, based on the division of the Admiralty following the Test Act 1673,[320] was constitutionally sophisticated. Before the Test Act of 1673 the Irish Court of Admiralty derived its root of title from the lord admiral of England and Ireland. But in 1673, when the Test Act made him ineligible, the duke of York resigned as lord admiral of England. However, while Prince Rupert became lord admiral of England, the duke of York continued to be admiral of Ireland.[321] Once the duke of York had resigned as admiral of England, two Admiralties, one English, the other Irish, had superseded the original unitary Admiralty. The separation into two distinct Admiralties had the effect, Petty argued, that the English court ceased to have supervisory jurisdiction over the Irish court.

The English civilian, William Trumbull, dismissed Petty's constitutional objection to the existence of an appeal to the English Admiralty Court, writing that it was 'clear both by law and practice uninterrupted that … an appeal lies from all admiralty courts in Ireland (as well as from the several vice-admiralties in England) to the High Court of Admiralty in England'. Furthermore, an appeal to the English court was a necessary safeguard against judges of unreliable ability. The English court was a higher quality tribunal: 'most cases both as to fact as law will be better judged in England than there'.[322]

---

319   Duke of York to Privy Council of Ireland, 13 July 1663 (TNA (PRO), ADM 2/1,745).
320   'An act for preventing dangers which may happen from Popish recusants', 25 Car. II, c. 2 (Eng.), 1673. Failure to take the prescribed oaths disqualified the recusant from any office in England, but not Ireland.
321   G.F. James and J.J. Sutherland Shaw, 'Admiralty administration and personnel, 1619–1714', *Bulletin of Institute of Historical Research*, 14 (1936), 10 & 166.
322   8 Mar. 1678 (Bodl., Rawlinson A 191, f. 174).

The appeal to England was vulnerable to abuse, particularly in seamen's wages cases. Early in 1679 Petty complained that 'an appeal had been brought unto the admiralty of England in case of poor seamen's wages, where so much as a probable tale could not be told in prejudice of the sentence given here for these poor seamen'.[323] The device of an appeal provided a means of evasion for masters seeking to avoid wages claims in the Irish court. The effect of an appeal was that the enforcement of the wages' sentence would remain in suspension.[324] There were also techniques available to the lower court in order to prevent the abuse of appeals. The usual procedure was to require that the appellant provide bail to prosecute the appeal. In 1671 the judge of the Munster Court, Dr Joshua Boyle, refused to admit an appeal in a wages case since he was not satisfied of the security offered by the defendant's proctor.[325] A stronger remedy was suggested by the English civilian Thomas Bedford. In response to a query by Sir William Petty, Bedford recommended that where the court apprehended an appeal, the sailor should be allowed his wages immediately. Allowing the sailor 'the wages on bail' would at least enable the sailor to have his wages without having to fight an appeal to obtain them.[326]

## THE NAVIGATION ACT 1670

Between 1670 and 1680 Irish transatlantic trade was regulated by the Navigation Act 1670.[327] The Navigation Act 1670 required that merchandise shipped from the colonies first be landed in ports in England, Wales, or Berwick on Tweed; it could not be landed in Ireland, and a vessel unloading in Ireland, and not at one of the authorized English ports, was liable to forfeiture.

The English Court of Admiralty was one of the courts entrusted with enforcing the legislation. Orders for the arrest of vessels infringing the Act issued from the English court into Ireland with instructions that they be executed in Ireland. These English orders encountered heavy resistance when the officers of the Irish court attempted to execute them. In the *America*[328] (owned by the merchant, Humphrey Jervis) the marshal was unable to execute the arrest, the crew threatening to 'knock him down if he did attempt to arrest the said ship'. In the case of the *Dublin*[329] the

---

323  W. Petty to R. Southwell, 4 Jan. 1679, *Petty–Southwell Corr.*, p. 63. The case to which Petty (almost certainly) referred was *Pippard v. Furlong* a seaman's wages case (and the only case to come to London by way of appeal from the Irish court during the period that Petty held office) (TNA (PRO), HCA 3/54, f. 459 (5 May 1680)).

324  In 1673 an appeal was taken by the French master, Captain Bienvenue, against a sentence of the Court of Admiralty sitting at Kinsale. The High Court of Admiralty, upon the petition of the mariners, assigned the master's proctor to state the grounds of appeal. No appearance was made within four months and the case was dismissed. The French ambassador subsequently intervened. L. Jenkins to Charles II, 21 Apr. 1673, *Life of Jenkins*, ii, p. 772.

325  TNA (PRO), HCA 15/9.

326  T. Bedford to R. Southwell, 11 Apr. 1678 (BL, Add. MS 72,852, f. 152).

327  22 & 23 Car. II, c. 26 (Eng.), 1670.

328  Affidavit of Patrick Little and John Murphy, 8 Jan. 1679 (TNA (PRO), HCA 15/9).

329  Affidavit of Patrick Little, 3 July 1679 (TNA (PRO), HCA 15/11).

master, having been informed that the marshal had arrested the ship by virtue of a
warrant issued by the English Admiralty Court, replied that that was 'a foolish
thing, meaning the broad arrow, and contemptuously with his own hand rubbed
it'. The ship owners also sought the assistance of the courts of common law.
Following the arrest of the *Dublin* a bill of indictment was laid against one of the
deputy marshals of the Irish Court, Patrick Little, before the Dublin Court of
Quarter Sessions, charging him with causing thousands of pounds' worth of
damage to the cargo. The merchants also complained to the English Privy Council
about the discouragement to trade in Ireland resulting from these English
Admiralty Court processes being executed in Dublin.[330] Following the Irish
complaint, the English admiralty lawyers Thomas Exton and Richard Lloyd, were
summoned to a conference with the English Privy Council's Committee of Trade
and Plantations. Lloyd and Exton informed the committee that Irish ship owners
were, in collusion with the Irish customs farmers, fraudulently evading the
Navigation Act 1670. A proviso in the Act allowed masters in emergencies to land
colonial produce in Ireland when shipwrecked. Merchants, feigning shipwreck
were, it was alleged, using this proviso to illegally land produce in Ireland: 'it is not
without good cause that so strict a hand is kept for hindering of the irregular trade
the merchants of Ireland to your excellencies plantations who have of late ventured
upon pretence of shipwreck and other fraudulent devices to elude the several acts
of parliament here'. Exton and Lloyd asked that a royal letter be sent from England
directing the Irish administration to support the enforcement processes of the
English Admiralty Court, and that the processes of 'your majesty's Court of
Admiralty here may have due course and effect'.[331]

The Navigation Act 1670 entrusted enforcement powers to the English High
Court of Admiralty. The Irish Court of Admiralty had no independent
enforcement powers; authority was restricted to 'the court of the high admiral of
England' (and 'to any of his vice-admirals, or in any court of record in England').
The Irish Court of Admiralty was not '*the* court' of the high admiral of England.
Notwithstanding this, warrants to enforce the legislation were issued out of the
Court of Admiralty of Ireland. The Dublin merchant Sir John Rogerson was
alleged to have imported a cargo of 460 hogsheads of tobacco from Virginia directly
into Dublin on board the *Providence of London*.[332] A warrant had been issued by the
English Court of Admiralty for the arrest of the vessel, and for the seizure of its
cargo of tobacco. When the English warrant could not be enforced, Sir William
Petty, at his own initiative, then issued a second warrant of attachment. John
Rogerson, however, refused to permit Petty's men to enter his premises. One of the
marshals alleged that:

330  23 Apr. 1679, *Cal. S.P. Dom. 1679–1680*, p. 128.
331  W. Coventry to J. Ormond, 19 June 1679 (Bodl., 39 Carte MS, f. 55).
332  Affidavit of Patrick Little and John Murphy, 8 Jan. 1679 (TNA (PRO), HCA 15/9).

About one of the clock, in order to serve and execute another warrant …
from the said High Court of Admiralty of Ireland upon the said tobacco, [he]
demanded entrance into the said Rogerson's cellars or warehouses, where the
said tobacco lay, but was not suffered to enter there into, though the said
Patrick showed the said attachment unto the said Rogerson, and told him the
contents thereof, the said Rogerson answering and confessing that there was
in his hands certain quantities of tobacco which he had from the said
*Providence of London*, but withal refusing to give obedience unto the said
attachment.[333]

Colonial vice-admiralty courts, particularly American vice-admiralty courts,
compensated for lean periods in instance business in the late seventeenth and early
eighteenth centuries by the business generated in enforcing the Navigation Acts.
The involvement of the Irish Court of Admiralty in the enforcement of the Acts
was much more short-lived and indirect.

## THE ADMINISTRATIVE AND REVENUE JURISDICTION OF THE COURT: FISHING LICENSING, BALLASTAGE AND PASSES

### Fishing licensing

Fees extracted for the licensing of fishing constituted the most important of the
court's revenue streams. In 1667, Dr John Topham, seeking office as judge of the
Leinster Admiralty Court, calculated that the licence fee generated '£80 a year
amongst all the officers, judge, registrar and marshal, and this is the only perquisite
belonging to the court'.[334] In 1680 Sir William Petty's factotum, Thomas Dance,
recorded 'the reckoning … about the herring licences'. There was 'due to Sir
William the sum of forty five shillings to complete the sum due for the season 1679
and before'.[335] In 1686 Sir Paul Rycaut noted in his diary that he had 'signed forty
fishing licences, being judge of the Admiralty'.[336] When attempting to encourage
his nephew to assume the office of surrogate, Rycaut calculated that the office
'might yield [£]40 or [£]50 year to a man who were industrious to bestow himself
in it, and active to gather the money arising from fishing licences'.[337] The following
year Rycaut implored his intended surrogate 'with God's help be prepared before
the fishing season comes in, the licences for which, if well managed, produce the
greatest profit'.[338] September was the critical month during which fishing licences
were issued. When in September of 1686 Rycaut wrote to his agent in London

---

333  Ibid.
334  J. Topham to E. Conway, 14 May 1667, *Cal. S.P. Ire. 1666–1669*, p. 362.
335  4 Aug. 1680 (BL, Add. MS 72,893, f. 56).
336  4 Sept. 1686, *Rycaut's memoranda*, p. 131.
337  P. Rycaut to W. Mayne, 4 Mar. 1691 (BL, Add. MS 1,153 D, f. 35).
338  P. Rycaut to W. Mayne, 22 Apr. 1692 (BL, Add. MS 1,153 D, f. 208).

looking for his patent of appointment, he stressed urgency since the fishing licensing period was imminent.[339] An entry in the commonplace book of Dudley Loftus (Rycaut's surrogate) recorded that he 'then signed 10 fishing licences and delivered them to Mr Mallam the deputy marshal'.[340] The licence might, on occasion, be obtained by an unofficial payment in kind. In a note to his friend Sir Peter Pett, Sir William Petty proudly disclosed that 'we hath gotten 6 [shillings] and 8 [pence] for a licence to dredge oysters and are promised ... a hundred of oysters for granting it a little before the piscine day, under colour of helping a poor old seaman'.[341]

There were, however, suggestions that the licence fee might not have a sound legal basis. The admiralty fishing licence was unknown in England, and opinion in Doctors' Commons was highly sceptical about this Irish practice. In 1663 an opinion prepared by two English civilians questioned whether the licence fee was authorized by the admiral's warrant:[342] 'as to the licensing of vessels employed in the herring fishing, the same being mentioned neither in the vice-admirals' nor judges' patents, they can neither of them pretend to it, but they are carefully to examine that business'. Some Irish judges thought that their patent of appointment did justify the fee; the lord high admiral's patent entrusted him in vague terms with 'command' over fishermen.[343] Since the patent of the judge of the Irish Admiralty Court designated him commissary of the lord admiral it followed that the admiralty judge acquired the administrative powers of the lord admiral. In a letter to Sir Allen Apsley, Petty argued that the entitlement was 'expressly within' his commission: 'I am not only judge of the admiralty, but also commissary of his royal highness in all maritime matters, and particularly of fishing'.[344]

*Ballastage in Dublin, 1682–1707*

The power of levying a fee from vessels taking ballast on the Thames – ballastage – was 'a very ancient office' which belonged to the lord high admiral. In 1594 the lord admiral re-assigned the perquisite of ballastage to the Crown which, in turn, assigned it to Trinity House – 'being a company of the most experienced seamen being fittest to take care of the river'. In return Trinity House undertook to maintain seamarks and beacons on the Thames.[345] A similar transfer of functions occurred later in Dublin. Ballastage continued to be levied by the Admiralty in

---

339   4 Sept. 1686, *Rycaut's memoranda*, p. 167.
340   12 Aug. 1691 (Marsh's Library, MS Z.R.5.14).
341   W. Petty to P. Pett, 26 Aug. 1676 (McGill, Osler MS 7,614).
342   James, duke of York, to G. Wentworth, 10 Dec. 1663 (TNA (PRO), ADM 2/1,755).
343   The lord admiral's patent of 1611 provided: 'He is simply the officer of the greatest power and strength in the kingdom, having at his command all the shipping, mariners, seamen, fishermen ...', G.F. James and J.J. Sutherland Shaw, 'Admiralty administration and personnel, 1619–1714', *Bulletin of Institute of Historical Research*, 14 (1936), 10 & 166.
344   9 Sept. 1676 (McGill, Osler MS 7,612).
345   11 June 1594 (Magdalene, Pepys MS 2,879, f. 609).

Dublin long after the Admiralty in England had lost its connection with the imposition. However, in the early eighteenth century the Admiralty assigned the perquisite to a specialist Dublin agency, the Ballast Office.

Legal opinions were commissioned from Leoline Jenkins and Dudley Loftus who confirmed that the power to levy ballastage was intrinsic to the wider admiralty power, and could be levied in Dublin. In May 1682[346] a grant of the right to extract ballastage ('strengthened with a king's letter to the lord deputy') was issued by the lord admiral to Peter Ashton.[347] In what was probably a reference to the Ashton grant, Petty, in a note to the duke of York's secretary, mentioned that he had 'received notice of a warrant from his royal highness about ballastage, but none hath been yet brought to me'.[348] The collection of the toll was undertaken by the marshal of the court and his staff of under-marshals. However, the Corporation of Dublin had 'revived their ancient right to the said ballast'.[349] The fight between the court and the corporation continued throughout the 1680s. It was this dispute which lay at the background of the arrest and replevin of the *Jacob* in the early 1680s.[350] In 1688 Dublin Corporation 'presented Francis Robinson, marshal of the High Court of Admiralty for procuring several ship masters' – who presumably had refused to pay the ballastage toll – 'to throw ballast and other rubbish into the channel, and within the harbour of the city, to the great damage of the said harbour and river for his private gain'.[351]

The imposition by both the Court of Admiralty and the corporation of this new charge in Dublin port angered English ship owners who traded with Dublin. In March 1683 a petition, subscribed by owners of ships belonging to Liverpool, Chester and Whitehaven, was laid before the English Privy Council complaining of 'the proceedings of the lord mayor of Dublin, and others joining with him, in molesting and interrupting them in their trade [there] with vexatious suits to enforce on them the new imposition they have laid on every ton of ballast taken in the river of Dublin, in high water mark … contrary to former practice'.[352]

In 1700 the Irish administration addressed the issue. The outcome was a defeat for the Admiralty. A committee of the Irish Privy Council reported in favour of diverting the imposition from the Admiralty to a ballast office maintained by the

---

346  9 May 1682 (TNA (PRO), ADM 2/1,755, f. 39).
347  P. Ashton to H. Styles, 13 Dec. 1683 (TNA (PRO), ADM 1/3,676, f. 346).
348  W. Petty to J. Werden, 6 [?] Aug. 1683 (McGill, MS 7,612).
349  4 Sept. 1676, *Cal. anc. rec. Dub.*, v, pp 118–19: 'That by the charter of King John, given to this city about four hundred years and sixty years since, and which charter has been by several of his royal successors from time to time confirmed to this city, all ways, waters and strands within the liberties and franchises of this city are by the aforesaid charters granted and confirmed to this city. That the river Liffey is likewise granted to this city … that this city have, by a late assembly held in July last, revived their ancient right to the said ballast, and have referred the consideration of a ballast office, the profits whereof is intended for the King's Hospital, to a certain committee'.
350  See p. 68 above.                                351  RIA, Haliday MS 12/E/2, f. 432.
352  28 Mar. 1683 (TNA (PRO), PC 2/69, f. 666).

city of Dublin ('whose interest it will always be to have the work proposed effectively perfected'). The money levied by the ballast office would be used to construct 'a pier, fort and light house, to be by them made and maintained, on the South Bull of the harbour'. This, it concluded, was 'not only proper to be done but is absolutely necessary for the preservation of the trade of the port'.[353] The Admiralty continued to insist that ballastage belonged to it, and threatened to veto the transfer of the perquisite unless a 'proper application [was made] to his royal highness'.[354] Dublin Corporation, in order to soothe the feelings of the lord admiral, undertook to deliver yearly to the lord high admiral 'for ever, one hundred yards of Dutch-style sail cloth'.[355] The Dublin Ballast Office Act[356] received royal assent in 1707. The lord admiral's power to levy ballastage was replaced with a statutory levy (12*d*. per ton of ballast extracted below Salmon Pool, and 15*d*. per ton of ballast extracted above Salmon Pool, with foreign ships paying one-third extra on these sums).[357] The legislation marked the end of one of the court's useful sources of supporting revenue.

*Algiers, Tripoli and Tunis passes*

A standard clause, common in many seventeenth-century peace treaties, guaranteed safe passage to vessels carrying an official pass confirming the nationality of the vessel and crew. The treaties with Algiers, Tunis and Tripoli[358] required that the pass, which guaranteed immunity from aggression by Barbary vessels, be granted by the lord admiral. Rules regulating the administration of passes in Ireland were promulgated by the Committee for Trade and Plantations.[359]

To the annoyance of the Irish Court of Admiralty, the lord lieutenant was entrusted by the English Admiralty with the function of issuing these passes. The Irish court queried why it was the lord lieutenant, and not it, which had been entrusted with this function. In 1676 William Petty complained to Sir Allen Apsley that 'the king and council in England did, last March, make rules for giving of passes to ships, appointing the admiral to be principal therein, without mention of

353  24 Oct. 1700 (TNA (PRO), PC 1/1/72).
354  Josiah Burchett to Benjamin Burton, 5 Sept. 1707, *Cal. anc. rec. Dub.*, vi, 619.
355  Petition to Prince George of Denmark, n.d., ibid.
356  6 Anne, c. 20 (Irl.), 1707.                    357  S. 4.
358  *A complete collection of the treaties and conventions at present subsisting between Great Britain and foreign powers*, ed. L. Hertslet (London, 1820), i, p. 128.
359  22 Nov. 1676 (TNA (PRO), SP 63/337, ff 187, 189). The rules prescribed that an adequate supply of blank passes be sent to the lord lieutenant. These were, in turn, to be passed on to the lord mayor of Dublin and the chief magistrates of the other ports. No pass was to be granted unless the ship had been surveyed by the chief patent officer of the customs. No pass was to be granted if the vessel was in some other port. Two-thirds of the crew were required to be nationals. No pass was to be granted unless any former pass had first been handed up. A bond of £100 was to be supplied. A pass was to be granted only where the proprietor was from Ireland. The lord lieutenant was to maintain a register of all passes granted, and to return that record to the lord admiral in London.

the lord lieutenant. But my lord lieutenant acts therein without any power (what I can hear of)'.[360] The intervention convinced the Admiralty, and in 1683 the administration of Algiers passes (described by an eighteenth-century judge who had consulted the courts' records as a 'profitable branch')[361] was entrusted to the officers of the Irish Court of Admiralty.[362] In 1686 the judge lost this revenue-generating perk when the function was re-assigned to the secretariat of the lord lieutenant.[363]

360  W. Petty to A. Apsley, 9 Sept. 1676 (McGill, Osler MS 7,612, f. 209).

361  R. FitzGerald to the commissioners of Admiralty, 29 June 1756 (TNA (PRO), ADM/1/3,883, f. 13).

362  In a note to Sir John Werden, dated 4 Aug. 1683, Petty mentioned that he had disposed of eight passes (McGill, Osler MS 7,612).

363  R. FitzGerald to the commissioners of Admiralty, 29 June 1756 (TNA (PRO), ADM 1/3,883, f. 13).

CHAPTER THREE

# 'Indolent' Dr Hawkshaw and 'mad' Dr Baillie, 1708–56

FOR THE FIRST FOUR DECADES of the eighteenth century the Irish Court of Admiralty operated unobtrusively, surviving on a diet of a tiny quantity of instance work, and presided over by the inactive, aged Dr John Hawkshaw. Then unexpectedly, starting about 1745, there commenced a period of excitement. That change in tempo coincided with the appointment to the office of judge of the Admiralty Court of a highly combative and indiscreet Scotish émigré, Dr Hugh Baillie. After no more than eleven years, and having managed to provoke every interest group connected with the court – especially the commissioners of Admiralty in England and the justices of the Irish Court of King's Bench – Dr Baillie was dismissed.

## THE JUDGES OF THE COURT OF ADMIRALTY OF IRELAND, 1708–56

*Dr John Hawkshaw*

Dr John Hawkshaw, a civilian lawyer from a Cheshire family which had settled in Ireland in the late seventeenth century[1] replaced Dr William King as judge of the Irish Court of Admiralty in December 1708,[2] and served as judge from 1708 to 1744. The level of instance work transacted by the court in the early decades of the eighteenth century was negligible. In 1720, the judge of the English Court of Admiralty, Henry Penrice, noted that 'the Doctor [Hawkshaw] has no salary and the fees arising from his office are so very small that he assures me they do not amount to £20 *per annum*, a sum so trivial that I am ashamed to mention it'.[3] The rate of deterioration accelerated. In 1744, immediately after the death of Dr Hawkshaw, the registrar of the court, who was more qualified than anyone to measure the court's activity, calculated that the court's profits had fallen to £10 a year, about half of what it had been twenty years earlier.[4]

---

1 T. Barnard, *A new anatomy of Ireland* (Oxford, 2003), p. 158.
2 Order continuing appointment, 25 Dec. 1708 (TNA (PRO), ADM 2/1,050, f. 12).
3 H. Penrice to T. Jobber, 17 Sept. 1720 (TNA (PRO), ADM 1/3,670 f. 56). Jobber was admiralty solicitor, 1718–23.
4 W. Sheil to T. Corbett, 22 Dec. 1744 (TNA (PRO), ADM 1/3,990). Thomas Corbett was admiralty secretary, 1741–51.

The inability of the judge of the Irish Court of Admiralty to generate an income from its low fee revenue prompted claims for a salary. In 1714 a petition seeking a salary was submitted by an impoverished Dr Hawkshaw. Hawkshaw alleged that he had been assured by the former English judge, Charles Hedges, that he would be granted a stipend 'but the said Sir Charles Hedges dying, and your petitioner not having since the countenance of the government in Ireland until his majesty's late accession'.[5] The issue of the salary entitlement of the Irish judge resulted in a constitutional impasse. In 1728 the lords justices of Ireland accepted in principle the argument presented by Hawkshaw, and recommended that he be paid a salary of £200 *per annum*. However, because they did not see why they should subsidize a judge who was not an officer of the kingdom of Ireland, but a mere delegate of the English Admiralty, they re-directed their recommendation to the Admiralty in London. The Admiralty, on the other hand, claimed that it did not have the revenue at its disposal to fund the court in Ireland, and that the court operated for the benefit of the Irish administration.[6]

At the beginning of his tenure Hawkshaw's conscientiousness was publicly praised. In 1715 he was able to procure a petition subscribed by almost thirty established Dublin merchants who testified as to his conscientiousness.[7] However, as Hawkshaw aged, the condition of the court also deteriorated. By the end of his career in the 1740s the general consensus was that Dr Hawkshaw had become inactive, 'very indolent'[8] and possibly senile: it was alleged that he was 'for some years before his death quite weak in his understanding'.[9] His successor, Dr Baillie, later alleged that the Court of Admiralty had undergone 'an interregnum'. Potential litigants were avoiding the court. Dr Hawkshaw's registrar agreed that it had 'sunk to nothing', was in 'great disrepute', and was 'but little used'.[10]

## Dr Hugh Baillie

News of Hawkshaw's death, and of the consequential vacancy in the court, was a cause for celebration by at least one of the court's practitioners. For the previous

5  *Calendar of Treasury Books, 1714–1715*, ed. W.A. Shaw and F.H. Slingsby (London, 1957), p. 426; NAI, M. 2447, ff 165–67 (petitions of Hawkshaw, John Rogerson and merchants of the city of Dublin).

6  'Their lordships [of the Admiralty] make no doubt that his excellency [the lord lieutenant of Ireland] will do therein as he shall find necessary, but that their lordships do not think it proper for them to concern themselves in matters which relate to the revenue of that Kingdom'. J. Burchett to J. Hawkshaw, 6 Aug. 1728. Burchett was secretary to the Admiralty 1694–1741 (TNA (PRO), ADM 2/1,053, f. 44).

7  'Dr John Hawkshaw as judge of the Admiralty of Ireland hath for the several years past (as occasion did require) duly attended his court of judicature for determining maritime causes where suits of great moment have been heard and determined'. Petition of Dublin merchants, 30 Mar. 1715 (NAI, M 2447, ff 166,167).

8  J. Potter to T. Corbett, 1 Mar. 1743 (TNA (PRO), ADM 1/3,990).

9  H. Baillie to commissioners of Admiralty, 21 May 1745 (TNA (PRO), ADM 1/3,990). H. Baillie to the Admiralty, 21 May 1745 (TNA (PRO), ADM 1/3,990).

10  W. Sheil to T. Corbett, 22 Dec. 1744 (TNA (PRO), ADM 1/3,990).

five years a frantically ambitious Scottish civilian practitioner, Dr Hugh Baillie, had been pestering the commissioners of Admiralty for an appointment to succeed old Dr Hawkshaw. Dr Baillie was a virulently anti-Jacobite[11] Scottish advocate from Monkton in Ayrshire. Baillie had been called to the Scottish bar in 1717, where he had practised as an advocate until 1740.[12] Well-connected, and privately wealthy, he had come into a fortune when he married in 1720. He had inherited a number of estates and had built himself a grand house, the famous Orangefield House, in Ayrshire.[13] One of Baillie's chief patrons was John Dalrymple, the earl of Stair. Baillie had been a member of Stair's extensive ménage when Stair was ambassador to Paris and Baillie took great pride in this connection.[14] This admiration even survived a disastrous intervention by Stair in 1720; Stair had advised Baillie, who was setting out to London to dispose of his considerable shareholding in the South Sea Company, to retain the shares – a piece of advice which resulted in Baillie having to sell sections of his estates.[15] Baillie, who mixed in church circles, had by the early 1740s come into contact with another important patron, Hugh Boulter, the archbishop of Armagh. Boulter had a policy of preferring British over Irish appointments to judicial posts in Ireland and encouraged Baillie[16] to develop a legal career in Ireland. Baillie settled in Dublin in the early 1740s. The move was a success. In 1744 a Scottish contact referred to Baillie as having 'for some time, been fixed at Dublin where … he's in very good business'.[17] Here he practised as a civilian[18] and launched a series of public lectures in Trinity College Dublin in civil law (attended by the young Edmund Burke).[19] Baillie set his sights on the office of judge of the Court of Admiralty. Unable to persuade Dr Hawkshaw to resign, Baillie began pressurizing Hawkshaw into accepting his acting as his 'coadjutor'.[20] At this stage at least, he appears to have impressed the administration in Dublin. Representations (probably solicited by Baillie himself) were made by the lord

---

11  Baillie claimed that he had given 'early proof of his zeal and duty to the Crown by raising and maintaining a company of men in Scotland 1715, cheerfully venturing his life'. Petition of Hugh Baillie, 1756 [?] (TNA (PRO), ADM 1/3,882). He repeated this in *A letter to Dr Shebear: containing a refutation of his arguments concerning the Boston and Quebec Acts of Parliament: and his aspersions upon …* (London, 1775), pp 48, 52.

12  'Petition of Hugh Baillie' (Oct. 1745) (TNA (PRO), ADM 1/3,990).

13  *A genealogical account of Ayreshire*, p. 31. The house is now the site of Prestwick airport.

14  H. Baillie, *A letter to Dr Shebear*, pp 10, 43–4. On the household in Paris see *Annals of the Viscount and the first and second earls of Stair*, ed. J.M. Graham, 2 vols (Edinburgh, 1875), ii, p. 2.

15  *A genealogical account of Ayreshire*, p. 31.

16  'I was brought over here to this country from North Briton by his grace, the late primate, to practise as a civilian'. Baillie to the commissioners of Admiralty, 17 May 1745 (TNA (PRO), ADM 1/3,990).

17  Charles Erskine to James Erskine, 20 Dec. 1744 (NAS, GD 124/15/1,555/1).

18  'Petition of Hugh Baillie to Lord Anson', n.d. (TNA (PRO), ADM 1/3,883, f. 16).

19  E. Burke to R. Shackleton, 31 Jan. 1745: 'I have a ticket to attend Dr Baylie's lectures on the civil law'. *The correspondence of Edmund Burke*, ed. T. Copeland, 10 vols (Cambridge, 1958), i, p. 40.

20  J. Potter to T. Corbett, 1 Mar. 1743 (TNA (PRO), ADM 1/3,990).

mayor and the local mercantile community in support of his petition to be appointed coadjutor.[21] Sources close to the lord lieutenant reported support for the proposal and predicted that 'if the request should be granted by the lords commissioners of Admiralty, when laid before them, it is very likely the business of the court may go on much better than it does at present'.[22] Baillie would probably have been appointed earlier had Hawkshaw not been reluctant to abandon the office. The lord admiral, Lord Winchilsea, 'required [Hawkshaw's] consent to the thing',[23] and since Hawkshaw would not consent to sharing power with Baillie, Baillie was forced to wait for Hawkshaw's death. However, on 3 January 1745 Baillie's ambition to be judge of the Court of Admiralty was (apparently with the help of his old friend, John Dalrymple) realized;[24] the commissioners of Admiralty appointed Baillie judge of the Court of Admiralty of Ireland. Baillie, by contrast with his immediate predecessors, was sincerely committed, almost obsessively so, to the institution. He dedicated himself full time to the position – sitting every day, for five or six hours – and abandoned his practice as a civilian.[25] There followed eleven highly eventful years.

### THE COURT OF ADMIRALTY OF IRELAND IN THE EARLY-EIGHTEENTH CENTURY: ITS ADMINISTRATION AND PERSONNEL

By the eighteenth century St Patrick's Cathedral had become the established place of business of the Irish Court of Admiralty.[26] The court also sat in improvised conditions, sometimes in Baillie's own home in Aungier Street:[27] in 1750 Dr Baillie wrote that 'he [had] appointed a court in my own house and admitted the vice-marshal'.[28] In February 1754 Baillie, who was under arrest for debt, held court in

21  'You know the lord mayor and merchants here of most consequence desired me for coadjutor in Dr Hawkshaw's time'; H. Baillie to T. Corbett, 14 Mar. 1745 (TNA (PRO), ADM 1/3,990).
22  J. Potter to T. Corbett, 1 Mar. 1743 (TNA (PRO), ADM 1/3,990).
23  H. Baillie to T. Corbett, 21 May 1745 (TNA (PRO), ADM 1/3,990). The earl of Winchilsea was Admiralty commissioner, 1742–4.
24  *A letter to Dr. Shebear*, p. 50; H. Baillie to the duke of Dorset (n.d.) (TNA (PRO), ADM 1/3,882). R. Osborn to H. Baillie, 3 Jan. 1745 (TNA (PRO), ADM 2/1,054, f.287). Osborn was deputy admiralty secretary, 1744–56.
25  H. Baillie to the commissioners of Admiralty, 16 Nov. 1745 (TNA (PRO), ADM 1/3,990). Petition of Hugh Baillie (n.d.) (TNA (PRO), ADM 1/3,883, f. 16).
26  'St Patrick's Church' was described as 'the usual place of holding said court' in an affidavit signed by the admiralty advocate, Dr Richard Clarke, in 1745 (TNA (PRO), ADM 1/3,990). The Court of Admiralty probably occupied the building which had been erected on the south close of the cathedral by Marmaduke Coghill to house the Court of the Prerogative and Faculties, the Consistorial Court and the Court of the Dean of St Patrick's. See W.M. Mason, *The history and antiquities of the Collegiate and Cathedral Church of St Patrick's* (Dublin, 1820), p. 16.
27  Dr Baillie's Dublin home was on Aungier Street (TNA (PRO), HCA 42/30, f. 1,075 & HCA 42/32, f. 454).
28  22 Mar. 1750 (TNA (PRO), ADM 1/3,882).

a sponging house (the 'house of the sheriff's officer').[29] On another occasion the court sat in the private residence of William Conolly, in St Mary's Abbey.[30]

The court's tangible assets were small. It possessed a seal.[31] But there is no reference to the Irish court possessing a symbolic silver oar. There was certainly no Irish admiralty oar in existence at the beginning of the century when Dr William King arrived in Dublin to begin his tenure as judge.[32] It is unlikely that the court would have been in a financial position to have one manufactured later in the century. Record-keeping, at least during the tenure of Dr Hawkshaw, was also poor. Baillie alleged that Dr Hawkshaw 'kept no regular records for reasons I have been told not so much to his honour'.[33]

Along with the judge, the court's personnel was composed of the judicial surrogate, the registrar and the marshal. Baillie sometimes ceded his power (as his patent permitted him to) to a surrogate. The practice appears to have been to nominate one of the leading civilians for the task. In 1745, for instance, Dr Edward Bullingbrooke was reported as acting as Baillie's surrogate.[34] The surrogate was constituted under a formal warrant of surrogacy.[35]

The position of registrar was occupied during the first part of Dr Hawkshaw's tenure by Thomas Wilkinson, the highly regarded and experienced officer, who had held the position since 1683 when Sir William Petty left the court. Towards the end of his career Wilkinson was assisted by a deputy registrar, Benjamin Mead.[36] In 1718 Thomas Wilkinson was replaced by Thomas Medlicott[37] who served until

29  W. Sheil to J. Clevland, 7 Feb. 1754 (TNA (PRO), ADM 1/3,882).

30  TNA (PRO), HCA 42/30, f. 1480.

31  A seal of the Irish Court of Admiralty is enclosed with the prize appeal papers in the *Gran Sultan* and the *St Francis* in 1747 (TNA (PRO), HCA 42/35 & HCA 42/30).

32  See p. 59 above.

33  H. Baillie to the commissioners of Admiralty, 17 May 1745 (TNA (PRO), ADM 1/3,990).

34  *St Philip of the Isle of Dieu* (TNA (PRO), HCA 42/44).

35  The 1745 warrant constituting Edward Bullingbrooke as surrogate in the absence of Dr Baillie read: 'To all Christian people to whom these presents shall come, Hugh Baillie esq. doctor of laws, judge and president of the High Court of Admiralty of Ireland sendeth greeting: know you that I, the said Hugh Baillie, have deputed, nominated and constituted, and by these presents do depute, nominate, and constitute Edward Bullingbrooke esq. doctor of laws my lawful deputy, or substitute in the office of the judge of the Admiralty in Ireland, hereby delegating and committing unto him the said Edward Bullingbrooke full power and authority of hearing and determining all, and all manner of, causes and controversies pertaining to the admiral's function in as full and ample manner as I myself being present might or could do, he the said Edward Bullingbrooke proceeding according to the laws and customs of the Admiralty Court, hereby empowering him to receive all manner of fees, perquisites, and other profits of right belonging, and accustomed, to the said office for my use and benefit to be held, executed and enjoyed by him during my absence from the said kingdom of Ireland, or during my pleasure only' (TNA (PRO), HCA 42/44, f. 894).

36  In 1716 Benjamin Mead described as 'gent. and notary public, deputy registrar of his majesty's High Court of Admiralty in Ireland' made a return to a committee of the House of Lords investigating court fees (*Eighteenth Report*, p. 101).

37  Thomas Medlicott was appointed on 2 Mar. 1718 (TNA (PRO), ADM 2/1,052, f. 122).

his death in 1743, and who, in turn, was replaced by William Sheil (who also acted as registrar of the Consistorial and Metropolitan Court of Armagh).[38]

Seven officers held the office of marshal between 1709 and 1751.[39] The marshal occupied two positions; firstly, he undertook the ordinary functions of marshal of the court: arresting vessels and attending sales. Secondly he also served as water bailiff. This purely administrative, tax-collecting post was highly remunerative. Although the power of collecting the duty of ballastage had been taken from the water bailiff by legislation in 1707,[40] the water bailiff was still entitled to the remunerative toll of anchorage. By the early eighteenth century the office was, for this reason, keenly sought after. Baillie noted that 'by reason of the great increase of the number of ships which arrive at this port of Dublin, the profits amount to about £300 a year'.[41] In the 1750s, following litigation in the Common Pleas, the marshal was instructed to cease collecting anchorage. With the loss of the right of levying anchorage in Dublin the office of marshal reverted, once more, to that of a minor court official. By the early 1760s the marshal, Richard Reade was reporting that the 'office of marshal is worth no more than twenty pounds a year'.[42] Although entitled to fees, the marshal was not paid a salary. When John Warham, deputy marshal to John Nicholas, applied for compensation for the 'insults and hardships which he had incurred' he was told that nothing was available from the navy budget.[43]

Until the loss of anchorage in the 1750s the office of marshal was held by political placemen, who would then delegate the administrative functions of the marshal and water bailiff, together with a portion of the profits, to a sub-marshal.[44] The deputy marshal to James Palmer was Francis Sherlock who was described as 'having been bred to the sea and captain of a private ship of war during the last war'.[45] It was the marshal (or more usually the deputy marshal) who carried out the dangerous function of executing the processes of the court. In 1719 a deputy marshal, Thomas Gower, described how he was injured during a physical confrontation near the Customs House with the sub-sheriff of Dublin (Thomas Cole).

---

38  Sheil was appointed on 30 Mar. 1743 (TNA (PRO), ADM 2/1,054, f. 118). The succession list produced as Appendix 3 to the *Court of Admiralty Commission Report, 1864* is inaccurate.

39  The office of marshal of the Court of Admiralty was occupied by: Francis Lake, appointed 29 Dec. 1709 (TNA (PRO), ADM 2/1,051, f.13); Samuel Adams, appointed 20 Aug. 1712 (TNA (PRO), ADM 1/1,051, f. 151); Francis Lake, appointed 15 Dec. 1714 (TNA (PRO), ADM 2/1,052, f. 9); John Nicholas, appointed 16 June 1721 (TNA (PRO), ADM 2/1,052, f. 232); James Palmer, appointed 20 Feb. 1727 'in place of John Nicholas dismissed' (TNA (PRO), ADM 2/1,053, f.3); earl of Bessborough, appointed 6 Mar. 1750 (TNA (PRO), ADM 2/1,055, f. 135); Richard Reade, appointed 9 May 1751(TNA (PRO), ADM 2/1,055, f.187).

40  6 Anne, c. 20 (Irl.), 1707. See p. 108 above.

41  H. Baillie to the commissioners of Admiralty, 1749 (TNA (PRO), ADM 1/3,882).

42  'The humble petition of Richard Reade of the city of Dublin, esquire' (TNA (PRO), ADM 1/3,883, f. 138).

43  J. Burchett to E. Thompson, 21 Apr. 1730 (TNA (PRO), ADM 2/1053, f. 103).

44  The arrangement is referred to in 'The memorial of Richard Reade' (n.d.) (TNA (PRO), ADM 1/3,883 f. 138).

45  Petition of H. Baillie (n.d.) (TNA (PRO), ADM 1/3,882).

The sub-sheriff with 'a great many assisting him' carried the arrested merchandise 'by virtue, as he said, of a replevin ... notwithstanding that [the marshal] told the said sub-sheriff that they were in his custody by virtue of the said warrant [of the Court of Admiralty]'. When the marshal insisted on retaining the vessel he 'was wounded and three of his fingers cut'.[46] A later deputy marshal, Francis McDonnell, described how he was prevented from arresting a vessel by two foot soldiers who had been enlisted by the master to prevent the execution of the warrant of arrest:

> on his attempting to enter the said ship, which lies in the river opposite the house of Mr John Power in Rogerson's Quay Dublin, he was prevented from entering and opposed by two foot soldiers, one of whom presented his musket with a bayonet fixed to the end to the deponent's breast and forbade the deponent at his peril to enter; upon which the deponent produced his warrant to them, and read the same word for word to the corporal who said he commanded them, there being four sentinels under arms.

At that point the captain of the *Italian Merchant* arrived with a writ from the King's Bench:

> immediately after which the said George Bribie, captain ... alighted out of a coach by the ship side and ... running up to the sentinels and addressing himself to them, 'I am just come from the lord chief justice; at your peril do not let any person aboard this ship'.[47]

The court, of course, did not have a prison and the governor of the Marshalsea refused to permit prisoners attached by the Court of Admiralty to be detained there. In 1750 Dr Baillie complained that 'the other prison keepers of the town often refused to receive prisoners from the marshal of the Admiralty'.[48] The marshal was forced to resort to improvising places of confinement in rooms in private houses.[49]

In 1747 Dr Richard Clarke was appointed to the office of king's advocate in the Court of Admiralty.[50] By the early 1750s the office politics of the court had become

46  Affidavit of Thomas Gower, in the *Sea Horse*, 5 Mar. 1719 (TNA (PRO), ADM 1/3,699, f. 370) & 5 June 1719 (TNA (PRO), ADM 2/1,052, f. 140).
47  Affidavit sworn 8 Mar. 1745 (TNA (PRO), ADM 1/3,990).
48  H. Baillie to the commissioners of Admiralty, 22 Mar. 1750 (TNA (PRO), ADM 1/3,882).
49  In 1745 a complaint was made that the captain of the *Italian Merchant*, the impugnant in a mariner's wages case, had been confined under a writ of attachment by the deputy marshal in his own house. R. Osborn to H. Baillie, 19 July 1745 (TNA (PRO), ADM 2/1,054, f. 358). In 1748 a prisoner attached for contempt by the court was reported as having been detained in the private house of one James Coleman in Bull Alley. 'Case relating to certain proceedings in the Court of Admiralty in Ireland against Mr Thomas Edwards, who was attached for contempt by Dr Hugh Baillie the judge of that court', c.1751 (TNA (PRO), ADM 1/3,882).
50  When news of his appointment (which had been made without the sanction of the Admiralty commissioners) came to the notice of the commissioners, it was immediately rescinded in favour

strained. Baillie complained that the registrar had told him that Clarke had formed a project to be 'judge himself and to have the proctor of office [Ephraim Carroll] registrar'.[51] By the early 1750s Clarke had been admitted to practise in the common law courts, and was making his expertise in admiralty law available to clients wishing to frustrate the work of the Court of Admiralty by common law remedies. The deputy marshal, Francis Sherlock reported[52] that the 'said Dr Clarke is continually harassing the court with prohibitions and replevins to promote his business at the common law, and to lessen and deprecate the Court of Admiralty'. He instanced one case, the *Nancy*, where, after the sentence in the Court of Admiralty, Clarke acted on behalf of the proprietors in the common law courts. In August 1751 the secretary of the Admiralty wrote to Clarke asking him to account for the allegations that he was attacking the court in the common law courts. When no satisfactory explanation was offered Clarke was dismissed and replaced by James Sheil.[53] Richard Clarke was one of a small number of specialist civilian lawyers who had emerged in the 1740s.[54] Others in this group included Dr Edward Bullingbrook; Dr James Sheil; Dr Richard Jackson LLD; Dr Thomas Radcliffe; and Dr Nathaniel Bland (the senior member of the group and a future judge of the Prerogative Court).[55] All held the degree of LLD from Trinity College Dublin, and three of the five (Clarke and James Sheil being the exceptions) were pure civilians who did not practise at the bar of any of the courts of common law.

VICE-ADMIRALTY COURTS

*The Court of Admiralty of the province of Munster*

The Admiralty Court of Munster was re-constituted in 1709: the Revd Dr Rowland Davies was constituted judge with Garrett Fitzgerald as registrar and Samuel Denys as marshal.[56] In 1716 Thomas Farren (who had served as judge in the late seventeenth century) was re-appointed judge with James Weeks acting as

of Edward Bullingbrooke LLD. This provoked yet another constitutional fight. Baillie protested claiming that his warrant allowed him to appoint every officer 'excepting the registrar and marshal' and, by implication, allowed him to appoint the admiralty advocate (TNA (PRO), ADM 1/3,881). However, within a month, Bullingbrooke had resigned and Clarke was reappointed; Admiralty commissioners to H. Baillie, 20 Nov. 1747 (TNA (PRO), ADM 2/1,054, f. 612).

51   H. Baillie to the commissioners of Admiralty, 20 Jan. 1752 (TNA (PRO), ADM 1/3,882).
52   Memorial of Francis Sherlock, 1751 (TNA (PRO), ADM 1/3,882).
53   J. Cleveland to T. Salisbury, 11 Feb. 1752 'whereas we have thought fit to appoint James Sheil, Bachelor of Law, to be advocate of the Admiralty in Ireland in room of Doctor Richard Clarke' (TNA (PRO), ADM 2/1,055, f. 225).
54   LLD (Dub.) 1744, Irish Bar, 1749. *Alumni Dublinenses*, p. 154.
55   LLD (Dub.) 1744, *Alumni Dublinenses*, p. 110. LLD (h.c., Dub.) 1749, Irish bar, 1746. *Alumni Dublinenses*, p. 747. LLD (Dub.) 1745, *Alumni Dublinenses*, p. 433. LLD (Dub) 1745, *Alumni Dublinenses*, p. 691. LLD (Dub.) 1727, *Alumni Dublinenses*, p. 73.
56   11 Mar. 1709 (TNA (PRO), ADM 2/1,050, f. 27).

his registrar.[57] In the late 1720s the long-serving Thomas Farren was replaced by John Love,[58] who also served as admiralty droit collector, or 'agent of the rights of the Admiralty'.[59] Love held office until 1750 when he, in turn, was replaced by William Austin[60] who though a 'practising attorney in the courts of law and equity' was also an absentee '[who] constantly resides in Dublin during the law terms'.[61]

The early eighteenth-century Munster judge, Dr Rowland Davies, reported that the authority of the court was effectively defunct: 'the admiralty jurisdiction in those parts is almost forgotten and lost'. He recommended that 'whoever be appointed judge be obliged to hold courts in the counties of Kerry and Limerick, Clare and Waterford at least twice a year in each county and by that means the jurisdiction will be better observed'.[62] As had been the case in the seventeenth century, the admiralty pretensions of the port towns continued to be a significant impediment. In 1717 warrants for the appointment of Farren as judge, and James Weeks as registrar of the court, were sent to the mayor of Cork with instructions to administer the oaths to the incoming office holders.[63] But the mayor of Cork, in an effort to keep the Munster Court of Admiralty out of the city, refused to administer the oaths. A correspondent of Edward Southwell reported that 'it seems that the mayor and his brethren, apprehending that this cause would be a check and discouragement to their trade ... declined to obey their lordships' order'.[64]

The important maritime town of Kinsale continued, as it had in the seventeenth century, not to recognize the court and asserted its own independent admiralty jurisdiction. Right into the mid-eighteenth century, Kinsale held regular admiralty courts, appointed a water bailiff, and even had its own ceremonial admiralty silver oar.[65]

Waterford also continued to press its claims to admiralty jurisdiction, going as far as to assert jurisdiction to hold a prize court. When in 1755, the French prize the *Brilliant of St Domingo* was brought in by a Waterford fishing vessel (the *Catherine*), the Corporation of Waterford claimed that its chartered court of admiralty was competent to adjudicate the prize suit. The Admiralty commissioners settled the issue by directing that the ship be taken from Ireland, and

---

57  4 Mar. 1716 (TNA (PRO), ADM 2/1,052, f. 68). E. Moore to E. Southwell, 14 June 1717 (BL, Add. MS 38,152, f. 50).
58  19 Aug. 1729 (TNA (PRO), ADM 2/1,053, f. 86).
59  'Instructions to be observed by John Love esq, agent of the rights of admiralty' (BL, Add. MS 38,152, f. 82).
60  Austin was appointed 22 Mar. 1751 (*Court of Admiralty Commission Report, 1864*, Appendix G, p. 78).
61  Petition of Dr Baillie (*c.*1755) (TNA (PRO), ADM 7/298, f. 509).
62  R. Davies to E. Southwell, 25 Feb. 1709 (BL, Add. MS 38,151, f. 114).
63  E. Moore to E. Southwell, 14 June 1717 (BL, Add. MS 38,152, f. 50).
64  Ibid.
65  A presentment laid in 1738 recorded the appointment of a water bailiff and instructed the bailiff to 'attend the sovereign with his silver oar ... at all courts of admiralty ...' 30 Sept. 1734, *Calendar of Kinsale Documents, vol. 6*, ed. M. Mulcahy (Kinsale, 1998), p. 12.

docked in London, for the purpose of condemnation by the English High Court of Admiralty.[66] The Corporation of Waterford entered an appeal to the prize appeal commissioners, claiming that prize disputes fell within the terms of its charter grant of admiralty jurisdiction and contesting the right of the English court to adjudicate in Waterford-related litigation.[67]

In addition to these local tensions, the Munster court was also in competition with the Court of Admiralty in Dublin. In 1709 Rowland Davies wrote to Edward Southwell, expressing concern that Dr Hawkshaw's grant as admiralty judge extended throughout all of Ireland and included the province of Munster. He enquired whether Southwell might use his influence so as to exclude Munster from this grant.[68] The central court, for its part, had become interested in extending its influence into Munster. Encroachments in Munster by the national court resulted in at least three incidents.

The first of these conflicts occurred in 1745, and involved the question of the entitlement of the judge of the national admiralty court to nominate deputies to operate in the province of Munster. The nominal judge of the Munster court in the 1740s was John Love. It is not clear how actively Love was discharging any judicial duties. The likelihood, in fact, is that Love never administered judicial (as opposed to purely administrative functions in collecting admiralty perquisites). He does not appear to have been a practising lawyer.[69] Furthermore, there was, at this time, no registrar of the Munster court, and, of course, without a registrar there could have been no court.[70]

In the meantime, Dr Baillie had advised the Admiralty that he intended to re-establish the provincial vice-admiralty structure in order to make the court 'a public benefit to the nation'[71] and appointed two deputies. St John Browne (a clergyman and LLD)[72] was appointed to administer a sub-branch of the national court at Kinsale, and a second deputy was appointed to preside in Cork city. Both were appointed with jurisdiction in cases where the value of the claim was less than £50.[73] Dr Baillie claimed that he made these appointments in response to requests

66  J. Clevland to H. Baillie, 27 July 1756 (TNA (PRO), ADM 2/1,055, f. 426).

67  Waterford Corporation delayed until 1762 (the maximum period permitted by the rules of the commissioners for prize appeals) to enter that appeal. By 1764 its proctor had died and the corporation was said to be anxious to withdraw its appeal. P. [?] Crespigny to P. Stephens, 4 June 1764 (TNA (PRO), ADM 1/3,883, f. 405).

68  R. Davies to E. Southwell, 25 Oct. 1709 (BL, Add. MS 38,152, f. 12).

69  Petition of John Love, Oct. 1745 (TNA (PRO), ADM 1/3,990).

70  J. Fitzmaurice to E. Southwell, 17 Nov. 1748 (BL, Add. MS 38,152, f. 98).

71  17 May 1745 (TNA (PRO), ADM 1/3990).

72  Baillie wrote in defence of Dr Browne: '[the judge of the Munster Court] insinuates as if I had named an improper person for Kinsale by saying he is a clergyman, but he forgets taking notice of this likewise, that he is a Doctor of Law and reckoned the best civilian in that part of the country. He was recommended to me by my Lord Kinsale as the fittest person to be named and was a person agreeable to everybody's inclination' (TNA (PRO), ADM 1/3,990).

73  Ibid.

made by the mercantile community in Cork: 'I thought it my duty to comply with what seemed the desire of these trading places because by that means they got justice without stirring from home, and if any injustice was done they could appeal to me'.

Remarkably, Baillie appears to have been unaware of the existence of the judge of the Munster Court of Admiralty, John Love. This was to be the cause of his first serious embarrassment with his administrative superiors. Soon after Baillie had made his own Munster appointments, Love memorialized the Admiralty in London complaining of the encroachments committed by the Dublin court, and alleging that Browne had, in some way, threatened him.[74] Dr Browne, on the other hand, pleaded ignorance of Love's existence.[75] Baillie, as soon as he was called upon by the Admiralty to explain his actions, cancelled the deputations; like Dr Browne, Baillie claimed that he had never heard of Love.[76]

There are grounds for believing Baillie's excuse. The confusion appears to have been a consequence of a change in constitutional practice in London – a change which was designed to emphasize the inferior status of the Irish court. The practice in the late seventeenth century was that a warrant for the appointment of a judge of vice-admiralty would issue to the Court of Admiralty in Ireland. The office of the national court would then draw up the patent of appointment. This practice ceased in the early eighteenth century. The warrants to draw up patents of appointment were, instead, directed to the judge of the Court of Admiralty in London. The change was a consequence of the English theory that the Court of Admiralty of Ireland was merely a co-ordinate court of vice-admiralty; it was inappropriate that an inferior court should issue the warrant of appointment to what was merely another court of co-ordinate jurisdiction. As a result of this change in practice, the warrant of appointment of the judge of the Munster court would not have appeared in the files of the Court of Admiralty in Dublin. Instead, what Baillie did find on the files, and what probably suggested the appointments, was a much older series of instruments constituting local appointments made by Sir William Petty in the 1670s.[77] It was these which inspired Baillie's Munster appointments. Though the probability is that Dr Baillie had acted entirely innocently, a notice of official censure was directed to Baillie by the commissioners of Admiralty in October 1745.[78] Baillie was instructed to 'recall and cancel the deputation aforementioned ... which interfere with the jurisdiction and privileges of other judges of the vice-admiralty courts in the kingdom of Ireland, and not to grant any such deputations to any persons for the future'.

---

74  Petition of John Love, Oct. 1745 (TNA (PRO), ADM 1/3,990).
75  Answer of Dr Hugh Baillie, 1745, ibid.
76  Ibid.
77  Dr Baillie specifically referred to the appointment (dated 29 Sept. 1677) by William Petty of Thomas Palmer as 'deputy judge' of the Admiralty Court of Ireland along the coastline from the town of Bantry to the town of Tarbert (TNA (PRO), ADM 7/298, f. 509).
78  Commissioners of Admiralty to Baillie, 15 Oct. 1745 (TNA (PRO), ADM 2/1,054, f. 389).

Further conflict arose when the Court of Admiralty in Dublin attempted to exercise jurisdiction in a case involving wreck found in Kerry. In 1748 one of the Munster Admiralty's Kerry deputies, John Fitzmaurice, seized some wrecked barrels of wine and the hulk of an abandoned ship. On legal advice, he then brought the find to the attention of the Court of Admiralty in Dublin. When John Love discovered the proceedings he travelled, livid, to Dublin to warn Dr Baillie to stay out of Munster. The court was in the midst of proceedings when 'came Mr Love of Cork ... as judge of Admiralty of Munster' who 'claimed the judging of this matter as his right'.[79] The general view in Ireland was that Love was not qualified to be granted an exclusive admiralty jurisdiction in Munster:

> The officers here say that Mr Love cannot judge it, for that he has no registrar in his court, which, it seems, is an officer without whom nothing can be done; and, besides that, the court here has a universal jurisdiction over the whole kingdom. Mr Love left the town in a disposition to have the clashing of jurisdictions determined by the lords of the Admiralty.[80]

Trouble surfaced once again in the early 1750s when the marshal of the national court was granted a warrant to seize a wreck stranded near Limerick.[81] A complaint at the court's acting in Munster was raised by William Austin, Love's successor as judge of the Munster Vice-Admiralty. The complaint was transmitted through Edward Southwell (then vice-admiral of Munster) to the admiralty commissioners. This earned Baillie a second official reprimand.[82]

Baillie, for his part, became more assertive.[83] What troubled him was the constitutional theory which treated the national court not as the superior of the provincial court but merely as its equal. The co-ordinate jurisdiction theory was, Baillie perceived, the corollary of a much more sinister notion: that the Irish Court of Admiralty was a mere court of vice-admiralty (which in Baillie's view it emphatically was not):

> those belonging to the Admiralty in England either don't, or will not, understand the constitution of the Court of Admiralty here. They imagine, or pretend to direct, that we are only a vice-admiralty court dependent on

79  J. Fitzmaurice to E. Southwell, 17 Nov. 1748 (BL, Add. MS 38,152, f. 98).
80  Ibid.
81  'The Petition of Hugh Baillie' (TNA (PRO), ADM 1/3,885).
82  'The Honourable Mr Southwell, Vice-Admiral of the Province of Munster, having transmitted to my Lords Commissioners of the Admiralty a complaint made against you by Mr Austin, judge of the Vice-Admiralty Court of the said Province, for interfering within that jurisdiction, their lordships command me to let you know that, after their order to you dated the 10th October 1745, they are not only surprised but displeased with your conduct in presuming to meddle with the jurisdiction and privileges of the Vice-Admiralty Court of Munster, which [being] a separate province you have no power in.' J. Clevland to H. Baillie, 13 Nov. 1751 (TNA (PRO), ADM 2/1,055, f. 206).
83  Petition of H. Baillie (TNA (PRO), ADM 1/3,882).

them and have ordered their directions oftentimes in the case of appeals as to a vice-admiralty court.[84]

Although recruited to serve in Ireland in the 1740s by Archbishop Boulter, one of the leaders of the English interest in Ireland, Baillie had by the 1750s become the first eighteenth-century judge to begin articulating the patriotic campaign against vice-admiralty status. However, the theory that the Court of Admiralty of Ireland was merely one of vice-admiralty, and not a high court, was precisely the view being taken in Doctors' Commons. The law officers of the Admiralty met to consider Baillie's memorial and, in reply, reasserted their view that the Irish court had no jurisdiction to interfere with the business of the Munster Vice-Admiralty.[85] The law officers repeated the theory of concurrent and subordinate jurisdiction of the several Irish admiralty courts. They were

> jurisdictions independent of each other, and derived from the same original power, and each vice-admiralty court within the limits of its province has as full and ample jurisdiction as Dr Baillie, with this difference only, that Dr Baillie has not a particular limited jurisdiction, but a general concurrent jurisdiction throughout the kingdom of Ireland, equal with each vice-admiral in his particular province, being a jurisdiction more extensive, but in no [way] superior.

The complaints coming from Ireland prompted the law officers to map out a detailed set of principles for determining the constitutional inter-relationship between the local and central courts of admiralty. First, it was recognized that there were certain issues which were peculiarly apposite for the courts of vice-admiralty, particularly questions relating to admiralty droits. 'We are humbly of opinion that the care and cognizance of the rights of Admiralty are [e]specially incumbent on every admiralty court within the extent of its province'.[86] Second, in cases of overlapping jurisdiction, priority would be determined by the application of the principle of the 'preoccupancy of the case'; in other words, the suit belonged to the court in which it was first instituted.

Within ten years this elaborate scheme of jurisdictional relations between the Dublin and Munster courts had become irrelevant: William Austin was the last appointment to the Admiralty Court of Munster; thereafter that court was closed for good.

*The campaign for the revival of the vice-admiralty courts in the other provinces of Ireland*

The 1630s' experiment of commissioning vice-admiralty courts in all four of the provinces of Ireland had been terminated by the 1690s. Courts of vice-admiralty

---

84  Ibid.
85  C. Crespigny, G. Belles, S. Seddon to the commissioners of Admiralty, 3 Feb. 1752 (TNA (PRO), ADM 1/3,882).                    86  Ibid.

had ceased to operate in the three provinces of Ireland outside Munster. The isolation of the other provinces from the central court prompted occasional demands for the re-establishment of local courts of vice-admiralty, and particularly for the revival of the once-active Admiralty Court of Connacht. In 1748, the vice-admiral of Connacht, Thomas Eyre, wrote to the commissioners of Admiralty petitioning them to re-establish the court. He had two nominees prepared to accept appointment – the Revd Richard Annesley, who would act as judge, and John Hall who would act as registrar.[87] The application was turned down. A brief minute subscribed to Ryan's petition read: 'there is one judge of the Admiralty Court in England, the lords do not consider it appropriate to appoint more in Ireland'.[88]

Subsequently, Stratford Eyre renewed the application for the appointment of a judge of Vice-Admiralty of Connacht. The principal cause of the demand was that without an admiralty court it was impossible for the vice-admiral to effectively perfect the processing of admiralty wreck. This was particularly problematic since, it was alleged, the Court of Admiralty of Ireland in Dublin was unhelpful to provincial vice-admiralties.[89] Eyre complained that although he had 'often applied to Doctor Baillie, Doctor Clarke and Mr Ephraim Carroll for the aid and countenance of courts' it had been to 'no effect'. The necessity for a court to assist the vice-admiral had become more urgent due to a rise in the number of claimants disputing the right to maritime wreck: 'the many grants since from the Crown to the subject, and the multiplicity of laws, has quite altered the case at this day and has given a candle to so many claimants that the vice-admiral cannot with security to himself act, but in his court'.

However, London was committed to its policy of winding down the provincial vice-admiralty judicature in Ireland. The Admiralty (inaccurately)[90] informed Eyre that 'there never' was a vice-admiralty court in the province of Connacht, and that '[the commissioners of Admiralty] do not think it proper to establish one there'.

### THE INSTANCE JURISDICTION OF THE MID-EIGHTEENTH CENTURY COURT OF ADMIRALTY

Like the High Court of Admiralty of England, the Court of Admiralty of Ireland was merely a court of limited jurisdiction subject to the limitations which had been propounded by the English Court of King's Bench in the late sixteenth century, and with its activities subject to the continuing supervision of the Irish Court of

---

87  A. Ryan (admiralty secretary) to J. Seddon (admiralty solicitor), 31 Mar. 1748 (TNA (PRO), ADM 1/3,676, f. 87).

88  Ibid.

89  Memorial of Stratford Eyre (TNA (PRO), ADM 1/3,882). Eyre nominated John Loftus of Loughrea as judge, and Peter Kilkenny, a King's Bench attorney, as registrar of the revived court.

90  See p. 17 above.

King's Bench by prohibition. The effect of this extensive withdrawal of jurisdiction by prohibition was that like its English equivalent, the Irish Court of Admiralty was not a court of general maritime jurisdiction. It was not permitted to hear suits involving ordinary maritime contracts like bills of lading or charter parties. The court had only a limited jurisdiction: claims involving wages, maritime collisions,[91] and wrongful seizure of vessels.[92] Despite the restricted jurisdiction allowed to it, Dr Baillie managed to stir controversy on two fronts. First, in respect of one of those few matters over which the court did have jurisdiction – mariners' wages – complaints about Baillie's allegedly partial and pro-mariner stance became the subject of a campaign agitated by mercantile interests. Second, in respect of those matters over which the court did not have jurisdiction (charter parties and bills of lading), Baillie boldly encouraged fictitious devices in order to extend the court's jurisdiction.

*Mariners wages suits*

In the mid-eighteenth century the principal work undertaken by the English Court of Admiralty involved claims by crew members against masters for unpaid wages; in the early 1750s the English court seems to have done very little work other than wages claims.[93] While the records of the Irish Court of Admiralty for the seventeenth and eighteenth centuries have been lost,[94] those sources which do survive (principally appeals taken to the High Court of Admiralty in London)

91  Two mid-eighteenth-century Irish appeals to the English Court of Admiralty involved collision cases. The impugnants in the *Nostra Signora de Olivea St Antonio Muras* had been ordered to pay for damage done by their ship, the *Janor of Whitehaven*. An appeal was submitted on two grounds: that the damage had occurred accidentally, and not by any negligence on the part of the impugnants; and, secondly, that the promovents (George St Ledger and Theobold Shea) had failed to prove their interest in the damaged vessel. The *Success of Appledore*, another collision case, was also of little doctrinal interest. The *Success* had been condemned by the court following a finding of damage done to the *Susanah of Waterford*. The impugnants appealed, claiming that the court had exaggerated the extent of the damage. The decree, it was alleged, should have been for £104 (and not the £162 which had been decreed). Act book of the High Court of Admiralty (Eng.), 18 Oct. 1745 (TNA (PRO), HCA 3/74, f. 74) & 3 Mar. 1747 (TNA (PRO), HCA 3/74, f. 293).

92  In *Lutwidge v. Vatable* (1713) Burrell 300; 167 ER 582 Dr Hawkshaw had condemned the defendant, the owner of a privateer vessel, the *Whitehaven*, in the sum of £780 as damages for the wrongful seizure, near Newfoundland, of an Irish vessel, the *Jane*. An appeal to the English Court of Admiralty was successful but only to the extent that the award of damages was reduced to £750. A further appeal to the Court of Delegates was initiated but not prosecuted.

93  In the first session of Easter 1751, 25 of the 29 cases recorded in the act book of the High Court of Admiralty were suits by mariners against masters. In the first session of Michalemas term 1751 the act book records that 32 of the 36 cases were suits by mariners against masters or vessels *in rem* (TNA (PRO), HCA 5/119).

94  By the mid-nineteenth century, only records of the Irish Court of Admiralty composed after 1747 survived: *Report of the Deputy Keeper of the Public Records and of the Keeper of the State Papers in Ireland* (*1869*), p. 37. In 1922, following the catastrophic explosion in the Irish Public Records Office, these too were lost. No original records of the court now survive.

confirm that the Court of Admiralty in Dublin was also, predominantly, a court for the relief of unpaid sailors.[95]

Despite the cliché that freight was the mother of wages, customary maritime law held that a mariner was only entitled to a portion of his wages when freight was earned on the unloading of cargo. As a disincentive to desertion, the right to full wages was postponed until the crew had taken the vessel back to the port from which it had originally set out. Although the sailor was entitled to a portion of the wages on delivery of the cargo, there was uncertainty as to precisely what proportion of his wages the mariner was entitled.[96] Under the English Piracy Act 1721[97] a master was forbidden from paying more than one half of the wages at the foreign port, but that measure was not in force in Ireland. The *Italian Merchant*[98] provides some evidence as to the mid-eighteenth-century Irish understanding of the law on the accrual of mariners' wages. The *Italian Merchant*'s articles provided that wages were payable only on the return of the vessel. The vessel discharged cargo at Leghorn and then set sail on its return journey to England. Conditions on board started to deteriorate. It broke its journey at Gibraltar. Rations began to run low and the sailors were put on a half allowance of bread; the ship then encountered a storm during which the sailors were obliged to throw overboard their clothes and sea chests. On disembarking at George's Quay in Dublin, the men asked the master, Captain Ribbie, for their wages. He apparently responded that 'they could go to the devil for he would not give them a thing'. When the crew then petitioned in the Court of Admiralty for wages, Dr Baillie ruled, firstly, that as a customary rule mariners were entitled to half wages on unloading at the port of destination: 'I was of opinion that supposing Leghorn was reckoned their second delivering port ... and that by the marine law they had been entitled to half their wages'. He held, secondly, that the customary rule – half-wages on unlading – could be displaced by a prior provision in the contract: here '[the mariners] had cut themselves off from that demand by the contract with the captain'. Baillie's third proposition was that the sailors were, notwithstanding the agreement, entitled to advance payment for necessaries. Baillie, accordingly, ordered that they be paid three guineas each, one half of which was to be spent on clothes and the other moiety on lodging and other charges. That sum was to be set off against the wages owing to the sailors on their return to England.

By contrast with the *Italian Merchant*, the master of the *Freda* was not permitted to demonstrate to the court that the right to part payment on unlading had been overridden by a contrary provision: in 1751 two Swedish sailors, Nyberg and Berg, crew members of the *Freda* of Stockholm which had docked in Dublin,

95   The *George*, 27 May 1755 (TNA (PRO), HCA 5/124); the *Jane*, 3 June 1756 (TNA (PRO), HCA 15/124).
96   A. Browne, *A compendious view*, ii, p. 178. C. Abbott, *A treatise on the law relative to merchant ships and seamen* (London, 1802), pp 365–8.
97   8 Geo. I, c. 24 (Eng.), 1721.
98   Memorial re the *Italian Merchant*, 1745 (TNA (PRO), ADM 1/3,996).

libeled for wages. Under the mariners' regulations promulgated by the king of Sweden in 1748 the master was obliged to pay the sailor no more than one month's wages when the ship's freight was discharged; full payment was to be postponed until the ship returned home. Captain Berg, the master of the *Freda* wished to argue, therefore, that under the Swedish mariners' wages regulation no wages were payable, the sailors having been paid more than one month's pay in the harbour of Dublin. The master had not retained a proctor 'as he was unwilling to put his owners and the ship to any expense'. Baillie refused to admit the evidence on the grounds that the master was not represented by a proctor. The master not having been allowed audience, and the Swedish regulations not having been opened to the court, the court decreed for the sailors. Baillie's ruling against the master in the *Freda*, and his refusal to admit a sound defence, prompted a pamphlet campaign against the court. James Digges La Touche,[99] the Dublin cloth merchant and a trading partner with the Swedish proprietors, produced two broadsheets[100] which he distributed about the precincts of the House of Commons during its sitting in May 1752, detailing the proceedings in the *Freda* and petitioning Parliament for a legislative remedy against the court's interference with the Irish shipping industry. La Touche complained of the embarrassment caused by the court issuing its processes against foreign vessels. The jurisdiction of the court was, he argued, properly restricted to claims made by crews of domestic vessels; it was not entitled to exercise jurisdiction in cases involving foreign crews.[101] La Touche argued that 'foreigners are discouraged from coming to this port, to the great discredit of the justice of the nation, and to the manifest detriment and loss of its trade'. The effect of the extension of the wages jurisdiction to sailors in foreign vessels was 'that the trade and navigation of [Dublin] doth receive great prejudice by the encouragement which is given to foreign sailors to desert the service of their master and to sue for wages in the High Court of Admiralty'.

The La Touche petition also alleged (a complaint which also featured in a number of appeals in the period 1745–56 to the English High Court of Admiralty) routine procedural unfairness towards shipmasters. The Court of Admiralty, he claimed, issued warrants of arrest virtually as a matter of course, and without the sailor promovent being required to specify the allegation on oath. The court acted 'upon the least application to any proctor in that court, and a complaint, in general terms by word of mouth, either of an assault or want of wages'. It was alleged that 'a sailor may procure an arrest of his master's ship, without it being necessary for the sailor to specify his demand, or on what his complaint is grounded; without any

99 James Digges La Touche (d. 1763) cloth merchant, parliamentary lobbyist, member of prominent banking family, and fine art connoisseur: D. Dickson & R. English, 'The La Touche Dynasty', in D. Dickson (ed.), *The gorgeous mask; Dublin, 1700–1850* (Dublin, 1987), p. 17.

100 J.D. La Touche, *The case of Frederick Berg, Master of the Freden of Stockholm* (Dublin, 1751); J.D. La Touche, *The humble petition of James Digges La Touche in behalf of himself and others, the merchants of the city of Dublin* (Dublin, 1751).

101 *The humble petition of James Digges La Touche* (Dublin, 1751).

oath; or even certificate of money being due to him'. Procedural rules were biased against the vessel master. The master was, as in the *Freda*, obliged to obtain legal representation; the sailor was not. No costs were awarded against the unsuccessful sailor. Instead, even where the master won, he still carried the burden of legal costs: 'the fees of proctors, of warrants, arrests, discharges &c. do fall on the master, and that no damages or costs are decreed in the said court against sailors when they are cast'.

Dr Baillie characterized La Touche (rather unfairly given La Touche's Huguenot background) as merely one of a gang of 'popish merchants' who were attempting to frustrate the court in carrying out one of its central functions – as a guardian against the abuse of mariners by vessel owners. With a touch of grandeur he boasted of the contempt with which, he claimed, the pamphlet was received in the Irish Commons:[102] 'They had the assurance some days ago to print a paper attacking the Court of Admiralty and a merchant, one Digges La Touche, distributed copies amongst the members of the House of Commons, but their folly and roguery were sufficiently exposed by acquainting some of the members of the facts, so they were laughed at'. Motivating the merchants' campaign, he alleged, was anger at the court's role in exposing the ill-treatment of sailors: 'what vexes them is that the Court of Admiralty is what hinders them from illicit trade and cheating the poor sailors out of their wages'. La Touche's understanding was rather different – Parliament had been inhibited from acting on purely constitutional grounds. Although there was strong support in principle for his proposal that the court's wages jurisdiction be reformed, the Court of Admiralty, as an agent of the English high admiral, was understood to be beyond the constitutional competence of the Irish legislature: 'the above petition was not brought in: those who had encouraged it, amongst whom I could name some of the most considerable men in the House of Commons … were dissuaded from the attempt, as it was doubted whether the Court of Admiralty would own any dependence on the legislature of Ireland'.[103]

La Touche was not the only person making charges about the court's partiality in wages cases. The allegations of bias against masters which had been made by La Touche were corroborated in a number of Irish appeals to the Court of Admiralty in London. For instance, the libel of appeal in the *George*[104] in 1752 expressly accused Baillie of having 'too much favour[ed] the party of the said Peter Johnston, John Anderson and Neal Kelly [the sailor promovents] more than he ought by law' and had 'not in the least regard[ed] the requisites and forms of law and judicial proceeding'. In the *Maidenhead of Ballycastle*[105] the Court of Admiralty decreed for the sailors, but without, it was alleged, allowing the proctor or the impugnant sufficient time to swear and examine a material witness who had just come to the notice of the proctor for the master.

102  H. Baillie to the commissioners of Admiralty, 12 May 1752 (TNA (PRO), ADM 1/3,882).
103  *The humble petition of James Digges La Touche* (Dublin, 1751).
104  Libel of appeal, 2 Dec. 1752 (TNA (PRO), HCA 15/124).
105  Act book of the English Court of Admiralty, 23 Aug. 1746 (TNA (PRO), HCA 3/74, f. 206).

*Maritime contracts and bills of lading*

The courts of common law had, in the sixteenth and seventeenth centuries, ensured that courts of admiralty could not exercise jurisdiction over the most important categories of commercial maritime litigation. Under the locality doctrine[106] a court of admiralty only had jurisdiction over disputes occurring on the high seas; accordingly, maritime agreements contracted on land (suits involving charter parties and bills of lading) could not be heard in a court of admiralty. In 1669 in *Jurado v. Gregory*[107] the English King's Bench had held that a bill of lading suit (involving failure to deliver wines from Malaga) could not be dealt with by the Court of Admiralty. The court only had jurisdiction over disputes occurring on the high seas. Since the bill of lading was contracted on land, the courts of common law alone had jurisdiction. The Irish King's Bench had also adopted the locality principle, regularly issuing writs of prohibition against the court when it acted outside the restrictions prescribed by the common law.[108]

The locality principle continued to be implemented by the courts of common law into the eighteenth and nineteenth centuries. The mid-eighteenth-century English Court of Admiralty never processed suits involving bills of lading or charter parties. However, there is some evidence that, despite the incontestable illegality of its so doing, the Irish Admiralty Court attempted to evade the restriction on its exercising jurisdiction in suits involving alleged breaches of contracts of lading. The technique used to obtain this jurisdiction was fictitious pleading: the libel would assert that the contract had been negotiated on the high seas.[109] In 1754 the court was about to hear a suit arising out of a contract of lading for the transport, on board a vessel called the *Friendship*, of a cargo of salt and malt between Lyme Regis and Dublin.[110] A writ of prohibition was obtained from the King's Bench on the ground that the promovent had used the collusive technique of 'warily and craftily libelling and suggesting' that the contract had been made on the high seas. In fact, it was alleged, the contract had been agreed on land 'in Lyme Regis in the county of Norfolk, and within the body of Norfolk, in that part of Great Britain called England, and not upon the high seas and within the jurisdiction of the said Court of Admiralty aforesaid, as by the libel … supposed'.

In the *Planter* in 1755 the Irish Court of Admiralty accepted a suit involving alleged damage to merchandise being carried between Lisbon and Dublin – a bill of lading dispute which, on orthodox principles, the court was not permitted to hear.[111] The defendant complained that the court had improperly acted upon a feigned allegation contained in the libel, that the contract had been concluded on the high seas, and not, as the defendant insisted, had really happened: following a bargain negotiated in Lisbon.

---

106  See p. 33 above.          107  (1669) 1 Ventris 32, 86 ER 23.          108  See pp 99–100 above.
109  This device had been used in England in the early-sixteenth century. J. Baker, *The Oxford history of the laws of England, vol. vi: 1483–1558* (Oxford, 2003), p. 214.
110  Eighteenth-century admiralty and ecclesiastical precedent book (King's Inns MS, f. 42).
111  Ibid., f. 39.

## Royal fish, wreck and the Court of Exchequer

The adjudication of title to maritime wreck continued to form one of the routine components of the court's work. In 1725 barrels of wine and brandy were picked up from the sea by the *William and Mary of Topsham* and taken to New Ross where they were, it was alleged, prematurely condemned as flotsam by the judge of the Court of Admiralty, Dr Hawkshaw, without first 'remain[ing] a year and day in the custody of the marshal of the Admiralty'.[112] In 1751 the claim of the judge of the Munster court to condemn a wreck found near Limerick led to a clash with the national court, which had also been preparing to condemn the same wreck.[113] Earlier in 1748 the Munster admiralty judge, John Love, had protested when Dr Baillie had begun adjudicating wines and the hulk of a ship which had been found on the coast of Kerry. In 1752, the judge of the Munster court, William Austin, reported that he had retrieved the hulk of a vessel, together with a quantity of rum, which had been discovered floating near the harbour at Schull.[114]

In the early eighteenth century the court occasionally exercised its arcane power to adjudicate claims to royal fish. In 1728 the vice-admiral of Connacht reported that a large whale had been washed up at Durras in County Mayo, and that the Admiralty's claim was being resisted by a Mr Dillon who 'pretends a right to it by virtue of a patent granted to Sir Arthur Shane'.[115] In the late 1750s, a Mayo man called Patrick Boyd, took the trouble of travelling all the way to London to inform the Admiralty commissioners that a whale had been washed up at Ross. The commissioners, while informing him that the more appropriate course of action was to bring the matter to the attention of the Court of Admiralty in Ireland, recommended that Boyd 'being in indigent circumstances and being obliged to go back again' should be awarded a reward for his conscientiousness.[116] By the mid-eighteenth century the Irish court appears to have abandoned the royal fish jurisdiction. In 1752 Dr Baillie commented that 'by my commission it likewise appears that the court has a right to certain fishes taken but as to this I believe that it has been in desuetude for many years past, so I did not attempt to revive it'.[117]

The jurisdictional contest between the Court of Admiralty and the customs over the right to abandoned maritime goods continued into the eighteenth century.[118] The theatre of conflict had moved from the coast of Munster to the Irish Sea. Typically, the Court of Admiralty would claim the goods were admiralty flotsam (and that the proper legal process was condemnation in the Court of Admiralty). The customs would counter-argue they had been cast off by smugglers

---

112   Commissioners of admiralty to Hawkshaw, 12 Aug. 1725 (TNA (PRO), ADM 2/1,052, f. 476).
113   The petition of Hugh Baillie, 1753 [?] (TNA (PRO), ADM 1/3,885, f. 192).
114   J. Cleveland to W. Austin, 9 Apr. 1752 (TNA (PRO), ADM 2/1,055, f. 237).
115   J. Burchett to St George, 3 Sept. 1728 (TNA (PRO), ADM 2/1,053, f. 46). Dr Hawkshaw was
       instructed to enquire into the validity of the claim made by Dillon.
116   J. Cleveland to S. Seddon, 8 Oct. 1759 (TNA (PRO), ADM 2/1,056, f. 182).
117   H. Baillie to the commissioners of Admiralty, 9 Dec. 1752 (TNA (PRO), ADM 1/3,882).
118   See p. 99 above.

illegally running goods from the Isle of Man into Ireland (and that, under the customs acts, the proper process was condemnation in the Court of Exchequer).[119]

Early in 1750 Dr Baillie[120] complained that after goods found floating on the Irish Sea had been condemned by the court as admiralty perquisites, an order had been issued by the Court of Exchequer requiring the admiralty registrar to hand over the proceeds. The Court of Exchequer claimed that the goods were within its jurisdiction, being smuggled goods thrown overboard when the vessel was being pursued by customs officials. There were, it was claimed, several cases pending where similar claims – cases where admiralty droits were claimed to be smuggled goods – were being made against the Court of Admiralty. Dr Baillie's complaint was referred to the English attorney general (William Murray) and solicitor general (Dudley Ryder), who responded unsympathetically, dismissing Dr Baillie's request for intervention as constitutionally improper:[121] 'the application by way of complaint of the common law courts in Ireland to the lords of the Admiralty is very improper. Nor can their lordships interpose in matters of justice at the instance either of the judge of the admiralty or of the party to any suit there'. They impatiently informed Baillie that if the court was 'injured by any judgment of the [Court of] King's Bench or Exchequer there, [it] must have [its] proper remedy, and must, as all other subjects, be left to that remedy, and [it] can't want advice there what that remedy is or how to apply it, without the assistance of their lordships'.

Baillie complained again in 1752 that 'in the Exchequer our right of judging in flotsams and jetsams … is controverted … without any colour of law'.[122] Revenue officers had intercepted a vessel which appeared to be smuggling goods from the Isle of Man.[123] Several casks of brandy were thrown overboard ('in order to lighten the load or save the boat being confiscated') which the revenue officers retrieved. The officers then 'carried [the brandy] to the Customs House, and exhibited an information against them upon the statute as goods intended to be run'.[124] Two sets of proceedings were opened concurrently. Proceedings to condemn the goods were initiated in the Court of Exchequer. At the same time, a suit concerned with the same goods was initiated in the Court of Admiralty. To Baillie's disappointment, the English law officers advised that the question of whether the goods seized were admiralty perquisites, or were, instead, illegally smuggled goods, should be determined by the Court of Exchequer:

---

119   The Customs Act 1725 (12 Geo. 1, c. 28 (Eng.), 1725). For the procedure regulating prosecution *in rem* of illegally imported goods in the Court of Exchequer, G. Howard, *A treatise of the Exchequer and Revenue of Ireland* (Dublin, 1776), pp 260–72.

120   H. Baillie to the commissioners of Admiralty, Jan. 1750 (TNA (PRO), ADM 7/298, f. 440).

121   Opinion of D. Ryder and W. Murray, 23 Jan. 1750 (TNA (PRO), ADM 7/298, f. 438).

122   9 Dec. 1752 (TNA (PRO), ADM 1/3,882).

123   The Customs Act 1725 (12 Geo. 1, c. 28 (Eng.), 1725) provided for the forfeiture of goods and vessels smuggling goods from the Isle of Man (s. 22).

124   J. Smith to S. Seddon, 13 July 1752 (TNA (PRO), ADM 1/3,676, f. 355).

where suits are in both courts, as to the same goods, and dispute is between the common law and Admiralty, whether the goods are flotsam etc. the common law court, and particularly, the Exchequer has the preference and must finally determine it … in all cases of this kind the true merits will be, whether from the all the evidence and circumstances, the goods so found in the sea appear to have been really on board a ship guilty of illicit trade, and would, if found on board, have been forfeited by the laws relating to the customs.[125]

Furthermore, the Court of Exchequer was entitled to issue writs of prohibition against the Admiralty Court in order to assert its entitlement to determine whether the goods were smuggled or were wreck:

the manner in which that superiority is exercised is either by prohibition, or order of the Exchequer Court not to proceed in the admiralty, and if they do notwithstanding, attachment will be granted against the contemnors of such prohibition or order … the proper remedy, as that case now stands, is by application to the Court of Exchequer for an order to the officer of the Admiralty Court to whom the money was paid, to repay that sum to the custom house officers who paid it, and to stay all further proceedings in that court – a late case of [*Foster v. Cockburne*][126] in the Exchequer here … should be fully stated and sent over with copies of the orders to the commissioners of the customs.

Baillie continued to attempt to enlist the sympathy of the admiralty commissioners. He accused the chief baron of the Irish Court of Exchequer, John Bowes, of bullying and alleged that he had 'threatened to attach the then advocate of office [James Sheil] … for appearing for the [Admiralty] Court against the commissioners [of customs] unless he showed a power for so doing from their lordships [the commissioners of Admiralty].'[127] The aggressive claims of the customs had, he claimed, wiped out the court's wreck business:[128] 'for these 2 years past we have lost the principal branch of the admiralty perquisites by such seizures, which may amount to betwixt £1,000 to £2,000 a year'.


PRIZE JURISDICTION IN EARLY EIGHTEENTH-CENTURY IRELAND

*The constitutional controversy*

No prize commission had been given to the Irish court since the second Anglo–Dutch War (1665–7). The conventional English position was rehearsed in 1744, on

125  Opinion of D. Ryder and W. Murray, 12 July 1752 [?] (TNA (PRO), ADM 1/3,676, f. 359).
126  Subsequent proceedings in this case are reported in (1744) Park 70; 145 ER 716.
127  H. Baillie to J. Clevland, 1 Jan. 1753 (TNA (PRO), ADM 1/3,882).
128  Ibid.

the outbreak of hostilities with France, when Dr Hawkshaw (in the final months of his life) had enquired about the extent of his power to condemn a French prize ('laden with gold and fish') which had been taken from Newfoundland into Dublin.[129] The judge of the English court, Henry Penrice,[130] emphasized the elimination of the Irish court from any role in prize work: first, he advised, prize commissions could be issued to Irish privateers (such as the famous Luke Mercer) – but only from the English court:

> letters of marque may be granted here, for Dublin or any port in Ireland ... as they are for Bristol, Liverpool, Edinburgh, or any distant port in Great Britain, by virtue of a warrant directed to me from my lords commissioners of Admiralty in the usual form. Instances of this kind are frequent. One very lately was to Luke Mercer of Dublin.

Second, the sole judicial function allowed to Irish officers was in the administration of interrogatories issued by the English court in order to assist prize proceedings in the English Court of Admiralty. Third, the Irish Court of Admiralty had no power to process claims to prize captures:

> there are already standing commissions granted to Dublin, and other ports in Ireland where prizes may be brought in, to examine witnesses ... which examinations, when taken, are to be transmitted to the High Court of Admiralty, and proceedings are thereupon to be had in the same manner as if the examinations were taken at Portsmouth or Plymouth; and this has been the ancient course of proceedings upon prizes brought into ports in Ireland, and I do not know that the vice-admiralty court of Dublin or any other vice-admiralty court in Ireland have proceeded to condemn prizes; neither do I conceive that they have any authority to do so.[131]

Acting on Penrice's advice, the commissioners directed Dr Hawkshaw not to act in prize cases.[132] This prompted Dr Hawkshaw to make a full confession. Throwing himself upon the mercy of the commissioners, he admitted that he had recently condemned a prize. He had been pressurized by the prize captor 'that their prize was in no condition to sail and their fish perishing'.[133] He had 'searched into the precedents in my registry and found several condemnations by this court, and also consulted my patent'.[134] But he now acknowledged that he had been mistaken. This was 'my last and only condemnation'.

---

129  J. Hawkshaw to the commissioners of Admiralty, 28 Aug. 1744 (TNA (PRO), ADM 1/3,990).
130  Sir Henry Penrice was judge of the Court of Admiralty of England from 1715 to 1751.
131  H. Penrice to the admiralty solicitor, 19 Sept. 1744 (TNA (PRO), ADM 1/3,990).
132  J. Burchett to J. Hawkshaw, 20 Sept. 1744 (TNA (PRO), ADM 2/1,054, f. 258).
133  J. Hawkshaw to Corbett, 6 Oct. 1744 (TNA (PRO), ADM 1/3,990).
134  Ibid.

Predictably, however, his successor, Dr Baillie, was more demanding. He determined to obtain prize jurisdiction. Within days of his appointment in January 1745, he had written to the commissioners of Admiralty inquiring as to his power to exercise prize. The commissioners replied, rehearsing the conventional position that the power of condemning prize was contingent on an express prize commission, and that none had been issued to the Irish court: 'It is no part of your patent, but a power given by special commission which does not take place in Ireland'.[135]

But Dr Baillie persisted. In March 1745 he wrote again to the commissioners, arguing that there was a strong mercantile interest in the grant of a prize commission, and that the concession of this entitlement would act as an incentive to Irish ship owners to seek letters of marque and assist in the war effort against France. Indiscreetly, the secretary of the Admiralty admitted to Baillie that the conferment of prize jurisdiction on the Irish court was likely to cause diplomatic problems in London, with the English court objecting to a measure which would reduce the profits derived from their prize business: 'The High Court of Admiralty here act by virtue of such a special power, and as it is a considerable perquisite to these officers, they will probably be glad to appropriate it to themselves'.[136]

Baillies's campaign was supplemented by an elaborate memorial addressed to the English Privy Council.[137] Although the memorial was submitted under the name of the 'merchants of Dublin concerned in fitting out privateers to distress his majesty's enemies', it looked suspiciously like it had been manufactured by Baillie himself.[138] Baillie also maintained an insistent letter-writing campaign. He based the claim on three legal arguments. First, a search of the Irish court's archives had uncovered four precedents from the early 1690s[139] in which the Irish court had condemned prize captures. These condemnations had been processed despite the fact that the court had not been granted any prize commission: 'Neither from the books, the registrar, the practitioners, nor anybody else, can I find that the condemnations here were by any other authority than that of the judge admiral's commission as such'.[140] These precedents, he argued, proved that the court did not require an express commission. This interpretation was, he claimed, supported by

135   R. Osborn to H. Baillie, 22 Jan. 1745 (TNA (PRO), ADM 2/1,054, f. 292).
136   R. Osborn to H. Baillie, 14 Mar. 1745 (TNA (PRO), ADM 2/1,054, f. 311).
137   'The petition of the merchants of Dublin concerned in fitting out privateers to distress his majesty's enemies' (TNA (PRO), PC 2/102).
138   The fact that no names were subscribed to the petition suggests doubts about whether this was really the work of 'the merchants of Dublin'. The arguments in this petition corresponded to those that Baillie had earlier made: that Irish privateers taking captured vessels into Irish ports endured delay and expense in having to await condemnation by the busy English court.
139   The *Two Williams of Bordeaux* & *St Laurence of Bordeaux* (11 July 1691, Dr Dudley Loftus, surrogate of Sir Paul Rycaut); the *Swallow of St Malo* (17 Nov. 1691, Dr Dudley Loftus) & the *St Michael of Dunkirk* (17 Dec. 1691, Dr Dudley Loftus), H. Baillie to the commissioners of Admiralty, 17 May 1745 (TNA (PRO), ADM, 1/3,990).
140   H. Baillie to T. Corbett, 21 May 1745 (TNA (PRO), ADM 1/3,990).

senior legal opinion in Ireland: 'indeed I laid the case before the prime serjeant, and some of the lawyers here of the best reputation, and they thought no more necessary'.[141] Second, he relied on the Scottish position; he pointed out that the judge of the Court of Admiralty of Scotland acted without a special patent to condemn prizes.[142] Third, and this was probably his strongest argument, Baillie made the point that the Naval Prize Act of 1744 implicitly assumed that the Court of Admiralty of Ireland was intended to enjoy prize jurisdiction.[143] The recital, with which the Act of 1744 opened, declared that privateers were to have 'the sole interest and property of, and in, all [prize]' which had been condemned by one of a number of prize courts. That schedule of courts included the Admiralty Court of Ireland:

> being first adjudged lawful prize in any of his majesty's Courts of Admiralty of Great Britain *or Ireland* or any of his plantations in America or other Dominions of Great Britain …

The explicit mention of the Irish Court of Admiralty as a prize court was the key to Baillie's argument. It provided him with a strong foundation from which to contend that the legislative assumption in 1744 was that the Irish court should exercise prize jurisdiction.

In May 1745 the secretary of the Admiralty commissioners wrote to Baillie asking him to provide 'an account of the authority by which prize cases were tried in the Wars of King William and Queen Anne'. Baillie returned a list of four vessels condemned in 1691 during Sir Paul Rycaut's tenure, together with the one condemnation by Sir William Petty in 1677 following the Third Anglo–Dutch War.[144] While five instances over a period of almost forty years hardly amounted to proof of a notorious jurisdiction, the commissioners were showing signs of relenting. On 4 June 1745, overruling English legal opinion,[145] the commissioners met and directed that a prize court be established in Dublin.[146]

This historic concession to Ireland was soon under attack. In the following year, 1746, the whole question was re-opened. It was prompted when the Commissioners for Prize Appeals raised the question of whether they had, under the terms of their commission, jurisdiction to determine appeals from prize decisions arising in Ireland. An appeal had been brought before the commissioners by the claimants in

141  Ibid.
142  William Murray advised the Admiralty that 'it was not the usage to issue such special notifications to the High Court of Admiralty of Scotland' and that 'the judges of that court have sufficient authority to proceed in the trial and condemnation of prizes without any special commission from the lords of the Admiralty for that purpose'. Opinion of W. Murray & G. Lee, 29 Oct. 1746 (TNA (PRO), ADM 1/3,885, f. 591).
143  17 Geo. II, c. 34 (Eng.), 1744.
144  *Golden Salmon*, 29 Oct. 1677 (TNA (PRO), ADM, 1/3,990).
145  W. Strahan to the commissioners of Admiralty, 10 June 1745 (TNA (PRO), ADM 1/3,990).
146  TNA (PRO), ADM 2/1,054, f. 339.

the *St Philipe of Isle Dieu* (which had been seized by Ireland's most active privateer, Luke Mercer). The commissioners, when they had been established in 1689, were given jurisdiction to hear appeals from Great Britain and the American Plantations, but none from the jurisdictions which had most recently been granted prize jurisdiction – Ireland and Gibraltar.

A sub-committee, consisting of the English solicitor general, William Murray, and the king's advocate, Dr George Paul,[147] was established. The obvious solution was to amend the terms of the commission by including Ireland. But instead the law officers proposed a much more radical suggestion: that the grant of prize jurisdiction to the Irish court simply be rescinded. Parliament, they argued, had not seriously considered the implications of constituting a prize court in Ireland when it enacted the Prize Act 1744, and there were policy objections to such an extension:

> it is advisable to supersede the commission given to the said vice-admiralty court in Ireland to try prize causes. When the Acts which passed in the sixth year of Queen Anne and in the 13th and 17th of his present majesty, for giving prizes to the captor and ascertaining the method of trial, were made, it is manifest the legislature did not think any such jurisdiction would ever be exercised in Ireland; and we apprehend that there are many objections to the making this innovation now.[148]

However the Admiralty commissioners, for the moment at least, stood their ground. They defended their previous decision[149] to grant admiralty jurisdiction on the ground of the expense and delay involved in the alternative of an exclusively English-based prize court:

> their lordships are of opinion (notwithstanding the advice of the learned gentlemen … to supersede their lordships' commission) that it will be a very great hardship and discouragement to the fitters out of privateers, not to be allowed to have such prizes as they bring into Ireland tried there, if they desire it, considering the expense and delay attending their transmitting the necessary papers and evidence over to England, and prosecuting their prizes in a court where trials will thereby be so multiplied, that the proceedings upon them may be drawn into inconvenient length.[150]

147  George Paul (King's advocate, 1727–55) and William Murray (solicitor general, 1742–54).
148  Report of Murray and Paul, 28 Mar. 1746 (TNA (PRO), PC 1/5/102, f. 5).
149  The commissioners acknowledged that they had been influenced by the Dublin merchants' petition (see fn. 137 above): '[The Admiralty commissioners] do not indeed find that the Court of Admiralty in Ireland was ever vested with any legal power to try causes (though the judges of that court have sometimes erroneously done it) before the commission granted by their lordships dated the 4th June last which was done upon a petition of merchants in Dublin concerned in fitting out privateers for the reasons mentioned in their petition'. Report of the commissioners of Admiralty to the Privy Council, 7 May 1746 (TNA (PRO), ADM 2/1,054, f. 443).
150  Ibid.

The Privy Council overruled the law officers' recommendation, preferring the advice of the Admiralty that the *status quo* be maintained. The Irish prize court lasted for three years. Between 1745 and 1748 the Irish Court of Admiralty enjoyed that lucrative prize jurisdiction – Baillie's fee income doubled from about 50 to 100 guineas per year –[151] which it had been denied since the 1660s. This concession was, however, to be merely temporary.

*1756: illegal prize condemnation and the dismissal of Baillie*

In 1755, on the eve of the outbreak of the Seven Years War, Baillie mentioned his concern that 'the vice-admiral of Munster intends to apply for a commission to condemn prizes should war occur with Spain'.[152] The English advocate, Charles Pinfold, anxious that prize business be retained exclusively in the hands of the English Court of Admiralty, set out as the principal policy argument against constituting prize courts anywhere in Ireland: the risk that captors would engage in forum-shopping, taking their captures to weaker Irish courts:

> [Litigants] often occasion many improper methods to be used in order to obtain causes and business to be brought before a particular court. In prize causes the reasons against concurrent jurisdictions are much stronger because the parties concerned are foreigners living at a great distance, ignorant of the nature of [the] jurisdiction, and ought therefore to be subject to one known, settled place of judicature, where they may be supposed to have agents to enter their claims in cases of captures and proper assistance; for which reasons before the last war no instance appears of any power being granted to any court in Ireland to consider prizes.[153]

On 18 May 1756 hostilities with the French were formally proclaimed. Instructions were issued to the English Court of Admiralty to try and condemn prize captures. Similar commissions were issued to the eighteen American and Caribbean vice-admiralties, and to Gibraltar and Minorca.[154] The notable omission was the Court of Admiralty of Ireland. Parliament also took the precaution of excluding the Irish court. The prize legislation of 1744 had expressly included the Irish court in its schedule of prize courts; the Prize Act of 1756 did not.[155]

On the day following the proclamation of war, a French ship, the *Brilliant*, sailing from St Domingo, and freighted with sugar and indigo, got into trouble in the Irish Sea. She was piloted into Passage, Waterford by a fishing vessel. On reaching Passage she had first been seized by the tide surveyor. She was then taken

---

151  Petition of H. Baillie, *c.*1752 (TNA (PRO), ADM 1/3,882).
152  Petition of H. Baillie, 1755 (TNA (PRO), ADM 7/298, f. 509).
153  Opinion of C. Pinfold, 5 May 1755 (TNA (PRO), 7/298, f. 513).
154  5 June 1756 (TNA (PRO), ADM 2/1,055, f. 402).
155  'An act for the Encouragement of Seamen', 29 Geo. II, c. 34 (Eng.), 1756.

by a group of soldiers from Duncannon Fort. Four claims to the prize were submitted: by the surveyor, by army officers at Duncannon, by the fishermen (for salvage) and by the Corporation of Waterford (by reference to the admiralty jurisdiction in its patent). The judge of the Admiralty Court of Munster (William Austin) had become involved, claiming that he was entitled to judge the suit. On 25 May both Baillie and James Sheil, the admiralty advocate in Ireland, wrote to the Admiralty commissioners informing them that the precaution had been taken of issuing a mandate for the arrest of the ship;[156] they were careful not to claim that the Irish court had the right to judge the suit. The Admiralty in London, anxious to avoid 'doubts about jurisdiction', ordered that the ship be taken out of the hands of the Irish court, and that the she and her cargo be taken over to Deptford to be proceeded against in the English court.[157]

But, on the second occasion that a prize was taken into Ireland, the Irish court became more assertive. In July 1756 the *Anson*, an English privateering vessel, captured a French vessel, the *Young Alexander*. The *Young Alexander* was taken into Kinsale, where the master, 'preparing to go out on another cruise', and wishing to dispose of the vessel, gave instructions to his agent to notify the Irish court and to initiate a prize suit. A prize court duly assembled on 28 August 1756.

A preliminary objection was made to the competence of the court on the ground of its lack of a prize commission. Dr Baillie overruled this objection, employing a strained argument based on the wording of the Prize Act 1756. Baillie's principal argument was based on an implication in the phrase 'or elsewhere' in section 3 of that Act. The Prize Act 1744 had assumed that the Irish court would have prize jurisdiction. Parliament had been careful not to expressly include the Irish court in the Prize Act of 1756. But, while not explicitly mentioned, Baillie thought that the Irish court was still implicitly included in the 1756 Act. Section 3 of the 1756 Act imposed a statutory duty, punishable by a £500 fine, on judges to process prize seizures within five days of the capture being taken in. The courts of admiralty which were identified as subject to this statutory duty were the *'judges of his majesty's courts of admiralty in Great Britain*, or in his majesty's plantations in America *or elsewhere'*. Dr Baillie's argument was that although the Irish court was not, of course, one of his 'majesty's courts of admiralty in Great Britain', it was of one of his majesty's courts of admiralty *'elsewhere'*. Diverting responsibility from himself, he suggested that he had been threatened by the advocate who acted for the captor with the penalties under section 3: who had 'humbly insisted that unless the judge of the court proceeded herein, that he was subject to the penalty of £500':[158]

156  TNA (PRO), ADM 1/3822; TNA (PRO), ADM 2/1055, ff 420 & 428.
157  S. Seddon to the commissioners of Admiralty, 14 June 1756 (TNA (PRO), ADM 1/3,677). Seddon was admiralty solicitor, 1749–8.
158  TNA (PRO), ADM 1/3,883, f. 18.

the said advocates and counsel prayed and humbly insisted that this court should, and ought *ex debito justitiae*, proceed in the said condemnation without delay, pursuant to the act of Parliament lately made in the 29th year of his present majesty's reign,[159] and humbly insisted that unless the judges of the court proceeded herein, that he was subject to the penalty of £500 in the said act mentioned. and to the damages which should be sustained by the [captor] by the said courts not proceeding pursuant to the said act.

A fortnight later the Irish court began hearing a prize suit involving a second (unnamed) French vessel, also brought in by the Cork privateer the *Anson*.[160]

Intelligence that the Irish court was again proceeding in prize was passed to the Admiralty in London by the proprietors of the privateering vessel. This privateer had become concerned after receiving a legal opinion in England that, since there existed no lawfully commissioned prize court in Ireland, a prize condemned in Ireland was void, and would give him no proper title. Extremely anxious about the validity of his title, the owners sought clarification from the Admiralty as to the legality of the proceedings in Ireland.[161]

The Admiralty, alerted to what was happening in Dublin, begun taking soundings at the highest level.[162] A consultation was undertaken with the attorney general, William Murray, to discuss the problem of 'the judge of the Admiralty Court in Ireland having lately condemned two prizes in Ireland, without a commission authorizing him to do so'.[163] An opinion was also commissioned from the admiralty advocate, Charles Pinfold, who, unsurprisingly in the light of his long opposition to the Irish Admiralty Court, enthusiastically confirmed the illegality of the proceedings. Baillie, becoming increasingly reckless, responded combatively to Pinfold's opinion. Reprising his constitutional position that, whatever the position in the colonies, the Irish court was not a mere court of vice-admiralty, he complained that 'that gentleman' (Pinfold) had 'thought fit to treat your lordship's High Court of Admiralty of Ireland as a vice-court of admiralty depending on the Court of Admiralty in England'.[164] He mocked Pinfold's vice-admiralty theory: 'by the reasoning of the said doctor in his said opinion we have only in Ireland a vice-Chancellor, a vice-King's Bench, a vice-Court of Common Pleas and a Vice-Exchequer …', and condemned the opinion as an attack on Ireland's constitution:

159  The Prize Act of 1756.
160  These proceedings were effected on 14 Sept. 1756 (TNA (PRO), ADM 1/3,882).
161  14 Sept. 1756 (TNA (PRO), ADM 1/3,882).
162  On 3 September 1756 the secretary to the admiralty commissioners, John Clevland, wrote to Dr Baillie transmitting the Admiralty commissioners' direction that he 'give them an account by virtue of what authority you have proceeded to the condemnation of any ship or vessel taken as prize in the present war'. J. Clevland to H. Baillie, 3 Sept. 1756 (TNA (PRO), ADM 2/1,055, f. 441).
163  10 Sept. 1756 (TNA (PRO), ADM 1/3,883, f. 124).
164  22 Oct. 1756 (TNA (PRO), ADM 1/3,882). The same objection to the characterization of the Irish court as a vice-admiralty court was made in an earlier letter (11 June 1756) to the Admiralty,

This attempt ends not only to take away the rights of the judge and members of the Court of Admiralty here, but also is an attack on the common law lawyers here, who are employed before the Court of Admiralty in almost every prize cause where there is controversy; nay it is an attack on the nation's privileges, by endeavouring to prevent our having a right to do what the courts of admiralty in the meanest plantation abroad had a right to do.

He then compounded the affront by accusing the English court of greed: 'one should think that as the Court of Admiralty in England condemns some score of prizes they would not grudge us the possession of our just rights'. He requested a hearing, in which he would be allowed legal representation, 'in order to convince you of the truth and in order to free ourselves from any encroachments'.

On 1 November 1756 the secretary to the Admiralty, John Clevland, wrote to Baillie: 'I have communicated to my lords commissioners your letter of the 22nd and am to acquaint you that your whole proceedings relating to prize causes is under consideration, and you may soon expect their lordships instructions thereupon'. Two weeks later, on 14 November 1756, the decision was taken to dismiss Dr Baillie, and to replace him with Robert FitzGerald. The news was conveyed to Baillie in a short communication which set out as the ground for his dismissal his 'extraordinary proceedings of late in prize cases, all of which was illegal'.[165]

### Prize procedure in Ireland in the mid-eighteenth century

For three years, between 1745 and 1748, the Irish court enjoyed the lucrative prize jurisdiction which it had been denied since the 1660s: a jurisdiction to condemn prize under a commission granted by the lord admiral. The proceedings before the Court of Admiralty would open with a monition advising potential claimants, wishing to object, of the proceedings against the cargo or the vessel. Claims were to be returned within twenty-one days. In Dublin the monition would be posted 'upon one of the pillars of the Tholsel of our city of Dublin at the usual time of the public resort of merchants thither'.[166]

The principal evidential source used in prize proceedings was the examination of the crew of the captured vessel carried out by reference to standing interrogatories. The administration of these standing interrogatories was conventionally delegated to prominent members of the municipal establishments of Cork,

---

Baillie arguing that both the English and Irish courts were courts of co-ordinate jurisdiction under the same parent: the lord high admiral (TNA (PRO), ADM 1/3,882).

165   'I am commanded by my lords commissioners of Admiralty to let you know that they have taken into consideration your extraordinary proceedings of late in prize causes, all of which was illegal, as having no authority so to do, and have thought fit to dismiss you from your employment as judge of the Admiralty Court in Ireland'. J. Clevland to H. Baillie, 23 Nov. 1756 (TNA (PRO), ADM 2/1,055, f. 459).

166   The text of an Irish prize monition may be found amongst the papers in the *Gran Sultan* appeal to the commissioners for appeals in prize cases (1747) (TNA (PRO), HCA 42/35, f. 12).

Waterford and Dublin. In 1757 Ussher Philpot, mayor of Cork, and the Revd Richard Beare were acting as prize examination commissioners in Cork city; earlier a commission had been issued to 'one Mr Scott a surgeon'.[167]

Concurrently with these Irish prize commissioners, prize examiners appointed by London, and attempting to poach business for the English court, were also stationed in Ireland. This resulted in complaints of encroachment on the autonomy of the Court of Admiralty of Ireland. James Sheil, the admiralty advocate, formulated his protest in constitutional terms. The practice was 'the only case in which any court has interfered in the proceedings in this island, where a proper tribunal has been established here for the decision of it'.[168] He asked the commissioners to take account of 'the inconveniency of scrambling for jurisdiction and the consideration of lowering the office of court here'.

Since it was the established view in Doctors' Commons that the English Court of Admiralty operated concurrently with the Irish court, the appointment of prize examination commissioners by the Court of Admiralty in England was, in the view of English admiralty lawyers, entirely lawful. Captors who had taken vessels into Ireland were free to sue either in the English or Irish courts:

> The jurisdiction of the judge of the High Court of Admiralty extends to Ireland as well as in England; therefore he had a power of granting the commission in question, and the judge of the Admiralty Court of Ireland hath a power of doing the like, so that the proceedings may be in either court the captor pleases.[169]

Prize examination commissions continued, despite Irish protests, to issue from London as late as the 1770s.[170]

These preparatory examinations furnished important evidence about the ownership of the vessel and its cargo. The claimant's case in the *St Francis of Dublin* in 1749 raised issues about the reliability of this testimony. The *St Francis* had been seized in the port of Dublin by the *Dublin Yacht*. The ship's cargo of paper and brandy was alleged to have been shipped from Bordeaux. The case turned on the reliability of the examinations extracted from the crew. Nathaniel Bland, the advocate who appeared for the claimants, alleged that the crew's statements had been compelled under threats of criminal prosecution (for corresponding with the enemy), and threats of violence and of impressment. The captors repeatedly, it was claimed, told the crew to say 'Bordeaux'. The court rejected the evidence and issued a decree against the captors.[171]

---

167  TNA (PRO), HCA 45/5; Memorial of John Love, 16 Apr. 1745 (BL, Add. MS 38,152, f. 89).
168  J. Sheil to the commissioners of Admiralty, 26 May 1757 (TNA (PRO), ADM 1/3,882).
169  6 June 1757 (TNA (PRO), ADM 2/1,055, f. 510).
170  12 July 1779 (TNA (PRO), ADM 1/3,885, f. 437).
171  TNA (PRO), HCA 42/30.

A variety of other sources were also used for establishing the origins of goods. The court admitted translations of the ships' papers;[172] or reports of the cargo undertaken by commissions of mercantile experts appointed by the court.[173] In the *D'Adventure*, in 1758, it was alleged that the mercantile commissioners were biased and incompetent.[174] One of the inspectors, Paul Mayler, was, it was alleged, a book keeper and agent to several of the privateers who were taking ships into Cork harbour, and the other two were, it was alleged, 'in poor, low and indigent circumstances of life'. All, it was claimed, were unskilled in identifying the provenance of sugars. Translators also played an important function in prize litigation; a John Fitzgerald was employed as a translator of Spanish in prize proceedings.[175]

### INTERFERENCE BY PROHIBITION AND REPLEVIN

Intervention by the common law courts in the proceedings of the Court of Admiralty of Ireland continued into the eighteenth century. Replevin remained in eighteenth-century Ireland, as it had been in the seventeenth century, a particularly effective anti-admiralty strategy – Baillie complained that 'every little man of the common law … by replevins and other contrivances take causes of all kinds from the jurisdiction of the court'.[176] Replevin was particularly effective because the marshal did not have the technical legal know-how to resist the process. In 1755, Francis Sherlock, the admiralty marshal, reported that replevin had been issued to re-take vessels from his custody in two recent cases. He had not entered an appearance in the proceedings, and costs had been awarded against him. The admiralty solicitor, writing from London, observed that the source of the difficulty was Sherlock's 'own unskill in the common law proceedings and his backwardness in getting proper advice and assistance'.[177] In 1750 Baillie requested the opinion of the English law officers on the question of 'what is the judge to do when by replevin from any other court an attempt is made to carry off goods or persons subject to the jurisdiction of admiralty …?'[178] The attorney general and solicitor general supplied the obvious answer that a replevin was only an initiatory step. The party granted the replevin was then obliged to pursue an action to prove the illegality of the marshal's possession of the vessel. At that trial, the marshal should plead that he had made a lawful arrest under the legitimate authority of the Admiralty Court:

---

172  The *Vast Betrauwen* (TNA (PRO), HCA 45/1). The court issued a commission to commissioners to inspect goods and to distinguish which parts 'were the growth of France'.
173  Ibid.                                  174  TNA (PRO), HCA 45/4.
175  *St Francis* (TNA (PRO), HCA 42/30, f. 1,112).
176  Petition of H. Baillie 1753 [?] (TNA (PRO), ADM 1/3,885, f. 192).
177  14 Aug. 1755 (TNA (PRO), ADM 1/3,676, f. 488).
178  Opinion of D. Ryder and W. Murray, 23 Jan. 1750 (TNA (PRO), ADM 7/298, f. 439).

as to replevins; if they are not well founded, the truth of the case may be
returned or pleaded, and the court of common law where that shall be tried
can alone determine the justice of such plea, or return. If they find it really
a matter of prize they will not take cognizance of it but they will leave it to
the Admiralty Court. But they must first determine whether it is a matter of
prize according to such return or plea.

Dr Baillie, however, had his own preferred method of dealing with the problem:
he would issue attachment against those using the process of replevin.[179] In 1747
Baillie reported that a ship arrested as prize had been re-seized by a replevin issued
by the Sheriff's Court in Dublin; in response he had 'granted warrants for
attaching those persons who had the chief hand in entering the ship, if they did not
show cause to the contrary at the next court day'.[180] He used the same technique in
the *St Antonio*. This arrest precipitated the most aggressive response taken by a
common law court in the history of the Admiralty Court in Ireland. The *St Antonio*,
a Spanish prize, had been taken into Dublin by the foremost privateer in mid-
eighteenth-century Ireland, Luke Mercer. It was arrested pending prize
condemnation proceedings. In order to avoid condemnation as prize, one of the vessel
owners (John Mernaugh) re-seized the vessel by means of replevin (returnable into
the Common Pleas). The process of reaction and counter-reaction, which the replevin
set in motion, resulted in four subsequent sets of legal proceedings. Firstly, the Court
of Admiralty responded. A rule of attachment for contempt issued out of the court
against Mernaugh (who had procured the replevin); the following day the acting
deputy marshal of the Court of Admiralty arrested Mernaugh. The court had no
prison, so the marshal was compelled to detain Mernaugh in improvised
accommodation – the kitchen of an alehouse owned by an innkeeper called Joseph
Coleman in Bull Alley in central Dublin.

The attachment induced a second legal process. Friends of Mernaugh moved
quickly to rescue him, obtaining a collusive writ of *latitat* (predicated on an action
for debt) from the Court of King's Bench authorizing the arrest of Mernaugh. The
purpose was to use this writ to spring Mernaugh from the custody of the admiralty
marshal. At about five o'clock on the evening the house was raided by Thomas
Edwards, a Dublin merchant (and a companion of Mernaugh), and John Hussey,
an attorney, carrying their King's Bench writ. There was an unpleasant confrontation between Mernaugh's friends and the marshal. Hannah Muckleby, the
pregnant spouse of the deputy admiralty marshal, described how Edwards 'pushed
[me] away with great violence; and Catherine Scanlan, or some person belonging
to the house, crying out: that the woman was with child, the said Edwards made
answer "I don't care if she be with child of the devil"'.[181]

---

179  This technique had also been controversially employed by Dudley Loftus in the *Jacob of Dublin*
     case in the 1680s; see p. 69 above.
180  H. Baillie to the commissioners of Admiralty, 15 Aug. 1747 (TNA (PRO), ADM 1/3,881).
181  'Case relating to certain proceedings in the Court of Admiralty in Ireland against Mr Thomas

1 Sir Adam Loftus, lord chancellor, and judge of Court of Admiralty of Ireland, 1612–19, 1628–38 (photograph courtesy of the National Gallery of Ireland).

2  Sir William Petty, judge of the Irish Court of Admiralty, 1676–83. This portrait by
Edwin Sandys was completed in 1683, the year that Petty resigned from the Irish court.

3 Sir Paul Rycaut (after Sir Peter Lely). Rycaut was an absentee for the greater part of his tenure between 1686 and 1698.

RIDENTEM DICERE VERUM, QUID VETAT? Hor.

W. KING, LL.D. Æt.49.

T. Cook sculp

4  Dr William King, English civil lawyer and judge of the Irish Admiralty Court from
1701 until 1707/08 (image courtesy of the Department of Early Printed Books, Trinity
College Dublin).

5 Jonah Barrington, judge of Court of Admiralty of Ireland from 1797 until his dismissal in 1830 (image courtesy of the National Library of Ireland).

6 Anonymous cartoon *c.*1830, based on the story in the Book of Jonah, showing Jonah Barrington being ejected from the Court of Admiralty (image courtesy of the British Museum).

7 The admiralty proctor Henry Richardson, 1758–1855, in old age. Regarded as 'the most active and responsible officer of the court', Richardson practised from the late-eighteenth to the mid-nineteenth century.

8 John Fitzhenry Townsend who served as judge from 1867 to 1893. Townsend was the last judge of the independent Court of Admiralty of Ireland; following his death the court was integrated into the High Court (Freemasons' Hall, Dublin).

News of Mernaugh's escape was reported to Baillie by Luke Mercer (the captor of the *St Francisco* and *St Antonio*). This led to a third set of proceedings (and a second attachment). Describing the proceedings in the King's Bench as a sham, Baillie issued an attachment against Edwards (who had obtained the writ of *latitat* by means of which Mernaugh had been rescued).[182] Then Edwards (anxious to avoid a spell in Coleman's kitchen) himself then moved in the King's Bench, for a writ of prohibition to stop the attachment proceedings in the Court of Admiralty. The King's Bench acceded to the application. The court held that the power to issue attachment for a rescue was limited to cases where the attaching court had jurisdiction to detain the rescued person.[183] But the Court of Admiralty had no jurisdiction to attach Mernaugh for exercising his legal right to procure a replevin. Accordingly, it could not punish others for his rescue. The judge of Admiralty had no jurisdiction to 'punish a rescue, but as a matter incidental in a cause which he has originally jurisdiction'. Here the judge did not have 'original jurisdiction'. It was Baillie, not Mernaugh, who had acted illegally. But Baillie had not just acted illegally; he had interfered with the process of the Court of King's Bench. Accordingly, an order was made committing the judge of the Court of Admiralty to the custody of the marshal of the King's Bench Marshalsea. Baillie was told 'from the bench that the court [of King's Bench] did not mean to interfere with the jurisdiction of the Admiralty but that they had attached [Dr Baillie] for misbehaviour in his office'.[184]

At first Baillie appeared to relish the chance of martyrdom. He grandly rejected advice that he apologize and apply for his discharge. He preferred to suffer imprisonment and challenge the imprisonment – apparently by writ of error, in the King's Bench in England.[185] Despite his defiance Baillie had begun to suffer physically. Within a few weeks his physicians had certified that he required fresh air, and requested the marshal to allow him temporary respite from prison.[186] The following month he was granted temporary release by the King's Bench on the strength of the report of two physicians who had certified that he was in bad health.[187] In July 1752 Baillie was granted temporary release (on payment of personal sureties on condition that he come up for judgment on the first day of next term).

Edwards, who was attached for contempt by Dr Hugh Baillie, the judge of that court' (TNA (PRO), ADM 1/3,882).

182 Edwards had submitted three arguments against the attachment: (i) that Mernaugh was arrested under a good writ of the King's Bench; (ii) that the arrest of Mernaugh had been illegal by virtue of the inhibition issued by the prize appeal commissioners, which had terminated the Irish Court of Admiralty's jurisdiction in that case; (iii) that the deputy marshal, Alexander Muckleby, had not been lawfully appointed. Baillie overruled all of these objections.

183 W Sheil to the commissioners of Admiralty, 23 Apr. 1752 (TNA (PRO), ADM 1/3,882).

184 Ibid.

185 H. Baillie to the commissioners of Admiralty, 25 Apr., 7 May, 12 May, 3 June 1752 (TNA (PRO), ADM 1/3,882).

186 Ibid.                                    187 Ibid.

The constitutional crisis was now being closely monitored by the Admiralty commissioners in London. The crisis was 'of so much importance' as to demand 'the ablest advice'. Relations between the courts of common law and Court of Admiralty had hardly been warm – they had been involved in jurisdictional running battles since the sixteenth century – but they had never involved the imprisonment of the judge of the Court of Admiralty. The law officers of the Admiralty recommended a diplomatic response, advising that Baillie's counsel[188] should argue that Baillie's period of confinement in the Marshalsea had now sufficiently exhausted his contempt 'because upon all the circumstances of the case, if Dr Baillie's conduct has not, in all respects, been prudent, yet he seems to have met with pretty severe treatment considering his station'.[189] In the end, the King's Bench was not so forgiving. Baillie was discharged after 40 days in prison,[190] and only on undertaking to provide £100 by way of compensation to Edwards.

THE WITHDRAWAL OF THE COURT'S MARITIME REVENUES:
ANCHORAGE AND FISHING LICENCES

Up until the mid-eighteenth century the court had been supported by the revenue derived from a series of maritime taxes: ballastage, fishing licences and anchorage. In the 1750s the revenue stream of the court was diminished by a series of decisions in which the Irish Court of Common Pleas held that two of the Admiralty Court's most important maritime taxes – the power to levy anchorage in Dublin harbour, and the power to grant fishing licences – were unlawful.

*The Dublin anchorage case*

In the first decade of the eighteenth century the Court of Admiralty had ceded the ballastage toll to Dublin Corporation.[191] The next target of Dublin Corporation was anchorage. Dublin was the only port in which anchorage continued to be levied. Campaigns of resistance to the collection of anchorage by the Corporations of Waterford and Cork had been successful in the early eighteenth century, and 'by the means aforesaid the marshal has been in no possession of fees of any port but that of Dublin'.[192] The marshal of the court continued, despite the protests by the corporation,[193] to levy anchorage in Dublin. Anchorage fees (at the rate of 3*s.* and 4*d.*)[194] were levied in return for the services of the water bailiff in maintaining buoys to guide the navigation of ships in the port of Dublin. But there were

188  The admiralty advocate, Dr Clarke.
189  S. Seddon to the commissioners of Admiralty, 4 Oct. 1752 (TNA (PRO), ADM 1/3,676, f. 363).
190  H. Baillie to S. Clevland, 25 Mar. 1756 (TNA (PRO), ADM 1/3,882).
191  See p. 108 above.
192  Petition of William Bodens, 1711 (TNA (PRO), ADM 1/3,668, f. 27).
193  *Cal. anc. rec. Dub.*, vi, p. 383 (4 Apr. 1708).
194  Memorial by H. Baillie, n.d. (TNA (PRO), ADM 1/3,882).

constant complaints about the inefficiency with which the marshal performed his navigational duties. In 1728 Dublin Corporation presented a memorial to the lord lieutenant, Lord John Carteret, seeking an end to the practice of levying anchorage toll, and complaining of the threat to navigational safety caused by the marshal's incompetence:

> all ships entering the harbour pay a duty of anchorage for the erecting and keeping up of such sea marks, which duty has, of late, been demanded by an officer called the marshal and serjeant-at-mace of the admiralty ... that the exercise of admiralty jurisdiction in this harbour by any private person, who depends chiefly on the profits arising from the employment for his support, will always be attended with fatal consequences, in regard the number of ships which have of late years been lost in entering the harbour must be attributed to the neglect of not keeping up and repairing the usual sea marks, and the loss of the ship called *The Friendship* of Bristol, which was stranded on the North Bull on the 26th of January last, was entirely owing to this cause.[195]

Concerned by the report from Dublin, the commissioners of Admiralty demanded sight of the letters patent of the marshal of the Admiralty Court 'wanting to be informed whether the marshal and water bailiff is not by his patent obliged to take care of the buoys in that kingdom'.[196] Six years later James Palmer, the marshal of the Irish Court of Admiralty, was formally censured for being 'very negligent' and failing to secure navigational aids in the port of Dublin.[197] In May 1745 a petition was submitted to Dr Baillie complaining that buoys were not being properly laid in the Liffey.[198] In the 1750s Edward Southwell, the vice-admiral of Munster, was asked to inquire into a complaint by the pilots of the harbour of Kinsale that the harbour 'is entirely filled up with mud, by the using unlawful drag nets'.[199]

In 1751 a decision was taken by Dublin Corporation to test the marshal's right to collect anchorage. On the recommendation of a sub-committee appointed to 'take and use proper methods for discovering and recovering such of the city's lands, royalties, tenements, royalties and rights', the corporation decided to appoint its own water bailiff (Thomas Taylor). In 1752 the attorney of the Corporation of Dublin informed Baillie that it intended to challenge the Admiralty's power of raising anchorage.[200] The corporation's legal strategy was then put into action.

195  'The memorial of the lord mayor, sheriffs, commons, and citizens of the city of Dublin', 15 Feb. 1728, *Cal. anc. rec. Dub.*, vi, p. 408.
196  J. Burchett to S. Browne, 28 May 1728 (TNA (PRO), ADM 2/1,053, f. 34).
197  J. Burchett to J. Palmer, 25 May 1734 (TNA (PRO), ADM 2/1,053, f. 233).
198  Baillie instituted a judicial inquiry, and having examined several witnesses, including the captain of the *Dublin* yacht, Captain Waller concluded that the marshal was not at fault. H. Baillie to the commissioners of Admiralty, 17 May 1745 (TNA (PRO), ADM 1/3,990).
199  J. Clevland to E. Southwell, 31 Jan. 1754 (TNA (PRO), ADM 2/1,055, f. 286).
200  Richard Reade to the commissioners of Admiralty, 17 & 22 Aug. 1752 (TNA (PRO), ADM 1/3,676, ff 342, 344).

Taylor having prevailed upon the proprietors of several vessels to pay anchorage to him, they, in turn, refused to pay a second set of anchorage duties to the admiralty marshal. In retaliation, the marshal distrained some of the rigging. The ship owners then obtained a replevin from the Sheriff's Court for the recovery of the rigging from the Admiralty Court.[201] Subsequently, the proceedings were removed into the Court of Common Pleas in order to test the legality of the anchorage levy.[202]

An opinion on the question of the legality of the power was commissioned from the king's advocate, Dr George Paul.[203] Paul advised that neither the corporation nor the court had the power to levy anchorage.[204] His opinion was premised on the contention that admiralty jurisdiction was exclusively concerned with matters *super altum mare*; it did not extend to 'lands and water joined in ports' or 'as described by the writers on maritime affairs … the land and water between a peninsula, or promontory of land'.[205] Anchorage – a cismarine toll – did not engage matters arising *super altum mare*, and, accordingly, was not an admiralty matter. The charter of 1582 entrusted Dublin with 'the office of admiralty'; but anchorage was not a perquisite of the 'office of admiralty'; accordingly, Dublin could not levy anchorage:

> the most material defect is that [the] grant [in the charter of 1582] precedes from the thing given which is droit or perquisite of admiralty. If it cannot appear that anchorage was ever deemed a perquisite of admiralty then there is nothing given. I have examined the *Black Book of the Admiralty*, a valuable piece of antiquity, and many of the writers upon admiralty affairs. I cannot find that anchorage was ever taken to be a perquisite of admiralty, but always a right inherent in the Crown.

The problem was that this opinion equally undermined the basis of the claim of the Irish Court of Admiralty. If anchorage was not a perquisite of the 'office of admiral' claimable by the corporation then neither was anchorage a perquisite claimable in right of the Admiralty Court. The issue was tried in the Common Pleas which found for Dublin Corporation, though on grounds more straight-forward than those suggested in Paul's opinion: it simply held that the right of

201  Ibid.
202  R. Reade to S. Seddon, 30 Oct. 1752 (TNA (PRO), ADM 1/3,676, f. 370).
203  George Paul, king's advocate, 1727–55. An opinion, dated 6 Mar. 1753, by Dudley Ryder was also to the effect that anchorage did not belong to Dublin: the 'non-payment of this anchorage duty to the city and the constant payment of it to the patentees of the Crown is a very strong proof that it is not one of the droits or perquisites of the Admiralty and does not belong by the charter of 27 Elizabeth' (TNA (PRO), ADM 7/298, f. 485).
204  Opinion of Dr Paul, 28 Feb. 1753 (TNA (PRO), ADM 7/298, f. 475).
205  Dr Paul defined ports as 'those places on the sea coasts which as described by the writers on maritime affairs to be the land and water between a peninsula, or promontory of land, when the sea and land join together, and from which places furthest extends into the sea, a direct line may be drawn to the next projecting line, on the same coast'. Ibid.

anchorage had been transferred to the city of Dublin by the admiralty grant in the charter of 1582. The outlawing of anchorage was a severe loss to the officers of the court: the marshal's profits dropped from about £300 per year to £20 per year.[206]

Dublin Corporation's right of levying of anchorage was short-lived. By statute in 1763, the anchorage duty was converted into an additional ballast charge.[207] The 1763 Act, reciting the need to make 'provision for preventing the many great losses happening for the want of skilful pilots', authorized the levying of fees on vessels using the harbour. The revenue was to be used for appointing pilots, and haven masters, and constructing navigational signals.[208]

*The court of admiralty's fishing licensing power*

In the early 1750s Dr Baillie had begun charging fishermen 5s. and 10d. for the licence to operate fishing vessels.[209] The tax was well established in the seventeenth century, but may have fallen into desuetude in the early part of the eighteenth century. In 1752, it was reported that 'it is alleged by those who dispute this power of granting licences to fishermen that it is a power but lately exercised'.[210] Baillie's reassertion of this recondite taxation power resulted in another suit before the Common Pleas.[211] The case concerned the owner of a dredger fitted for oyster fishing who had obtained a fishing licence from the court. Subsequently a row had occurred between the oyster fisherman and the owner of an oyster bed in Wexford. The oyster bed owner launched an attack from a ferry and threatened the crew 'with severe ill-usage if it ever trespassed again'.[212] The licensed proprietors of the dredger then complained to the Court of Admiralty. The court, in another extravagant exercise of power, directed the arrest of the Arklow ferry. The proprietors were forced to seek relief from the courts of common law – by means of a replevin issued from the Common Pleas to secure the return of the vessel. When called upon by London to justify this uniquely Irish admiralty toll, Dr Baillie relied on the wording of his warrant of appointment, which, rather unconvincingly, he claimed, entrusted him with the 'care of fisheries' and on the 'long usage in the matter'. The Admiralty's legal advisers in London were

206  Memorial of Richard Reade (TNA (PRO), ADM 1/3,882).
207  3 Geo. III, c. 15 (Irl.), 1763.
208  This Act, which effectively superseded the water bailiff, was, in turn, repealed and replaced in 1786 by 26 Geo. III, c. 19 (Irl.), 1786.
209  C. Crespigny, G. Bellas and S. Seddon to J. Clevland, 3 Feb. 1752 (TNA (PRO), ADM 1/3,882).
210  J. Smith to S. Seddon, 1 Aug. 1752 (TNA (PRO), ADM 1/3,676, f. 357). John Smyth was a Dublin attorney appointed by the commissioners of Admiralty to investigate the proceedings against the court in the early 1750s.
211  There had been an earlier case in the Common Pleas: a fisherman who, having been cited to appear in the Court of Admiralty for using a fishing vessel without a licence, was ordered to pay the marshal's costs, and to take out a licence to recover the boat. The fisherman then initiated proceedings in the court of Common Pleas for the recovery of costs and licence money. Baillie lost on a pleading point. J. Smith to S. Seddon, 1 Aug. 1752 (TNA (PRO), ADM 1/3,676, f. 357).
212  Ibid.

embarrassed by Baillie's claim. The right of the subject to fish in the high seas and tidal waters was well established;[213] fishing 'without licence is lawful to all the king's subjects',[214] and the Admiralty Court had no jurisdiction to regulate the exercise of this popular right:

> There is no doubt but that every Admiralty Court has power of punishing the occupiers of unlawful nets and fishers at unlawful seasons; but with respect to the power of granting licences for fishing boats, several of which licenses the Doctor says were given by the court of late … fishing … without licence is lawful to all the king's subjects … The seizure of the boat for fishing without licence is not to be justified; and we humbly submit to their lordships' consideration, whether or not a demand of five shillings and ten pence claimed to be due for granting every such licence can be properly supported out of the public money.

Following a direction from the Admiralty commissioners, Baillie withdrew from the litigation. The Common Pleas made an order of costs against him.[215]

DR BAILLIE'S FINAL YEARS

Hugh Baillie lived for another twenty years after his dismissal from the office of judge. His bitterness was aggravated as all attempts to obtain alternative office were rejected. Baillie's reputation had been so badly damaged that he had come to be regarded as a figure of fun. One admiralty official, in correspondence with Robert FitzGerald (his successor as judge, in 1759) cruelly recalled one of Baillie's eccentric military strategic proposals in which a regiment of bulldogs would be raised for fighting in India. Baillie, he suggested, was not so much corrupt as mad:

> I should [take notice] if the Doctor's character was confined to dishonesty alone, but I really believe the man is mad. And I am much mistaken if the first preferment his scheming had acquired to himself be not in Moorfields. Some time ago there came to my hand a proposal for fighting the Indians with an army of bulldogs which was supported by many learned quotations.[216]

213  *Warren v. Matthews* (1703) 1 Salk 357; 91 ER 312.
214  C. Crespigny, G. Bellas and S. Seddon to J. Clevland, 3 Feb. 1752 (TNA (PRO), ADM 1/3,882).
215  'The memorial and humble petition of Hugh Baillie esq, judge in the High Court of Admiralty in Ireland', (n.d.): 'When the cause was ready for hearing he found by letter from Mr Secretary Clevland that it was your lordships' pleasure that he should not defend that privilege, upon which he immediately went to the Court of Common Pleas and gave it up, but, notwithstanding, the court ordered costs against him; but the Lord Fitzwilliam who supported the suit against the court has not demanded them' (TNA (PRO), ADM 1/3,885, f. 192).
216  R. Wood to R. FitzGerald, 31 May 1759 (PRONI, T 3,075/1/40). Robert Wood was the under-secretary to the Southern Department.

Baillie certainly suffered from defective self-awareness. He had also become an irritant. At least some of the sympathy he had earned with the Admiralty through his period in prison under attachment was cancelled when petitioning John Clevland, the secretary of the commissioners of Admiralty, for a salary he used the ambivalent phrase 'if you can manage this for me, I shall as I wrote you formerly, convince you that I am not ungrateful'. Affronted, Clevland reprimanded Baillie for the insinuation that he might be accessible to bribery: 'what could induce you to think me so mean or dishonest a person as to accept of a bribe I am at a loss to guess'.[217] Incredibly, he repeated the offence in 1755, again requesting a salary and promising Clevland a gratuity of '£100 for your trouble'. At that point the Admiralty secretary severed his relationship with Baillie completely, informing him that he had 'communicated his note there offering me £100 to the Lords of the Admiralty who are equally offended' and instructing him 'not to write to me again'.[218] The touches of paranoia and exaggeration in the correspondence which he transmitted at such a manic rate to the Admiralty in the mid-1750s indicate some degree of psychological disturbance.

The disastrous period in the mid-1750s tainted Baillie's reputation for the next decade. In 1757 he wrote to the lord lieutenant, the duke of Bedford, complaining of his unjust dismissal from the Admiralty. He bitterly complained about the appointment of Robert FitzGerald as his successor, which he identified as a political favour given in return for FitzGerald's support of the Bessborough faction in Parliament, and sought compensation, 'being in the decline of life and deprived of his judicial appointment, being moreover distressed in his personal circumstances'. He identified appropriate compensation as nothing less than appointment to the office of baron of the Court of Exchequer in Ireland.[219] That rather over-ambitious request was turned down. In 1759 an attempt to take up practice in Doctors' Commons was frustrated by the insistence of Doctors' Commons (some of whose members may have recalled Baillie-related incidents from the 1750s) that only lawyers holding an LLD from Oxford or Cambridge were entitled to be admitted. Baillie's qualification was Scottish and he was not eligible.[220] He continued to depend on his 'private fortune'[221] and in the early 1760s may have commenced practice at the Irish chancery bar.[222]

217  J. Clevland to H. Baillie, 25 May 1752 (TNA (PRO), ADM 2/1,055, f. 242).
218  31 July 1755 (TNA (PRO), ADM 1/3,883, f. 40).
219  H. Baillie to the duke of Bedford, 18 Jan. 1757 (PRONI, T 2,915/1/14). A.P.W. Malcomson, ed., *Eighteenth-century Irish official papers in Great Britain* (Belfast, 1990), ii, p. 165.
220  G.D. Squibb, *Doctors' Commons* (Oxford, 1977), p. 41.
221  H. Baillie to the commissioners to Admiralty, 9 Dec. 1752 (TNA (PRO), ADM 1/3,882).
222  'I plead before the chancellor in Ireland'. H. Baillie to Clevland, 11 Mar. 1764 (TNA (PRO), ADM 1/3,883).

However, by the early 1760s relations with the Admiralty had improved and he was considered fit for office again. Firstly, in 1763, Baillie was appointed to the Vice-Admiralty Court of Quebec.[223] However, for reasons which are unclear, he never took up this appointment. Then in 1764, Baillie, while on a visit to London, called on the commissioners with the news that Richard Morris, judge of the Court of Admiralty in New York had died, and volunteered his services as a successor: 'I could make a good deal there as a lawyer where a little knowledge goes a long way'. Surprisingly, he succeeded in persuading the admiralty commissioners that he was fit to be appointed to this important court of admiralty, and in 1764 he was appointed a judge of the Court of Admiralty of New York. However, his bad fortune had not dissipated. His New York appointment was immediately rescinded. Embarrassingly, it turned out that Baillie's intelligence about the demise of Richard Morris was inaccurate. Morris was alive. The admiralty solicitor's record book contains the pathetic entry:[224] 'whereas we thought fit to appoint Richard Morris esq. to be judge of the Vice-Admiralty Court of New York, Connecticut, and the East and West Jerseys in America, in the room of Dr Hugh Baillie, who was lately appointed judge of the said court, upon an erroneous report of Mr Morris being dead'.

In the absence of alternative employment, Dr Baillie survived on his considerable private income, settling in London, where it has been said that his company was sought after 'by the literati being very intelligent and full of anecdote'. His life picked up after the disasters of the 1750s and 1760s: he remarried at the age of eighty, his new bride, Frederica Spence, 'render[ing] his latter days comfortable'.[225] He indulged his recreational interest in foreign affairs, producing a pamphlet promoting the cause of the American colonists and condemning the conciliation of French Catholic Canadians made by the Quebec Act of 1774.[226] Right to the end of his life he regarded the period that he had been judge of the Irish Court of Admiralty as having been his life's principal achievement, and he continued to be embittered by his treatment.[227] He had, he complained in the preface to his 1775 pamphlet on American affairs, not received so much as a sixpence for his work in the Irish court, and yet had been dismissed in favour of a mere political appointee.[228]

---

223   19 Dec. 1763 (TNA (PRO), ADM 2/1,057, f. 159).
224   28 Apr. 1764 (TNA (PRO), ADM 2/1,057, f. 171).
225   *A genealogical account of Ayrshire*, p. 32.
226   *A letter to Dr Shebear: containing a refutation of his arguments concerning the Boston and Quebec Acts of Parliament: and his aspersions upon* ... (London, 1775).
227   Baillie died 15 Aug. 1776; *The Faculty of Advocates in Scotland, 1532–1942*, ed. F.G. Grant (Scottish Records Society, Edinburgh, 1944), p. 8; TNA (PRO), Prob 11/1,022.
228   *A letter to Dr. Shebear*, p. 50.

# CHAPTER FOUR

# Constitutional re-organization and public scandal, 1756–1830

## THE JUDGES OF THE COURT OF ADMIRALTY, 1756–1830

### Robert FitzGerald

HUGH BAILLIE WAS SUCCEEDED as judge of the Court of Admiralty by the barrister (and MP for Dingle) Robert FitzGerald.[1] Embittered, Baillie attributed the appointment of FitzGerald to the politically powerful Ponsonby family. The appointment was FitzGerald's repayment for having voted with the Ponsonbys 'in party questions here'.[2] Although Baillie's judgment was often unreliable he was, on this occasion, correct. Robert FitzGerald's precise point of contact within the faction was John Ponsonby, the speaker of the Irish House of Commons. As an exceptional concession, the first lord of the Admiralty, George Anson, had allowed the power of nomination of the judge to be transferred to the lord lieutenant of Ireland. The lord lieutenant, the duke of Devonshire, was the brother-in-law of John Ponsonby, and was happy to approve Ponsonby's nominee – FitzGerald. This part of the work done, Ponsonby wrote to FitzGerald relating the good news:[3] 'I wrote to you at least a month ago from Chatsworth that Lord Anson had been so good to give the duke of Devonshire the naming a judge of the Admiralty [Court] in Ireland and that his grace had, upon my solicitation, told me he would serve you in it'.

The second part of the process required the confirmation of the Admiralty. This was more of a struggle. The Admiralty was not entirely satisfied that FitzGerald was sufficiently qualified in civil law to serve as their judge in Ireland. Ponsonby had been forced to exaggerate FitzGerald's competence and 'to be your godfather that you are the best civilian in the world'.[4] The first lord of the Admiralty, George Anson, insisted, as a minimum requirement, that FitzGerald obtain a more meaningful civilian qualification. Ponsonby conveyed to FitzGerald the necessity

---

1   13 Nov. 1756 (TNA (PRO), ADM 1/3,677, f. 125).
2   H. Baillie to duke of Bedford, 18 Jan. 1757, *Eighteenth-century official papers in Great Britain*, ed. A.P.W. Malcomson (Belfast, 1990), p. 155.
3   J. Ponsonby to R. FitzGerald, 16 Nov. 1756 (PRONI, T 3,075/1/25).
4   J. Ponsonby to R. FitzGerald, 23 Oct. 1756 (PRONI, T 3,075/1/24).

of obtaining an LLD:[5] 'you must take a doctor of civil laws degree as soon as possible. Lord Anson has been vastly good to me upon this occasion'.[6]

There was a further problem. There had been a change of ministry in England in 1756 and the Admiralty commissioners who had approved FitzGerald's appointment were about to be replaced. Confirmation of FitzGerald's appointment was one of the last acts undertaken by the outgoing commissioners before Pitt's government assumed power:

> You are extremely lucky that I happened to be in London upon the present revolutions in the ministry. Lord Anson and the whole Admiralty is changed, and the signing your commission was the very last act done by them. My brother Duncannon has been extremely kind about it, and went with me to Lord Anson and we got it done the very day before he resigned, which I think was a nick, and entirely owing to my being on the spot and with my brother. I heartily give you joy of it.[7]

Ponsonby stressed again to FitzGerald the embarrassment which would be caused if he did not immediately obtain an LLD degree: 'I have promised the Admiralty and the duke of Devonshire that you would take your degree in civil law and qualify yourself for it, which I have no doubt you will do for your own honour as well as mine'.

The fact that the office of judge of the Admiralty Court of Ireland was entirely unsalaried was particularly frustrating to Robert FitzGerald, a government loyalist who had amassed a collection of remunerated government offices (including an office as commissioner of revenue appeals, controller of customs for Dingle, and a place on the linen board).[8] FitzGerald began a campaign to have a salary attached to the position, beginning with a petition to the lords of the Admiralty. He complained that the sum which he had received by way of fees (£40 arising out of instance litigation, and £43 from prize) had not even been sufficient to cover the expenses which he had incurred in renting a room for the court:

> I have at my own expense rented a court and pay a considerable diurnal rent for it insomuch that in the year ending last December, which was my first year, I was out of pocket by the employment. This your lordships will admit is an uncommon case but upon my honour it is true. The profits of the judge arise from small profits upon the proceedings in court and do not, exclusive of prize, amount to £40 a year, and the judge's fees in prize causes in that year are somewhat short of £43.[9]

5   Ibid.
6   Soon after his call to the Bar, FitzGerald had, in 1744, obtained the degree of LLD *hon causa* from Trinity College Dublin, G.D. Burtchaell & T.U. Sadlier, *Alumni Dublinenses* (Dublin, 1935), p. 286. The Admiralty may have had in mind a more meaningful course of study than the Trinity LLD.
7   J. Ponsonby to R. FitzGerald, 16 Nov. 1756 (PRONI, T 3,075/1/25).
8   W. Hunt, *The Irish Parliament, 1775* (Dublin, 1907), p. 19.
9   R. FitzGerald to the commissioners of Admiralty, 29 June 1758 (TNA (PRO), ADM 1/3,883, f. 13).

When the Admiralty declined to attach a salary, FitzGerald re-directed the pressure to the lord lieutenant, the duke of Bedford. Bedford's objection was that the position could not be paid for by the Irish administration so long as the court remained constitutionally subordinate to the commissioners of Admiralty. In 1756 the lord lieutenant had already been allowed, as a special concession, to nominate the judge. He now insisted, as the condition to placing the judge on the civil list, that that arrangement be made permanent. FitzGerald was informed that 'if the Admiralty will consent that the lord lieutenant of Ireland shall have the nomination to that employment, his grace will agree to the fixing a salary upon it'.[10] There was a constitutional issue of 'general principle, and certainly a very right one: that the government of Ireland shall not pay any officers but such as are of their own appointment'. The Admiralty agreed to the Irish demand for the right of nomination. An arrangement was negotiated between the lord lieutenant and the Admiralty and in 1759 FitzGerald was placed on the civil list on a salary of £300 *per annum*.[11] The 1759 agreement was the beginning of a process in which the constitutional link between the court and London was gradually weakened, and the Admiralty Court was re-orientated from an English to a local institution.

Despite his reputation as a placeman, FitzGerald was not a mere sinecurist. At the beginning of his tenure he worked conscientiously. Later he began delegating the function to the lawyer and MP John Hatch, but when he employed a surrogate he insisted that he was kept briefed about the day-to-day business of the court.[12] By contrast with his chaotic predecessor Baillie, he kept his head down and rarely troubled London with complaints or requests for assistance. In 1757 the Dublin publisher Richard Watts dedicated his *Practice of the Court of Admiralty in Ireland and England*[13] to Robert FitzGerald, noting the 'growing reputation of the court under your administration'.[14] FitzGerald, after two years in office, drafted a glowing self-assessment:

> Doctor Hawkshaw and Doctor Baillie my immediate predecessors filled that post for 48 years but did not bring any great honour or reputation to it. And unquestionably when I had the honour of being appointed by [the Admiralty] to that employment I found it in very low esteem in which many causes have concurred. I flatter myself that since my commencement no complaint hath been made of the denial or delay of justice and that I have at least brought back some regularity to the court. I am very sensible of my want of ability but in assiduity and integrity I cannot yield to any man.[15]

10  R. Rigby to R. FitzGerald, 22 Feb. 1759 (PRONI, T 3,075/1/37).
11  Duke of Bedford to the commissioners of Treasury, 17 Sept. 1759 (TNA (PRO), T 1/397, f. 221).
12  J. Hatch to R. FitzGerald, 21 Aug. 1759 (PRONI, T/3,075/1/43). Hatch was MP for Swords, and the seneschal of the Liberty of St Sepulchre's. Johnston-Liik describes Hatch as 'a lawyer who made his living by looking after the affairs of absentee landlords'. *History of the Irish Parliament*, iv, pp 380–2.
13  Dublin, 1757.                          14  Ibid., p. 3.
15  R. FitzGerald to the commissioners of Admiralty, 29 June 1758 (TNA (PRO), ADM 1/3,883, f. 13).

By the mid-1770s FitzGerald's commitment to the office appears to have been weakening. He increasingly relied on John Hatch to act as his surrogate.[16] In 1776 he settled for retirement. The chief secretary, John Blaquiere, reported that Robert FitzGerald had intimated a desire to retire from the three public offices he held, including the judgeship of the Admiralty Court, in order to 'accommodate [the] government'. FitzGerald did well out of the arrangements for his retirement, receiving a very generous pension of £1,400.[17]

### Warden Flood

In accordance with new constitutional arrangements made between the Irish government and the Admiralty in 1759, the nomination of FitzGerald's successor was placed in the hands of the lord lieutenant. The lord lieutenant informed the prime minister that he was proposing to nominate Warden Flood to the office of judge.[18] The nomination was confirmed in London, and on 15 May 1776 the Admiralty instructed the judge of the English court, George Hay, to draw up a patent for the appointment of Warden Flood as 'judge of the admiralty in Ireland, in the room of Robert FitzGerald esq who has desired leave to resign'.[19] Warden Flood originally demanded a salary of £600 per annum for taking up the post.[20] In the end, the salary was increased, though not quite to the extent desired by Flood, to £500.[21] Warden Flood's background was similar to that of his predecessor. He was a barrister, and a well-connected MP.[22] Warden's cousin, Henry Flood MP, to whom he was close,[23] was vice-treasurer of Ireland, and this cousin's influence may have assisted Warden's appointment.

16   John Hatch LLD is referred to as surrogate of Robert FitzGerald in the papers accompanying the *Venus* appeal to the English Court of Admiralty in 1776 (TNA (PRO), HCA 16/62/340).

17   S. Harcourt to Lord North, 4 May 1776 (TNA (PRO), SP 63/438, f. 185). Johnston-Liik misdates the year of FitzGerald's retirement as 1774 (*History of the Irish Parliament*, iv, p. 157).

18   S. Harcourt to Lord North, 4 May 1776 (TNA (PRO), SP 63/438, f. 185).

19   Commissioners of the admiralty to G. Hay, 15 May 1776 (TNA (PRO), ADM 2/1,058, f. 346).

20   TNA (PRO), SP 63/438, f. 185.

21   A king's letter authorizing the increase was sent on 7 June 1776. The £500 was paid in four instalments: on the feast of St Michael the Archangel; the Nativity; the Annunciation of the Blessed Virgin Mary and the feast of St John the Baptist. In addition to his salary, Flood was also entitled to all the judges' fees without any requirement to account. See the king's letter of appointment, 11 Jan. 1785 (TNA (PRO), HO 100/5, f. 108).

22   *History of the Irish Parliament*, iv, pp 192–4.

23   A contemporary account described Warden Flood as 'a follower of Mr Henry Flood's, and with as much violence but less parts – his object is to be counsellor to the commissioners of revenue': W. Hunt, *The Irish Parliament, 1775* (Dublin, 1907), p. 21.

Within six years, Flood had lost the confidence of the English government. In 1782 the Admiralty began to make preparations for the dismissal of Flood. The law officers were asked to advise on the legal consequences of his dismissal. A copy of Flood's commission was enclosed, and the attorney general was asked whether the Act of Settlement 1701[24] might pose a bar in case 'it shall be found expedient' to remove 'A.B. from his said office without proof of malegestion first made in due course of law?' and 'whether the said A.B. under the said Act can support a right in the said office or to the fees or can he maintain any … actions against any persons on that account and … especially against the judge of the [English] Court of Admiralty for affixing the great seal of the Admiralty to a patent granting the said office to another person?'[25] The law officers advised that Flood's office was during pleasure only, that he was not protected by the Act of Settlement 1701, and that, were he dismissed, he would have no cause of action.

The whole incident is a mystery. There was no firm indication as to what was the cause of this proposed move against Flood. One possibility is that the commissioners were considering dismissing Flood for the same reason that they had dismissed Baillie – that, notwithstanding the absence of a prize commission, he had illegally exercised prize jurisdiction. The Irish court had not been included in the commission issued to all courts of vice-admiralty in 1780 to try captures of Dutch vessels.[26] Notwithstanding the court's exclusion from prize competence, Flood appears to have processed prize captures.[27]

Flood survived the threat of dismissal and the following year was involved in constitutional agitation against the court's connection with the English Court of Admiralty. The Irish Appeals Act 1783[28] had explicitly recognized the judicial sovereignty of Ireland. The Court of Admiralty, deriving its title from the lord admiral of England, and not from the kingdom of Ireland, was an anomaly within this theoretically autochthonous legal system. Henry Flood, the patriot politician (and cousin of the judge) had become determined to add the Court of Admiralty to the catalogue of constitutional grievances. In 1783 the lord lieutenant, Earl Temple, reported that Henry Flood was being assisted in his research into the Court of Admiralty by his cousin, Warden the judge: 'Henry Flood [is] very angry and desponding, but indefatigable by means of his cousin in searching the Admiralty Court in order to proceed upon it, when Parliament meets'.[29]

The Irish administration anticipated the constitutional attack by enacting the Court of Admiralty Act 1783[30] which removed the principal sources of external

---

24   The Act of Settlement 1701 (11 &12 W & M, c. 2 (Eng.), 1701).
25   Opinion of W. Wynne and L. Kenyon, 17 July 1782 (TNA (PRO), ADM 7/300, ff 275, 277).
26   22 Dec. 1780 (TNA (PRO), ADM 2/1,060, f. 306).
27   The *Johannes*, 1781 (TNA (PRO), HCA 41/6).
28   23 Geo. III, c. 28 (Eng.), 1783.
29   Earl Temple to W. Grenville, 22 Jan. 1783 ('The manuscripts of B. Fortescue esq', *Thirteenth Report, Appendix III* (HMC, London, 1892), p. 183).
30   23 & 24 Geo. III, c. 14 (Ire.), 1783.

influence: the right of appointment, previously formally vested in the lord high admiral (but in practice since 1759 exercised by the lord lieutenant of Ireland) was transferred to the government of the kingdom of Ireland; the right of dismissal was transferred from the lord high admiral in London to the Irish Parliament, and the right of appeal was transferred from the High Court of Admiralty in England to a Court of Delegates in Ireland. Despite the consideration given in 1782 to dismissing Flood, George III, acting under section 1 of the Court of Admiralty Act 1783, re-appointed Warden Flood.[31] Flood used the power given by his patent to appoint surrogates, appointing first John Christian,[32] and then the politician and distinguished civil lawyer, Dr Patrick Duigenan. He continued in office until his death, after a long illness, in March 1797.

*Sir Jonah Barrington*

In early February 1797 'common fame alleged [Warden Flood] to be in a dying state'.[33] Without even waiting for him to die, three applications for appointment to his office were submitted to the government. One of these petitions came from the judge of the Prerogative Court, Patrick Duigenan:

> I have been for many years, and before I ever sat in Parliament, his majesty's advocate in the Court of Admiralty. I have never, since I sat in Parliament, asked or received any favour from government. My attention to the interests of the Crown in Parliament … and the civil law has always been my particular interest and study. I would not ever now solicit government in this account were it not that I conceive the passing me over in the disposal of this employment (my present station considered) would tend to lessen me in the eyes of the public.[34]

Duigenan did not, however, offer to resign his other, better-remunerated office of judge of the Prerogative Court. Duigenan's claim to a second judgeship may have been unattractive to a government concerned to distribute its patronage more widely. The member of Parliament for Tuam, Jonah Barrington,[35] who felt that he deserved something more elevated than the only office which he did hold (the

---

31  TNA (PRO), HO 100/5, f. 108 (11 Jan. 1785). On 16 May 1785 the king appointed by letters patent under the great seal of Ireland the four officers of the court: Hugh O'Neill (marshal), Thomas Tisdall (registrar), William Robnet (proctor) and Robert Day (advocate) (TNA (PRO), HO 100/16, f. 366 (16 May 1785)).

32  John Christian LLD is referred to as surrogate of Warden Flood in the 1777 Irish appeal, the *Callabogy* (TNA (PRO), HCA 16/65/3,75A).

33  P. Duigenan to E. Cooke, 2 Feb. 1797 (NAI, OP 29/1/2).

34  Ibid.

35  Jonah Barrington, originally from Athy, had been called to the Irish bar in 1787. His marriage to Catherine Grogan, the daughter of a well-to-do Dublin silk mercer, facilitated his rise in the world, including the purchase of his parliamentary seat, T. Reynolds, *The life of Thomas Reynolds*, 2 vols (London, 1839), ii, p. 351.

sinecure office of clerk of the ships' entries for the port of Dublin ('a position quite inconsistent with my situation')[36] had also petitioned the lord lieutenant;[37] Flood's office 'though little superior in emolument to my own it is in the line of my profession and therefore more valuable to me'. He asked the lord lieutenant to 'oblige though not a very old yet a very faithful servant who has never [had?] any favour from his government'.

There was a strange reference in Barrington's petition: Barrington wrote of 'a vacancy [which] will probably take place immediately in the office of judge of the ecclesiastical courts by the death of Warden Flood'. There was no vacancy in 'the ecclesiastical courts'. The dying Flood was judge of the Admiralty Court. Barrington seems to have been confused about the basic identity of the office for which he was applying. At any rate, notwithstanding the possibility that he stumbled into the position by mistake, Barrington was appointed judge of the Court of Admiralty of Ireland.[38] On 13 April 1797 a warrant issued to draw up the patent constituting Jonah Barrington judge of the Court of Admiralty of Ireland.[39] Barrington certainly had no knowledge of civil or admiralty law. By his own admission he 'was neither a doctor of law nor an advocate when I was appointed'[40]

36  J. Barrington to E. Cooke, 1 Feb. 1797 (NAI, OP 29/1/1). 'At the time Doctor Barrington accepted said office, he had held the office of the ships' entries of Dublin, which had been previously held by Mr George Ponsonby, and was executed solely by deputy, said office being a total sinecure', *Eighteenth Report*, Appendix 2, p. 58.

37  J. Barrington to E. Cooke, 1 Feb. 1797 (NAI, OP 29/1/1).

38  The former lord lieutenant, the earl of Westmoreland, promoted Barrington's application. In 1795 Westmoreland had written to Barrington: 'I have not failed to apprise Lord Camden of your talents and spirit, which were so useful to my government on many occasions'. Anon., *The Georgian era; memoirs of the most eminent persons who have flourished in Great Britain*, 4 vols (London, 1833), ii, p. 337.

39  '… Whereas we are well assured of the loyalty, integrity and ability of our trusty and well beloved Jonah Barrington esq. we are graciously pleased to constitute and appoint him to be judge of our High Court of Admiralty of Ireland in room of Warden Flood esq. deceased; our will and pleasure therefore is that, upon receipt hereof, you do forthwith cause effectual letters patent to be passed under our great seal of our said kingdom for constituting him, the said Jonah Barrington, judge of our High Court of Admiralty in our kingdom aforesaid, to have, hold and enjoy the same unto him the said Jonah Barrington so long as he shall behave himself well therein, with all the rights, powers authorities, jurisdictions, salaries, profits and emoluments to the said office belonging and appertaining in as full and ample manner as the said Warden Flood, or any other person heretofore hath, or of right ought to have held and enjoyed the same. And likewise with power to him the said Jonah Barrington to depute and surrogate in his place one or more deputy or deputies as often as he shall think fit, and such substitute and substitutes at pleasure to revoke, and to exercise, expedite and execute all and singular the premises or any of them by his aforesaid deputy. And you are to cause to be inserted in the said letters patent a clause saving and reserving unto us our heirs and successors the right of constituting and appointing all officers and ministers whatsoever to our High Court of Admiralty of Ireland appertaining and belonging' (TNA (PRO), HO 100/71, f. 245). Several years later the chief justice of the King's Bench, Lord Norbury, expressed doubts about the legality of Barrington's patent. J. Barrington to G. Ponsonby [?] undated, 1806 (NAI, OP 214/111).

40  J. Barrington to C. Lyons, 28 May 1823 (NAI, Frazer MS, No. 6 (73)).

and one contemporary suggested that he had acquired the position 'partly by purchase' and 'partly by his parliamentary interest'.[41] Although the Irish secretary, Thomas Pelham, had originally assured him that the appointment to the Court of Admiralty was to be a purely temporary one,[42] he held office for the next thirty-three years.

Within just two years of his appointment the Irish administration had begun to lose confidence in Barrington. The lord chancellor, John FitzGibbon, had formed an early loathing of Barrington.[43] The first serious conflicts with the government and the lord chancellor concerned prize. In 1798, despite repeated advice that the Irish Court of Admiralty was not competent to process prize captures, Barrington accepted jurisdiction over a rich prize capture, a Greek vessel, the *Madonna*, carrying a Dutch cargo, which had been seized near Dingle.[44] The proceedings were only stopped when the lord chancellor, FitzGibbon, issued a writ of prohibition preventing the Admiralty Court from acting any further. The first signs of the roguery for which Barrington was to be so notorious[45] can be traced to the *Madonna*, where Barrington was alleged to have appropriated hundreds of pounds out of the proceeds of the prize.[46]

There was no restriction on judges of the Admiralty Court practising at the bar,[47] and Barrington, throughout the early years of his career as judge, continued to appear at the common law bar.[48] Between 1790 and 1800 he was also a member of Parliament (sitting between 1790 and 1797 for Tuam, and between 1798 and 1800 for Clogher). By 1801 he was complaining that he did not find being a lawyer sufficiently fulfilling and was threatening a return to politics. However, an attempt to re-enter public life by obtaining a seat in Dublin failed,[49] and Barrington was forced back on his career as a lawyer and judge. He was also suffering serious money troubles. In August 1804 he had entered into an arrangement with a Dr Rankin, under which he borrowed £2,409. The loan was to be repaid by way of an assignment of Barrington's salary to a receiver who would collect the salary from Dublin Castle. With his salary diverted to his creditors, and desperate for cash, he commenced in 1805 a campaign to quadruple the salary attached to the office. A memorial seeking a pay rise was referred to the judge of the English court, William

41  T. Reynolds, *The life of Thomas Reynolds*, 2 vols (London, 1839), ii, p. 351.

42  J. Barrington, 'Statement as to the High Court of Admiralty and the judge thereof' (NAI, CSORP, 1828/983).

43  See p. 191 below.                    44  NAI, OP 65/7.

45  Reynolds, *The life of Thomas Reynolds*, ii, p. 353. The Reynolds' memoir describes an incident in which money lent to Barrington's son in Portugal was never re-paid.

46  Evidence of Henry Richardson, *Eighteenth Report*, Appendix 21, p. 195.

47  'To his majesty in council the humble memorial of Jonah Barrington, esquire, LLD one of his majesty's counsel at law, and judge of his High Court of Admiralty of Ireland', 1806 (NAI, OP 214/11).

48  J. Barrington to G. Ponsonby, 11 July 1806 (NAI, OP 214/11). He ceased to practice in April 1805 on faith of a promise that his judicial salary would be increased.

49  *History of the Irish Parliament*, iii, p. 137.

Scott. Scott helpfully recommended to the Irish Secretary, Nicholas Vansittart, that Barrington's demand be met. He was

> strongly impressed with the reasonableness of Dr Barrington's application, and think a compliance with it essentially connected with the purity and reputation of the administration of justice in an important part of its jurisprudence … if an act of Parliament should be deemed necessary, it shall have my hearty support. I know of no person here, who has expressed any opinion at all upon the augmentation of salary, that has objected to £2,000 as unreasonable.[50]

Barrington's principal argument was that the salary of £480 *per annum* attached to the office[51] was so insufficient that the judge was forced to continue legal practice. This, in turn, prevented the court from functioning on a full-term basis: 'the indispensable attendance of the admiralty judge to his professional duties as a barrister, during terms, and on circuits, render punctual and uninterrupted sittings of the Admiralty Court quite impracticable; and consequently, the sittings are irregular and decisions protracted'. Another consequence of being obliged to practise as a barrister was that he necessarily took instructions from solicitors, who then reappeared as proctors when he sat as judge of the Admiralty Court. This compromised 'the due distance of judge and proctor'.[52] Barrington also complained of under-payment relative to other judges of comparative rank. He was paid 'five times less than the puisne judges of the superior courts of common law' and made the ludicrous claim that the office of judge of the Irish Admiralty Court was attended 'with more constant labour, and much greater responsibility'.

Sensing that he was unlikely to be favoured by the Irish administration,[53] Barrington, in 1805, deputed his judicial business to a surrogate, Dr William Thomas, and departed for London in order to pursue his application for a salary rise before the Treasury. This was a move which caused offence on all sides. The lord lieutenant was angered by Barrington's going directly to London, and not first making his application in Dublin. The lord chancellor, Baron Redesdale (who had as low a regard for Barrington as his predecessor, FitzGibbon) censured Barrington for going behind the back of the Irish administration, and 'an attempt to carry a measure by solicitation in England in opposition to the Irish government'.[54]

50  11 May 1805 (NAI, OP 214/11); Barrington to Hardwicke, 19 June 1805 (BL, Add. MS 35,760, f. 76).
51  In addition there was a retirement annuity of £400 attached to the office of judge of the Irish Court of Admiralty (40 Geo. III, c. 69 (Ire.), 1800).
52  Memorial of Jonah Barrington, 1806 (NAI, OP 214/11).
53  The application had originally been referred to the Irish lord chancellor and the chief justice of the Court of King's Bench, William Downes, the chief justice of the Court of Common Pleas, Baron Norbury, and the chief baron of the Court of Exchequer, Standish O'Grady. Hardwicke to Baron Redesdale, 27 Aug. 1805 (BL, Add. MS 35,761, f. 219); Hardwicke to Hawkesbury, 4 Sept. 1805 (BL, Add. MS 35,761, f. 281).
54  Baron Redesdale to the earl of Hardwicke, 2 Nov. 1805 (BL, Add. MS 35,718, f. 160).

He was also accused of deliberately deceiving senior figures in the Irish administration into believing that the request had been sanctioned by the lord lieutenant (when it had not).[55]

Barrington had taken up residence in London in order to advance his campaign. This was not Barrington's first prolonged absence from judicial duties,[56] and it provoked Baron Redesdale to remark that Barrington's casual abandonment of the court compromised his assertion that his work had expanded so significantly as to justify an augmentation in salary: 'some surprise has been expressed at your remaining so long in England if the business of the Court of Admiralty is of so important and pressing a nature as represented by you'.[57] Redesdale warned Barrington to return to Ireland: 'I therefore think it my duty to tell you that if you imagine that by staying in England you are acting in conformity to any wish of the Irish government you are much deceived'.

Baron Redesdale, who believed Barrington unfit for office, advised the lord lieutenant, the earl of Hardwicke, that the salary could only be increased on condition that the post was handed to a judge more reliable than Barrington; it was 'highly imprudent to do so without putting the office of judge of the admiralty in better hands'.[58] Late in 1805 a report by the senior Irish judges (the lord chancellor, Redesdale; the chief justice of the Court of King's Bench, William Downes; the chief justice of the Court of Common Pleas, Baron Norbury; and the chief baron of the Court of Exchequer, Standish O'Grady) recommended that no increase in the salary of the judge of the Admiralty Court be conceded.[59]

In 1806, following the change of government in London, and the election of the Fox-Grenville 'ministry of all the talents', Barrington renewed his campaign with the incoming government. He claimed that he had been victimized by the previous administration, particularly Redesdale, and hinted that this prejudice had its origin in other matters 'not fit to be committed to writing'.[60] Between April and July 1806 he presented the new lord chancellor of Ireland, George Ponsonby, with seven separate applications. Barrington's argument was quite convincingly organized. He argued that the Admiralty judge was comparatively under-paid: the judge of the Prerogative Court sat for 100 days and was paid £2,000; puisne judges sat for 110 days and were paid £2,000 *per annum*; yet the Admiralty judge who, he

---

55  Baron Redesdale to J. Barrington, 23 Oct. 1805: 'Mr Vansittart, I understand, considers himself as misled by the representation made to him that the application was made by you in England under the sanction of his excellency's approbation' (NAI, OP 214/11).

56  In 1802 Barrington ceased to sit in protest against physical conditions in the court. See p. 186 below.

57  Baron Redesdale to J. Barrington, 23 Oct. 1805 (NAI, OP 214/11). In 1805 the Danish consul had also complained that 'there is no judge and the power is exercised by the petty officers'. G. Eskildson to A. Marsden, 17 Sept. 1805 (NAI, OP 200/8).

58  Baron Redesdale to Earl Hardwicke, 5 Sept. 1805 (BL, Add. MS 35,718, f. 141).

59  Baron Redesdale to J. Barrington, 23 Oct. 1805 (NAI, OP 214/11).

60  J. Barrington to chief secretary's office, *c.* 1806 (NAI, OP 214/11 (2)).

claimed, sat for between 80 and 100 days was paid only £484.[61] The remuneration of the judge of the Admiralty Court of Scotland had been raised to nearly £1,000, while the salary of the comparable judge of the Irish Admiralty Court was half that amount.[62]

This campaign was a complete success. The new Irish lord chancellor, George Ponsonby, recommended a doubling of the judge's salary. In 1807 the lord lieutenant justified his decision in a memorandum to the prime minister, Lord Grenville:[63]

> His salary upon the civil list is but five hundred pounds a year, subject to deductions. The lord chancellor ... made particular investigation into the duties of that court, and, after full consideration, has stated to me his opinion that one thousand pounds is but a fair and reasonable remuneration for the services which are to be performed, and that the judge of the Court of Admiralty in Scotland receives now by act of Parliament as large a stipend, and has probably not as much duty to perform. His lordship has also represented that, from the length of time this matter has been depending, he thinks it just that the additional salary should commence from as early a period as it may be granted.[64]

By 1809 Barrington's arrangements with his creditors were becoming even more chaotic. Barrington entered into a further series of loan agreements, this time with a wealthy Dublin saddler, Fennel Collins. Collins lent Barrington £5,080 in exchange for an assignment of his judge's salary, and, as security, Barrington deposited the seal of office of judge of the Court of Admiralty with Collins.[65] This, of course, was the very same arrangement to which he had committed himself to Rankin in August 1804.[66] Rankin, who at this stage knew that Barrington was in a 'very embarrassed state', instructed Dublin Castle to ignore the assignment to Collins.[67] Collins then waited on Barrington who breezily agreed that he had swindled him.

In an even more outrageous move, Barrington managed to regain the salary he had assigned to Rankin. An opinion by the attorney general, William Saurin, confirmed that the assignment of Barrington's salary to Rankin infringed the Sale of Offices Act 1809 (which made void agreements for the sale of an office which 'touched or concerned the administration of execution of justice').[68] Accordingly, the

---

61 J. Barrington to G. Ponsonby, 11 July 1806 (NAI, OP 214/11).
62 J. Barrington to G. Ponsonby, 8 June 1806, ibid.
63 Duke of Bedford to Lord Grenville, 6 Jan. 1807, *Report on the manuscripts of J.B. Fortescue, IX, 1807–1809* (HMC, London, 1915), p.6.
64 Barrington claimed that Ponsonby had undertaken that the salary would be further increased to £2,000 when Barrington ceased private practice at the Bar (NAI, CSORP, 1828/983).
65 Petition of Mrs Anne Collins, 1824 (NAI, CSORP, 1824/9,665). A petition was sent to Sir Robert Peel on 17 Apr. 1829 (NAI, OP 611/15).
66 See p. 158 above.                    67 BL, Add. MS 40,234, f. 84.
68 The Sale of Public Offices Act 1809 (49 Geo. III, c. 126) had extended the Sale of Offices Act 1551 (5 & 6 Edw. VI, c. 16 (Eng.)) to Ireland.

assignment to Rankin was void. Barrington presented Saurin's opinion to the Treasury, which then stopped paying Rankin. The payments to Barrington resumed.

With his salary restored, Barrington departed Ireland and the Court of Admiralty, settling first in London. Barrington's official excuse for departing Dublin was his medical condition. He complained of suffering 'severe indispositions ... [of having] been affected by an acute nervous disorder and other bodily complaints'.[69] He claimed that his 'life has been several times despaired of' and that he needed to escape 'damp or cold seasons or climates'. He did not explain why he found London (or his other retreat, Beaumaris in Wales) a more effective relief from the 'damp or cold seasons' which threatened his life in Ireland. In 1811 he was, on the nomination of the kindly William Scott (a relationship which Barrington carefully cultivated throughout his life) admitted *speciali gratia* to the English bar.[70] His new objective appears to have been to exchange his Irish Court of Admiralty appointment for a place on the colonial legal service.[71] In receipt of his salary once more, he was described as 'living as it seems in very great comfort and engaging in all sorts of amusements'.[72] This security was threatened when his creditor, Rankin, tracked him down, and commenced proceedings in England; although judgment was obtained, it could not be executed. Barrington took elaborate precautions to avoid execution; it was reported that he:

> almost daily chang[ed] his residence ... he also, as it has been ascertained, [was] employing parties constantly to search the sheriff's books that they might appraise him of any measures taken against his person.

In 1812 Barrington skipped the jurisdiction, settling first in Boulogne-sur-Mer, home to a large expatriate population, and a favourite refuge of the early nineteenth-century British debtor.[73] The persistent Rankin followed him to France, and in 1818 commenced proceedings to recover the Irish debt.[74]

Prior to his departure in September 1810, Barrington drew up a commission of surrogacy to the barrister and civilian advocate, Ninian Mahaffy.[75] (Mahaffy was exceptionally tall; according to an innocent contemporary witticism, with Mahaffy in charge, the court was now 'very fitly called the *High* Court of

69  J. Barrington, 'Statement as to the High Court of Admiralty and the judge thereof' (NAI, CSORP, 1828/983).

70  In 1827 Barrington noted 'the most flattering eulogies written to me by Lord Stowell [William Scott] on my book', J. Barrington to C. Lyons, 10 Aug. 1827 (NLI, MS 1,723, f. 16).

71  Rankin's petition, 15 July 1814 (BL, Add. MS 40,234, f. 84).

72  Ibid.

73  'One of the chief British colonies abroad', *A handbook for travellers in France* (London, 1843), p. 12.

74  J. Barrington to C. Lyons, 10 July 1818 (NAI, Frazer MS No. 6 (44)).

75  The patent of surrogacy was dated 15 Sept. 1810 (*Fourth Report*, p. 28; *Eighteenth Report*, p. 6). Mahaffy had been called to the bar in 1788, and acquired an LLD in 1798, *Alumni Dublinenses*, ii, 547; *Stewart's Almanack 1802*, p. 67.

Admiralty'.)[76] Mahaffy undertook the responsibility of deputizing for Barrington from motives 'of private friendship'[77] and certainly not for reasons of private gain since he was entitled to no salary and received only the token sum generated by fees. The fees received by Mahaffy for the three years ending in 1814 amounted to no more than £12 13*s*. 4*d*. In order to relieve the burden on Mahaffy, further auxiliary commissions were granted to the senior advocates of the court: Doctors Duigenan, William Vavasour and William Ridgeway.[78] Ridgeway proved unsuitable and in 1818 Barrington granted a deputation to Dr Jameson, the receiver of the Chancery, to sit with Mahaffy in a two-judge court.[79] Jameson also, on occasion, sat as sole judge.

The principal surrogate, Mahaffy, appears, however, to have been slow, and there were complaints about his competence. In 1817 a piece in the English daily, the *Morning Chronicle*, was highly critical

> a gentleman, a circuit barrister, has occasionally attended in the law term, as if to do the duty of the court, but not having an interest in the performance of that duty, nor a competent knowledge of the law and practice of the court, the business is managed in such a manner as to give no manner of satisfaction, and attended with such delays, and consequent expenses, that merchants and ship owners have an horror of entering into contest in the court.[80]

In 1818, a memorial subscribed by the proctors of the court criticizing the state of the court, was presented to the chief secretary. In the following year, a memorial containing the same complaint, presented by a group describing itself as 'the merchants of Dublin', was submitted to Dublin Castle.[81] The problem was aggravated by the fact that the registrar of the court, Daniel Pineau, was also acting through a deputy, John Robinson, who himself was frequently absent and inefficient.[82]

By 1823 Mahaffy was terminally ill. In light of the 'incapacitation' of his surrogate Barrington was obliged to replace him.[83] The first of his nominees was

---

76  *London Literary Gazette*, 15 July 1820.        77  *Fourth Report*, p. 30.
78  *History of the Irish Parliament*, iv, pp 84–7. William Vavasour was, along with William Ridgeway, the senior advocate of the court at the time of Barrington's departure: *Eighteenth Report*, Appendix 22, p. 212. Ridgeway is best remembered as a law reporter responsible for *Reports of cases upon appeals of Writs of error in the High Court of Parliament since the Restoration of the Appellate Jurisdiction* (Dublin, 1795); P. O'Higgins, 'William Ridgeway (1765–1817): law reporter', *NILQ*, 18 (1967), 208.
79  J. Barrington to C. Lyons, 1 June 1818 (NAI, Frazer MS, 6 (42)). Jameson was receiver general of the Court of Chancery. J. Barrington, 'Statement as to the High Court of Admiralty and the judge thereof' (NAI, CSORP, 1828/983). *1828 Accounts*, pp 2–3.
80  *Morning Chronicle*, 6 Dec. 1817.
81  NAI, OP 503/4. These documents no longer survive.
82  *Eighteenth Report*, Appendix 13, p. 107.
83  J. Barrington to C. Lyons, 28 May 1823 (NAI, Frazer MS, No. 6 (73)).

the barrister Holwell Walsh, but objections were made to Walsh on the ground that he lacked the basic civil law qualification of LLD.[84] When the nomination was vetoed, Barrington privately recalled that 'I was neither a doctor of law nor an advocate when I was appointed and acted as judge; nor is any such qualification necessary by the patent'.[85]

In 1824 it was reported that Barrington had been about to engage in another of his money-making schemes, this time trading his office to 'a friend of his, in exchange for a considerable sum of money'.[86] The other party to this furtive scheme was Sir Henry Meredyth. The arrangement seems to have involved Barrington resigning the office, Meredyth being appointed by the government, and Meredyth paying Barrington an annual pension in exchange for Barrington surrendering his office. The price requested by Barrington – an annual payment of several hundred pounds per year – was excessive[87] and Barrington and Meredyth fell out badly; by 1823 Barrington complained that Meredyth showed 'not the least good will' to him.[88] However, later in the year, Meredyth[89] was appointed as Barrington's surrogate. Meredyth presided until Barrington's dismissal in 1830. In 1828 it was alleged in the House of Commons that Meredyth attended 'very occasionally at three o'clock upon a very few days in the year, to the great prejudice of suitors and the encouragement of the plundering of wrecks'.[90] This seems an unfair assessment. The general view amongst practitioners was that Meredyth was highly conscientious. In 1830 a Dublin proctor, writing to Daniel O'Connell, commended the 'attention and assiduity unprecedented' with which Meredyth administered the office:[91]

> Whenever business in any way required it, whether in vacation or in term, [Meredyth] was ready to sit, and his house was open to the public and practitioners as a court for which he never received any remuneration. Thus no *public* complaint can be made on this score.[92]

84  Walsh is referred to as a doctor of laws in *Wilson's Dublin Directory 1822*, p. 172. There is no reference to Walsh having such a degree in *Alumni Dublinenses*.
85  J. Barrington to C. Lyons, 28 May 1823 (NAI, Frazer MS, No. 6 (73)).
86  Petition of Anne Collins (NAI, CSORP, 1824/9,665).
87  J. Barrington to C. Lyons, undated, 1829 (NAI, Frazer MS, No. 6 (89)). 'Sir HM and I could not come to any close because I wanted my retiring pension to be so increased as to make it worth my while to resign and that could not be done –the case stands thus'.
88  J. Barrington to C. Lyons, 28 May 1823 (NAI, Frazer MS, No. 6 (73)).
89  Meredyth had a practice in the ecclesiastical, though not admiralty, courts. *Select Committee*, pp 56, 58.
90  Sir John Newport MP, *FJ*, 16 Feb. 1828.
91  Mathew Anderson to Daniel O'Connell, 16 March 1830, *The correspondence of Daniel O'Connell*, ed. M.R. O'Connell, 8 vols (Dublin, 1977), iv, pp 138–9.
92  A report prepared for the House of Commons in 1828 recorded that 'Sir Henry Meredyth is always ready to sit when the court assembles, and he never quits the bench whilst there is anything to do; and he generally sits two or three hours at a time … and he has frequently sat until seven

## THE DISMISSAL OF JONAH BARRINGTON

Meanwhile, Barrington, living in 'great splendor and affluence', continued to receive, while others did his work, an annual salary of £1,000.[93] He was now spending much of the year in Paris, where, he reported, the title of judge of the Admiralty Court of Ireland carried some social cachet: 'the name of the office', he wrote to his Dublin solicitor, 'gives me considerable weight here'.[94]

Barrington had managed to avoid being called to account for his abuse of office for three decades. The government's file of complaints against him had been accumulating. Two successive lord chancellors, FitzGibbon and Redesdale, had concluded that Barrington was unfit for office. Sir Robert Peel was certainly aware, as far back as 1814, from the petitions submitted by his creditors, Collins and Rankin, that Barrington had been raising money by selling his salary. In 1815 the problem of delays in the Irish court had been brought to the attention of the lord lieutenant, Charles Whitworth, by a claimant in the salvage case, the *Redstrand*, which had remained undetermined for five years.[95] The government had also been reminded, by the proctors' and Dublin merchants' memorials of 1818 and 1819, of Barrington's continued desertion. By the late 1820s Barrington's corruption and dereliction of office had spread to the public domain. In 1827 he was referred to in the English newspaper, the *Examiner*, as 'a reptile, a condemned liar and a swindling sharper';[96] in response he initiated proceedings for criminal libel.[97] In 1828, Dublin Chamber of Commerce launched a campaign for a public enquiry

o'clock in the evening. In the vacation time, when Sir Henry Meredyth sits in his own house (the courts then being shut) he uniformly sits at 11, and often *de die in diem* for a week or ten days; he has even sat at his own country house to dispatch foreign seamen. He has sat on Christmas Eve until a late hour to speed a cause; usually giving his judgment when the advocates finish, without waiting (as is usual in all civil law courts) to deliberate of judgment until next court day', *1828 Accounts*, p. 2.

93  In addition to his salary, he received £4,000 *per annum* under the will of his father-in-law (NAI, CSORP, 1824/9,665).

94  J. Barrington to C. Lyons, undated 1829 (NAI, Frazer MS No. 6 (89)).

95  Whitworth directed the king's proctor, William Richardson, to examine the petition (20 July 1830, Lords' *jn*, lxii, 907). The *Redstrand* was to feature again as one of the cases in which it was found that Barrington had appropriated suitors' funds.

96  *The Times*, 9 & 19 May, 10 Nov. 1828. Around the same period, Barrington's absence from the jurisdiction was publicly censured by the Irish lord chancellor, Anthony Hart, in litigation involving the appropriation of money which had been left to his daughter, Sybella, a ward of court, by her grandfather: *Barrington v. Grogan* (1828) Beatty 199. In the course of his judgment Hart LC (at p. 215) observed with regret that, by reason of his absence from the jurisdiction, Barrington was not subject to the process of the court.

97  In a letter to his Dublin solicitor, Charles Lyons, Barrington wrote 'you will perceive in the *Examiner* of 22 July the greatest and most atrocious libel upon me ever yet published – I shall first day of term apply for an information against Mr Hunt the editor … with the attorney general as my counsel. Pray retain him for me'. J. Barrington to C. Lyons, 10 Aug. 1827 (NLI, MS 1,723, f. 16). A rule for an information against the author was granted by the King's Bench, *Morning Chronicle*, 19 May 1828.

into the court, observing that the 'mercantile interests are universal against the protraction of suit and ruinous expense entailed in litigating there'.[98]

The process which ended in Barrington's dismissal four years later was set in motion by the energetic reforming member of Parliament for Waterford, Sir John Newport. Early in 1828 Newport had made it known that he intended to raise the state of the Court of Admiralty in Ireland in the House of Commons. The secretary to the Admiralty, John Croker, sought guidance from Sir Robert Peel (newly installed as the secretary of state for the Home Department):

> What is to be done as to Sir J[ohn] Newport's motion about the Irish Admiralty? I last year gave a pledge that the case should be enquired into. And I have since looked into the case and no doubt *something* must be done – the question is what? The matter properly belongs the government and should not, I think, be left in the hands of an opposition member.[99]

In the House of Commons, Newport criticized Barrington's absence, and sought a return of the number of days during which the court sat.[100] The chief secretary, William Lamb, agreed to the request for a return, adding ominously that it was 'not his intention to forestall the observations he would be forced to make on a future occasion'. Adding further to the pressure, some days after the debate in the Commons, a strongly worded petition was submitted to Parliament by the Dublin Chamber of Commerce. This alleged that litigants were being advised to avoid the court and 'that individuals, rather than encounter the delays, expense and vexation, usually attendant on suits in that court, abandon their rights altogether'.[101]

Barrington over-complacently reacted to Newport's motion for a return, describing Newport as a 'fidgety old gentleman who knew nothing of matters he presumed to meddle in', and predicted that Newport would back down as soon as 'Mr Lamb finds he was mistaken as blind'.[102] But Barrington had underestimated both John Newport and the chief secretary (and future prime minister) William Lamb. On 19 May 1828 the Commons approved a proposal by Newport that the royal commissioners (who had been established in 1815 to investigate the court system in Ireland)[103] should turn their attention to the Admiralty Court.[104] In fact,

---

98  Minutes of the Council of Dublin Chamber of Commerce, 22 Jan. 1828 (NAI, 1,064/3/3, ff 249–50). A memorial based on the report was presented to the Board of Trade. Minutes of the Council of Dublin Chamber of Commerce, 5 Feb. 1828 (NAI, 1,064/3/3, f. 253).

99  J. Croker to R. Peel, 2 Feb. 1828 (BL, Add. MS 40,320, f.1).

100  *FJ*, 16 Feb. 1828.                               101  *Commons' jn*, lxxxiii, p. 79 (18 Feb. 1828).

102  J. Barrington to C. Lyons, 16 Mar. 1828 (NLI, MS 1,723, f. 17).

103  The Royal Commission which had been established in February 1815 was already charged with investigating the Irish Court of Admiralty (HC 1814–15 (222), vii, 135).

104  In the course of his speech Newport complained of the exorbitant legal costs in the court (citing one case where costs of £160 had been charged in a seaman's wages case) and another case where the proceedings had taken two years to conclude. He noted that complaints were being expressed by English ship owners about the Irish court. Newport expressed the view that it would be

this stage of the inquiry was already in motion; in the spring of 1828 the commissioners of inquiry had begun investigating the Irish Court of Admiralty, and were collecting confidential information from aggrieved interest groups.[105] By May 1828 the intelligence which was to be the cause of Barrington's final disgrace – his misappropriation of suitors' funds lodged in the registry – had been disclosed to the commission.

The corruption charge had been revealed to the commissioners of inquiry on 16 May 1828. The registrar of the court, Daniel Pineau produced documentary evidence showing that Barrington had appropriated suitors' funds.[106] The litigation which had generated the suitors' funds in question involved two derelict cases – the *Nancy* and the *Redstrand*. Pending the determination of the cases, the vessels had been sold. The techniques allegedly used to obtain the money from the registry were quite crude. In the *Nancy* in 1806 Barrington ordered the registrar, Daniel Pineau, to hand over £200 from the suitors' fund. He had derived a further large sum by a court order dated 21 December 1805, which directed that £482 8s. 8d. be paid out of the suitors' fund to Patrick Hamilton (the king's proctor) ostensibly so that the sum could be invested in government securities. The real purpose was that the money would then be paid over to Barrington himself; Hamilton duly parted with £300 to Barrington. The effect of the two transactions in the *Nancy* was that Barrington managed to convert a sum of £500, made up of the £200 obtained from Pineau and the £300 provided by Hamilton. In the *Redstrand* in 1810, Barrington withdrew £200 from suitors' funds account in Gleadowe Newcomen's bank. Again the sum was never repaid.

News of the disclosures to the commission soon made its way to London. Three days later, William Lamb wrote to the commissioners informing them of the parliamentary address and suggesting that, in the light of the information which had three days earlier been disclosed about Barrington, they consider, in addition to the general report on the court, a separate report investigating the charges against Barrington.[107] Barrington was also informed of the course the inquiry was taking. He replied that his 'miserable state of health'[108] prevented his travelling, but

preferable to de-commission the court than to have it so badly administered. Lamb informed the Commons that an inquiry had already been established. *FJ*, 23 May 1828.

105  In April 1828 the secretary of the judicial commissioners, J. Fetherson, wrote to the Dublin Chamber of Commerce making it known that the commission would 'be happy to receive any information ... whether in the form of documentary evidence, or the suggestions of witnesses for personal examination'. Minutes of the Council of Dublin Chamber of Commerce, 3 Apr. 1828 (NAI, 1,064/3/3, f. 275). In response the council advertised a public meeting on the subject of abuses in the court; a document based on that meeting was sent to the commissioners. Minutes of the Council of Dublin Chamber of Commerce, 10 Apr. 1828 (NAI, 1,064/3/3, f. 279).

106  *Eighteenth Report*, Appendix 13, pp 140–3.

107  The commissioners explained that, in the light of the failure of Barrington to co-operate, they could not comply with Lamb's suggestion that they produce a special report on the judge. B. Mitford, W. Wynne, J. Driscoll, and P. Low to W. Gregory, 20 June 1828 (TNA (PRO), HO 100/222, f. 414).

108  J. Barrington to F. Leveson-Gower [?], 1 Aug. 1828 (NAI, CSORP, 1828/983).

promised a full refutation of the allegations when he had been furnished with the evidence. The promised defence was never submitted.

The report into the Admiralty Court, the *Eighteenth Report of the Commissioners on Duties, Salaries and Emoluments in Courts of Justice in Ireland*, was presented to Parliament in January 1829. The strength of the corroborating documentary evidence made the case against Barrington irresistible. In light of such powerful evidence the House of Commons was unlikely to just let the matter drop. In April 1829, the Commons agreed to 'go into a committee to consider the Eighteenth Report of the Commissioners of Judicial Inquiry in Ireland'.[109]

The select committee appointed to consider the charges against Barrington sat between 4 and 21 May 1829. Barrington, who had travelled from France to Westminster, had, at this point, become hysterical: 'I have committed no crime or wronged any body. I am punished in the severest manner and disgraced through Europe. I shall not long survive',[110] and claimed that he 'would rather to have cut my throat at once' than defend the proposed investigation.[111] During April and May 1829 he attempted to negotiate his way out of trouble with an offer of resignation. At first he offered a deal in which, in exchange for his voluntary resignation, he would be awarded an actual increase in pension. But when those terms of settlement were (not very surprisingly) refused, he re-submitted a request for resignation on the standard pension 'conceiving that my principal object had been attained, by undergoing a strict interrogation before the committee and that the credit due to the accuser Mr Pineau had been duly destroyed …'[112] The government had no interest in a settlement. Barrington's tormentor, the chief secretary, Leveson-Gower, facetiously expressed himself 'anxious' that Barrington should have 'every opportunity for deliberation on such a step', and returned Barrington's letter of resignation.[113] Barrington begged for a personal interview with the home secretary. Gower refused.

The select committee reported on 1 June 1829. Its conclusion was more directly expressed than the *Eighteenth Report* had been, finding that Barrington 'did in the years 1805 and 1806, under colour of his official authority, apply to his own use two sums, amounting to £500 9s. 2d., out of the proceeds of the derelict ship *Nancy*, then lodged in the hands of the registrar of that court; and that he did in the year 1810, in a similar manner, apply to his own use the sum of £200 out of the proceeds of the *Redstrand* derelict'.[114]

The documentary evidence assembled against Barrington was extremely cogent. The fraud in the *Nancy* involved the appropriation of two sums. The first was £200 withdrawn from the suitors' funds held by the registrar, Pineau. A minute in

109  *Commons' jn*, lxxxiv, p. 209 (7 Apr. 1829).
110  J. Barrington to F. Leveson-Gower, 25 May 1829 (NAI, RP 1829/10,247).
111  J. Barrington to C. Talbot, 29 May 1829, ibid.
112  J. Barrington to F. Leveson-Gower, 17 May 1829, ibid.
113  F. Leveson-Gower to J. Barrington, 19 May 1829, ibid.
114  *Select Committee*, p. 10.

Barrington's handwriting dated 2 September 1807 appeared to prove this allegation. The letter to Pineau urged him to make a false report that he had invested the money and promised 'upon your making such order, to account with, and pay you over, a sum of £190 … and I promise, upon demand by you, to give you my bond, payable forthwith for such sum'.[115] Barrington never denied the authenticity of this document. The second was the £300 withdrawn by the king's proctor, Patrick Hamilton. Again there was documentary proof. A Dublin proctor, Mathew Anderson, had been left a cache of papers by a Mr Whiteway, the former clerk to Patrick Hamilton. Anderson found, among those letters, some highly incriminating material, including an IOU note apparently from Barrington to Hamilton[116] on the subject of the *Nancy*. The note in Barrington's handwriting recorded: 'IOU Patrick Hamilton £300 9s. 2d. 23 December 1805. J. Barrington'. In the *Redstrand* case, where Barrington was alleged to have obtained nearly £200 from suitors' funds lodged with Gleadowe Newcomen's bank, there was also direct supporting documentary evidence: the bank's books showed both the lodgment of the money, and Barrington's withdrawals from the same account.[117]

Francis Leveson-Gower was determined to implement Barrington's removal from office. Even before the select committee had reported, Gower had advised him of his intention to initiate the process for his dismissal. The dismissal procedure took longer than Gower might have wished. Under section 2 of the Court of Admiralty Act 1783 the judge could only be dismissed following 'an address [to the king] of both houses of Parliament'. There was a delay of about a year during which the government obtained legal advice on the procedure to be followed in operating the 1783 Act.[118] On 10 May 1830, in accordance with the 1783 Act, a resolution recommending Barrington's dismissal was laid before the House of Commons.[119] For two days the House of Commons deliberated a request by Daniel O'Connell that Barrington should be permitted to appear at the bar of the house. The motion was resisted on the grounds that the evidence was so overwhelming that the outcome was unlikely to be altered by the accused's attendance.[120] Although Barrington himself was not allowed address the House, the right of audience was conceded to his counsel, Thomas Denman (the future chief justice). Denman made the constitutional argument that proceedings for removal could only be operated following a prior judicial (rather than parliamentary) finding of criminal misconduct. Here there had been no such judicial conviction, and the process was unconstitutional.[121] Otherwise the contributions made by Barrington's small group of sympathizers were very weak: it was argued that the

---

115  J. Barrington to W. Pineau, 2 Sept. 1807, *Select Committee*, p. 6.
116  The letter is reproduced in the *Eighteenth Report*, Appendix D, p. 100; *Select Committee*, p. 4.
117  *Eighteenth Report*, Appendix D, p. 109; *Select Committee*, p. 8.
118  NAI, RP 1830/4153.
119  'Resolutions of the whole house on the conduct of Sir Jonah Barrington' (HC 1830 (382) 4, 749).
120  *FJ*, 10 & 25 May 1830.
121  *Hansard 2*, vol. 24, col. 966 (22 May 1830).

practice of temporarily appropriating suitors' funds was merely a customary perk attached to the office,[122] and that it was unfair that the administration which had so long tolerated Barrington's absenteeism should now move to dismiss him.

On 25 May, the House of Commons voted in favour of the resolution for a conference with the Lords.[123] The first of the addresses required by section 2 of the Court of Admiralty Act 1783 had been put in place. On 25 May, a message was brought from the House of Commons by Francis Gower 'to desire a conference with this house upon a matter of high importance and concern, respecting the due administration of justice'.[124]

An investigation into the charges was conducted in the House of Lords between 14 June and 20 July. This enquiry was administered in the manner of a trial. Orders were made for the attendance of Pineau and Mathew Anderson and it was resolved that Barrington be permitted to be represented by counsel, and to cross-examine.[125] Barrington's counsel, Henry Dean Grady, undertook the cross-examination of Pineau. Grady pursued three lines of questioning: the first was intended to undermine the reliability of Pineau's rule-book. Grady showed that the entries in the rule book about the *Redstrand* case had subsequently been added, and that the orders relating to the *Nancy* contained suspect erasures.[126] Second, Grady produced a long schedule of twenty-six judgments entered against Pineau in the Common Pleas, Exchequer and King's Bench between 1804 and 1824,[127] and interrogated Pineau about his personal debts. The object of this line of examination was to show that Pineau could not have been in a position to conceal the withdrawals (by replacing the money Barrington had taken from the registry) in the way that he had claimed to have done. How, Grady asked, was Pineau in a position 'to advance money to that extent to Sir Jonah Barrington when you were not in a position to pay your own debts?'[128] Third, Pineau was interrogated as to why he had never mentioned the debt owed by Barrington in the course of a government-instituted inquiry into the *Redstrand* in 1816.[129] Grady's cross-examination of Pineau had been highly effective. But however unreliable Pineau might have been, the powerful effect of the documentary evidence derived from sources independent of Pineau – particularly the archive left by the king's proctor, Patrick Hamilton – could not be successfully impugned. In summing up the case for Barrington's removal, the lord chancellor, Baron Brougham, referring to the cross-examination of Daniel Pineau, conceded that from 'what took place on the cross-examination of that gentleman, he did not think it would be safe in their lordships to come to a determination against Sir Jonah on that evidence'. On the other hand, 'the support of those charges did not rest on the testimony of that

122  See D.W. Harvey MP, *Hansard 2*, vol. 24, col. 976 (22 May 1830).
123  *Hansard 2*, vol. 24, col. 1082 (25 May 1830).
124  *Lords' jn*, lxii, 528 (25 May 1830).                    125  *Lords' jn*, lxii, 602 (4 June 1830).
126  *Lords' jn*, lxii, 880–6, 891 (14 July 1830).            127  *Lords' jn*, lxii, 888 (14 July 1830).
128  *Lords' jn*, lxii, 887 (14 July 1830).                   129  *Lords' jn*, lxii, 889 (14 July 1830).

gentleman alone; they were supported by written documents signed by Sir Jonah himself'.[130]

On 20 July 1830 the Commons' address was re-read. The Lords resolved to 'agree with the Commons in the said address', by inserting the phrase 'lords spiritual and temporal and' before the phrase 'Commons in Parliament assembled' in the Commons' address.[131] The address of both houses of Parliament was then ceremonially carried by four MPs, the lord chamberlain and the lord steward to St James's Palace. The king returned a communication to Parliament: 'I cannot but regret the circumstances which have led to this address. I will give directions that Sir Jonah Barrington be removed from the office which he holds of judge of the High Court of Admiralty in Ireland'.[132] The procedure formally concluded with the issue by the king of a warrant directed to the lord lieutenant to pass letters patent to rescind Barrington's patent of 1797.[133]

Barrington refused to accept the parliamentary findings. He attempted to petition the king against exercising his prerogative to dismiss. This letter was, he claimed, intercepted: the duke of Wellington, whom he called 'a most consummate rascal', had suppressed the letter which he had written to the king.[134] He complained that 'no evidence was offered for me, I was nearly dying in bed, and the case was cut short without attending to my last petition'.[135] He repeatedly, and perhaps unfairly, blamed his barrister, Henry Dean Grady who had been 'over-confident', had failed to cross-examine witnesses, and had 'acted as if at nisi prius'.[136] Barrington resolved to re-open the matter by a further petition to the Houses of Parliament, where his ultimate object was 'to destroy Dan Pineau for my own sake, and I have ample materials'.[137] He was confident that the duke of Sussex would take up his case in the Lords.[138]

One twentieth-century commentator[139] vaguely suggested that Barrington may have been mistreated: 'from beginning to end of this affair, the real defence, if any, was never developed, and the impression is left that there may really have been a defence'. But it cannot convincingly be claimed that Barrington was not permitted an opportunity to develop a defence. He was allowed four such opportunities: in advance of publication of the commissioners' report, before the select committee, in the Commons and in the Lords. Barrington's own instructions to his solicitor as to his grounds of defence were opaque.[140] Admittedly, his barrister made some

130  *FJ*, 24 July 1830.
131  *Lords' jn*, lxii, 908 (20 July 1830).
132  *Lords' jn*, lxii, 915 (22 July 1830).
133  TNA (PRO), HO 100/235, f.10.
134  J. Barrington to C. Lyons, 15 July 1831 (NLI, MS 1,723, f. 21).
135  J. Barrington to C. Lyons, 26 Jan. 1831 (NLI, MS 1,723, f. 20).
136  J. Barrington to C. Lyons, 15 July 1831 & 12 Jan. 1832 (NLI, MS 1,723, ff 21 & 22).
137  J. Barrington to C. Lyons, 15 July 1831 (NLI, MS 1,723, f. 21).
138  J. Barrington to C. Lyons, 26 Jan. 1831 (NLI, MS 1,723, f. 20).
139  A.D. Gibb, *Judicial corruption in the United Kingdom* (Edinburgh, 1957), p. 72.
140  Barrington requested his solicitor to 'compare, connect and consolidate the evidence of Mathew Anderson and William Richardson' and complained that 'my letter to Pineau, mentioning a confidential communication to you, was represented by the chancellor as a confession to you of

progress in undermining the integrity of Pineau, and if the only evidence had been Pineau's, Barrington would have had a case for acquittal. But other items of incriminating documentary evidence, particularly the manuscripts found amongst the papers of Patrick Hamilton, and the records of the Dublin banks, which had been discovered by the commissioners in 1828 and by the select committee in 1829, were never seriously challenged. Even those sympathetic to Barrington, such as Daniel O'Connell (who confessed that he would 'have rejoiced to find anything in it advantageous to Sir Jonah Barrington, for he [was] now old and in circumstances of great difficulty, dropping into the grave')[141] were unable to identify any basis of exoneration.

At the age of seventy-four Barrington had to face the prospect of life without a regular income. The winter of 1830 was particularly hard: he complained that his remittances from Ireland had dried up, and that he was 'utterly destroyed', 'Lady B's heart [was] breaking fast', and he feared 'dying of want in a French prison'.[142] However, by the summer he had a spring in his step once again. He had been forced to give up his old house, but his new accommodation – a 'most excellent small house' – was 'extremely pretty and roomy'. He was feeling 'vastly better than before'[143] and was, in his mid-seventies, still productive and was excited by the appearance of his final work of history, *The rise and fall of the Irish nation*.[144] He died three years later, in 1834, at Versailles.

THE CONSTITUTIONAL STATUS OF THE IRISH COURT OF
ADMIRALTY, 1756–1800

Two premises underlay the understanding of the constitutional status of the Irish Court of Admiralty up to the late eighteenth century. First, the Irish court was not an autochthonous Irish institution. Instead it derived its title from a high officer of the Crown of England, the lord admiral. Second, the court created by the lord admiral was a purely subordinate court, subject to the admiral's principal court, the English Court of Admiralty, which exercised supervisory and concurrent jurisdiction over its Irish agent.[145] These two propositions were the source of a number of sub-principles which undermined the independence of the Irish court: (a) Because the court derived its title from the lord high admiral it was the admiral, or the Admiralty commissioners, who (though after 1759 only formally) appointed the judge of the Irish Court of Admiralty; (b) because the court was inferior to the English Court of Admiralty, decisions of the Irish court were subject to correction

    my own guilt and was the confession he relied on'. J. Barrington to C. Lyons, 26 Jan. 1831 (NLI, MS 1,723, f. 20).

141  *FJ*, 29 May 1830.
142  J. Barrington to C. Lyons, 26 Jan. 1831 (NLI, MS 1,723, f. 20).
143  J. Barrington to C. Lyons, 15 July 1831 (NLI, MS 1,723, f. 21).
144  Paris, 1833.                          145  See pp 11–12 above.

on appeal by the English Court of Admiralty; (c) because the English court was superior, it was entitled to exercise its own process within Ireland. The form of intrusion which caused most irritation was that under which the English court authorized commissioners to take evidence in Ireland. In 1779, Warden Flood complained about officers of the English court operating in Ireland, carrying out in Ireland examinations relating to prize cases in the English court.[146] The judge of the English court, Sir James Marriott, reminded Flood that there was no comity between the two courts; the English court was dominant and the Irish 'only a court of vice-admiralty and consequently a subordinate court generally in all matters relative to Admiralty jurisdiction'.[147] However, within four years, the Irish Parliament had enacted the Court of Admiralty (Ireland) Act 1783, and the principle stated by Marriott had been displaced.

## *The Court of Admiralty (Ireland) Act 1783*

The Irish Admiralty Act 1783 reorientated the constitutional basis of the Irish Admiralty Court. The Crown in right of Ireland replaced the lord admiral of England as the constitutional root of title of the court. In 1759 the power of nomination of the judge had been transferred to the Irish government.[148] This process was formalized by section 1 of the 1783 Act which entrusted the right of appointment to the Crown, in place of the admiral (or commissioners of Admiralty). Under section 2 the power of removal of the judge was withdrawn from the Admiralty in London, and judges were given the protection of the Act of Settlement 1701. A judge could be removed by the Crown but only 'upon the address of both Houses of Parliament'. Section 3 abolished the right of the English Court of Admiralty to hear appeals. Instead there was to be a right of appeal to a local court of delegates appointed by the lord chancellor of Ireland.

Fundamental constitutional changes in the 1780s had made the Irish Admiralty Court an institutional anomaly. In 1783 Ireland was granted judicature sovereignty. The Irish Appeals Act 1783 had withdrawn the power of English courts to exercise supervisory jurisdiction over Irish courts, and had given formal recognition to the constitutional proposition that Ireland had 'exclusive rights' in 'matters of judicature'.[149] But the constitutional character of the Irish Admiralty Court infringed this general principle of judicature sovereignty: it was an external institution – an English-instituted court dropped into the Irish judicature in the late sixteenth century, with its decisions subject to appeal in London. By 1783 this anomaly was about to be targeted by the patriot party. The patriot politician, Henry Flood, in collaboration with Warden Flood, began researching the constitutional

---

146  Commissioners of Admiralty to W. Flood, 28 Oct. 1779 (TNA (PRO), ADM 2/1,060, f. 184).
147  J. Marriott to the commissioners of Admiralty, 12 July 1779 (TNA (PRO), ADM 1/3,885, f. 437).
148  See p. 153 above.
149  23 Geo. III, c. 28 (Eng.), 1783.

status of the court with the intention of agitating about it when parliament re-assembled.[150] The government took pre-emptive action. The Admiralty Court Act 1783 was drafted by the government in anticipation of the expected campaign by Flood and his supporters 'in order to remove the objections against the judicature'.[151] The lord lieutenant (the earl of Northington) informed the home secretary, Lord North, that reform of the constitutional character of the Court of Admiralty was a necessary consequence of the principle of judicature independence:

> The independence of the legislature and jurisdiction of Ireland being fully established, other regulations are to be considered as consequential arrangements, not as fresh demands. In this view, an establishment of a new Court of Admiralty … must be immediately settled. The commission of the judge of the Vice-Admiralty Court is under the seal of the lords' commissioners of the Admiralty, and the final appeal lies to the king in his High Court of Chancery in England. I am therefore of opinion that a bill must be brought in to the Irish Parliament in order to remove the objections that will be raised against this judicature.[152]

The preparation of the legislation was organized by the chief secretary, Thomas Pelham, with the lawyer and parliamentary speaker, Edmond Pery, contributing to the drafting.[153] By 23 September the bill was ready. The lord lieutenant outlined the principal features of the legislation:

> The judge of the High Court of Admiralty might, in future, be commissioned by the king under the great seal of Ireland, and his office held during good behaviour or during pleasure, as his majesty might direct. Powers similar to those of the judge of the High Court of Admiralty might be vested in him. Appeals from his decisions may lie to the king in the High Court of Chancery in Ireland, and the chancellor empowered to appoint commissioners or delegates for the final determination of such appeals.[154]

In order to stress the conversion in the constitutional status of the court from that of a mere vice-admiralty, it was re-titled 'the *High Court* of Admiralty in this

150  Earl Temple to W. Grenville, 22 Jan. 1783 (*The manuscripts of B. Fortescue, I, 1698–1790* (HMC, London, 1892)), p. 183; James Kelly, *Henry Flood* (Dublin, 1998), p. 339.
151  Earl of Northington to Lord North, 23 Sept. 1783 (TNA (PRO), HO 100/10, f. 106).
152  Ibid.
153  Pery returned a draft of the proposed Admiralty Court Bill to Pelham requesting, as his handwriting was recognizable, 'that these papers shall remain with you, and that my name not be mentioned … for I am apprehensive lest the gentlemen, whose draft I have made free with, for whom I have a very high esteem, and whose opinion I respect, should take umbrage at it'. E. Pery to T. Pelham, 14 Sept. 1783 ('Manuscripts of the Earl of Onslow', *Fourteenth Report, Appendix IX* (HMC, London, 1895), p. 179).
154  Earl of Northington to Lord North, 23 Sept. 1783 (TNA (PRO), HO 100/10, f. 106).

kingdom'. Section 1 defined its jurisdiction in a way which suggested that its competence was wider than it had been when it had been a mere court of vice-admiralty. The court was to have jurisdiction to 'hear and determine all and all manner of civil, maritime, and other causes to the jurisdiction of the said court belonging'. This last phrase – 'other causes to the said court belonging' – implied that the court's jurisdiction was not restricted to 'civil, maritime' causes, as it had been in its pre-1783 days, and that its jurisdiction might extend to other categories of work, including (as some Irish civilians would subsequently argue) prize work. Section 3 of the 1783 Act, continuing the process of pushing the English Court of Admiralty out of Ireland, provided that appeal was to be to the 'king of this kingdom'. Where an appeal was taken, the chancellor of Ireland was to assemble a court of delegates, granting a 'commission or delegacy to some discreet and learned persons of this kingdom'. The demand, first made by the Catholic Confederates in the 1640s, for the abolition of the admiralty appeal to London had eventually been accomplished.[155] The bill quietly passed through Parliament without controversy or debate between 6 and 10 December 1783.

## *The Court of Admiralty and the constitution of 1782*

Over the years 1782 and 1783 Ireland was granted judicature independence from England: the King's Bench and the House of Lords of England no longer had power to hear appeals from Irish courts, while the Irish Appeals Act 1783[156] confirmed the 'exclusive rights' of the courts of Ireland 'in matters of judicature'. The Irish Admiralty Court Act 1783 converted the court into an autochthonous institution and cut the connection with the English Court of Admiralty. However, throughout the 1790s the English court, despite advice from Ireland, seemed not to have grasped the consequences of this new constitutional dispensation. The issue arose in 1795 when a number of Dutch vessels were taken into Limerick.[157] Apparently not perceiving any difficulty about its competence to act within Ireland, the English Court of Admiralty issued a commission to the Irish court instructing it to process a prize capture. However, the lord lieutenant, Camden, advised that the commission be discreetly rescinded;[158] following the constitutional changes of 1783 the English court was no longer competent to operate in Ireland. Camden explained that the pre-1783 arrangement, under which the English Court of Admiralty was able to operate in Ireland, had been a casualty of that constitutional re-organization: 'Previous to the year 1783 the admiralty jurisdiction subsisted under a court of vice-admiralty, the judge whereof held by commission from the lords of the Admiralty'. It was a consequence of the constitutional independence of the Irish judicature that the commission of the English Admiralty Court no longer ran in Ireland: 'it will be necessary to show that the authority of the

---

155  See p. 13 above.                           156  23 Geo. III, c. 28 (Eng.), 1783.
157  See p. 188 below.
158  Earl Camden to the duke of Portland, 30 Oct. 1795 (TNA (PRO), HO 100/59, f. 60).

commission now issued is consistent with the laws of Ireland'. Camden warned the English government of the political dangers in attempting to operate the processes of the English Admiralty Court in Ireland; the issue 'should it be taken up in Parliament will certainly give rise to much popular clamour'. But the anachronistic pre-1783 view continued to be maintained in England for some time afterwards; it was confidently reasserted in 1800 during the *Madonna* controversy[159] by Sir John Nicholl, the king's advocate in the English court. Nicholl (writing as if nothing had changed after 1783) described the jurisdiction of that court as extending into Ireland: 'The Court of Admiralty [of England] has a jurisdiction co-extensive with that of the lords commissioners of Admiralty and is competent to take cognizance of all captures wherever made'.[160] The position was, as we shall see, finally settled in favour of the Irish position in the *Jamaica* controversy of 1823.[161] The next great constitutional upheaval in Ireland, the Act of Union 1800, also affected the Court of Admiralty.

### The Act of Union 1800 and the prize competence of the Court of Admiralty

The Court of Admiralty made an appearance in the Act of Union 1800.[162] Indeed, the humble Court of Admiralty had the distinction of being the only court explicitly referred to in the Act of Union. There was no reference to the Court of Admiralty in the original plans for an act of union drawn up in 1798.[163] But in its final form, Article 8 of the Act of Union made a special reference to the court:

> provided that from and after the union there shall remain in Ireland an instance court of admiralty for the determination of causes civil and maritime only ...

In making the court a tribunal 'for the determination of causes civil and maritime *only*' the intention was to deal finally with claims being made by the Irish court that it had prize jurisdiction.[164] Sir Henry Meredyth, in his evidence to the courts' commissioners in 1828, confirmed that the intention was to suppress the court's claim to act as a prize court: 'I conceive that the enactment of this Article of Union was calculated and intended to define the jurisdiction of the court, and to prevent the exercise of any other jurisdiction but that of an instance court of admiralty'.[165] The Act of Union 1800 settled a debate of over two-hundred-years standing.

### The Act of Union 1800 and the independent Court of Admiralty

Under the Act of Union Irish parliamentary sovereignty had been ceded to London. But had the principle of an independent admiralty judicature been ceded

159  See p. 190 below.
160  J. Nicholl to the duke of Portland, 7 July 1800 (TNA (PRO), 30/42/18/4).
161  See p. 177 below.
162  40 Geo. III, c. 38 (Ire.), 1800; 39 & 40 Geo. III, c. 67 (Eng.), 1800.
163  NLI, MS 887, f. 7.     164  See p. 191 below.     165  *Eighteenth Report*, Appendix 5, p. 80.

as well? In the mid-1820s it was settled that the Irish Admiralty Court retained its post-1783 sovereignty in Ireland. The master of a private merchant vessel, the *Jamaica*, had been spotted at Whitehaven illegally displaying a naval pendant. On being asked by a customs officer to remove it, the master (Alexander Miller) returned 'an indecent and insolent message' and proceeded to Dublin. A warrant for Miller's arrest was issued under the Smuggling Act 1822[166] from the English Admiralty Court. The defendant was arrested by the Dublin police and after spending a night in the Police Office, was transferred to Newgate prison. On 24 November 1823 Miller's attorney made an application to the King's Bench in Dublin for *habeas corpus*,[167] and Miller was discharged on the basis that there was a technical defect in the warrant.[168] Although the King's Bench did not deal with the constitutional point, a high-powered committee of English and Irish law officers[169] (which included the attorney general and solicitor general of England and the attorney general and admiralty advocate of Ireland) concluded that the English court had no power to issue its processes to Ireland. The Act of Union 1800 was to be read strictly. Only those aspects of the sovereignty of Ireland which had been expressly ceded by the Act of Union were withdrawn. The Act of Union had not diminished the admiralty judicial sovereignty of Ireland established in 1783; accordingly the exclusive jurisdiction of the Irish court within Ireland remained intact:

> But since the English statute 6 Geo. 1, c. 5 [the Declaratory Act 1720] (which had asserted the subordinate character of Ireland), had been repealed by the [Renunciation Act 1782] ... which was understood to be a recognition of her rightful independence; since likewise the [Irish Appeals Act, 1783] has taken away the appellate jurisdiction of the English courts; and since, in fine, the Act of Union has practically admitted the independence of Ireland as a contracting party, it seems to follow that the Courts of Admiralty in England and in Ireland have now become mutually independent, and have therefore the same jurisdiction in the waters of the other island which belongs to either in the waters of any foreign state.

However, some governmental figures considered that an entirely independent Irish Court of Admiralty was an anomaly in the post-Union constitution. In 1805 the Irish lord chancellor, Baron Redesdale, told Jonah Barrington that he was at a loss to reconcile the idea of 'an independent Court of Admiralty ... with a union of the two countries in one kingdom'.[170] Redesdale's support for assimilation prompted Jonah Barrington (who was, at the time, campaigning for a salary increase) into a

---

166  3 Geo. IV, c. 110 (Eng.), 1822.      167  *FJ,* 25 & 29 Nov. 1823.      168  *FJ,* 29 Nov. 1823.

169  Opinion of J.S. Copley, C. Wetherell, W.C. Plunket, J.L. Foster, 18 Aug. 1825, *Cases and opinions on Constitutional Law,* ed. W. Forsyth (London, 1869), p. 104. *R. v. Miller* (1823) 1 Hag Adm 197, 166 ER 71.

170  Baron Redesdale to J. Barrington, 23 Oct. 1805 (NAI, OP 214/11).

fit of judicature unionism, developing a scheme for re-attaching the Irish court to the English court. Barrington suggested to the lord lieutenant, the earl of Hardwicke, that the Irish court would benefit from re-establishing a formal link with the English court, under which the English court might be able to give advisory determinations on matters before the Irish court:[171] 'the Irish court would then go on without embarrassment and the opinion of the British judge would become an unquestioned precedent – it is my earnest wish to have the Irish court as dependent upon that of England as circumstances will admit of'.

### THE OFFICERS OF THE COURT OF ADMIRALTY OF IRELAND

*The registrar of the Irish Court of Admiralty*

In 1760 the chaise which was carrying William Sheil, the registrar of the court, overturned. Sheil cracked his skull and died.[172] Both the judge, Robert FitzGerald, and the king's advocate, James Sheil (the late registrar's son) pressed to have another member of the Sheil family, Osborne Sheil, made registrar.[173] Osborne Sheil was appointed by Robert FitzGerald as a temporary replacement while the court awaited the decision of the Admiralty in London.[174] However, the Admiralty refused to perpetuate a Sheil family dynasty, and appointed Thomas Tisdall instead.[175]

Under the post-1783 constitutional re-arrangement, the power to appoint the registrar was transferred from the Admiralty in London to the Irish government. The duke of Rutland re-appointed Thomas Tisdall,[176] who served as registrar for the next ten years. Tisdall had always regarded the office as a sinecure: between 1777 and 1781[177] he delegated the duties to a deputy, John Coen. Subsequently, Thomas Mangan served as Tisdall's deputy registrar until 1798.

Henry Fitzgerald was the twelve-year old son of the MP and serjeant, James Fitzgerald.[178] In 1798 the lord lieutenant, Camden, concerned that 'he had no opportunity of expressing his good will' towards Henry, appointed him to the

---

171  J. Barrington to the earl of Hardwicke, 29 Oct. 1805 (BL, Add. MS 35,763, f. 58). Barrington's scheme was composed of three points: first, an assimilation of practice between the two courts; second, the creation of a procedure equivalent to a consultative case stated from the Court of Admiralty of Ireland to the English court; and third, in cases involving the construction of points of international law, an appeal by way of bill of review from Ireland to the English Privy Council.

172  R. FitzGerald to the commissioners of Admiralty, 22 May 1760 (TNA (PRO), ADM 1/3,883, f. 92).

173  R. FitzGerald and J. Sheil to the commissioners of Admiralty, 5 Aug. 1760 & 22 May 1760 (TNA (PRO), ADM 1/3,883, ff 91 & 95).

174  R. FitzGerald to the commissioners of Admiralty, 5 Aug. 1760 (TNA (PRO), ADM 1/3,883, f. 81).

175  J. Clevland to R. FitzGerald, 11 Aug. 1760 (TNA (PRO), ADM 2/1,056, f. 290). John Clevland was secretary to the Admiralty between 1759 and 1763.

176  On 16 May 1785 the King appointed Thomas Tisdall by letters patent drafted by the prime serjeant and solicitor general (TNA (PRO), HO 100/16, f. 366).

177  *Watson's Almanack 1777*, p. 63.

178  Henry Fitzgerald grew up to become the dean of Kilmore.

sinecure office of registrar.[179] This earned young Henry about £60 per annum. A series of sub-registrars discharged the function on his behalf – first, John Barrett and then the senior proctor, John Hawkins. Subsequently, John Robinson took over the position of sub-registrar in the early part of the Barrington régime, filling the office between 1799 and 1803.[180] When Henry Fitzgerald tried to dismiss Robinson on the ground that he 'had not acted to his satisfaction' Robinson threatened to sue. Litigation, Henry's father feared, 'would subject the patentee to a suit the expense of which would exceed the value of the office'.[181] In order to neutralize the Robinson threat it was decided that young Henry Fitzgerald would resign. James Fitzgerald recommended that the position be transferred to Daniel Pineau, a Dublin proctor (whose sister had been a governess to the Fitzgerald family).[182] In his testimonial Fitzgerald wrote: 'I wish that a new patent be granted to Mr Daniel Pineau'. Pineau was 'a gentleman of character' who 'will himself discharge the duties of the office and thereby prevent the necessity of a disagreeable suit'.[183]

Daniel Pineau, who turned out to be far from a 'gentleman of character', served as register from 1805 to his death in 1837. For most of this period he officiated in person, except for a period between 1815 and 1819[184] when he delegated the function to John Robinson (the son of the proctor whose inefficiency had been the cause of Pineau's own appointment).[185] Robinson, as his father had been, was again dismissed for inefficiency.[186] Pineau attended the court on three days a week. Otherwise he conducted business from the admiralty registry, an office in his home in St Stephen's Green, from where he also conducted his other professional occupation as an attorney. The annual income generated by fees was on average about £300, and he was sufficiently busy to engage two clerks to assist him.[187]

The continued existence of a system of registry fees was the ground of one of the principal complaints made against the court. In 1828 Dublin Chamber of Commerce reported that the court was an anomaly, being 'one of the few courts now left in Dublin from which fees are not abolished'. The system of fees, it claimed, gave the court's officials a 'direct interest in the protraction of suits'. The report suggested that the registrar was guilty of 'bias in adjusting costs where one party may be wealthy and another a pauper'.[188]

179  James Fitzgerald to unnamed, 2 Dec. 1804 (NAI, OP 176/9).
180  NAI, OP 65/7; *Wilson's Dublin Directory 1802*, p. 74; Robinson was an early victim of Barrington's venality: Robinson apparently accommodated Barrington with loans, of which nearly £400 was never repaid. *Eighteenth Report*, Appendix 21, p. 196.
181  J. Fitzgerald to unnamed, 1 Dec. 1804 (NAI, OP 176/9).
182  Deposition of Sir Jonah Barrington, 16 Jan. 1829, *Select Committee*, Appendix A, p. 78.
183  J. Fitzgerald to unnamed, 1 Dec. 1804 (NAI, OP 176/9).
184  *Eighteenth Report*, Appendix. 13, p. 106. Pineau's corruption in office is described at p. 205 below.
185  Deposition of Sir Jonah Barrington, 16 Jan. 1829, *Select Committee*, p. 76.
186  *Eighteenth Report*, Appendix 13, p. 106.
187  Ibid., p. 107. His fee income for 1825 was £320; for 1826 was £310; and for 1827 was £280. His clerks were named as Samuel Stephens and James McGulk.
188  Minutes of the council of Dublin Chamber of Commerce, 22 Jan. 1828 (NAI, 1,064/3/3, f. 249).

Most seriously of all it also pointed out that 'there are large sums in the hands
of the registrar'. The insinuation that the practice whereby the registrar held
suitors' funds might prove a temptation to corruption would, of course, prove
accurate. The judicial commissioners, who sat in Dublin in the spring and summer
of 1828, also strongly criticized the registrar's administration of suitors' funds. By
contrast with the court's rule-books, which appear to have been meticulously
maintained, no book of accounts of fees was kept. The registrar's accounts, instead,
were described as consisting of:

> sheets of paper loosely stitched together, purporting to contain the accounts
> of the proceeds in different causes; the earliest commencing in the year 1805;
> but without any arrangement, and omitting a great number, which, the
> officer states, have not yet been collected or made out … the payments
> appearing therein are not stated to have been made under any particular
> order; and the entire presents a mass of irregularity and confusion.[189]

There was no requirement (as with suitors' funds in the Court of Chancery) that
the funds be deposited in the Bank of Ireland. The profits of sale were usually
lodged in the registry, and, if deposited in a bank, were lodged in the registrar's
personal account.

Non-payment of sums owed to suitors enhanced the opportunity for
corruption. Some litigants, particularly salvors in remote areas unaware that an
order had been made in their favour, complained of never being paid.[190] Such
inefficiency in transmitting money to suitors left the registrar with a fund of
unclaimed cash available for irregular purposes. It seems to have been an
acknowledged perquisite that the registrar was entitled, in the interval between
deposit and the order, to make use of the proceeds.[191] Sir Henry Meredyth
conceded that the registrar was entitled to exercise a discretion over suitors'
moneys in his registry and that 'there is nothing in the law or practice of the court
to control him'.

The levying of fees by court officers for unnecessary, or fictional, duties, and for
useless paper work, was routine in all the courts in early nineteenth-century
Ireland. The registrar of the Admiralty Court, though probably not the worst
offender in the Irish judicature, also engaged in such practices. Suitors were
burdened with unnecessary scriveners' functions. The registrar was entitled to a
charge for every page transcribed; he charged a sheet fee for every page of ninety
words. Since his fees were determined according to the number of sheets
generated, techniques were used to multiply the size of the paper work. When
suitors sought copies of depositions, the libel which was the foundation of the
litigation would be laboriously reproduced on the deposition 'thus compelling a
party demanding a copy of depositions to take out and pay for a copy of a pleading

189  *Eighteenth Report*, p. 20.    190  Ibid., pp 22, 23.    191  Ibid., p. 89.

which he has … filed himself'.[192] The registrar of the Admiralty Court was also guilty of the common offence of charging suitors for documents which they did not actually need. A suitor could not obtain a decree unless he also paid for an attested copy of that decree. The commissioners of inquiry sensibly recommended that 'the party should be left to his own discretion as to the necessity for taking out a copy of his decree; and if not taken out, it should not be charged for'.[193]

## The marshal of the Court of Admiralty

Richard Reade served as marshal from 1751 to his death in 1774. But after the loss of the fishing and anchorage revenues, Reade found [it] of no value whatsoever'.[194] He took no interest in the office, and 'never sought to renew his grant at the accession of his present Majesty'. Instead he relinquished the functions to a deputy, Hugh O'Neill. On the death of Reade, Judge FitzGerald pressed the claims of Hugh O'Neill with a glowing reference:

> The court, indeed, could not carry on its ordinary business without a marshal, and if there is not one duly appointed the court must of necessity assume one, for otherwise the justice might stand still. Mr Hugh O'Neill is the acting marshal. I found him in that office when I was first appointed judge just 18 years ago, and he is perhaps the most diligent, active and upright officer to be found in any court in this kingdom.[195]

In July 1774, O'Neill (who had the constitutional distinction of being the last officer of the Irish court to be appointed by the lord admiral under the old system) succeeded Richard Reade.[196] It appears that, by contrast with his predecessor, O'Neill at least discharged the functions personally.[197] When O'Neill died in 1792 the office became a sinecure once more. The office was handed on to Henry LeFanu who just two years later relinquished office in favour of his nephew, William LeFanu.[198] In reality, the duties were delegated to the proctor, Henry Richardson. Barrington reckoned Henry Richardson 'the most active and responsible officer of the court'.[199]

Following the loss of the revenues generated by fishing licensing in the mid-eighteenth century, the value of the office diminished. For the three years ending

192  *Eighteenth Report*, p. 15.                    193  Ibid., p. 17.
194  R. FitzGerald to the commissioners of Admiralty, 3 June 1774 (TNA (PRO), ADM 1/3,884, f. 353).
195  Ibid.
196  Warrant dated 28 July 1774 (TNA (PRO), ADM 2/1,058, f. 366).
197  It was the practice of the *Watson's Almanack* to identify the deputy marshal of the Irish Court of Admiralty. The absence of a reference to a deputy during O'Neill's time suggests that he acted in person.
198  A. LeFanu to S. Hamilton, 8 Dec. 1794 (NAI, OP/14/13).
199  Second statement and deposition of Sir Jonah Barrington, 8 July 1828 (NAI, CSORP, 1828/983). Lefanu was succeeded for a short interval by Thomas Mullock. However, Mullock's

in 1817 the average gross fees earned by the marshal were £161 *per annum*. The earnings of the deputy marshal were only a fraction of the marshal's: the net average earning of the deputy marshal for the three years ending 1827 was a pitiful £53 18s. 6d.[200] Fees were charged for services which were fictional. Where several different suits were taken against the same vessel, an equivalent number of warrants issued; the marshal then levied separate fees for executing the same arrest.[201] He also charged separate fees for detaining the vessel and the cargo. The commissioners condemned such multiplication of fees for the one transaction. Customarily the marshal received a fee for 'release' (for releasing a vessel after the promovent's libel was dismissed, or where the suit was settled). But he also charged for something called a 'discharge'. In fact, there was no difference between the function of 'release' and the new function of 'discharge'. Again the marshal was receiving multiple fees for the same function. There was also double-charging in the administration of commissions of appraisal: the marshal was entitled to a poundage (assessed at 5% of the first £100 and 2.5% of the remainder) paid on the sum realized by the sale; but he had also started charging a new 'day fee' of three guineas *per diem*. The day fee was charged for exactly the same function as he was paid poundage. In a petition, dated April 1824, the court's proctors protested against this new imposition.[202] The 1828 judicial commissioners also could find no justification for this duplicative day fee for which there was no equivalent in England.[203] The fees extracted by the marshal had, at least, enabled the acquisition of one addition to the court's physical resources – by the end of the eighteenth century the marshal had been issued with the traditional symbol of admiralty judicature authority, a ceremonial silver oar carried on board, when effecting arrest 'as the badge of office'.[204]

### The king's advocate

The king's advocate represented the interests of the Crown in prize suits, in suits where the Crown claimed entitlement to admiralty droits, and in admiralty criminal prosecutions.[205] In 1781 James Sheil, who had served as king's advocate

commission was revoked in 1815, and placed in the hands of Robert Simpson (*Eighteenth Report*, Appendix 16, p. 165). Simpson again discharged his duties through a deputy, Peyton Gamble Meares, under an arrangement in which he allowed his deputy one-third of the profits (ibid.).

200  *Eighteenth Report*, Appendix 20, p. 185.        201  Ibid., p. 38.
202  The petition is set out in the *Eighteenth Report*, Appendix 20, p. 189. It was subscribed by William Richardson, Henry Richardson, Robert Marchbank, Robert Archland Whiteway and John McLoughlin.
203  *Eighteenth Report*, p. 42.
204  *The city and country calendar ... 1795* (Dublin, 1795), p. 239. The silver oar had not existed at the beginning of the century; see p. 62 above. A later, silver-electroplated admiralty mace inscribed 'High Court of Admiralty Ireland' is now held by Trinity College Dublin. D. Bennett, *The silver collection, Trinity College Dublin* (Dublin, 1988), p. 122.
205  John Leslie Foster, who held the office 1816–30, described the functions as being to 'sign

since 1751, though senile and incapable of discharging the office, refused to resign. Robert Day (the future judge of the King's Bench) pestered his uncle (the retired judge of the Admiralty Court, Robert FitzGerald) into intervening on his behalf.[206] Day reported that Sheil was irrecoverably senile: he 'has in fact died a civil death … that he never can properly emerge and that it is understood a pension is granted for his subsistence'.[207]

However, no action was taken by the Admiralty. After a long interval during which the position was unfilled, Robert Day, in May 1785, at last obtained the office.[208] Day served as king's advocate until his appointment in 1789 to the more valuable office of chairman of the Co. Dublin Quarter Sessions. In 1789 Dominick Trant, a former MP for Kilkenny, and brother-in-law of the lord chancellor, John FitzGibbon, was appointed the king's advocate.[209] Trant served for only a short period and died after a severe illness in June 1790. In July 1790 the distinguished civil lawyer Patrick Duigenan succeeded Trant.[210] After 1783 the office was integrated into the government's system of patronage, and was a remunerated public office worth £300 in 1799.[211] However, with the withdrawal of prize jurisdiction by the Act of Union in 1800, the office declined in importance; once prize was removed from the court, the advocate merely acted as counsel in droit suits and the rare admiralty criminal prosecution.[212] In 1816 the barrister and member of Parliament for Armagh and Lisburn,[213] John Leslie Foster, was appointed to the office.[214]

*Admiralty practitioners*

In 1769 ten Dublin lawyers practised as advocates in the civil law courts. The size of the profession increased only very gradually. By 1780 the number of civilian (though not necessarily admiralty) advocates had increased to fourteen,[215] and by 1790 the figure had risen to nineteen.[216] In the mid-eighteenth century the civilian advocate operated as a separate profession, practising exclusively in the courts of civil jurisdiction; in 1769 eight of the ten advocates practised exclusively as advocates; only two practised as advocates and barristers concurrently.[217] However, as the eighteenth

---

pleadings, and act as counsel upon hearings and motions, and to advise as to the expediency of instituting droit suits when consulted by the king's proctor'. *Eighteenth Report*, Appendix 6, p. 94.

206  *History of the Irish Parliament*, iv, p. 33. Robert Day was a son of Robert FitzGerald's sister Lucy. He sat as an MP (firstly for Tuam, and subsequently for Ardfert) continuously between 1783 and 1798.

207  R. Day to R. FitzGerald, 21 Mar. 1781 (PRONI, T 3,075/4/54).

208  TNA (PRO), HO 100/16, f. 368.

209  *The Times*, 7 Oct. 1789; *History of the Irish Parliament*, vi, pp 433–4.

210  *The Times*, 9 Aug. 1790.

211  'List of offices tenable by members of parliament in Ireland' (NLI, MS 887, ff 59, 63).

212  *Eighteenth Report*, Appendix 7, p. 94.    213  *The Times*, 1 July & 22 Aug. 1818.

214  *Eighteenth Report*, Appendix 6, p. 94.    215  *Wilson's Dublin Directory 1780*, p. 116.

216  *Wilson's Dublin Directory 1790*, pp 119–20.

217  Archibold Montgomery and Barry Yelverton, *Wilson's Dublin Directory 1769*, p. 101.

century advanced, the separate civilian legal profession had begun to dissolve; it was superseded by a newer model of lawyer capable of practising interchangeably both as advocate and barrister. In 1801 twelve advocates practised at the Court of Admiralty.[218] All of these lawyers had been admitted to practise as barristers. This small admiralty bar was relatively distinguished – it included names like Arthur Browne (the prime serjeant whose work on admiralty law became an international authority),[219] Charles Bushe (the future chief justice of the King's Bench) and William Fletcher (the future chief justice of the Common Pleas).

Theoretically, the right of audience in the Court of Admiralty was restricted to advocates, while barristers were not entitled to appear. In practice, that civilian monopoly was not over-rigidly enforced: barristers were allowed audience (though not to sign pleadings) at the discretion of the court. Arthur Browne noted that 'the common lawyers, though not allowed to sign pleadings, are admitted to speak in these courts in Ireland; for in that kingdom the common lawyer is not much distinguished from the civilian: multiplicity of business has not produced division of labour'.[220]

The small number of proctors – just nine in 1782 – was tiny compared with the 850 lawyers who practised as attorneys in Dublin.[221] The size of the profession was tightly regulated. When ecclesiastical proctors began to appear in the Court of Admiralty in the late 1790s the court promulgated a general order intended to enforce the monopoly, providing that 'no person shall be admitted a proctor unless he shall have been duly indentured and served an apprenticeship to a proctor of admiralty'.[222] This rule facilitated the development of a monopoly; since admission depended on prior apprenticeship to an existing admiralty proctor, existing proctors were enabled to agree amongst themselves to limit the number of apprenticeships. In 1828, Dublin Chamber of Commerce identified as one of the causes of delays in the court 'the limitation of proctors'.[223] Most proctors also practised as attorneys. Jonah Barrington compared the position in England and in Ireland where the 'practitioners in the Court of Admiralty in Ireland are not, as in England, exclusively so; the proctors of admiralty also practise as attorneys and solicitors in all the other courts of Ireland'.[224] Of the leading proctors active in 1824

218  Patrick Duigenan LLD; Benedict Hamilton LLD; Ninian Mahaffy LLD; Arthur Browne LLD; W. Betty LLD; Charles Bushe LLD, William Ridgeway LLD; Robert Smith LLD; W. Vavaseur LLD (senior advocate); John Radcliffe LLD; J. Jameson LLD; W. Fletcher LLD (NAI, OP 130/2).

219  J.C. Sweeney, 'The Admiralty Law of Arthur Browne', *Journal of Maritime Law and Commerce*, 26 (1995), 59.

220  *A compendious view*, ii, p. 131.

221  Thomas Boland, Thomas Butler, John Coen, Phillip Collins, Thomas Dease, Armstong FitzGerald, Thomas Hackett, John Robinson, Francis Spotwood. Only the latter two were not included in the list of attorneys, *Wilson's Dublin Directory 1782*, p. 115.

222  General Order, 11 Oct. 1797; *In re Thompson* (1849) 5 Ir Jur 258.

223  Minutes of the council of Dublin Chamber of Commerce, 22 Jan. 1828 (NAI, 1,064/3/3, f. 249).

224  'To his majesty in Council, the humble memorial of Jonah Barrington, esquire, LL.D. one of his

(William Richardson, Henry Richardson, Robert Marchbank, Robert Archland Whiteway and John McLoughlin) only one (John McLoughlin) was not listed as a practising attorney.[225]

## THE PREMISES OF THE IRISH COURT OF ADMIRALTY, 1760–1830

At some point in the mid-eighteenth century, the court vacated its home in St Patrick's Cathedral and transferred to Christ Church Lane, part of the courts' complex at Christ Church Cathedral.[226] In Christ Church the court was accommodated in an office-sized premises, for which it paid a 'considerable diurnal rent'.[227] The issue of suitable and permanent accommodation for the court had been raised in the Irish House of Commons by Barrington when the Four Courts was under construction. FitzGibbon LC designated a home for the Court of Admiralty.[228] However, in 1801 the chamber originally assigned by FitzGibbon to the court in 1796 was transferred to the new Court of Exchequer Chamber, and the Court of Admiralty was evicted.[229] Barrington protested by suspending all admiralty proceedings:

> the Court of Admiralty in the Four Courts has been last term appropriated by the judges to the new Court of Error, and so altered as to make it altogether mis-adapted to the further occupation of the Court of Admiralty sittings – and as no new court has been since allotted for that purpose, I am to acquaint you that the proceedings of the Court of Admiralty must be necessarily suspended until a new court is appropriated and fitted up for that purpose. There is a chamber adjoining the Court of Exchequer which might be prepared to answer that purpose ...[230]

majesty's counsel at law, and judge of his High Court of Admiralty of Ireland' (NAI, OP 214/11).

225 These are the names subscribed to the proctors' petition of 1824 (p. 182 above). *Eighteenth Report*, Appendix 20, p. 189.

226 The address of the Court of Admiralty of Ireland is given as Christ Church Lane in documentation accompanying the 1776 appeal to the English Court, the *Venus* (TNA (PRO), HCA, 16/62 (340)). The lease to the Court of Admiralty is not recorded in the repertory of leases of Christ Church Dublin (RCB, C.6.1.17.5). This suggests that the arrangement may have been with the lessees of Christ Church, and not a direct arrangement with the Cathedral. On the history of the Four Courts at Christ Church see C. Kenny, 'The Four Courts at Christ Church, 1608–1796', in W.N. Osborough (ed.), *Explorations in law and history* (Dublin, 1995), p. 107.

227 R. FitzGerald to the commissioners of Admiralty, 29 June 1758 (TNA (PRO), ADM 1/3,883, f. 13).

228 2 Jan. 1803 (NAI, OP 154/1). *Third Report of the Commissioners of Public Records*, 1813, plate xvi (HC 1812–13 (337), xv.1).

229 *Reilly v. Anon.* (1801) Rowe 675.

230 J. Barrington to Castlereagh, 5 Apr. 1801 (NAI, OP 107/3).

The court returned to work after renting rooms belonging to the Common Pleas.[231]
In 1802 Barrington once again reverted to the strategy of closing the court:

> on the appropriation of the present courts, a suitable one was allotted to the
> admiralty department and occupied by it – but, on the new Courts of Error
> and Rolls being instituted, they were necessarily obliged to occupy the Court
> of Admiralty as being the only one sufficiently spacious for their occupation,
> and no new court of admiralty or any office for its records or officers has
> since been instituted. I am to remark to you that in consequence of such
> omission, causes of very considerable importance remain at a stand and
> vessels of value are now necessarily detained under arrest in different ports,
> and must remain so until a proper court be appropriated for causes to
> be adjudicated and processes to be returned … I have therefore been
> necessitated to suspend all business in the Court of Admiralty; I have
> received many petitions from suitors likely to be injured by delay but whom
> I am incapacitated from redressing by the reason I mention.[232]

The problem was addressed when an office off the entrance hall[233] to the Four
Courts became available and was assigned to the Admiralty Court. The room was
similar to the private chambers of the chief justices, with a bathroom attached, and
was probably never intended to function as a public court room. An editorial note
in the *Law Recorder* in 1827 regretted that:

> the Court of Admiralty of Ireland, in which cases of the greatest importance
> to the public are discussed and decided, should be obliged to sit in a
> wretched room adjoining the public entrance to the hall of the courts, and
> that even in this confined and inconvenient spot there is no description
> of accommodation for either practitioners or the public. Surely these
> inconveniences ought to be remedied.[234]

In 1812 Daniel Pineau reported that 'the records are lodged in a front parlour of
the registrar's house at Stephen's Green, Dublin'.[235] Private storage of records
risked destruction. In 1803 Barrington complained that in the absence of a public
office, 'the records of the court have all been nearly destroyed by [a] flood'.[236] The
extent of the loss of its archives had been considerable. When, in the mid-
eighteenth century, Hugh Baillie served as judge he was in a position to consult a

---

231 J. Barrington to unnamed, 2 Jan. 1803 (NAI, OP 154/1).
232 J. Barrington to the chief secretary [?], 19 Dec. 1802 (NAI, OP 130/9).
233 'Ground plan and entrance to the Four Courts, 1813' (*Third Report of the Commissioners of Public
    Records, 1813*, plate xv (HC 1812–13 (337) xv.1)).
234 (1827) 1 *Law Recorder* 28.
235 *Second Report of the Commissioners of Public Records, 1812*, p. 262.
236 J. Barrington to unnamed, 2 Jan. 1803 (NAI, OP 154/1).

set of records dating back to the 1670s;[237] however, by 1812 the registrar reported that the earliest records in the possession of the registry dated only from 1747.[238]

PRIZE LAW IN IRELAND, 1776–1800

*The American War, 1776–83*

Early in January 1776, Robert FitzGerald wrote diffidently to the commissioners of Admiralty noting that it was probable that American prizes would be taken into Ireland 'pursuant to the late act of Parliament for a commerce with the American rebels' and while carefully assuring the commissioners that he would not act in any prize cases 'without an express order', sought a commission to prize captures. The prize commission that he sought[239] was granted; in June 1776 the Irish court was invested with jurisdiction to process proceedings in respect of prizes captured under letters of marque granted against American vessels.[240] The amount of prize business processed by the court during the American war was lower than the periods during the 1750s when the court previously had prize jurisdiction.[241] When France joined the war, the Irish court, in August 1778, received the necessary commission to process captures of French prizes.[242] This was to be the last prize commission ever issued to the Irish Court of Admiralty. Thereafter, the policy towards Ireland changed. The Irish court was not included in the commission, issued in 1779 to virtually all other vice-admiralty courts, to exercise prize jurisdiction against Spanish captures.[243] Nor was it included in the commissions issued to courts of vice-admiralty in 1780 to try captures of Dutch vessels.[244] However, the Irish court appears to have ignored the legal consequences of its omission from the schedule of authorized prize courts and, on at least three occasions, exercised prize jurisdiction in the case of Spanish and Dutch captures.[245]

Offence was taken in Ireland by the practice of the English Court of Admiralty stationing its own prize commissioners in Irish ports. These commissioners were authorized to administer standing interrogatories for the purpose of proceedings

---

237  H. Baillie to the commissioners of Admiralty, 17 May 1745 (TNA (PRO), ADM, 1/3,990).
238  *Second Report of the Commissioners of Public Records, 1812* (HC 1812–13 (337) xv.1, p. 261).
239  R. FitzGerald to the commissioners of Admiralty, 3 Jan. 1776 (TNA (PRO), ADM 1/3,884, f. 231).
240  22 June 1776 (TNA (PRO), ADM 2/1,058, f. 355).
241  Only three appeals were taken to the prize appeals commissioners in the period 1776 to 1784, one fifth of the number in the period 1756–63: the *Victoria*, 1780; the *Henrietta Maria*, 1781, the *Johannes* 1781 (TNA (PRO), HCA 41/6).
242  15 Aug. 1778 (TNA (PRO), ADM 2/1059, ff 271, 272). Records from two Irish prize cases, both *c*.1778, the *Flora of Dunkirk* and the *Margaretta*, are included in the King's Inns eighteenth-century admiralty and ecclesiastical precedent book (King's Inns MS, ff 243–7, 248–51).
243  24 June 1779 (TNA (PRO), ADM 2/1,060, f. 139).
244  22 Dec. 1780 (TNA (PRO), ADM 2/1060, f. 306).
245  The *Victoria* (decree of 1780); the *Henrietta Maria* (decree of 1781); the *Johannes* (decree of 1781) (TNA (PRO), HCA, 41/6).

before the prize court in London. This continued to be a source of grievance. A letter of protest by Warden Flood (complaining that 'the jurisdiction of the Admiralty Court of Ireland has been invaded by the issuing of commissions from the High Court of Admiralty to persons in the towns of Kinsale and the city of Limerick for examining witnesses') was impatiently dismissed by the judge of the English court, Sir James Marriott.[246]

*The Irish prize question, 1795–7*

Prior to 1783 the accepted view was that the Irish court did not have intrinsic prize jurisdiction. However, section 1 of the Irish Admiralty Court Act 1783 unsettled this understanding. Section 1 defined the jurisdiction of the new court in a way which made it arguable that it was being given a wider competence: the court was to have jurisdiction not just 'to hear and determine all and all manner of civil, maritime [causes]' but was also empowered to adjudicate 'other causes to the jurisdiction of the said court belonging'. Was the ambivalent phrase 'other causes to the said court belonging' wide enough to include prize work? The issue was fought over in three cases in the late 1790s.

    The first of these involved three Dutch East Indian ships taken into the river Shannon in September 1795. A commission was issued by the commissioners of Admiralty in London to the judge of the Irish Court of Admiralty, Warden Flood, to have prize proceedings administered against the vessels in Ireland. The lord lieutenant, Camden, urged that the prize commission to the Irish court be rescinded: the 1783 Act gave the new Irish Admiralty Court power to adjudicate 'civil, maritime and other causes', but 'no power to that court to try prize causes'. Camden was concerned about another issue: the lack of an appeal.[247] The (English) Manning of the Navy Act 1793[248] provided for an appeal to the English Prize Appeal Commissioners. But this appeal did not apply to sentences originating in Ireland. This was problematic because Camden did not entirely trust the Irish court:

> there is no right of appeal from here, and as the Admiralty Court in Ireland cannot be expected to be perfectly acquainted with all circumstances which might guide its decrees, it may justly be apprehended that the decisions here may not always be consistent with the principles which govern the decision in Great Britain.[249]

    The same issue arose in 1797 when the *Deseada*, a Spanish vessel carrying rum and sugar from Havana, *en route* for Hamburg, was taken into Limerick harbour

---

246  J. Marriott to the commissioners of Admiralty, 12 July 1779 (TNA (PRO), ADM 1/3,885, f. 437). Sir James Marriott was judge of the English Court of Admiralty, 1778–98.

247  Earl Camden to the duke of Portland, 30 Oct. 1795 (TNA (PRO), HO 100/59, f. 60).

248  33 Geo. III, c. 46 (Eng.), 1793.

249  Earl Camden to the duke of Portland, 30 Oct. 1795 (TNA (PRO), HO 100/59, f. 60).

by the naval ship, the *Amphritite*.[250] A warrant for the arrest of the ship on behalf of the Crown was issued by the Irish Court of Admiralty. Concurrent with the proceedings in Dublin, a suit opened in the English Court of Admiralty. A rescript was issued by Sir James Marriott,[251] the judge of the English court, instructing the king's advocate in Ireland, the combative Patrick Duigenan, to terminate the Irish proceedings. Duigenan, however, simply refused to comply with the order of Sir James Marriott. The judge, Jonah Barrington, also objected, arguing that the Irish court had an inherent right to process prize captures.[252]

The impasse in Dublin was referred to Baron Loughborough, the lord chancellor of England who, in 'the leisure time of imperfect holidays' during Christmas 1797, considered the legal claims being advanced by the Irish court. Loughborough's position was a straightforward rehearsal of the traditional pre-1783 principle: the entitlement to administer prize jurisdiction was conditional on the receipt of a commission from the Crown, and none having been granted, the Irish court was incompetent.[253] Having first rehearsed Barrington's argument – that a 'court of admiralty had an inherent right of trying prizes, which in England has been modified by prize acts, but subsists in Ireland as an original and final jurisdiction' – he then went on to reprise the orthodox position:

> the same notion had once prevailed in Scotland where the admiralty jurisdiction is preserved separate and entire by the Act of Union. It is certain, however, that no court of admiralty has an original jurisdiction in questions of prize and the Court of Admiralty in England never pretended to it. The king appoints, by special commission issued upon each war, a judicature subordinate to the authority of his council to examine and determine in the first instance questions concerning the right of captures made at sea. That commission has usually been directed to the High Court of Admiralty, and it is by virtue of that commission alone that the court is enabled to take cognizance of a question of prize.[254]

The Irish lord chancellor discussed with his English counterpart the possibility of dismissing Dr Duigenan (who he described as a 'not very right-headed man nor yet a very practicable man'). Apprehensive that 'the bear' – Duigenan – 'was not to be tamed',[255] FitzGibbon urged the extreme measure of the king issuing a letter

---

250  E. Cooke to C. Grenville, 4 Feb. 1797 (TNA (PRO), HO 100/71, f. 106).
251  Barrington undertook to take no further steps towards condemnation. J. Barrington to T. Pelham, 23 Nov. 1797 (NAI, OP 24/18).
252  Barrington claimed that his approach had the support of Fletcher J and Lord Avanmore. 'Statement as to the High Court of Admiralty and the judge thereof' (NAI, CSORP, 1828/983).
253  Loughborough LC to FitzGibbon LC, 30 Dec. 1797 (NAI, OP 24/19).
254  Ibid.
255  FitzGibbon LC to T. Pelham, 19 Dec. 1797, *A volley of execrations*, p. 274.

directing Duigenan to desist: 'Such an order I presume he will not venture to disobey; and if he should, I should suppose Lord Camden would not feel any scruples in removing him from office'.[256] The Irish claim was also referred to the king's advocate general in the English court, William Scott. Scott, increasing the pressure on Duigenan, advised that the proceedings in the *Deseada* were 'cognizable exclusively in the prize court' in London.[257] In January 1798 the Irish court reluctantly gave up its claim to process the *Deseada* prize. Dr Duigenan tendered his resignation as king's advocate, and privately published a pamphlet, *The Case of the Deseada*, (described mockingly by FitzGibbon LC as a 'manifesto in a very nervous style'),[258] in which he set out the constitutional case against the English court's interference in the *Deseada*.

## The Madonna del Burso

The claims of the Irish court to prize competence were settled definitively in the *Madonna del Burso*. In the winter of 1797 the *Madonna*, a Greek vessel which had departed from the port of Patras with a cargo of currants and leather, had been blown off course and diverted into Dingle Bay. There she was seized by Edward King Hill (an officer with the commissioners of customs in Ireland). Hill was so determined to establish that the goods were Dutch, and therefore, prize,[259] that he allegedly invited the captain, an Albanian called Demetrio Antonopolo, 'to dine at his house in Dingle, with his pilot, where he made [him] an offer of the sum of six hundred pounds if [he] would declare the goods to be Dutch property'.[260] A considerable delay (designed to intensify pressure on the captain and crew to confess that the vessel was prize) was allowed to elapse between the time of the original capture in November 1797 and the institution of prize proceedings in February 1798. During this long period of inactivity, the vessel was damaged and the cargo deteriorated.[261] The Albanian captain, who had to pay for accommodation for the crew, was imprisoned for debt.[262] The crew was reduced to begging around the streets of Dublin, and a collection was taken up in the House of Lords on behalf of the starving Albanian sailors by the lord chancellor, John FitzGibbon.[263]

---

256  FitzGibbon LC to Loughborough LC, 15 Dec. 1797, *A volley of execrations*, p. 273.
257  FitzGibbon LC to Loughborough LC, 20 Dec. 1797, *A volley of execrations*, p. 275.
258  'Case of *The Deseada*', 20 Jan. 1798 (NAI, OP 24/ 10). FitzGibbon LC to Loughborough LC, 15 Dec. 1797, *A volley of execrations*, p. 273.
259  According to Duigenan's account 'some of the sailors made very strong affidavits before a magistrate that both ship and vessel belonged to Dutch merchants resident in Amsterdam (though she had false papers on board purporting that she was bound for Hamburg)'. P. Duigenan to unnamed official, 9 Apr. 1799 (NAI, OP 65/7); J. Barrington to Earl Spencer, 30 Oct. 1799 (NAI, OP 65/7).
260  Affidavit of Demetrio Antonopolo, 17 Apr. 1801 (TNA (PRO), HCA 32/757).
261  Barrington claimed that the deterioration had occurred during the period that a deputy marshal nominated by the owners, a Mr Ankettle, 'a total stranger to the court', had charge of the vessel. J. Barrington to Earl Spencer, 30 Oct. 1799 (NAI, OP 65/7).
262  Affidavit of Demetrio Antonopolo, 17 Apr. 1801 (TNA (PRO), HCA 32/757).
263  Petition of the 22 Greek sailors on *La Madonna*, Aug. 1800 (NAI, OP 84/7).

On 10 May 1798, without the knowledge of the government, a libel was exhibited by Duigenan against the cargo of the *Madonna* as a droit and perquisite to his majesty 'in his admiralty in Ireland'.[264] The proceedings dragged on for a year before, in February 1798, the claimants entered an exception to the jurisdiction of the Irish court, objecting 'that the Court of Admiralty, as constituted under the [Irish Court of Admiralty Act 1783] had no power or jurisdiction to proceed on any manner of captures and seizures, prizes, or reprisals, of any ships, or goods that shall be taken in the ports or creeks of Ireland'.[265] The claimants, knowing that they were bound to lose in the Irish Court of Admiralty, changed tactics and obtained a writ of prohibition out of the Court of Chancery. The application to the Chancery was unconventional – the Court of King's Bench was the traditional court for prohibiting excess of jurisdiction by courts of admiralty. It is likely that the Court of Chancery was selected on the ground that it was presided over by John FitzGibbon, who, following the *Deseada* controversy two years earlier, was known to be antipathetic to the Irish Admiralty Court. Barrington, aware of FitzGibbon's dislike of him, observed that 'the whole of the proceedings in the prohibition never could be supported in its present form in any other court'.[266] Barrington entered an appearance, where he defended the exercise of prize jurisdiction by his court on the ground that his court had 'original [prize] jurisdiction' and did not need a prize commission. He persisted in the argument that the court possessed an inherent jurisdiction to engage in prize matters even without a prize commission. In a letter to the chief secretary, Barrington pointed out that 'the rule books of this court show that such cases have been argued in Ireland for three hundred years'.[267] Inevitably, the Chancery dismissed Barrington's defence, holding that no such power was given by the Irish Admiralty Court Act 1783: 'the court could look for its powers only in the statute 23 Geo. III; and that by any other construction, it would have power of determining peace or war'.[268]

In 1801 the *Madonna* proceedings were transferred to the English Court of Admiralty.[269] The English court decreed that the cargo belonged to an innocent neutral – a disappointed admiralty official accounted for the decision on the ground 'that the court here is particularly tender of Turkish property on account of the ignorance of the Turks with regard to our laws'.[270] In 1802 the proprietor of

264  Duigenan had presumably withdrawn the resignation as king's advocate which he had submitted following his defeat in the *Deseada*.
265  'Letter from Dr Barrington, judge of the Admiralty to the right honourable Earl Spencer on the case of *La Madonna* in the High Court of Admiralty of Ireland', 30 Oct. 1799 (NAI, OP 65/7).
266  J. Barrington to E. Cooke, 23 Nov. 1798 (NAI, OP 48/15). Barrington alleged that FitzGibbon had 'wilfully misstated and mis-recited the proceedings' in the prohibition case.
267  J. Barrington to E. Cooke, 28 July 1800 (TNA (PRO), 30/42/18/4).
268  *A compendious view*, ii, p. 153.
269  The Irish admiralty proctor, Patrick Hamilton, was put in charge of taking the evidence which had been collected in Ireland to London, and for bringing Captain Hill and two crew members over to London; P. Hamilton to A. Marsden, 28 Jan. 1802 (NAI, OP 130/7).
270  E. Cooke to A. Marsden, 19 Dec. 1801 (NAI, OP 130/7).

the *Madonna* instituted an action in the English court for the economic loss caused
by the misconduct of the customs and the Admiralty Court in Ireland.[271] Judge
William Scott found that the three-month interval, between the seizure of the
vessel in November 1797 and the initiation of proceedings in February 1798,
rendered Hill liable for demurrage and for the damage to the freight which had
occurred in Dingle. A second period of actionable delay was the interval during
which the Irish court illegally proceeded without lawful prize jurisdiction against
the vessel. The ever-charitable Scott absolved Barrington and Duigenan of
misconduct: 'knowing the high character of the persons concerned, I consider
these proceedings as arising out of an unsettled state of things, in which those
gentlemen could not consider themselves, as conscientiously and honourably at
liberty to abdicate their claim of jurisdiction'.[272]

Nonetheless, Scott held that the neutral proprietor of the *Madonna* should not
have to bear the cost. Damages, which the government undertook to pay, were
decreed. Lord Hardwicke estimated that the sum payable by way of compensation
ran to thousands of pounds. The government was also obliged to support the
destitute Greek crew who had remained in Dublin.[273]

The *Madonna* litigation had permanent constitutional consequences. There had
been no reference to the obscure Court of Admiralty of Ireland in the original
outlines of the proposed post-union judicature, drawn up in 1798.[274] Between 1798
and 1800 the *Madonna* case had intervened. It is at this point that Article 8 of the
Act of Union 1800 appeared. Article 8 contained a very elaborate reference to the
court, providing 'that from and after the Union, there shall remain in Ireland, an
instance court of admiralty, for the determination of causes civil and maritime
only'. The inclusion of this emphatically restrictive description of the jurisdiction
of the court was intended to settle this prize claim once and for all.

*The title to captured prize*

Two Irish cases in the late-eighteenth century involved difficult issues of the legal
title to vessels after capture by privateers. In the first of these, the *Union* in 1779,
an American privateer, Gerard Sullivan, acting under a letter of marque from
Congress, had captured a vessel, and held it in his possession on the Atlantic for a
month before he was overpowered by the crew. The crew took the vessel back to
Ireland. The king's advocate argued that when the *Union* was taken by Sullivan it
had become an American enemy vessel. It was a basic rule of prize law that
captures of enemy vessels by non-commissioned persons vested in the Crown.[275]

---

271  The *Madonna del Burso* (1802) 4 C Rob 169; 165 ER 574.
272  Ibid., 180, 578.
273  Earl of Hardwicke to W. Wickham, 18 Oct. 1802 (PRONI, T 2627/5/E/81). I am grateful to Dr
     James Kelly for referring me to this item.
274  NLI, MS 887, f. 7.
275  *R. v. Broom* (1697) 12 Mod. Rep. 134; 88 ER 1217.

The first component of the rule was in place; the crew which had re-taken her was not commissioned by a letter of marque. The second, and more difficult, condition was that the *Union* have changed nationality when taken by Sullivan. If the American capture had changed nationality the crew had captured an enemy vessel (and the vessel vested in the Crown). The conventional test for determining whether a vessel had changed nationality was whether, after capture, the vessel had been taken into the territory and protection of the enemy (*infra praesidia*). Although the *Union* had not physically reached America, the king's advocate argued that, after so long a period, the vessel was constructively *infra praesidia*: 'for in respect of a voyage across the Atlantic and that a month's time was equal to being brought into any port and fitted out again'. However, Judge FitzGerald rejected this constructive definition of the *infra praesidia* principle. The *Union* had not been taken into an enemy port. The vessel remained the property of the original owners in the same way that vessels taken by pirates remained the property of the original owners. The owners were entitled to repossession of the *Union* (and the crew was entitled to salvage compensation).[276]

A sentence of condemnation was necessary to transfer title in a prize to a third-party purchaser. The doctrinal question which arose in the *Hanna* in 1799 was whether a sentence of condemnation was sufficient where it was issued by a prize court commissioned by a belligerent state operating not in the belligerent state, but in some third country. The *Hanna of Maryport*, a British-registered vessel, had been sailing from Belfast to Danzig when she was captured by a French privateer and taken to Christiansen in Norway, where the French had established an extra-jurisdictional prize court, and had condemned hundreds of British vessels.[277] She was then sold at a public auction in Christiansen to a Norwegian, Daniel Isaacson. It was registered as a Danish vessel, and proceeded to Belfast, where she was discovered by her former owners. The former owners then took proceedings in the Irish Court of Admiralty, *Wood v. the Hanna*,[278] for restoration of the vessel. These proceedings, in turn, prompted a diplomatic complaint by the Danish consul (who suggested that the challenge to the integrity of the sentence of the Christiansen prize court in the Dublin courts was an act of aggression against Denmark).[279]

276   W. Sheil to J. Dyson, 30 June 1779 (TNA (PRO), ADM 1/3,681, f. 180). FitzGerald's analysis was approved by the English civil lawyers William Wynne and George Harris (TNA (PRO), ADM 1/3,681, f. 181).

277   George Eskildson to Viscount Castlereagh, 7 May 1799 (TNA (PRO), HO 100/89, f. 15).

278   (1799) *A compendious view*, ii, Appendix, pp 29, 80; 'Report on the *Hanna*', 24 May 1799 (TNA (PRO), HO 100/89, f. 18).

279   The Danish consul complained that Barrington had been responsible for a 'great infraction of the [1670] Treaty [between England and Denmark] and long and uninterrupted friendship which has subsisted between the two nations'. He also excepted to the jurisdiction of the Irish court, arguing that 'the transaction (if any injury was done to the British subject) … was not committed on the high seas, but in the king of Denmark's dominions, and, as such, subject to the settlement

The king's advocate in the English Admiralty Court, Sir John Nicholl –
referring to litigation on precisely the same issue which was pending in that court
– advised the Irish government that 'it remains undecided whether the title of the
former owner is extinguished by a sentence of condemnation in France and a bona
fide sale to a neutral, the vessel never having been carried into the French
Dominions.'[280] That English case, the *Flad Oyen*, was decided the following
month.[281] In January 1799 the English Court of Admiralty held that sentences of
condemnation pronounced by French consuls in neutral countries were nullities.[282]
The *Flad Oyen* had been captured by a French privateer and carried into Bergen
in Norway where she was condemned following a sentence pronounced by the
French consul. William Scott dismissed the contention that a sentence pronounced
by a tribunal not operating in the belligerent country, but in a neutral country, was
competent to pass title. International law did not sustain the validity of any prize
court except (i) a court based in the state of the captor, or (ii) a court operating in
a neutral state by virtue of a reciprocal treaty binding each state to active mutual
military support. Neither of these rules applied here. The conveyance was a nullity
and the court ordered restitution to the original owner.

The decision in the *Flad Oyen* meant that the original owner of the *Hanna* was
now definitively entitled to restitution. The lord lieutenant, Castlereagh, sharply
informed the Danish consul, who had been complaining of the Irish proceedings,
of the decision in the *Flad Oyen*: 'sentences of condemnation pronounced by
French consuls in a neutral country have been held by his majesty's tribunals to be
mere nullities, and to found no valid title in a neutral purchaser'. Accordingly, 'the
British owner has just grounds to proceed by due course of law to recover
possession of his vessel'.[283]

Assuming then that such extra-territorial courts did not have jurisdiction to
pass title, and that the original owner of the *Hanna* was entitled to restitution,
which courts – the courts of common law or the Court of Admiralty – could effect
such restitution? *Wood v. the Hanna* was pending before the Irish Admiralty Court.
The Irish court, it was generally assumed, did not possess prize jurisdiction. But
did a suit for the restoration of an illegal prize capture 'savour' of prize so as to
engage the prohibition on the court acting in prize? Barrington had hesitated
before giving judgment until he could ascertain the result in the *Flad* case; but
before he got the opportunity to apply *Flad*, the master moved to the King's Bench
for a prohibition against the Admiralty Court hearing the restitution suit. The
King's Bench, expressing 'strong displeasure' at the proceedings on the ground
that the Admiralty of Ireland had no prize jurisdiction as had been 'lately

    of the two governments only'. George Eskildson to Viscount Castlereagh, 7 May 1799 (TNA
    (PRO), HO 100/89, f. 15).
280  Opinion of Sir John Nicholl, 10 Dec. 1798, ibid., f. 18.
281  (1799) 1 C Rob. 134; 165 ER 124.
282  Viscount Castlereagh to G. Eskildson, 2 July 1799 (TNA (PRO), HO 100/89, f. 87).
283  Ibid.

determined in the case of the Grecian ship [the *Madonna del Burso*]' granted an absolute order of prohibition.[284] Castlereagh firmly instructed Barrington to terminate the proceedings, writing to him in June 1799 that 'I am to intimate to you that it does not appear as this is a prize case that it can be determined without a prize commission, or that it can be determined anywhere but in a prize court of admiralty'.[285]

## THE INSTANCE JURISDICTION OF THE COURT OF ADMIRALTY IN THE LATE-EIGHTEENTH AND EARLY NINETEENTH CENTURY

In 1828 Sir Henry Meredyth reported to the commissioners of inquiry into the Admiralty Court[286] that the business of the court was made up of 'suits for seamens' wages, causes of collision, derelict and salvage causes, *respondentia* and bottomry bonds, causes of possession, causes of security between joint owners'.[287] However, he added, that two species of litigation arose more frequently than the others – suits for wages and suits for salvage.[288]

### Sailors wages

Wages suits probably generated the largest category of admiralty litigation in the late eighteenth century. In the period 1756 to 1783 most of the appeals taken from the Irish Court to London concerned wages cases.[289] But, despite making up the largest category of the court's work, the number of wages cases was, in an absolute sense, still low and uneven. In the 1820s the court was disposing of about ten wages suits *per annum*.[290]

---

284 Arthur Browne commented that the court had granted the prohibition 'on the last day of term, though to do so is contrary to all usual practice'. *A compendious view*, ii, Appendix, p. 85. Petition of George Eskildson, 27 June 1799 (TNA (PRO), HO 100/89, f. 83). The principle against the Admiralty Court being competent to adjudicate restitution following a sentence by an illegal prize court was applied again in *Drivar v. White* (1799 [?]) Rowe 189: a cargo of flax seed had, following condemnation by the French admiralty court at Bergen in Norway, been condemned as prize and purchased by a merchant, Mr Major, who consigned it to the defendant, a Dublin merchant. On arrival in Dublin it was seized under a writ of replevin at the suit of the original owner. In the King's Bench, Baron Kilwarden held that the Irish Admiralty Court would have had no jurisdiction, since the jurisdiction of that court was confined to purely instance matters, and did not include prize issues. The King's Bench went on to hold that the condemnation of the French court did not pass title, it being 'vain now to argue whether the foreign court, sitting in a neutral state, has competent jurisdiction'.

285 Viscount Castlereagh to J. Barrington, 3 June 1799 (TNA (PRO), HO 100/89, f. 31).

286 See p. 166 above.

287 *Eighteenth Report*, p. 81.                          288 *Eighteenth Report*, p. 82.

289 The *Fearns*, 1771 (TNA (PRO), HCA, 15/56); the *Albemarle of Dublin*, 1773 (ibid.); the *Russell* 1773 (TNA (PRO), HCA, 16/59/115); the *Bumper Squire Jones*, 1774 (ibid.); the *Venus*, 1775 (TNA (PRO), HCA, 16/62/340); the *Callabogy*, 1777 (TNA (PRO), HCA,16/65/395A).

290 *1828 Accounts*, p. 28.

The Court of Admiralty had merely concurrent jurisdiction in wages suits; the courts of common law, including local courts of conscience,[291] could also provide sailors with remedies. However, the perception, within admiralty circles at least, was that the common law courts were rarely used.[292] The preference amongst sailors for the Court of Admiralty was attributed to procedural advantages of admiralty process. First, the unpaid seaman could proceed *in rem*, and have the vessel itself seized, rather than having to proceed against the master personally. The admiralty proctor, Henry Richardson, described the advantage of proceedings *in rem*:

> if [the sailor] were left to his remedy *in personam* I think he would lose his wages nineteen times out of twenty, because in that case he would be obliged to sue the owners of the ship who might be thirty-two in number, or the captain; and in the case of suing the captain he might not be within the jurisdiction of the Court, he might die, or he might leave the country.[293]

Second, by contrast with the position at common law, a group of seamen could consolidate their action, thus reducing the costs and court fees incurred in the litigation.[294] Third, wages suits were prioritized over other business. Arthur Browne wrote that 'in general, seamen's wages are heard with particular favour and expedited with the utmost dispatch'.[295] The requirement for a written petition might be dispensed with; in place of written pleadings the court would admit a statement of claim *ore tenus*.[296] Fourth, suits for wages were not vulnerable to interference by prohibition by the courts of common law. The Irish King's Bench, like its English counterpart, refused to apply the locality principle to wages suits: contracts for wages, although made on land, were allowed to proceed in the Admiralty Court. In a late eighteenth-century case, *Boulger v. Ship Anne*,[297] the Irish King's Bench dismissed an application for a prohibition against wages

---

291  In the 1835 report into municipal corporations in Ireland it was noted that the Dublin Court of Conscience, which exercised jurisdiction in cases of claims under 40*s.*, was processing sailors' wages cases: *Appendix to the Report of the Commissioners appointed to inquire into municipal corporations in Ireland* (HC 1835 (25) xxvii 1, 53).

292  Henry Meredyth, giving evidence in 1828, considered suits at common law for sailors wages rare, *Eighteenth Report* (1829), Appendix 5, p. 92.

293  *Eighteenth Report* (1829), Appendix 21, p. 203.

294  In *Wells v. Osmond* (1705) 6 Mod 238, 87 ER 987 the English Queen's Bench, in declining to issue a prohibition against an admiralty wages case, stated that 'the true reason why seamen may sue in the Admiralty, though the contract be made on land, is that there the ship itself is made liable to them; and besides, there they may all join in the suit; neither of which may be at common law, and yet both are much to the ease of poor seamen'. In the *Eliza, FJ*, 8 Dec. 1858, Kelly J said that the 'strong reason always urged for selecting [the Admiralty Court] as the best tribunal in such cases was that, in it only, all, no matter how many, plaintiffs might join in one suit, and thereby an accumulation of costs be saved to owners'.

295  *A compendious view*, ii, p. 188.            296  *Eighteenth Report* (1829), Appendix 5, p. 90.

297  (n.d.) *A compendious view*, ii, p. 188.

proceedings in the Court of Admiralty. The promovent's argument – 'that it was a contract made on land' – was dismissed as 'of no weight'. A seaman was entitled to sue *in forma pauperis*, on swearing that his means were less than £5. The Stamp Act 1815[298] also provided an exemption from stamp duty in the case of wages suits. The court might attempt to induce a settlement of the dispute before taking the more drastic step of arresting the ship. In 1808 the admiralty proctor, Henry Richardson, testified that, having received a petition seeking recovery of a 'trifling sum' he had postponed arresting the vessel, and had instead 'applied to Pritchard [the master] … for payment of the seaman's demand'. It was only after '[Pritchard] came to his office after receiving his letter … and threatened to strike him' that Richardson resolved to have the vessel arrested.[299]

The court's handling of wages suits taken against masters of foreign vessels continued to attract complaints from consular representatives. In 1805 the Danish consul to Ireland, George Eskildson, complained that the *Johanna Maria* had been arrested by the Irish Court of Admiralty in a wages suit contrary to the terms of the Anglo–Danish Treaty under which the capacity of the court to hear a claim against a Danish master was 'solely entrusted to my decision as his Danish majesty's consul'.[300] The Irish commercial community also continued to complain that ship owners were being harassed by specious wages claims. In 1828 the Dublin Chamber of Commerce petitioned the House of Commons that:

> masters and owners of vessels are frequently summoned by sailors on the most frivolous pretexts, and there is reason to believe, at the instigation of individuals, whose sole object is to extort costs from masters or owners through the instrumentality of pauper clients …[301]

This was a direct attack on the integrity of the proctors, and, in response, an emergency meeting of the practising proctors was convened in the court.[302] A resolution was passed complaining that Dublin Chamber of Commerce 'imputed to us motives' in seamen's wages suits. The proctors resolved to solicit the support of John Foster LLD, John Doherty LLD, George Moore LLD, Thomas Wallace LLD and John Henry North LLD (all admiralty advocate practitioners, who were also MPs) to 'use their influence to prevail on the House to suspend its judgment upon the charge in the petition until the facts should be inquired into and the truth or falsehood ascertained'.

The late eighteenth-century court has left a small body of jurisprudence on seamen's wages. The most interesting of these was *Harrison v. The George* which considered the wages entitlements of sailors who agreed to act as hostages.[303] In

---

298  55 Geo. III, c. 78 (Ire.), 1815, Schedule.
299  J. Dunn to J. Nail, 22 Jan. 1808 (NAI, OP 267/4).
300  Petition of George Eskildson, 17 & 24 Sept. 1805 (NAI, OP 200/8).
301  *Commons' jn*, lxxxiii, p. 79 (18 Feb. 1828).
302  NAI, OP 611/19.                    303  (n.d.) *A compendious view*, p. 546.

1796 Harrison had undertaken to serve as mate on a voyage from Liverpool to Oporto, and from there to Dublin. The vessel was captured by a French privateer; it was then released on the master's undertaking to pay a ransom on the arrival of the ship. Harrison was left behind in Dunkirk as security. The master promised to pay Harrison £10 4s. 9d. per month for the time spent in captivity. Having abandoned Harrison in France, the master forgot about the promise of wages. A suit was initiated in the Irish court by Harrison's wife who libelled to the effect that her husband (who had been granted permission by his captors to write to her) had been a prisoner for five months in Dunkirk, and that no money had been paid in pursuit of the arrangement. The master contested the claim, arguing that the contract between the captain and Harrison was void by reason of section 2 of the Ransoming of Ships Act 1781.[304] Section 2 provided that 'all contracts which shall be entered into *for* ransom thereof, or of any merchandise or goods on board such ship shall be absolutely void'. The interpretative issue was whether the contract between the captain and Harrison was 'for' the ransom of the vessel (and, therefore, statutorily void), or merely, as the promovent argued, collateral to the ransom agreement. The Admiralty Court held that the second interpretation corresponded to the circumstances and decreed for Harrison. That sentence was then upheld on appeal by the Court of Delegates.

*Material-men*

The processing by the Irish court of suits initiated by unpaid suppliers or fitters (so-called 'material-men') provided the principal comparative difference between the instance work undertaken by the Irish and English Courts of Admiralty in the early part of the nineteenth century. The subject matter of an admiralty material-man suit was a claim arising upon default in payment to the supplier of services and materials ('necessaries') in the fitting out of a vessel prior to its departure. These contracts were made on land and the common law, on the usual territorial grounds, held that such suits were outside the competence of the English court.[305] The competence of the English Admiralty Court had been temporarily restored by the resolutions of February 1633.[306] The third Article of the 1633 protocol provided that in cases involving the 'necessary victualling of a ship' where the suit was 'against the ship itself, and not against any party by name' no 'prohibition [was] to be granted, though this be done within the realm'. However, following the Restoration, the courts of common law reverted to their traditional aggressive

---

304  21 & 22 Geo. III, c. 54 (Ire.), s. 2.

305  In *Leigh v. Burley* (1609) Owen 122; 74 ER 946, a material-man who had sold sails to the master of a ship at St Catherine's dock, London, was prohibited by the Court of King's Bench from pursuing a claim in the Admiralty Court on the ground that the contract had been made *infra corpus comitatus* and, therefore, outside the jurisdiction of the court.

306  See p. 37 above.

stance, repeatedly issuing prohibitions[307] to the point that the English court ceased to exercise jurisdiction in such cases, and this category of business dried up.

In the early nineteenth century, the English court refused (subject to one exception)[308] to hear claims by unpaid maritime suppliers. But the Irish court went further than its English counterpart. In Ireland, the Admiralty Court was open to material-men. In the *Defiance* in 1828 a supplier named O'Hogan, who had provisioned a vessel with whiskey, soap, beer, thread, pipes, tobacco, butter, snuff, bacon and candles, obtained a warrant for the arrest of the vessel. The impugnant challenged the court's jurisdiction and invited the promovent, to 'show in the English practice, or that of this country, any one case wherein a similar case was instituted'. Sir Henry Meredyth refused, however, to strike out the libel.[309] In 1828 Meredyth informed the judicial commissioners that 'suits by material-men have been frequently commenced and prosecuted in that court; and there are many instances to be found in the registry of such suits'.[310] He did, however, express a worry that Irish practice was out of alignment with the English position: 'I have great doubt such suit is cognizable by the court in the first instance, and I believe it is held not to be so in the English Court of Admiralty'.

*Bottomry*

By the late seventeenth century even the hostile Court of King's Bench had been prepared to concede to the Admiralty Court jurisdiction over bottomry bonds – the maritime security under which masters abroad were enabled to pledge their vessel in return for emergency supplies and repairs.[311] The ability of the foreign creditor to enforce these bonds in the Court of Admiralty was, the King's Bench conceded, an essential support for this system of international maritime credit. The court, by its *in rem* jurisdiction, provided the creditor with his most effective remedy, possession of the ship: 'the party has no other remedy; [the Court of King's Bench] cannot give him remedy against the ship'.[312] Accordingly, the English Court of King's Bench had held that the bottomry bond was an exception to the

---

307  *Hoare v. Clement* (1684) 2 Show 338, 89 ER 974; *Justin v. Bellam* (1702) 2 Ld Raym 805, 92 ER 38.
308  The court would accept jurisdiction where the unpaid supplier appeared as an intervenient (but not where it was the principal suitor). In the *John* (1801) 3 C Rob 288; 165 ER 466 the primary suit was a wages action taken by a sailor; the unpaid supplier appeared as an intervenient. William Scott distinguished suits by suppliers as primary parties (where the court could not hear the suit) and suits by suppliers as interveners (where it would accept jurisdiction): 'it has continued to be the practice of this court to allow material-men to sue against remaining proceeds in the registry, notwithstanding that prohibitions have been obtained on original suits instituted by them'. The principle in the *John* – the capacity of suppliers to litigate as intervenients – was also accepted in Ireland (*Eighteenth Report*, Appendix 5, p. 91). However, the *John* was overruled in the *Neptune* (1835) 3 Knapp 94; 12 ER 584.
309  *FJ*, 1 Apr. 1828.
310  E.g., the *Foveran* (1828) described in the *Eighteenth Report*, Appendix 21, p. 202.
311  *Cossart v. Lawdlry* (1688) 3 Mod 244; 87 ER 159.
312  *Johnson v. Shippen* (1703) 2 Ld Raym 982; 92 ER 154.

usual bar against the Admiralty Court adjudicating complaints concerning any
'contract, plea or quarrel within any county of the realm' (as the 1391 admiralty
statute had put it). However, mid-eighteenth-century Irish admiralty practitioners
adopted a precautionary approach to the risk of prohibition, pleading fictionally
that the security had been pledged on the high seas. For instance, in *Richard Kent
v. Good Hope*[313] the creditor alleged that he had lent the master (Lawrence Smith)
£194 for repairs, and pleaded fictionally that the security had been pledged on 'the
high seas and within the jurisdiction of this honourable court' where the parties
'duly [made] and execute[d] the hypothecation of the said ship or bottomry bond'.
However, by the late eighteenth century the Irish court indicated that the 'high
seas' recital was unnecessary: in *Corish v. Murphy*[314] it was objected that the libel
did not positively state that the bond had been executed on the high seas. Allowing
the case to proceed, the court held that it had jurisdiction whether the agreement
was made on land or on the high seas 'since the parties could not have the same
remedy in courts of law, the sentence of this court going *in rem*'.

*The adjudication of Crown droits*

Maritime derelict generated by transatlantic trade – in particular the timber trade
– with North America had become the main source of derelict coming before the
Irish court in the early nineteenth century.[315] In addition to these cargoes of
American wood, more traditional derelicts continued to be processed by the
court – casks of wine or spirits found floating at sea, and beached whales proceeded
against as royal fish.[316] But the level of business generated by droit suits was
relatively modest and irregular; in 1812 proceedings were initiated in four droit
cases; between 1815 and 1822 no warrant of arrest issued in a droit case. In 1828
the admiralty proctor, William Richardson, asserted that 'as to the business of the
Crown … it is at a stand'.[317]

      One reason for this low level of activity was the lack of a formal system of
reporting of derelict. Although the King's proctor maintained 'his correspondents
on the coast'[318] there was not, until the mid-1830s, any established arrangement
between the proctor and the board of customs by which the customs would apprise
the proctor of admiralty derelict.[319] As a result many derelicts were seized
informally without the King's proctor in Dublin being informed. In one case in the

313  Eighteenth-century admiralty and ecclesiastical precedent book (King's Inns MS, f. 251).
314  [1796?] *A compendious view*, p. 531.
315  Evidence of J.L. Foster, *Eighteenth Report*, Appendix 7, p. 95.
316  *The King against butter found derelict and brought into Cork* (1812), *The king in his office of
      Admiralty against a royal fish brought to the strand at Lacken* (1826), *John Cullen, master of the brig
      Hannah, of Dublin, mariner against three casks of claret wine, found derelict at sea* (1825) (*1828
      Accounts*, pp 6, 12, 14).
317  Evidence of William Richardson, *Eighteenth Report*, Appendix 22, p. 212.
318  Evidence of J.L. Foster, *Eighteenth Report*, Appendix 7, p. 95.
319  NAI, CSORP, 1840/T 9,930.

early 1820s, a justice of the peace had retained a hoard of gold coins wrapped in a sock, the property of a passenger on the *Albion* of New York, which had been found buried in sand.[320] The finders petitioned the lord lieutenant, who, in turn, requested a legal opinion from Sir John Nicholl. Nicholl advised that the petitioners were not entitled to 'any grant or dispositions of this money 'til the title of the Crown is established by the sentence of the proper Admiralty Court pronouncing it to be derelict and droits of the admiralty'.

*Bill of lading suits*

The Irish Court of Admiralty had (though its competence to do so was dubious) begun handling bill of lading cases in the mid–eighteenth century.[321] Some support for this jurisdiction may have been obtained from the 1783 Act which entrusted the court with jurisdiction over 'all manner of civil maritime and other causes'. In addition, the warrant issued to appointees under the 1783 Act entrusted judges with authority over 'ladings of ships and all other matters and contracts which relate to freight due for hire of ships'.[322] In his *Compendious view* Arthur Browne was optimistic that the jurisdiction had become implicitly tolerated by the courts of common law, which had ceased issuing prohibitions: 'to this day, suits on charter parties and by material-men, are often brought, and no prohibition'.[323] He illustrated this with an account of his success in the *Jenny of Pengally*:[324] the promovent, the consignor of a cargo of flour from Waterford to Dublin, alleged that the master had failed to deliver the flour in accordance with the bill of lading. Relying on the locality principle, the master argued that, since the contract had been made *infra corpus comitatus*, in Waterford, and not upon the high seas, the libel was outside the jurisdiction of the Court of Admiralty. In response Arthur Browne asked the court to consider the words of Article 2 of the protocol of 1633 which had admitted suits for 'charter parties' as within the jurisdiction of the Admiralty Court. Browne argued that the 'old and absurd notion of locality superseding the nature of the contract was long since exploded'. The Admiralty Court decreed that it had jurisdiction. Significantly, no prohibition issued from the King's Bench. In another of these cases, the *Fly*[325] had been hired to carry wine from Malaga to Dublin. The wine had been lost due to the master's breach of contract. Arthur Browne, in an opinion prepared for the importers, relied on Article 2 of the protocol of 1633, and advised his clients that the court had jurisdiction. Browne subsequently recorded with satisfaction that the 'advice was followed and succeeded'.

---

320  NAI, CSORP, 1824/1,0541.
321  See p. 128 above.
322  Commission to Warden Flood, 11 Jan. 1785 (TNA (PRO), 100/5, f. 108).
323  *A compendious view*, p. 122          324  Ibid., p. 32.
325  *The Case of the Fly Sloop* (n.d.), *A compendious view*, ii, p. 538.

However, the position described by Browne was still legally unstable, and even Browne conceded that there remained the 'risk of prohibition'.[326] By the late 1820s the lading and charter party branch of the court's instance jurisdiction had, it seems, once again disappeared. The detailed inventory of the instance work of the Admiralty Court conducted by the judicial commissioners in the late 1820s made no reference to the court hearing suits involving charter parties, or bills of lading.[327]

326 Ibid., p. 539.  327 *Eighteenth Report*, Appendix 5, p. 81.

CHAPTER FIVE

# Expansion and dissolution, 1830–93

## THE JUDGES OF THE IRISH COURT OF ADMIRALTY, 1830–77

BY THE MID-1830s the dereliction and corruption of the Barrington era had resulted in the court being regarded as so disreputable that its very existence was threatened. However, within thirty years it had managed to reverse that perception. Its refurbished reputation was as a busy, efficient commercial court, an important support to Ireland's mercantile prosperity. The court processed more litigation than ever before, and its speed and procedural reforms were praised internationally.

Despite its improved image, successfully concealed from the public, on two occasions, in 1837 and in 1867, senior officers of the court were found to have behaved disreputably. The first of these incidents involved the fraudulent conversion of suitors' funds by the registrar, Daniel Pineau. The second of these events – the involvement of the judge, Thomas Kelly, in embarrassing probate litigation – resulted in the dismissal of the judge of the Court of Admiralty. The Kelly dismissal was disguised from Parliament under cover of the most important piece of admiralty judicature legislation ever enacted for Ireland, the Admiralty Court (Ireland) Act 1867.

The period ended with the enactment of the Judicature Act 1877, which provided for the termination of the existence of the separate Court of Admiralty of Ireland, and its integration into a new consolidated High Court. The 1877 Act postponed the dissolution of the court until the death of the existing judge, John Fitzhenry Townsend. The exceptional longevity of Townsend kept dissolution in abeyance until his eventual death in February 1893. On 2 February 1893, the dissolution provided for in the judicature acts was activated; after 318 years, the independent Court of Admiralty of Ireland was disbanded.

### John Henry North

In 1830, three months before Barrington had been finally dismissed, a rumour was circulating in the Four Courts that his successor had already been chosen, and that he was the barrister and Tory MP, John Henry North.[1] This was precisely how it turned out. Sir Henry Meredyth, who had acted so conscientiously as surrogate for the previous eight years, was passed over by the duke of Wellington's outgoing Tory government. North's warrant was quickly prepared for signature by

1 *FJ*, 15 May 1830.

203

William IV, and then transmitted to Dublin.[2] North, who had recently lost the election for Dublin University, was about to fight a by-election for the constituency of Drogheda, against Daniel O'Connell's son Maurice. The official charged with organizing the draft of the warrant urged expedition since 'it is of the utmost importance (in consequence of the Drogheda election) that the warrant should reach me in time tomorrow to send off by the post'.[3] North sat as judge for the first time on 16 October 1830.[4]

North's ability as a civilian was highly regarded, and he had attracted a circle of devotees.[5] However, he was never allowed sufficient time to establish himself, and his single year's service as judge was not distinguished. He appointed a surrogate, the future Admiralty Court judge, Dr Joseph Stock,[6] and may not have sat full-time. Only a modest level of business was transacted. In the ten months between the date of his being sworn in and the end of August 1831, the court disposed of just six cases. These cases were its usual diet of salvage and wages cases.[7] John Henry North lasted barely a year in office, dying unexpectedly of a pulmonary condition in early October 1831.[8] North had certainly not managed to restore confidence in the court. Indeed, a movement for its abolition emerged. In October 1831 Dublin Chamber of Commerce resolved to prepare a petition describing the abuses which existed in the court and to urge Parliament to 'adopt such measures as they may deem expedient for its total abolition or its reform'.[9] In the House of Commons a few days later, Henry Grattan, the member of Parliament for Meath, promoted the case for abolition.[10] Referring to 'the inutility of the court', he pointed out that during the last year only five wages cases had been tried; he made the point that these might have been tried by magistrates, and queried why the judge was in receipt of a salary of £1,000 *per annum* when he was doing virtually no work. A defensive chief secretary for Ireland, Edward Stanley, had to concede that the salary was excessive and 'liable to reduction'. This agitation prompted the enactment of a provision in the Lord Lieutenant's Salary (Ireland) Act 1832[11] which halved the salary of the judge to £500 *per annum*. Lord Althorp, the chancellor of the exchequer, expressed the government's irritation with an institution which it plainly considered had ceased to justify its existence:

2   TNA (PRO), HO 100/235, f. 12.
3   C. Flint to M.[?] Phillips, 29 July 1830 (TNA (PRO), HO 100/235, f. 223).
4   (1830) 3 Law Rec (OS) 372.
5   J. Anster, *The Roman Civil Law. Introductory lecture on the study of the Roman Civil Law* (Dublin, 1851), p. 33.
6   *Watson's Almanack 1831*, p. 79.
7   'An account of the names and description of causes which have been tried and adjudicated in the Court of Admiralty in Ireland since the 1st day of August last past …' (HC 1831 (201) xv. 359).
8   *FJ*, 3 Oct. 1831. See obituary (1831) 4 Law Rec 307; and Robert McGhee, *A sermon on the death of the late lamented John Henry North Esq., M.P., judge of the admiralty, preached in the Magdalen Asylum Chapel* (Dublin & London, 1831).
9   Minutes of the council of Dublin Chamber of Commerce, 6 Oct. 1831 (NAI, 1,064/3/4, f. 92).
10   *FJ*, 10 Oct. 1831.                              11   2 & 3 Will. IV, c. 116, s. 1 (Ire.), 1832.

At the Union it was settled that that office [of judge of the Court of Admiralty] should be preserved; the salary, however, which was then £500 a year, has since been raised to £1,000; which looking at the business to be done by that court, appears to me to be much too high a rate of payment. Since, therefore, we are bound to preserve the office, I think we are fully justified in reducing it to its former standard of £500.[12]

*Sir Henry Meredyth, 1831–7*

North was succeeded in 1831 by Sir Henry Meredyth. Meredyth had been associated with the judgeship of the Admiralty Court since the 1820s. Meredyth's performance as surrogate (though blemished by an awkward attempt to purchase the office of judge from Barrington) had been highly regarded. However, he was overlooked when the government chose a successor to Barrington in 1830.[13] Meredyth's turn came in 1831 following North's death. Meredyth held office for seven years. He exercised his prerogative to appoint a surrogate, Dr Joseph Stock.[14] The barrister and legal writer John Finlay also deputized for Meredyth on occasion.[15] Meredyth resigned in 1837. The grounds of Meredyth's resignation were never made public. However, the year 1837 co-incided with the discovery of corruption within the court; Barrington's old registrar (and principal accuser) Daniel Pineau, had died insolvent. A search of Pineau's accounts recovered only £300 instead of the £1,100 which had been entrusted to Pineau as suitors' funds. This massive misappropriation of public money – far greater than that for which Barrington had been dismissed – must also have been very embarrassing for the judge who was open to censure for lack of supervision.[16] Meredyth, who had been manoeuvring for a place on the King's Bench when the Conservatives were in power,[17] was also out of favour following the return to power of Viscount Melbourne's government which wanted the position for one of their own. In return for resigning his office of judge of the Admiralty Court, Meredyth was appointed to the less glamorous office of secretary to the ecclesiastical commissioners.[18] He died in 1859.[19]

*Dr Joseph Stock, 1838–55*

Joseph Stock, a whig and an O'Connellite sympathizer, who had just fought a brave but unsuccessful campaign for the seat of Dublin University, was installed

12  *Hansard 3*, vol. 14, cols 941–2 (30 July 1832).
13  Meredyth was instead, in the autumn of 1830, appointed, by way of consolation, to the largely honorific office of king's advocate.
14  Dr Stock acted as judge in the mariners' wages case, *Stephenson v. the Catherine, FJ*, 21 July 1831.
15  *Watson's Almanack 1836*, p. 176.
16  The details were included in a paper submitted by an admiralty proctor, John Hamerton, 'Suggestions as to the High Court of Admiralty of Ireland', 29 Aug. 1842 (NAI, CSORP, 1842/O/11,758).
17  *FJ*, 20 Dec. 1837.
18  Church Temporalities Act 1833 (3 & 4 Wm IV, c. 37 (Ire.)).
19  *Illustrated London News*, 21 May 1859.

by Melbourne's administration in succession to Meredyth.[20] News of the appointment was carried in the press in December 1837 and confirmed in January 1838.[21]
Stock was well qualified for appointment, having been a leading admiralty
advocate, and a surrogate judge under Sir Henry Meredyth. He also held a busy
common law practice. The appointment was well received. The *Morning Chronicle*
observed that while Stock's appointment had 'given great annoyance to the faction
... they do not venture to query the fitness of the learned civilian'.[22] The *Freeman's
Journal*, approving of the new appointment, commented that 'the Admiralty
Court, however, stands in great need of reformation, and we doubt not that Doctor
Stock will endeavour to remedy all the defects of its practice and constitution'.[23]
However, Stock was over-committed, and was very much a part-time judge: the
queen's proctor in 1842 described 'the present judge of the court [as] a member of
parliament, one of her majesty's serjeants at law, a practising barrister and an
advocate with considerable business in the Court of Prerogative'.[24] Within seven
months of his appointment, Stock had been elected as MP for Cashel,[25] a seat he
retained until 1846. The House of Commons Disqualification Act 1821[26] which
barred judges from election to the Commons did not, anomalously, apply to judges
of the Court of Admiralty, and Joseph Stock (like John Henry North) was able to
carry on his parliamentary career while holding down judicial office. The strain on
Stock's time increased when, in 1842, he was promoted first serjeant. Under
pressure from his parliamentary commitments and his legal practice, Dr Stock
developed the practice of delivering his judgments *ex tempore*.[27] Although by no
means an absentee, sheer pressure of work required Stock to depute his judgeship
to surrogates: firstly, to the senior admiralty advocate, and judge of the Prerogative
Court, Joseph Radcliffe, and then to the admiralty advocate, Thomas Kelly.[28]
Stock's knowledge of technical navigational matters was also poor: he openly
confessed that he was 'unable to grapple with the nautical details' of collision
cases,[29] and he would delegate to the assessors the entire question of identifying
the party at fault in collision cases (rather than limiting their role to the provision
of technical advice). In the last six years of Stock's tenure, there was a steep decline
in activity: in the year ending 31 December 1850 the court sat on just thirty days;
in the year 1855 the court sat for only eight days.[30] This (by comparison even with

20   Stock polled 186 votes against the successful candidates, Shaw (852) and Lefroy (839).
21   *FJ*, 18 & 20 Dec. 1837. Stock's patent was dated 17 Jan. 1838. Report of H. Harding, Assistant
     Keeper of Public Records, 9 Nov. 1858 (NAI, CSORP, 1859/4,449).
22   *Morning Chronicle*, 21 Dec. 1837.        23   *FJ*, 18 Dec. 1837.
24   'Suggestions as to the High Court of Admiralty of Ireland' (NAI, CSORP, 1842 O/11,758).
25   *Parliamentary Election results in Ireland, 1801–1922* ed. B. Walker (Dublin, 1978), p. 67.
26   1 & 2 Geo. IV, c. 44 (Ire.), 1821 ('An act to exclude persons holding certain judicial offices in
     Ireland from being members of the House of Commons').
27   The *Victoria* (1854) 7 Ir Jur 94.        28   The *Allesandro* (1850) 3 Ir Jur 383; *FJ*, 8 Dec. 1855.
29   The *William* (1854) 7 Ir Jur 229, 232.
30   'Number of sittings of judge of the Court of Admiralty in Ireland and of warrants issued in the said
     Court, in each year, for the seven years ending 31st December 1855 and 1862' (HC 1863 (399) xlix.1).

the forty-seven days for which the court sat under Barrington's much-criticized surrogate, Ninian Mahaffy in 1822) amounted to a virtual collapse in activity.

*Thomas Kelly, 1855–67*

Joseph Stock died aged sixty-nine in October 1855.[31] He was succeeded by Dr Thomas Kelly.[32] Kelly was, at the time of his appointment, one of the leading advocates practising in the court. A former foundation scholar at Trinity College Dublin, he had qualified as a barrister but followed an unconventional path, combining legal practice with a professional bureaucratic career, serving as first secretary to the National Education Board,[33] and as chairman of the Dublin Marine Board. He also accepted a junior judicial appointment as a divisional magistrate in Dublin, where his criminal work made him well known to the newspaper-reading public. Although the Dublin Justices' Act 1808 prohibited divisional magistrates from practising before the courts of common law,[34] it did not (through a drafting oversight) prohibit practice before the courts of civil law. Dr Kelly took advantage of this omission to combine his career as a magistrate with practice before the Courts of Probate and Admiralty. By the mid-1850s Kelly had become the senior advocate of the Admiralty Court.[35] His appointment, following the recession in business during the final Stock period, was well received in some quarters. The *Freeman's Journal* was extravagant, commenting that 'if experience, special knowledge, long acquaintance with the classes of case of which the court takes cognizance, combined with those qualities that adorn the scholar … form any of the qualifications of a judge of the Admiralty Court, Dr Kelly, may with truth be said to be "the right man in the right place"'.[36] But Kelly's reputation within the wider profession was prejudiced by his failure to establish a practice at the bar, while his position as a divisional magistrate made him the target of social snobbery. In 1861, when the English law reform body, the Social Science Congress, held a major annual conference in Dublin, a paper on the subject of the Irish Court of Admiralty was read. One of the contributors from the floor tactlessly suggested that the reason that Parliament had been willing to reform the English[37] (but not the Irish) court was that the English court was presided over by 'one of the ablest men that ever sat in a civil court, Dr Lushington'; by implication, Kelly was not in the same league as his English equivalent. Judge Kelly was in the hall, and there

31  *Gentleman's Magazine* (n.s.), 44 (1855), 651.
32  Kelly's patent was dated 26 Nov. 1855 (NAI, CSORP, 1859/4,449).
33  R.B. McDowell, *The Irish administration, 1801–1914* (London, 1964), p. 249. *Irish Times*, 14 Aug. 1876.
34  48 Geo. III, c. 140 (Ire.), 1808. S.14 prevented divisional justices practising as a 'barrister in any court'. On a strict interpretation it did not prohibit a divisional justice practising as an 'advocate' in the Court of Admiralty.
35  *Irish Times*, 19 Aug. 1861.                    36  *FJ*, 9 Nov. 1855.
37  The powers of the English court had been extended by the Admiralty Court Act 1861 (24 & 25 Vict., c. 10 (Eng.) 1861).

was an awkward scene when, visibly hurt, he rose to counter the implication that
he was 'appointed to the bench without possessing that amount of knowledge
which was necessary to do credit to the office'.[38] Kelly pointed out that, far from
being incompetent, he had, before his appointment, been the senior practising
advocate in the court.

On appointment, Kelly relinquished his better-paid position as divisional
justice for that of the relatively under-paid office of judgeship of the Court of
Admiralty[39] (making what lord chancellor Chelmsford described as 'a sacrifice for
an advance of position').[40] Judge Kelly (as he liked to be called) turned out to be a
successful appointment. He administered the court for twelve years as a full-time
judge. By contrast with his predecessors, he performed his judicial duties
personally and only rarely employed a surrogate.[41] His greatest achievement was
in raising the scale of activity of the court. In the early 1850s it had sat for no more
than 30 days per year;[42] by 1859 it was sitting for 151 days. This was the Irish
court's highest ever recorded period of activity. Its public perception was
transformed. It was now recognized as a serious specialist commercial court, and
as an essential structural support for Ireland's increasing maritime traffic.[43] The
credit for the increase in the court's business was acknowledged to be due to Kelly's
efficiency and innovations.[44] The expansion in work was facilitated by Kelly's
willingness to receive suits outside the accepted limits of admiralty courts. The
court accepted cases involving bills of sale, demurrage and unpaid freight, all
categories of litigation which according to well-established doctrine were outside
the competence of the Admiralty Court.[45] Kelly was also a law reformer. He was
responsible for a series of procedural innovations which modernized and accelerated
the court's processes: pleadings were simplified; the rules relating to bail were
rationalized; and very rigorous four-day time-limits were imposed for the exhibition
by litigants of their libels and answers. He managed to produce his judgments

---

38  *Irish Times*, 19 Aug. 1861.
39  The position of admiralty judge was comparatively under-paid. In 1866 Kelly submitted a
    petition seeking an increase in his salary from its current level of £500 *per annum*. He contrasted
    that salary with the £4,000 paid to the judge of the English Court of Admiralty, and with the
    salaries paid to judges of the other specialist courts in Ireland: £2,500 to the judges of the Court
    of Bankruptcy and of the Landed Estates Court; £3,500 to the judge of the Court of Probate.
    'The High Court of Admiralty in Ireland; observations relative to the judge's salary 1866' (TNA
    (PRO), T1/6,627A).
40  *Hansard 3*, vol. 189, col. 1214 (9 Aug. 1867).
41  Clifford Lloyd occasionally sat as surrogate: the *Golden Eagle*, *FJ*, 26 July 1859.
42  30 days in 1850 and 1852; 29 days in the year 1854, 'Number of sittings of the judge of the Court
    of Admiralty in Ireland and of warrants issued in the said court, in each year, for the seven years
    ending 31st December 1855 and 1862' (HC 1863 (399) xlix.1).
43  P. Solar, 'Shipping and economic development in nineteenth-century Ireland', *Economic History
    Review*, 69 (2006), 717.
44  'The Court of Admiralty', *Irish Times*, 18 Oct. 1859.
45  *Robson v. Douglas*, *Shipping & Mercantile Gazette*, 23 Apr. 1859. The *William of Waterford*, *FJ*,
    24 Mar. 1859. The *Consul*, *Shipping & Mercantile Gazette*, 23 Aug. 1858.

rapidly. These were crisply reasoned, and he could call upon a wide range of international admiralty sources. Some of Kelly's judgments are still cited.[46]

Despite his success as judge, the government's plans for reform of the court had made Judge Kelly's position vulnerable. In 1866 it narrowly avoided total dissolution. Two rival approaches to the modernization of the Court of Admiralty were debated in the 1860s: an abolitionist approach (which proposed dissolution and consolidation with the Court of Probate) and a reformist approach (which proposed retention, modernization and jurisdictional expansion). The first threat to the court's existence occurred in the spring of 1866 when the Liberal attorney general, James Lawson, produced an Irish Admiralty Court Bill.[47] This measure would have provided for the transfer of the jurisdiction exercised by the court to the Court of Probate. However, there was no great enthusiasm in the House of Commons for the proposal to transfer admiralty jurisdiction to the Court of Probate, and the measure was the subject of two lukewarm speeches by two senior Irish lawyers.[48] It never progressed beyond its first reading early in May, and it lapsed when Russell's administration lost power the following month.

The following year the new administration switched to the alternative position – reform. The new Conservative government in 1867 made a renewed attempt at Irish admiralty legislation. This measure proposed modernization along the lines of the English Admiralty Court Act 1861, rather than abolition of the court. However, buried amongst the technical reforms was section 5, a stunning provision directly targeted at Kelly. Section 5 provided that on enactment 'the present judge … [was to] cease to hold [his] respective office'. In other words, Kelly was to be dismissed.

The government did its upmost to ensure that its legislative plans were withheld from Kelly for as long as possible. He only discovered that the government was planning legislative reform of the court in the newspapers, and 'anxious about its continuing welfare' requested the Irish chief secretary for an interview (pleading that 'my twelve years judicial administration of the court … may be my apology for this request').[49] He was not told of the details of the measure prior to its introduction in the House of Commons, and the attorney general refused Kelly's request to supply him with an advance copy of the bill. The fact that the attorney general who was refusing him access was Hedges Eyre Chatterton, one of the senior advocates of the Admiralty Court, who had until very recently practised before Kelly, can only have aggravated Kelly's humiliation.

46  Kelly J's judgment (on the relative priority between the victims of collision and unpaid sailors) in the *Duna* (1861) 5 LT(NS) 217 was quoted *in extenso* by David Steel J in the English Queen's Bench in the *Ruta* [2000] 1 WLR 2068. See p. 246 below.

47  Questions about the state of preparation of legislation were repeatedly asked in the House of Commons: *Hansard 3*, vol. 176, col. 279 (24 June 1864); vol. 177, col. 83 (8 Feb. 1865); vol. 181, col. 1,390 (2 Mar. 1866) ; vol. 185, col. 1,447 (7 Mar. 1867); vol. 187, col. 769–70 (20 May 1867).

48  Sir Colman O'Loghlen and James Whiteside both doubted the wisdom of transferring jurisdiction to the Court of Probate: *Hansard 3*, vol. 183, cols 280–3 (2 May 1866).

49  T. Kelly to Lord Naas, 3 June 1867 (NAI, CSORP, 1867/11,152/6).

Considerable effort was devoted to ensuring that the real grounds for the decision to remove Kelly were concealed from Parliament. In the House of Lords the English lord chancellor, Baron Chelmsford (Frederick Thesiger) struggled to justify section 5 (the dismissal provision): the reformed Admiralty Court, he said, would obtain parcels of new jurisdiction – freight, cargo and material-men. These were matters which, he argued, the court had not previously handled, and which Kelly would not be technically competent to administer:

> the Bill would introduce great improvements into the court, extend its jurisdiction and bring within its cognizance matters connected with the common law of which this gentleman had had no experience; therefore [Kelly] would not be competent to perform the large duties which would be thrown upon him.[50]

The lord chancellor was dissembling: the proposed additions to the jurisdiction of the court were insignificant. Some of these new categories of work (such as cargo and material-men litigation) were already being undertaken by the court. The private briefing given by the chief secretary of Ireland, the earl of Mayo, to the prime minister, the earl of Derby, was quite different to that being stated in Parliament:

> The Admiralty Court Bill was passed principally for the purpose of getting rid of this man who is utterly unfit for office – was a party to a case not long ago that was almost fraudulent, who owes money to every practitioner in his court who will trust him, and whose character is of the most questionable kind.[51]

The 'case which was almost fraudulent' was *Kelly v. Dunbar*, a probate suit which Kelly had taken in 1864. A widow named Mrs Seale had died at her summer home in Kingstown in Dublin after a long disabling illness. The Kellys and the Seales had been long-standing family friends, and Kelly had agreed to act as executor of Mrs Seale's will. Kelly did extremely well out of this will: he was made a residuary legatee, entitling him to about £8,000. However, Mrs Seale's nieces (the two Dunbar sisters) claimed that Kelly had exerted undue influence over Mrs Seale, who having suffered a stroke, was being plied with alcohol, and who had already lent several hundred pounds to Kelly. Kelly sued in the Court of Probate to establish the validity of the legacy.[52] The Dunbar sisters contested the residuary clause and retained a legal team led by James Whiteside QC and John Fitzhenry Townsend. Whiteside, who was at the height of his powers, performed devastatingly, effectively characterizing Kelly as a legacy hunter.[53] Whiteside's performance was so powerful that, before the case closed, Kelly withdrew his

---

50   *Hansard 3*, vol. 189, col. 1213 (9 Aug. 1867).
51   Earl of Mayo to earl of Derby, 29 Aug. 1867 (Liverpool Record Office, Derby Papers, 155/4).
52   *FJ*, 15 Nov. 1864.                              53   *FJ*, 14 Dec. 1864.

claim, and the case terminated without being sent to the jury. Extensive daily reports of *Kelly v. Dunbar* were carried in the newspapers, and the case prompted the government to take the decision to dismiss Kelly. The earl of Mayo recalled that Sir Robert Peel, who had been chief secretary of Ireland in 1864, 'had very nearly made up his mind to remove [Kelly] by an address of both Houses of Parliament'.[54]

Kelly was only in a position to organize a very late defence. On 9 August, he laid a petition before the Lords 'praying for the amendment of clause 5 of the Bill insofar as it purported to repeal sections 1 and 2 of the Court of Admiralty Act 1783 and to provide that the current judge should cease to hold office'.[55] Kelly had also managed to enlist the support of Baron Cranworth (who had been lord chancellor until 1866). The proposal to dismiss Judge Kelly had been under consideration since *Kelly v. Dunbar* in 1864, and it is likely that Baron Cranworth knew exactly what the background to the measure was. Cranworth proposed a motion 'that there be laid before this house, correspondence between the Irish government, and the lord chancellor and the lord chancellor of Ireland relating to that judge'.[56] Under section 2 of the Court of Admiralty Ireland Act 1783 the judge could only be dismissed 'upon the address of both Houses of Parliament'. Baron Cranworth argued that the government's proposal to dissolve the office of judge by statute was an unconstitutional attempt to avoid the security of the two direct resolutions prescribed by the 1783 Act:

> The judge of the Admiralty Court in Ireland held office under an act of Parliament which made him irremovable, except upon an address from both houses of Parliament; his tenure was therefore the same as that of the lord chief justice of the Queen's Bench; yet for the first time in the annals of English history, the enactment which fixed his tenure on this footing was to be repealed by this clause, in order that he might be immediately removed. If this gentleman was an unfit person to discharge the duties of the office, it would be proper to say so; but the judge defied anybody to show this. There had been a constitutional safeguard against the removal of judges, and it was now proposed to take it away.[57]

The same constitutional point was rehearsed in an impressive speech by the Irish Whig politician, the marquess of Clanricarde. Kelly, who had travelled to Westminster for the debate, passed a card to Cranworth which read 'I demand an enquiry into my conduct'. Cranworth rose again and suggested that if the government thought that Kelly was 'an unfit person to discharge the office of judge … it

---

54  Earl of Mayo to the earl of Derby, 29 Aug. 1867 (Liverpool Record Office, Derby Papers, 155/4).

55  *Lords' jn*, xcix, p. 568 (9 Aug. 1867).

56  Ibid. The motion was withdrawn when the lord chancellor informed the House of Lords that, following an enquiry, no such correspondence could be found: *Hansard 3*, vol. 189, col. 1212 (9 Aug. 1867).

57  Ibid.

should have stated so on the face of the Bill'.[58] The lord chancellor was reduced to lying to the House of Lords, denying that 'there was in the minds of those who had considered the subject any suspicion in regard to [Kelly's] conduct'. A final attempt by Cranworth and Clanricarde was made in the form of a 'dissentient' to the motion that the bill be read a third time:

> though the present judge of the Admiralty Court of Ireland held his office during good behaviour, and is removable only on an address of both houses of Parliament, this bill, without alleging either incompetency or misconduct, removes him from his office, and enables the Crown to appoint a successor, thus affording a precedent for unconstitutional interference with the independence of judges.[59]

In October 1867, after the measure had been enacted, and the matter was *fait accompli*, Kelly submitted a further application to Dublin Castle in which he set out once more the argument that the measure was equivalent to a dismissal from office, and that if the proper procedure for dismissal (an address of both houses predicated on a finding of unfitness) had been complied with, he would, at least, have been entitled to a hearing. He quoted Sir William Blackstone ('in this distinct and separate existence of the judicial power in a separate body of men … not removable at pleasure by the Crown consists one main preservative of the public liberty') and requested that the matter be referred to the judicial committee of the Privy Council to obtain its advice on the legality of the proposed termination.[60] The lord lieutenant, Abercorn, replied brusquely that Kelly had demonstrated no grounds for a reference to the judicial committee and added the information that 'a barrister' had already been appointed as his successor.[61] Kelly's tenure was terminated, by the operation of the Court of Admiralty Act 1867, on 3 November 1867. He died at his home in Sandycove, Dublin in 1876, his death passing unnoticed in the newspapers and legal professional press. The background to his removal from the court was never again publicly discussed.[62]

*John Fitzhenry Townsend, 1867–93*

Section 7 of the Court of Admiralty (Ireland) Act 1867 enabled the Crown to appoint a successor to Kelly.[63] There was panic in maritime circles that the position would be handed to a barrister with no background in admiralty law. A memorializing campaign was undertaken with the objective of keeping the position out of the hands of the common law bar. Petitions were directed to the lord lieutenant

---

58  *Hansard 3*, vol. 189, cols 1,215–16 (9 Aug. 1867).
59  *Lords' jn*, xcix, p. 568 (9 Aug. 1867).
60  'The petition of the Honourable Thomas Frederick Kelly,' Oct. 1867 (NAI, CSORP, 1867/21,623).
61  17 Oct. 1867 (NAI, CSORP, 1867/21,623).
62  Kelly died at his home in Co. Dublin, aged seventy-five on 30 Oct. 1876.
63  30 & 31 Vict., c. 113 (Ire.).

from 'the ship owners and merchants of Londonderry,' the mayor of Limerick, the 'important steam companies', 'the ship owners and merchants of Belfast', and from 'merchants, ship owners, foreign consuls, and others residing in the city and port of Cork'.[64] The Cork petition argued for the necessity of retaining admiralty adjudication in the hands of an admiralty specialist:[65] 'experience in these very peculiar branches of law and practice, and knowledge of nautical matters, are very essential qualifications, and such are not possessed by a great many eminent members of the bar who have not been practitioners in the court'. The government responded to the campaign by taking a deliberate decision to restrict the position to an admiralty specialist. The most aggrieved of those by the decision to appoint an admiralty civilian was Robert Longfield, the MP for Mallow, who had been co-drafter of an unsuccessful reforming Irish Admiralty Court Bill in 1863. Longfield had been promised a judgeship when the Conservative administration had come to power, and protested bitterly at the breach of the undertaking. The chief secretary, after a long meeting with the lord lieutenant, stood his ground, insisting that the office must be confined to an admiralty specialist. He enclosed a sample of the memorials[66]

> of the most influential character that have been presented to the government emanating from persons who represent to a very large extent the shipping interest of the country. I have myself consulted the heads of the legal profession both in this country and in England, and am bound to say that they unanimously agree with the opinion put forward by the memorialists, namely, that it is indispensably necessary that the judge who should preside in the Admiralty Court should have been a practitioner there, and should possess the technical knowledge which can alone be obtained by practice in that particular branch of the legal profession … were it the Landed Estates or Bankruptcy Court I should not have hesitated for a moment but this is a totally different case.[67]

The admiralty specialist selected by the government was John Fitzhenry Townsend. On 30 August 1867 Mayo wrote to Townsend, inviting him to accept the office of judge.[68] Townsend assented, expressing 'the hope that the new Admiralty Court will not disappoint the expectation of the public'. Townsend had

64   10 Aug. 1867 (NAI, CSORP, 1867/14,086). 27 Aug. 1867 (NAI, CSORP, 1867/15,127). 10 Aug. 1867 (NAI, CSORP, 1867/14,085); 8 Aug. 1867 (NAI, CSORP, 1867/14,096). 9 Aug. 1867 (NAI, CSORP, 1867/14,021).
65   Ibid.
66   Earl of Mayo to R. Longfield, 25 Aug. 1867 (NLI, MS 11,154/3).
67   Mayo concluded by suggesting that Longfield apply for the vacant office of mastership of the Exchequer. Longfield accepted the consolation prize of the chairmanship of Galway Quarter Sessions. *ILT & SJ*, 2 (1868), 216.
68   J. Townsend to the earl of Mayo, 3 Sept. 1867 (NLI, MS 11,158/22).

practised at the Admiralty Court since 1847. He had established his name as an admiralty expert when in his twenties he produced a book on the law of salvage,[69] and he had appeared in virtually all significant admiralty cases over the previous twenty years. His appointment, which had been known to the press before it was formally announced, was well received, the *Irish Law Times* comparing Townsend in ability to the judge of the English Court, Sir Robert Phillimore.[70] Townsend and Kelly were linked, not just by twenty years of years of practice in the court, but also by *Kelly v. Dunbar*, where Townsend had been a senior member of the legal team that had brought about Kelly's disgrace.

While arrangements were being made for his succession, Kelly was humiliatingly required to continue to serve as judge until 3 November 1867, when the 1867 Act came into force. On Friday 1 November 1867 the old, pre-reformed court sat for the last time. Charles Todd, the senior admiralty advocate paid a warm tribute to Kelly, thanking him, on behalf of the profession, for his courtesy and diligence. Todd acknowledged Kelly's achievement in increasing the court's business:[71] 'it is owing chiefly to your lordship's ability and diligence in the discharge of your duties that this court has risen to the high position it at present enjoys in the mercantile opinion of this kingdom'. He then passed on a message of goodwill from Townsend: 'I think it will be gratifying to your lordship to know that I have the authority of my friend who succeeds your lordship to say that he fully concurs in the sentiments I have already expressed towards your lordship on your retirement into private life'. But none of these gestures defused the awkwardness. Kelly 'who appeared to labour under deep emotion'[72] refused to let the issue of his dismissal rest, making a final valedictory statement of grievance:

> I have a right to feel indignant at the mode in which my retirement has been effected, and the almost merciless manner in which I have been treated. With that I am done. I only say that those who know me well will feel that this expression, whether expected or not, is a natural one. I thank the advocates, and I thank the proctors, in thus parting from the place where the most important part of my life has been spent.

Dr Townsend was sworn in on 4 November 1867.[73] Townsend served as an uncontroversial and gentlemanly judge. He implemented the new jurisdiction entrusted to the court under the Court of Admiralty (Ireland) Act 1867, and drew

---

69　*A treatise on the law of salvage in Ireland* (Dublin, 1840).
70　'[Townsend] is widely known as a mercantile and maritime lawyer of great soundness and experience as well as possessing great nautical knowledge'. *ILT & SJ*, 1 (1867), 622.
71　Ibid.　　　　　　　　　　　72　*Irish Times*, 2 Nov. 1867.
73　S. 3 of the 1867 Act provided that, 'except with respect to the appointment of officers', the Act was to come into force 'after the second day of November 1867'. A constitutional difficulty was spotted in September 1867 as the government prepared to perfect Townsend's patent. Townsend pointed out that under s. 3 only 'officers' could be appointed prior to the coming into force of the legislation. But under the 1867 Act the judge was not an 'officer'. Townsend, therefore, asked the

up the new rules regulating its practice. He served until his death aged eighty-two on 2 February 1893, preparing judgments just a few days before his unexpected death.[74] Townsend was the last judge of the independent Court of Admiralty of Ireland which had existed since the mid-1570s. In 1893 the court was integrated into the High Court.[75]

### LEGISLATIVE REFORM OF THE COURT OF ADMIRALTY, 1857–67

*Probate and Letters of Administration (Ireland) Act 1857 and Court of Admiralty Bill 1861*

Two competing positions underlay mid-nineteenth-century policy on the Admiralty Court issue. The first, the abolitionist view (found in measures proposed in 1857 and 1861), was that the court was irremediably weak, and did not justify being retained as an independent institution. The solution according to this view was to amalgamate the court with another tribunal of analogous jurisdiction. The first significant advance for the abolitionist approach occurred in 1857, when Parliament enacted section 14 of the Probate and Letters of Administration (Ireland) Act 1857.[76] Section 14 provided that upon the next vacancy in the Court of Admiralty in Ireland 'it shall be lawful for her majesty ... to appoint the person then being judge of the Court of Probate to be also judge of the said Court of Admiralty, and after the union of the said two offices they shall be thenceforth held by the same person'.

A rival approach proposed reform – rather than total abolition – of the Court of Admiralty. In March 1863 the MP for Dungarvan, John Francis Maguire,[77] and Robert Longfield, the MP for Mallow, introduced in the Commons a 'Bill to alter and amend procedure and practice of the Court of Admiralty in Ireland'.[78] Two ideas underlay Maguire and Longfield's Bill: the first was to increase the jurisdictional competence of the court. The bill proposed an extension of jurisdiction, with the court being granted jurisdiction over matters such as claims by maritime suppliers, claims for damage to cargo, and claims for salvage of life, identical to the

---

government to postpone his appointment until after the legislation came into force: 'Until the commencement of the Act, the present judge must be deemed to hold his office; and it seems questionable whether under the 7th section of the Act, a valid appointment can be made of a judge during the continuance in office of the present judge'. J. Townsend to T. Larcom, 24 Sept. 1867 (NAI, CSORP, 1867/16,811). The appointment was delayed until Monday 4 November 1867 when Townsend was sworn into office before the lord chancellor, and the reformed court commenced operations.

74  *ILT & SJ*, 27 (1893), 67 & 77.              75  See p. 219 below.
76  21 & 22 Vict. c. 79 (Ire.), 1857.
77  Maguire, who had been called to the Bar in 1843, was also the founder and editor of the *Cork Examiner* newspaper; *Who's who of British Members of Parliament: a biographical dictionary* ... ed. M. Stenton, 4 vols (Sussex, 1976), i, p. 256.
78  HC 1863 (45) l.5.

measures introduced in England by the Admiralty Court Act 1861. Second, the
Bill provided for modernization of the practice of the court: it was in the Maguire
and Longfield Bill that the proposals (later adopted in the Court of Admiralty Act
1867) for the giving of testimony *viva voce*, and for opening up the court to the
non-civilian profession, were first set out. The Bill's assimilationist ambitions were
warmly welcomed by Judge Kelly and within Irish business quarters.[79] The Bill
progressed as far as committee stage when it was withdrawn following a
representation by the solicitor general, James Lawson, that legislation would be
prepared by the government and introduced in the next session.[80]

The English trade journal, *Mitchell's Maritime Register*, identified the Treasury
as responsible for blocking the Maguire Bill. The Treasury wished, it alleged, for
purely penny-pinching reasons, to see the 1857 solution (the transfer of Admiralty
business to the Court of Probate) implemented. This, the journal alleged, was a
'pitiful economy'. The saving would be insignificant because the judge of the
Probate Court would demand an increase in salary for undertaking the extra duties.
Nor would the judge of the Court of Probate have the time to deal with the rising
scale of admiralty business:

> the wills business in the Court of Probate is also large, and will, in the normal
> course of things, increase. It frequently happens that one of these cases
> occupies a fortnight during which time, if the courts were amalgamated, a
> vessel, British or foreign, would be kept waiting.[81]

The plan to have admiralty jurisdiction transferred to the probate judge had to be
aborted due to the unwillingness of the sitting probate judge, Richard Keatinge, to
undertake the position. Keatinge, quite reasonably, argued that it would be
oppressive to impose upon him the extra burden of admiralty business.[82]

*The Admiralty Court (Ireland) Bills of 1866 and 1867*

In September 1863 a high-powered Royal Commission was established to
investigate the state of the Court of Admiralty of Ireland. That commission began
taking evidence in October 1863 and reported in May 1864. Its most important
recommendation was that the court should remain a separate institution, and that
the amalgamation solution, which had underlain section 14 of the Probate and

---

79  Dublin Chamber of Commerce appointed a sub-committee, which held a meeting with Judge
    Kelly, to consider the Bill. The Chamber was enthusiastically in favour of the measure,
    concluding that it was 'most beneficial and desirable'. A letter in support of the Bill was sent to
    the chief secretary, Robert Peel. Minutes of the council of Dublin Chamber of Commerce, 22 Apr.
    1863 (NAI, CSORP, 1,064/3/8, f. 447).
80  *Hansard 3*, vol. 171, col. 175 (1 June 1863).        81  *Mitchell's Maritime Register*, 10 Oct. 1863.
82  R. Keatinge to W.N. Hancock, 4 Feb. 1864, *Court of Admiralty Commission Report, 1864*,
    Appendix C, p. 59.

Letters of Administration Act 1857, should be shelved. The commission suggested that an expansion in jurisdiction along the lines accomplished by the Admiralty Court Act 1861 in England, where the scale of business had increased four- or five-fold, would result in a similar expansion in business in Ireland, and justified the retention of a separate Admiralty Court.

The report required implementation by statute. It was not until the spring of 1866 that the Liberal attorney general, James Lawson, managed to produce an Irish Admiralty Court Bill.[83] Quite unexpectedly, this Bill, to the dismay of both maritime interests and the court, did not implement the proposals of the Royal Commission. Instead it reverted to the rationalization approach of the Probate and Letters of Administration Act 1857, providing for the transfer of jurisdiction to the judge of the Court of Probate, and providing that 'the right honourable Richard Keatinge, judge of Her Majesty's Court of Probate in Ireland, or other person then being the judge of the said Court of Probate, shall be also the judge of the Court of Admiralty'.

The proposal to transfer admiralty jurisdiction to Richard Keatinge, a judge who knew little admiralty law and who had expressly said that he did not want the office, prompted a campaign of opposition. The matter was raised in Parliament: Jonathan Pim, the MP for Dublin City, questioned whether it was desirable to place the Admiralty Court under the jurisdiction of the Court of Probate, and informed the Commons that 'it was much feared in Ireland that this would be done'.[84] Dublin Chamber of Commerce wrote to the attorney general complaining that the proposal to vest the jurisdiction of the Admiralty Court in the Court of Probate would be 'highly inconvenient and injurious to mercantile interests'[85] since the Court of Probate 'was frequently monopolized for days and sometimes for weeks by a single record'. Judge Kelly argued that it was 'a theoretic economy' to 'transfer the administration of the court from experienced and energetic hands' – his own – 'in which, during these ten and a half years' labours, have reposed commercial confidence'. Richard Keatinge was not up to the job, being 'already full of other important matters and reluctant also, and to which the very nomenclature of this court should be a new learning'.[86] The attorney general defended the proposal for assimilation: the plan was to appoint a judge of top-rate ability to administer both courts, and this, he argued, would benefit the reputation of the Admiralty Court.[87] The 1866 Bill was presented to Parliament in May 1866, but lapsed soon afterwards.[88]

83  HC 1866 (133) I.7. Questions about the state of preparation of legislation were repeatedly asked in the House of Commons: *Hansard 3*, vol. 176, col. 279 (24 June 1864); vol. 177, col. 83 (8 Feb. 1865); vol. 181, col. 1390 (2 Mar. 1866); vol. 185, col. 1447 (7 Mar. 1867); vol. 187, col. 769 (20 May 1867).

84  *Hansard 3*, vol. 184, col. 1551 (26 July 1866).

85  Minutes of the council of Dublin Chamber of Commerce, 30 May 1866; 25 June 1866 (NAI, 1,064/3/9, ff 113, 126).

86  T. Kelly to the Treasury, 6 Apr. 1866 (TNA (PRO), T1/6,627A).

87  J. Lawson to F. Codd, 4 June 1866 (NAI, 1,064/3/9 f. 124).          88  See p. 209 above.

The earl of Derby's new Conservative administration made a fresh attempt at Irish Admiralty Court reform in 1867. In light of the protests which had followed the proposal to amalgamate the Admiralty Court with the Probate Court, the 1867 measure provided for the continuation of the court as a distinct institution under a specialist judge. The Irish attorney general, Hedges Eyre Chatterton, himself a leading admiralty advocate, introduced the Admiralty Court of Ireland Bill in June 1867. This reforming legislation swept through Parliament within two months without virtually any recorded debate on the technical reforms contained in the measure;[89] it received royal assent on 20 August 1867.

*The Judicature Act 1877*

In August 1877 the abolitionist theory prevailed once more. Parliament enacted the Supreme Court of Judicature (Ireland) Act 1877.[90] This historic measure provided for the abolition of the three-hundred-year-old Court of Admiralty in Ireland, and its assimilation into the High Court. The court's ultimate destination was to become part of the Probate and Matrimonial Division of the High Court.[91] The legislation envisaged that this end would be reached over two stages. First, the Admiralty Court was to become part of the High Court upon the death, or resignation, of the existing judge of the Court of Admiralty (John Fitzhenry Townsend). Second, the Admiralty Court was to form part of a new Probate and Matrimonial Division but only when the existing judge of that division (Robert Warren, who had replaced Richard Keatinge in 1868) had died.[92] Section 9 provided that if Warren was still judge when John Townsend died (the point at which the court was to become fused into the High Court) the Court of Admiralty was to form a separate division within the High Court. The insertion of the section, postponing the integration of admiralty jurisdiction into the Probate and Matrimonial Division until after the death of Warren, was made at committee stage.[93] The most obvious

89  *Hansard 3*, vol. 188, col. 559 (26 June 1867) [first reading]; vol. 188, col. 1,511 (15 July) [committee]; vol. 189, col. 78 (25 July 1867) [report]; vol. 189, col. 329 (29 July 1867) [third reading]; vol. 189, col. 405 (30 July 1867) [first reading, Lords]; vol. 189, col. 1,079 (8 Aug. 1867) [second reading, Lords]; vol. 189, col. 1199 (9 Aug. 1867) [committee, Lords]; vol. 189, col. 1304 (12 Aug. 1867) [report, Lords]; vol. 189, col. 1431 (13 Aug. 1867) [third reading, Lords]; vol. 189, col. 1633 (20 Aug. 1867) [royal assent]. *Hansard* overlooked the Second Reading of the Bill on 8 July 1867.
90  40 & 41 Vict., c. 49 (Ire.), 1877.
91  Opposition to the proposed amalgamation was, however, expressed by Sir Colman O'Loghlen on the ground that the measure infringed Article Eight of the Act of Union 1800 (which provided for perpetuation of the Irish Admiralty Court). He also pointed out that the adjudication of admiralty law required a 'peculiar knowledge which ordinary judges did not possess', *FJ*, 20 Feb. 1877.
92  S. 9 provided that if Warren was still judge when Townsend died, the Court of Admiralty was to form a separate High Court of Admiralty within the High Court. It was only upon the retirement or death of the judge of Probate that the court was to be amalgamated with the Probate and Matrimonial Division.
93  The Supreme Court of Judicature (Amendment) Bill 1877 [as amended in Committee] (HC, 1877 (184) vi. 607).

explanation for this amendment was that Warren, who had never practised in the Court of Admiralty, was considered unsuitable, or had refused, to be entrusted with admiralty work. In the end, the scheme under section 9 for a separate Probate, Matrimonial and Admiralty Division was never put into operation.[94]

*1893: the Admiralty Court of Ireland dissolved*

Townsend continued as judge until his death as the oldest sitting judge in Ireland, aged eighty-two, on 2 February 1893.[95] This event triggered the fusion of the Admiralty Court into the Supreme Court of Judicature in Ireland. The original intention had been that the court would ultimately become part of the Probate and Matrimonial Division of the High Court. However, under section 9 of the 1877 Act, integration into the Probate and Matrimonial Division was suspended until the death of the judge of the Probate and Matrimonial Division, and the appointment of a new judge of the Probate and Matrimonial Division. Since the judge of the Probate Court, Robert Warren, was still alive the consolidation remained in suspension. In the interval the court became a distinct Admiralty Division within the wider High Court. On 16 February 1893, the government nominated Mr Justice William Moore Johnson to be the judge of this temporary Admiralty Division.[96]

In 1897, the government reversed the original policy of creating a separate Probate, Matrimonial and Admiralty Division. In the end no such division was ever constituted in Ireland. Instead, the Supreme Court of Judicature (Ireland) (No. 2) Act 1897 amalgamated the Court of Admiralty with the Queen's Bench Division: section 6 provided that admiralty work was to be 'disposed of by one of the judges of the Queen's Bench Division to be assigned by the Lord Lieutenant'. Mr Justice Johnson was re-appointed under section 6 of the 1897 Act as the judge of the Queen's Bench Division charged with disposing of admiralty cases. Johnson disposed of admiralty litigation until his retirement in January 1910.[97] Johnson's successor was the former king's advocate and admiralty textbook author, Mr Justice Walter Boyd.[98] Boyd, whose fifty-two-year association with the court extended back to 1864, served as admiralty judge until his retirement in 1916.[99]

94  Under the Supreme Court of Judicature Act 1897 admiralty causes were assigned to one of the judges of the Queen's Bench Division (s. 6).
95  *ILT & SJ*, 27 (1893), 67 & 77.
96  J. Wylie, *The Judicature Acts* (Dublin 1895), p. 13.
97  *ILT & SJ*, 44 (1910), 2.
98  'Admiralty Business in Ireland', *ILT & SJ*, 44 (1910), 11.
99  *ILT & SJ*, 50 (1916), 96. Boyd was, in turn, succeeded by Justice John Gordon, who, as a practitioner, had been a prominent admiralty advocate, and served until 1922. *ILT & SJ*, 56 (1922), 236.

THE ADMINISTRATION AND PRACTITIONERS OF THE COURT

*Registrar*

In 1837 the corrupt Daniel Pineau was succeeded by John Anster. Anster was a more glamorous figure than the unassuming proctors who had previously held the office of registrar in Ireland: he was a civilian advocate, *littérateur*, translator of Faust, and professor of civil law in Trinity College Dublin. His appointment was understood to be a form of official bursary for his scholarly activities. The *Examiner* commended the government for this enlightened use of patronage:

> with the true feeling of an ardent lover and elegant cultivator of literature, Lord Mulgrave, in conferring this favour, has merely seized an occasion to pay a just compliment to a man of talents, who holds an honourable place among living poets. We rather think the official posts Mr Anster will have to perform are not of such a nature as to usurp the hours hitherto dedicated so successfully to letters.[100]

The personnel of the admiralty registry expanded in the early nineteenth century. Daniel Pineau had ceased carrying out the more prosaic functions of the office and had appointed two clerks to do this work on his behalf.[101] In 1839 Anster appointed a proctor, J. Taylor Hamerton, together with Hamerton's clerk, a Mr Moore, to undertake routine, scrivener-type functions: 'preparing attested copies, taking down formal rules'.[102] On the other hand, Anster personally undertook 'such other parts of the business of the registry as a barrister could effectively perform … – such as the taxation of costs, the examination of witnesses *in scriptis*, whether in town or under commissions to the country'.[103]

Despite the recommendations made by the Royal Commission in their *Eighteenth Report*[104] the procedures in the registry remained unreformed. Until 1867 the registrar continued to be paid by increasingly lucrative court fees.[105] Even more worryingly, the registrar continued to have personal custody of suitors' funds. Queries were raised through the Board of Trade about Anster's delay in releasing suitors' funds in a salvage award in a case in 1867.[106] The attorney general's sceptical conclusion that Dr Anster's response '[did] not tell the whole truth'[107] was embarrassing. Dr Anster died in June 1867.[108]

---

100  *Examiner*, 12 Apr. 1837.
101  *Eighteenth Report*, p. 12.
102  *Court of Admiralty Commission Report, 1864*, Appendix C, p. 61.
103  Ibid.                                104  See p. 180 above.
105  J. Anster to the solicitor general, 9 Feb. 1867 (NLI, MS 43,858).
106  Salvors in the *Pawnce of New York* complained that Anster had delayed between December and February before handing over an award of £232. Anster explained that the delay was caused by the illness of the salvor's proctor and the Christmas vacation. J. Anster to the solicitor general, 9 Feb. 1867 (NLI, MS 43,858).
107  H.E. Chatterton to Lord Naas, 11 Feb. 1867 (NLI, MS 43,858).
108  In recognition of his services to the court, business was suspended until his burial, *FJ*, 12 June 1867.

It was a measure of the increase in the court's activity that competition for appointment to the office after Anster's death in 1867 was so intense.[109] Eventually the government announced the appointment of Augustine Barton. Barton's appointment was the first to be made under the Admiralty Court (Ireland) Act 1867. Section 10 of the 1867 Act restricted the appointment to 'a fit person being an advocate, barrister at law, proctor, attorney or solicitor of ten years standing'. Barton had been secretary to the judge of the Probate Court, Judge Keatinge, and, although called to the bar, had never practised. The appointment was a purely political one, and Barton had no significant professional experience of the Admiralty Court. While the professional press described the appointment as one which would 'meet with general approval',[110] the attorney general, Hedges Chatterton, who as a leading admiralty advocate had a particular interest in the reform, was livid. The appointment of a Conservative placeman like Barton was, Chatterton protested, contrary to the reforming spirit of the 1867 Act:

> I have been just surprised by seeing that Mr A. Barton has been appointed registrar of the admiralty. With the political aspect of this I have, of course, nothing to do, so that I only mention it legally, and this I should not do but that I am the person who had charge of the Bill in the house. If not too late, I would again remind you that the appointment of a gentleman merely in name a barrister, but who has never even looked for practice, is certainly directly opposed in spirit, if not in letter, to the terms of the Act, and may probably be challenged in the house.

Chatterton stressed the importance of the functions performed by the registrar:

> One thing certainly should be distinctly stated: that the place is not a sinecure, but a really important and arduous office the duties of which must in future be performed in person, and not by deputy as it was before, to the great scandal of the court, and the registrar will be required to attend not only in court, but daily in his office during office hours as in other courts, and more especially during the absence of the judge in vacation.[111]

When the position became vacant again, following Barton's death in 1874,[112] the chief secretary, Michael Hicks Beach, fretting over money (and anticipating that the court would 'ultimately cease to exist') wrote to Townsend suggesting that the office of registrar be left vacant.[113] Judge Townsend patiently advised the chief secretary that a vacancy in the office would paralyze the court: under section 48 of the Admiralty Court Act 1867, suitors' money could not be withdrawn save by an

---

109  There were twenty-two applicants for the office (NLI, MS 11,252 (2)).
110  *ILT & SJ*, 1 (1867), 529.
111  H.E. Chatterton to earl of Mayo, 3 Sept. 1867 (NLI, MS 11,149 (6)).
112  NAI, CSORP, 1874/15,452.
113  M. Hicks Beach to J. Townsend, 24 Oct. 1874 (NAI, CSORP, 1874/15,452).

order of the registrar. But while it would not be possible to do away with the office of registrar, it would be possible to have the registrar administer other functions. Townsend's plan was that the existing clerk in court,[114] Charles Capel McNamara, should be appointed registrar, while continuing to perform (without any additional salary) the functions of clerk in court. McNamara was 'a barrister of more than twenty three years standing, who has for at least three years sat as my surrogate'. He had done so 'thoroughly to my satisfaction and is perfectly conversant with the court's business in all its details'. The amalgamation of the office of clerk with that of registrar would effect a saving of £400.[115] This suggestion was implemented and McNamara was appointed registrar. The appointment was a success. McNamara's association with the court endured almost as long as Townsend's, serving until his death in 1891. At the sitting following the announcement of McNamara's death, Townsend warmly described McNamara as his 'good friend' who had done 'everything in his power to save [me] trouble on all occasions'.[116]

*The clerk in court*

In 1848 Joseph Stock had modernized admiralty practice by relaxing the conventional procedure under which evidence was given by written deposition only. Under the court's new rule, evidence could, where both parties gave their consent, be supplied *viva voce*. That oral evidence would then become a record of the court by being transcribed by the registrar.[117] In practice, the registrar never undertook this transcription function; instead, a new office, the clerk in court (or actuary) was created. The functions of the clerk in court were 'to take notes of the evidence and judgment, transcribe them, and certify the transcript which became a record of the court'.[118] The first of these clerks in court was William Chamney, who began to undertake these 'most laborious duties' in the mid-1840s.[119] The actuary's fees, which were a first charge against funds in court,[120] were two guineas per day's attendance; and six pence per folio of seventy-two words. Chamney supplemented his official income by selling edited transcripts to the legal journals, the *Irish Jurist* and the (English) *Law Times*, as well as trade journals such as *Mitchell's Maritime Register*. In the late 1860s, the future registrar, Charles Capel McNamara replaced Chamney as clerk in court.

114  This office is described immediately below.
115  J. Townsend to M. Hicks Beach, 27 Oct. 1874 (NAI, CSORP, 1874/15,452).
116  *ILT & SJ*, 25 (1891), 578.
117  The court was required to have a full record of the evidence for the purpose of compiling a transmiss in case an appeal was taken to the Court of Delegates.
118  J. Townsend to M. Hicks Beech, 27 Oct. 1874 (NAI, CSORP, 1874/15,452).
119  'Statement on behalf of William G. Chamney', 9 June 1864 (NLI, MS 11,252 (1)); W. Chamney to the earl of Mayo, 28 June 1867 (NLI, MS 11,252 (1)).
120  General Order, 8 July 1861 (ibid.).

*Commissioners for taking affidavits*

Admiralty commissioners, whose functions were to take witness depositions and stipulations to hold to bail, were appointed at the principal outports, Belfast, Cork, Galway, Londonderry, Newry, Waterford, Wexford, and Dingle.[121] The court also appointed commissioners to take affidavits in London.[122] Those seeking to be appointed commissioners were required to prove that a new commissioner was necessary in the interests of suitors and practitioners, and that the appointment was approved by the proctors of the court.[123]

Besides depositions taken by specially appointed commissioners, the court also accepted depositions taken by magistrates (who had not been formally appointed commissioners by the court). The Irish court became uneasy about the legality of this following the decision of the Court of Criminal Appeal in England in *R. v. Stone* in 1853, where it was held that masters of the Court of Chancery (who had not been specifically appointed admiralty commissioners) were not empowered to administer admiralty depositions.[124] The *Stone* decision prompted a request by Dr Stock to the English Court of Admiralty as to the legality of admitting depositions taken by magistrates who had not been formally admitted as commissioners by the court. The English deputy registrar, H.C. Rothery, advised John Anster that, in light of the *Stone* decision, only those who had been specially appointed by the Admiralty Court as 'commissioners to administer oaths in admiralty' were competent to take depositions; the terms of magistrates' commissions were not sufficient to give them general competence in admiralty matters.[125]

*The marshal*

In 1862 the queen's proctor, Clement Lee Taylor, was appointed marshal.[126] With the increase of business in the mid-Victorian period, the office of marshal, generating fees of over £400 *per annum*, had become an attractive one. Taylor resigned the patent office of queen's proctor on the understanding that 'as the fees

121 *Thom's Irish Almanack and Official Directory 1853*, p. 501. In 1857 two petitions were submitted by lawyers seeking the office of commissioner for taking affidavits in Dingle. Judge Kelly accepted that, in light of increased maritime activity, Dingle required a commissioner. *Mitchell's Maritime Gazette*, 9 May 1857.

122 *FJ*, 4 Dec. 1856.          123 *Re Clement Taylor, FJ*, 28 June 1862.

124 (1853) 6 Cox CC 235.

125 *Notes on Four Admiralty Registry letter Books*, ed. K.C. McGuffie (London, 1964), p. 118. Anster had enquired: 'what is the practice of your court in regard to taking affidavits and stipulations for bail, and whether these acts are performed by commissioners specially appointed for the purpose, or whether by magistrates, or by both?'

126 Patent dated 15 Mar. 1862, *Court of Admiralty Commission Report, 1864*, Appendix C, p. 58. After Barrington's dismissal, the office of marshal continued to be held by Robert Simpson who executed it by a deputy, John McLaughlin. This arrangement continued until 1859. In February 1859 the lord lieutenant promoted McLaughlin marshal (T. Larcom to T. Kelly, 16 Feb. 1859 (NAI, CSORP, 1859/1,646)). McLaughlin, however, served for just two years. He fell ill in 1861 and died early in 1862.

of the office had increased for some years past, they would continue to do so'.[127] However, the business of the court, and the fees of the marshal, declined after their peak in the late 1850s, and Taylor protested that he had not been rewarded in the way that he had expected. Samuel Lee Anderson, who succeeded Taylor in June 1866, was another unimpressive appointment who was principally interested in fees.[128] Anderson regarded the appointment as a pure sinecure, awarded in compensation for his services as crown solicitor, and not meant to be performed in person: 'it was thought at the time but a small one for me to accept, but it had these advantages: that it was held for life by patent under the great seal, its duties could be performed by deputy and it did not interfere with my still labouring for the Crown as before'.[129] He protested when the Court of Admiralty (Ireland) Bill 1867 professionalized the office, and restricted the right to act by a deputy:

> Now after another year of unremitting toil and another special commission ... I find I am by a government measure to be deprived of an office (s. 5) the average emoluments of which have been £360 a year ... the Bill takes away my patent and makes me removable by the judge and lord chancellor (s. 10). It also imposes duties which seem to me to be almost impossible to perform – it empowers the lord lieutenant to appoint every quarter sessions a local court of admiralty. It enacts that the marshal is to be the officer of every such court (s. 86) and it forbids him to perform his duties by deputy (s. 12), unless in exceptional cases, and does not even allow him a clerk, although one is granted to the registrar (s. 14).[130]

The government settled the problem by inducing (by the promise, in exchange, of the office of crown solicitor for Waterford) Anderson to resign his position as marshal.[131] However, Anderson's replacement as marshal, Maurice Keating, was, again, not entirely suitable.[132] Keating was also the registrar to the judge of the Court of Probate, and retained that office after his appointment to the Admiralty

127  'Statement of the admiralty marshal, Clement Taylor', 1 Jan. 1864 (PRONI, D/2,777/7/1/A, f. 437).

128  The original patent of appointment survives in the Mayo papers (NLI, MS 11,291). The patent was enrolled in the Court of Chancery on 7 June 1866; it was exhibited in open court on 9 June 1866.

129  S. Anderson to H.E. Chatterton, 7 July 1867 (NLI, MS 11,146(2)). The following week he was pestering the chief secretary to amend the legislation to provide for a stipend of two guineas for each day spent attending local courts of admiralty: S. Anderson to H.E. Chatterton, 14 July 1867 (NLI, MS 11,146/3).

130  Ibid. By way of compensation for the increased duties, and the withdrawal of the right to act through a deputy, Anderson sought a salary of £400 *per annum*.

131  Opinion dated 15 Feb. 1869 (NAI, CSORP, 1868/17,547). The attorney general advised that under s. 10 of the 1867 Act the marshal could only be removed by the lord chancellor on the advice of the judge of the Admiralty Court, and not by the government.

132  In December 1868 Townsend wrote to the chief secretary to confirm that he had admitted Keating as marshal: J. Townsend to the earl of Mayo, 9 Dec. 1868 (NAI, CSORP, 1868/17,547).

Court. This pluralism drew public complaint and was investigated by the law officers.[133] Although the office was required by the 1867 Act to be executed in person 'except in case of temporary illness or other reasonable cause allowed by the judge',[134] Keating maintained the two offices by delegating his admiralty functions to a deputy. Judge Townsend put an end to Keating's abuse of office in the Queen (No. 1).[135] In that case Townsend disallowed the marshal's claim for expenses[136] where he claimed for functions which he had not discharged personally, but had been incurred by his deputy: 'the marshal is an officer of the court, and it is his duty to make the inventory in person, and not by a deputy. Had he from illness or other special cause been unable to go down, a special case should be made on his behalf, which was not done here'.

*Advocates of the Court of Admiralty*

A small group (the ecclesiastical lawyers Sir Thomas Staples, Arthur Gayer, Joseph Radcliffe and his brother-in-law, George Battersby; Thomas Kelly; William Monk Gibbon and his former devil, Hedges Chatterton; the textbook writer Edmund Hayes; and John Fitzhenry Townsend (the last judge of the independent Admiralty Court)) made up the most prominent members of the admiralty bar of the late 1840s and early 1850s. A slightly later generation of advocates included Isaac Butt, Walter Boyd, Clifford Lloyd, Joseph Elrington, William Corrigan, and Charles Todd. Admission to the Admiralty Court offered the junior barrister attempting to establish a practice an extra potential source of work outside the courts of law and equity. Hedges Chatterton recalled that he had been advised for this reason to join the admiralty bar early in his career by his master, the admiralty advocate William Gibbon. Junior barristers intending to practise in the Admiralty Court would take the degree of LLD in Trinity College, Dublin – the condition of admission to the court – in the lean years immediately after their call to the bar.[137] Some of these may have been drawn towards admiralty practice because of earlier professional maritime experience,[138] or because of a recreational interest in yachting. Chatterton was comfortable with admiralty law because he 'always had a love for the sea and

133  Law officers' opinion, 15 Feb. 1869 (NAI, CSORP, 1869/2,691).
134  S. 12.                                                            135  (1869) 8 Bar Reports 705.
136  Under s. 16 of the 1867 Act the marshal was provided with a fixed salary of £100 'besides such travelling and other expenses necessarily incurred in the execution of his duty as the judge, with the approval of the commissioners of Her Majesty's Treasury, shall allow'.
137  In his evidence to the select committee on legal education in 1846 the Professor of Feudal and English Law, Mountifort Longfield related that there were no educational conditions to acquisition of the degree of LLD; candidates, he said, 'just … go through some disputations, which are considered matters of form'. When asked whether the course might be improved, he replied 'I would not consider it improving the course, but creating the course' (HC 1846 (686) x.1, p. 220).
138  Monck Gibbon had served in the merchant navy in his youth. His career at the admiralty bar progressed when an early success in a maritime case before magistrates at Wexford brought him to the notice of James Watt, the queen's proctor. C. Haliday, *The Scandinavian kingdom of Dublin* (Dublin, 1882), p. cxx.

had a little knowledge of seamanship as far as some yachting taught me'.[139] Many of these advocates (of whom Gayer, Battersby, Townsend and Radcliffe were outstanding examples) were prominent as ecclesiastical advocates. But the older model of advocate who practised exclusively as a civilian had disappeared: all of these nineteenth-century advocates carried on practice concurrently before the courts of common law and equity.

In addition to those admitted as advocates, barristers, not entered on the Admiralty Court's roll of advocates, were occasionally given special leave to appear.[140] However, before 1867 common law barristers enjoyed no right of audience; the court was entitled to refuse admission. The discretion to admit non-advocates 'lay altogether within the authority and practice of the court'.[141] The demand for opening the profession to barristers grew, particularly after the enactment of the English Admiralty Court Act 1861, which removed the advocates' old monopoly in England.[142] In 1867 barristers in Ireland were, for the first time, allowed the right of audience in the Admiralty Court. Section 25 of the Admiralty Court Ireland Act 1867 provided that 'all barristers-at-law were to be entitled to practise as barristers before the Court of Admiralty and to enjoy the rights and privileges of practising in the said Court of Admiralty as advocates now have'. In practice, representation continued to be by those who had been leading advocates before de-regulation in 1867. The *Irish Law Times* noted in 1868 that 'the monopoly of the happy family of advocates has not, as yet, been very seriously interfered with, in consequence of the changes introduced in the recent Act'[143] and admiralty litigation continued, at least until the mid-1870s, to be dominated by the five leading advocates of the pre-1867 generation.

*Proctors*

No more than a handful of lawyers traded as proctors in the 1830s; in 1833 there were just six admiralty proctors in practice in Dublin.[144] In the following decade, however, corresponding with the rise in admiralty litigation, the number of proctors had virtually doubled: in 1845 eleven lawyers were recorded as admitted to practise as proctors.[145] The admiralty proctors fought to maintain a monopoly. Their chief support was the court's rule of practice of 1797, which restricted admission to persons who had served as apprentices with admiralty proctors.[146] This enabled the proctors to regulate the size of the profession; admission as an apprentice required the prior permission of the court, and since the court would

---

139  H.E. Chatterton biographical sketch (TCD MS 6,401/1, f. 13).

140  In the *Eliza* (1858) 11 Ir Jur 58 Francis W Brady BL appeared for the promovents.

141  *Re W. Russell*, *FJ*, 3 July 1862.        142  'The Court of Admiralty', *Irish Times*, 18 Oct. 1859.

143  *ILT & SJ*, 2 (1868), 382.

144  *Wilson's Dublin Directory 1833*, p. 192. The proctors were: Mathew Anderson, John McLoughlin, Henry Richardson, John Cooke Rogers, Clement Taylor and James Watt.

145  *Thom's Irish Almanack 1845*, p. 302: Mathew Anderson, Joseph Doran, J. Taylor Hamerton, R.C. Lee, John McLaughlin, A. McCorkell, Henry Richardson, J.C. Rogers, George Swettenham, Clement Taylor, James Watt.

146  See p. 184 above.

refer that application to the proctors, the proctors could restrict the size of the profession.[147] When an ecclesiastical proctor, George Frederick Thomson (who had not served an apprenticeship with an admiralty proctor) sought admission in 1849, the existing proctors intervened, requesting the court to enforce its general order of 1797.[148] They argued that there were already sufficient proctors and that the English court restricted admission in the same way. Dr Stock inclined towards the view that the 1797 Order should be enforced, and the petition was withdrawn.

Through over-use of its veto, the profession failed to reproduce itself. By 1867 the number of proctors had dropped to six.[149] The leading admiralty proctor of the mid-Victorian period was John Hamerton, the queen's proctor. The next most successful was William Richardson[150] (who also prepared a textbook on the practice of the court).[151] Section 25 of the Admiralty Court Act 1867 broke the monopoly of proctors and opened the court to solicitors. Section 121 of the Court of Admiralty Act 1867 authorized the Treasury to provide the existing proctors with compensation for the economic loss caused by the end of their monopoly. In 1867 four admiralty proctors, John Hamerton, Robert Lee, Joseph Doran and William Richardson, made applications for compensation for loss of earnings.[152]

*The premises of the Court of Admiralty*

In 1868 the court moved to a small room on the top floor of the Four Courts.[153] The room was cramped, unventilated and a health hazard. The *Irish Law Times*[154] carried accounts of incidents in which the claustrophobic conditions in the court had caused fainting (and of another chaotic occasion in which a spectator's clothes had become stuck to the recently painted jury box).[155] It was described in 1890 as:

> like a court scene in private theatricals. Everything seems to be out of proportion. The material court is too mean for the high sound of the tribunal … The nautical assessors are cooped up in one corner of the bench and the crier in endeavouring to keep at a respectful distance from the judge, is forced to take up his position in the other corner, which is also occupied by the window and its draughts.[156]

---

147   When the queen's proctor moved for permission to take an apprentice, the court referred the petition to the senior proctor. *FJ*, 11 Aug. 1859.
148   *In Re Thompson* (1849) 5 Ir Jur 258. See p. 184 above.
149   *Thom's Irish Almanack 1867*, p. 941.
150   Hamerton was appointed Queen's Proctor in 1862; *FJ*, 26 Mar. 1862. In the period 1862 to 1867 Hamerton acted as proctor in 184 suits, and Richardson in 118 cases (TNA (PRO), T1 (1867) 20,042). Other proctors such as Joseph Doran and Robert Lee had only half the practice of Hamerton and Richardson.
151   *Irish Times*, 23 Aug. 1867; *Court of Admiralty Commission Report, 1864*, p. 68.
152   TNA (PRO), T1 (1867) 20,042.      153   NAI, OPW/5HC/1/23 (1836).
154   'An unventilated grievance', *ILT & SJ*, 2 (1868), 382.
155   Ibid.                 156   Rhadamanthus, *Our judges* (Dublin, 1890), p. 106.

The habit of using models in collision litigation increased the pressure on space:

> there is a little black table, with white lines and figures, showing the points of
> the compass; and on the registrar's desk stands a model of a ship, for all the
> world like a toy of Lawrence's window, but intended to illustrate to the
> unskilled advocate the important distinction between the port and starboard
> side of a vessel.

### LOCAL COURTS OF ADMIRALTY

*The Recorders' Courts of Cork and Belfast*

Local courts of admiralty had not operated since the Munster Court of Admiralty
ceased to function in the mid-eighteenth century.[157] Part IV of the Admiralty Court
(Ireland) Act 1867 instituted a modern system of local admiralty courts. Section
74 provided that local courts, defined[158] as the Recorders' Courts of Belfast and
Cork, were to have admiralty jurisdiction where the value of the dispute did not
exceed £200; or, in cases of a higher value, where the parties consented to the
matter being tried by a local court. However, it was not for a further seven years
that these local courts were eventually put into operation. In 1874 an English
vessel-master wrote to the *Shipping and Maritime Gazette* complaining that the
recorder of Cork had refused to exercise the jurisdiction given under Part IV of the
Act of 1867 and 'assigns the reason, as I am informed, his pay was not stated'.[159]
The background to the delay was a dispute between the lord chancellor's office in
Dublin and the Treasury in London over the scale of fees to be charged to suitors
using these local admiralty courts.

   Under section 82 of the 1867 Act the local admiralty courts could only come
into operation when a schedule of fees had been 'prescribed by General Orders'.
Seven years were spent in a tedious argument before a scale of fees was eventually
drawn up, and the courts allowed to operate. The cause of the dispute was that
while the Treasury was concerned that the fees should be substantial enough to
make the courts self-financing, the admiralty judge, John Townsend, was
concerned that the fees should not deter small claims. In 1869 a scale of fees was
drafted by Townsend, after a conference with the recorders of Belfast and Cork.
This scheme, which set charges at a rate lower than that imposed in the central
Court of Admiralty, was transmitted to the Treasury on 4 December 1869.[160] The
Treasury, concerned that the fees were 'entirely insufficient to cover the expenses
of the court',[161] enquired why fees in local courts were less than those of the central

---

157  See p. 122 above.                    158  S. 2 of the Admiralty Court (Ireland) Act 1867.
159  13 Apr. 1874 (NAI, CSORP, 1907/15,859). A complaint was also received from Lloyds (ibid.).
160  C. Palles to Hartington, 2 July 1873 (ibid.).
161  W. Law to the under-secretary for Ireland, 25 Oct. 1873 (NAI, CSORP, 1907/15,859).

court when carrying out the same functions.[162] For a period of three years the lord chancellor's office in Dublin failed to reply to the Treasury's query. It was only in 1873, after pressure from business groups in the affected cities, particularly Belfast,[163] that negotiations were re-opened. Embarrassed by the delay in establishing the local admiralty courts, the attorney general, Christopher Palles, urged action 'so that the powers conferred by local courts so far back as 1867 should not remain inoperative'.[164] When communications re-opened, Townsend explained that the rationale behind the reduced scale of fees in local courts was to encourage smaller claims. The Treasury, however, refused to accept this argument and suggested that the way to ensure that the courts were used by litigants with smaller claims was to introduce a system of differential fees, distinguishing high-value and low-value cases.[165] Townsend accordingly drew up a revised scale of fees, differentiating according to the value of the claim. However, the Treasury remained dissatisfied, complaining that the schedule of fees proposed for the local courts were still uneconomical.[166] Finally, in 1874, following pressure in the House of Commons, the Treasury relented and sanctioned the table of fees drawn up by judge Townsend for the courts of Belfast and Cork.[167] The local admiralty courts then, after a seven-year delay, came into operation.

*Demands for extension of local admiralty jurisdiction*

The 1867 Act empowered the government to extend, by order in council, local admiralty jurisdiction to the recorder or chairman of quarter sessions in port towns outside Belfast and Cork.[168] Almost as soon as the 1867 Bill was published, Dublin Chamber of Commerce identified the flaw in the proposal: admiralty jurisdiction, because of the emergency nature of its processes, required continuous availability; however, recorders or chairmen sat too irregularly to provide continuous admiralty jurisdiction.[169] A number of applications for the extension of local admiralty courts submitted in the late 1860s were rejected for this reason. In 1867 the Chamber of Commerce of Waterford petitioned for the establishment of an admiralty court. The attorney general advised that there 'are serious difficulties as there is no recorder in Waterford and the chairman of the county sits in Waterford only a few days'.[170] In

---

162  G. [?] Hamilton to under-secretary for Ireland, 14 Jan. 1870 (ibid.).
163  J.H. Otway to Burke, 5 Jan. 1870 (NAI, CSORP, 1907/15,859).
164  C. Palles to Hartington, 2 July 1873 (ibid.).
165  W. Law to the lord chancellor, 19 Sept. 1872 (ibid.).
166  W. Law to the under-secretary for Ireland, 15 Oct. 1873 (ibid.).
167  W. Law to the under-secretary for Ireland, 10 Feb. 1874 (ibid.).
168  S. 84 Court of Admiralty (Ireland) Act 1867.
169  The chamber suggested that the local judge be a local stipendiary magistrate (J. Bagot to H.E. Chatterton, 11 July 1867 (NLI, Mayo MS 11,146/3)).
170  Petition of the Chamber of Commerce of Waterford, 4 Nov. 1867; attorney general's opinion, 11 Nov. 1867 (NAI, CSORP, 1907/15,859).

1869 the Corporation of Limerick initiated a similarly unsuccessful campaign.[171] Once again the solicitor general advised that jurisdiction could not be conferred since the recorder did not sit permanently, while the queen's advocate[172] pointed out that, due to the necessity of not delaying shipping, it was necessary that there be a permanent judge: 'in the case of Cork and Belfast the difficulty could be arranged, as the recorders are resident, but it seems to me a serious objection to the vesting of admiralty jurisdiction in any Court of Quarter Sessions'.[173]

*The Court of Admiralty (Ireland) Amendment Act 1876*

A high proportion of the vessels which were the subject of litigation in the central Court of Admiralty of Ireland had docked in Belfast, and in Cork.[174] But it took three or four days for litigants in these ports to obtain a warrant of arrest (or bail) from the court in Dublin. The MP for Cork City, N.D. Murphy, argued that, in emergencies, these delays could be avoided were the recorders' courts in Belfast and Cork to be given powers of arrest and bail. This power would be distinct from local admiralty jurisdiction; it would have functions purely ancillary to proceedings being litigated in the Dublin court:

> A cause, or supposed cause, of action arises against a vessel while in the port of Cork. The vessel is about to sail and has its cargo on board. Without any previous notice, a warrant issuing from the High Court of Admiralty, Dublin, is put in force by the marshal of that court through his deputy in Cork, and the vessel is seized and arrested. A period of three or four days must elapse in the ordinary course of practice before the necessary formal proceedings and completion of bail can be perfected, and the order for the vessel's release obtained … and in the meantime … lose perhaps, by the delay, the advantage of a charter party which she would be entitled to on her arrival.[175]

171  Petition of the mayor, aldermen and burgesses of Limerick, 11 Jan. 1869; petition of Limerick Chamber of Commerce, 16 Jan. 1869 (NAI, CSORP, 1907/15,859).
172  'Case on behalf of the Crown submitted to the queen's advocate in admiralty in Ireland, 18 May 1874' (NAI, CSORP, 1907/15,859).
173  In 1871 a memorial was presented by Waterford Chamber of Commerce seeking the appointment of the chairman of the Quarter Sessions, Dr Lloyd (who had previously served as Judge Kelly's surrogate) as president of a Waterford Court of Admiralty. The mayor told a meeting supporting the petition that the necessity of litigating in the court in Dublin involved considerable expense and that he had been informed that a suit of £10 had cost £1,300. The 1871 petition was rejected by the law officers on the standard ground of lack of continuity of sitting (*ILT & SJ*, 5 (1871), 16; NAI, CSORP, 1907/15,859). A further petition in 1878 was also rejected.
174  *Return of number of causes and warrants of arrest in proceedings 'in rem' in the Court of Admiralty (Ireland), 1868–75* (HC 1875 (202) lxx.1).
175  N. Murphy to M. Hicks Beach, 23 Apr. 1875, *Papers relating to admiralty courts for Cork and Belfast* (HC 1876 (321) lxi. 323).

In 1876 the solicitor general, David Plunket, oversaw the enactment of the Court of Admiralty (Ireland) Amendment Act 1876.[176] The Act enabled recorders in Cork and Belfast to arrest vessels which were the subject of cases intended to be removed to the central Court of Admiralty. There followed a delay of almost a year, caused once again by problems in obtaining approval for the rules, until the legislation came into effect.[177] But the legislation, when eventually implemented, was certainly not the success that had been hoped. The number of applications for arrest made under the 1876 Act was tiny; in Cork the figure never exceeded two per year.[178]

## INSTANCE JURISDICTION OF THE COURT OF ADMIRALTY, 1830–77

The early 1860s was a time of optimism at the admiralty bar. In 1861 the advocate Dr Clifford Lloyd read a paper to the Social Science Congress meeting held in Dublin in which he noted that the 'shipping trade of the country had greatly increased' and argued that Parliament should respond by modernizing the Court of Admiralty of Ireland along the lines effected in England.[179] Lloyd told the meeting that the jurisdiction of the Irish Admiralty Court now 'chiefly comprised suits for the recovery of damages for collision, suits for wages, suits for materials supplied to vessels, and suits of possession'. Collision cases, which in the 1820s were virtually unheard of, had became the principal constituent of the court's business, while cases involving wages (once the staple of the court) were declining in importance.[180]

In addition to the rise in collision and salvage work, the court was also acquiring commercial work by straying outside the limits prescribed by the common law. In the late 1850s a suitor before the Irish Court of Admiralty could obtain the court's intervention in a complaint relating to unpaid freight or demurrage;[181] or one concerned with unpaid towage fees;[182] or payment for supplies, or repairs undertaken for the benefit of a foreign vessel;[183] or damage to cargo, or loss of cargo.[184] Judge

---

176  39 & 40 Vict., c. 48 (Ire.), 1876. There was short debate on the second Commons reading: *Hansard 3*, vol. 228, cols 1,885–6 (28 Apr. 1876).

177  Questions by McCarthy Downing MP: *Hansard 3*, vol. 232, col. 827 (22 Feb. 1877), & vol. 234, col. 618 (10 May 1877).

178  *Return of number of Admiralty Cases in Local Admiralty Courts of Cork and Belfast, 1877–79* (HC 1878–79 (349) lix. 327).

179  *Irish Times*, 19 Aug. 1861.

180  In 1863 the court heard 18 salvage cases; 22 cases involving damage by collision; merely 5 wages suits; 5 cases of claims by unpaid suppliers; 2 bottomry cases; and 2 cases involving possession. *Court of Admiralty Commission Report, 1864*, Appendix D, pp 62–3.

181  The *Catherine & Alice, Shipping & Mercantile Gazette*, 27 Aug. 1858; the *Consul, Shipping & Mercantile Gazette*, 23 Aug. 1858.

182  The *San Giovani Teologos, Shipping & Mercantile Gazette*, 12 Feb. 1858.

183  The *Shannon* (1852) 6 Ir Jur 82; the *Moffatt* (1859) 11 Ir Jur 22.

184  The *Cinq Freres, Mitchell's Maritime Register*, 25 July 1857.

Kelly admitted that, even before the introduction of the legislative reforms of 1867, the Irish court had already assumed the very jurisdiction which the legislation proposed to give it: the new additions were 'subject matters which, by its ancient practice, had been considered within it already, and adjudicated upon by me'.[185]

With the boom in law reporting, decisions of the Irish court, derived from copy provided by the clerk in court, began to be reported extensively. The court's proceedings were carried in the *Irish Jurist* from the time of that journal's inception in the late 1840s; reports were also carried in English journals – the *Law Times* and *Bar Reports* – and in trade journals – the daily *Shipping and Mercantile Gazette* and the weekly *Mitchell's Maritime Register*. In a small number of these the court made contributions of original doctrinal significance.[186] Most, however, were routine applications of the principles of maritime navigation in collision cases, and of the principles for assessing the quantum of salvage awards.

### *Collision*

One of the effects of the significant rise in maritime traffic around the Irish coast between the late 1840s and the late 1870s[187] was an increase in the scale of collision and salvage cases being adjudged by the Court of Admiralty.

A high evidential burden was carried by the promovent. The Admiralty Courts of Ireland and England adopted the same widely criticized maritime rule of apportionment: if the victim was in some way at fault – no matter how minor – the loss was borne equally by the two parties, and not proportionately according to degree of fault.[188] The promovent could only fully recover where he could establish that he was entirely blameless, completely clear of 'willful neglect or gross negligence'.[189] Dr Stock shared the commonly expressed complaint that this rule was crude – a *judicium rusticorum*.[190] It meant that a liability could be thrown upon the injured part out of all proportion to the extent of its blameworthiness.[191]

Once the promovent had discharged the burden of showing both injury and lack of fault, the burden would then shift to the impugnant to show that it had not sailed with 'want of ordinary skill and caution'. Dr Stock, in the *Victoria*,[192] described the process of transfer of the burden of proof:

---

185  T. Kelly to the Treasury, 6 Apr. 1866 (TNA (PRO), T1/6,627A).

186  The *Clytha* (1849) 5 Ir Jur 317; the *Romolo* (1854) 8 Ir Jur 462; the *Berlin* (1849) 4 Ir Jur 11.

187  P. Solar, 'Shipping and economic development in mid-nineteenth-century Ireland', *Economic History Review*, 69 (2006), 717.

188  The *Woodrop (Sims)* (1815) 2 Dods 83; 165 ER 1422.

189  The *Victoria* (1855) 7 Ir Jur 94 (per Dr Stock). The rule that a promovent guilty of any contributory fault was entitled to one half only of the damage sustained was applied by the Court of Delegates in the *William* (1854) 7 Ir Jur 354.

190  *De Vaux v. Salvador* (1836) 4 Ad & El 420; 111 ER 845 (per Denman CJ).

191  The *Victoria* (1855) 7 Ir Jur 94.

192  (1855) 7 Ir Jur 94.

> If [the promovent] can get so far and show a severe injury or loss resulting from the act of their opponent, they themselves being clear of fault, then the onus is thrown upon the other side and the defendants must show that they are clear of all culpability and free from a want of ordinary skill and caution …

In determining 'want of ordinary skill and caution' the court was (imitating the English practice of assistance by elders of Trinity House) assisted by maritime assessors.[193] The role of the assessors was 'in the nature of opinion and advice only, which the court, in the exercise of sound discretion, was free to disregard'.[194]

Until 1863 the principal source of the rules of 'ordinary skill and caution' were the customary rules of maritime navigation which had been settled through the case law of the English court. The leading principles of this code included the rule that a vessel at berth be securely anchored;[195] the principle that a vessel keep a proper look out;[196] that a vessel exhibit effective lights;[197] that where vessels on opposite tacks met, the vessel on the port side should give way to the vessel on the starboard side;[198] that when two vessels met, one close-hauled and going against the wind, and the other not, that the vessel having the wind should yield to the close-hauled vessel;[199] that a vessel's look out should be increased where the vessel was travelling at night, at speed or in a busy shipping area.[200]

Rules for the meeting of ships were given statutory force by section 296 of the Merchant Shipping Act 1854[201] which provided that vessels meeting each other should put their helms to port. The rule of port-helm was applied in the *Cambria*:[202] the promovent (the lawyer and political economist Mountifort Longfield) was the owner of the yacht, the *Foam*, which had been seriously damaged by the *Cambria* steamer during the Royal Irish Yacht Club regatta in June 1857. Judge Kelly, assisted by the nautical assessors, dismissed Longfield's suit, finding the yacht responsible for the collision by not sufficiently porting towards the East Pier of Kingstown harbour.[203]

---

193  The *Jersey Tar* (1854) 8 Ir Jur 317 (Captain Daniel and James Dombraine); the *Cambria* (1858) 10 Ir Jur 443 (James Dombraine and Captain Crosby, merchant navy); the *Irishman* (1859) 11 Ir Jur 24 (Capt McClintock RN, and Capt Carpenter, merchant service).

194  The *American Union, FJ*, 4 Feb. 1860.    195  The *Alessandro* (1850) 3 Ir Jur 383.

196  The *Carlota* (1849) 4 Ir Jur 237.    197  The *Victoria* (1854) 7 Ir Jur 94.

198  The *Jersey Tar* (1854) 8 Ir Jur 317.    199  Ibid.

200  The *Londonderry*, 4 Notes of Cases, Suppl. xxxi.

201  17 & 18 Vict., c. 104, 1854. In addition to the provisions regulating steering under the Merchant Shipping Act 1854 rules and bye-laws promulgated under local harbour acts provided a further source of regulation. In the *William* (1854) 7 Ir Jur 354 an infringement of the by-laws made under the Kingstown Harbour Act 1836, prohibiting vessels anchoring in a designated triangle at the entrance to the port, was found to have been committed.

202  (1858) 10 Ir Jur 445.

203  A suit instituted by the owner of a smack damaged following collision with a steamer, the *Irishman*, at Poolbeg, was lost when it was established that the smack had starboarded instead of porting its helm. The *Irishman* (1858) 11 Ir Jur 24.

More extensive regulation followed the enactment of the regulations 'for preventing collisions at sea' prescribed in Table C of the Merchant Shipping Amendment Act 1862.[204] These regulations, which came into force in 1863,[205] replaced the provisions under Part IV of the Merchant Shipping Act 1854, and established the standards for lights, signals, and for meeting and crossing. The application of the 1863 regulations dominated collision litigation after 1863. Article 13 set out the rule to be observed where two steam vessels met, requiring that both vessels put to port. In the *Louisa v. The City of Paris*,[206] a tug and steamer which had collided on the river Suir were both held to have been at fault for not having ported their helms as required by Article 13. Originally, under section 296 of the Merchant Shipping Act 1854, a steamship and a sailing vessel meeting each other had been required to put their helms to port.[207] Under Article 13 of the 1863 rules this rule was amended: the sailing vessel was required to take its course, and the steam vessel to keep out of the way. In the *Iron Duke*,[208] Judge Kelly, noting the difference between the 1854 and 1863 régimes, held that a steamship had acted unlawfully in not taking sufficient measures to keep out of the way of a sailing vessel with which she had collided. In the *Belle*,[209] a steamship which had collided with a sailing cutter near Ringsend, was held to have complied with the rule by stopping and reversing. In the *General Lee*[210] a case concerning a sailing vessel which had collided with a steam ship near Howth harbour, the court held that, as soon as the risk of collision was apparent, the steamer was bound to keep out of the way by 'throwing off steam or reversing her engines'.

*Salvage of vessels in peril*

By the Wreck and Salvage Act 1846 local justices were entrusted with jurisdiction over salvage, concurrent with that exercisable by the Court of Admiralty.[211] By section 21 of the 1846 Act any claim where the sum involved was less than £200 could be determined by two local justices of the peace residing at a place where such service has been performed. The salvor could alternatively proceed in the Court of Admiralty. However, in the following decade that concurrent jurisdiction was abolished. Section 460 of the Merchant Shipping Act 1854 provided for exclusive jurisdiction by magistrates in the case of salvage disputes where the amount claimed was less than £200. Judge Kelly summarized the policy underlying the 1854 Act:[212] 'it was the object of the Merchant Shipping Act 1854, under

204  25 & 26 Vict., c. 63, 1862.
205  S. 25 of the Merchant Shipping Act 1862 provided that the regulations laid down in Schedule C would come into operation on 1 July 1863. The rules of 1863 were followed by a later set of rules promulgated in 1879: Order in Council for Preventing Collisions at Sea, 14 Aug. 1879.
206  W. Holt, *Rules of the road* (London, 1867), p. 14.
207  The *Irishman* (1858) 11 Ir Jur 24 (petition by a smack damaged by steamer in Dublin bay dismissed; sailing vessel had starboarded his helm on meeting steam vessel).
208  *FJ*, 1 Dec. 1863.                          209  (1872) 6 *ILT & SJ* 153.
210  (1869) 3 *ILT & SJ* 226.                     211  9 & 10 Vict., c. 99, 1846.
212  The *Union* (1857) 10 Ir Jur 462.

which the magistrate had exercised the jurisdiction in question, to prevent cases of salvage of small amount coming before the High Court of Admiralty of either country, and to curtail, as far as possible, the expense when the amount of salvage was small'. In 1862[213] a further restriction was imposed on the jurisdiction of the Court of Admiralty: the court was only to have jurisdiction where the value of the property saved was worth in excess of £1,000.[214]

A second legislative technique designed to divert salvors away from the Court of Admiralty was the costs' penalty created by section 460 of the 1854 Act. Where a case was litigated in the Admiralty Court and the value of the vessel was in excess of £1,000, but the salvors failed to recover more than £200, the salvors would have to bear their own costs. The only exception to this penalty arose where the court had certified 'that the case is a fit one to be tried in a superior court'. In the *Fenix*[215] Dr Lushington in the English Court of Admiralty read the 'fit to be tried in a superior court' formula as meaning that the Admiralty Court would only refuse to certify in a case where 'there is not some difficulty'. He included, within this category of 'difficult' cases, allegations of misconduct or neglect against the salvors. The *Fenix* was adopted in Ireland: by Judge Kelly in the *Lisbon*, and by Judge Townsend in the *Cherubim* and in the *Avenir*, all cases where it was alleged that the plaintiff salvors had been guilty of misconduct.[216] The rule produced the strange outcome of appearing to advantage misbehaving salvors, and was vigorously criticized in the *Irish Law Times*: 'does the doctrine come to this, that … a defendant can never raise the question of negligence in a salvor, but at the risk of having to pay all the costs in case the latter recovers £5?'[217]

The salvor's entitlement to recover was restricted where, at the time of salvage, the parties had pre-negotiated a fixed sum for the assistance; that agreement was conclusive of the amount owed for services.[218] In legal advice circulated to the coast guard of Ireland in 1840, the queen's proctor warned that:

> no agreement should be made as to any assistance in the way of salvage, with captain, crew, or any other person. The act of going out and rendering such assistance must be voluntary. Any agreement precludes the salvors from obtaining any sort of remuneration in the Court of Admiralty.[219]

In the *Elizabeth*[220] it was reluctantly acknowledged that a salvage contract had superseded the salvor's admiralty claim, even though the court thought it a

---

213 By section 49 of the Merchant Shipping (Amendment) Act 1862, the summary jurisdiction of magistrates was increased to 'extend to all cases in which the value of the property does not exceed one thousand pounds as well as the cases provided for by the principal Act'.

214 The *Empire Queen* (1869) 3 *ILT & SJ* 137.     215 (1855) Swab 14; 166 ER 992.

216 (1867) IR 1 Eq 144; (1869) IR 2 Eq 172; (1869) 8 Bar Reports 52; (1868) 2 *ILT & SJ* 105; (1868) 7 Bar Reports 157.

217 *ILT & SJ*, 2 (1868), 180.

218 The *Mulgrave* (1827) 2 Hag Adm 77, 166 ER 172; the *True Blue* (1843) 2 W Rob 176, 166 ER 721.

219 1 Feb. 1840 (NAI, CSORP, 1840/T 9,930).     220 (1856) 8 Ir Jur 340.

'hardship that they should not be entitled to more'. There were two exceptions to the rule: firstly, it was necessary that the agreement have been clearly understood and assented to by the salvors[221] – the court considered one alleged salvage contract so unfavourable to the salvors that they would have 'proved themselves such simpletons' if they really had agreed to the proposal.[222] Secondly, a salvage contract would not supersede the right to seek general salvage compensation from the Admiralty Court where a radical change of circumstances – 'a totally new and unforeseen emergency'[223] – had arisen after the contract had been negotiated.

The general principles settled by the English High Court of Admiralty for determining the quantum of the sum to be awarded by way of salvage,[224] were adopted by the Irish court: the skill of the salvors;[225] the degree of danger to which the property was exposed;[226] the degree of labour and skill which the salvors incurred and displayed;[227] the value of the property saved,[228] the time occupied,[229] and the fact that the salvage operation was successful.[230] Weighting was attached to the danger to which the salvors were exposed.[231] In the *Amazon*, magistrates at Arklow had taken into account the danger encountered by the salvors when awarding a group of Arklow fishermen £700, one-sixth of the value of the cargo. An editorial in the *Shipping and Mercantile Gazette*[232] condemned the award as extravagant. An appeal by the owners duly followed[233] in which the Admiralty Court, finding that the justices had exaggerated the element of danger, reduced the award. In the *Lisbon*[234] Kelly quoted from the American textbook, Marvin's *Law of wreck and salvage*[235] in support of the principle that 'salvage is a recompense resting entirely upon equitable considerations; and the salvor must present his claim with clean hands'. The quantum awarded might be reduced, or no award at all might be made, where the salvors had been guilty of plunder or misconduct.[236] On the other hand, a salvage award could be increased in recognition of the praiseworthy conduct of the salvors. In the *Amazon*,[237] where nearly 400 men had participated

221  The *Salacia* (1829) 2 Hag Adm 262; 166 ER 240.

222  The *Jane Anderson* (1848) 3 Ir Jur 293.          223  The *Briton* (1848) 5 Ir Jur 170, 176.

224  The *Clifton* (1834) 3 Hag Adm 117; 166 ER 349.

225  In the *Jane* (1852) 5 Ir Jur 31 Dr Stock acknowledged that the salvors, who had pumped considerable quantities of water and had plugged up holes in the hull of the vessel had shown 'great activity and bravery as well as intelligence'.

226  The *Elizabeth Bibby* (1847) 3 Ir Jur 257; the *Berlin* (1849) 4 Ir Jur 11; the *Empire Queen* (1868) 8 Bar Reports 576.

227  The *Sansone* (1847) 3 Ir Jur. 258.          228  The *John Bryant* (1851) 5 Ir Jur 233.

229  The *Elizabeth Bibby* (1847) 3 Ir Jur 257 ('three days and two nights during which the salvors underwent great hardship with goodwill and cheerfulness'); the *Rutland Derelict* (1848) 3 Ir Jur 283.

230  The *Eliza* (1858) 11 Ir Jur 58; the *Flamingo, FJ,* 24 Apr. 1862.

231  The *Amazon* (1860) 2 LT (NS) 140.          232  2 July 1858.

233  The *Amazon* (1860) 2 LT (NS) 140.          234  (1867) IR Eq 144.

235  W. Marvin, *A treatise on the law of wreck and salvage* (Boston, 1858).

236  The *Sarsfield* (1850) 5 Ir Jur 213; the *San Nichola* (1853) 6 Ir Jur 90; the *Magnolia* (1857) 9 Ir Jur 235; the *Lisbon* (1867) IR 1 Eq 144.

237  (1860) 2 LT (NS) 140.

in a rescue operation in Arklow, Kelly took the salvors' earnest conduct into account in increasing the award. The *Shipping and Mercantile Gazette*, while observing that the salvors were from a community whose 'reputation for honesty has at best hitherto been doubtful', commended the ruling as 'one which is best calculated to produce the best results and should be noticed favourably and liberally'.[238]

As a general principle only actual participants in the salvage operation were entitled to a salvage award.[239] There was, however, one exception: the owners of steamships, though not personal participants in the salvage, were entitled to significant compensation for economic loss incurred when their vessels delayed their journey to assist in salvage operations.[240] In the *Nimroud*[241] the court rehearsed the policy argument underlying the legal principle: the 'general interests of commerce, as well as the obvious policy of encouraging owners of large and powerful steamers to permit the employment of them in salvage services, required that salvage remuneration should be always adequate, and even liberal'. By the mid-nineteenth century, the owners of steamships were often the principal beneficiaries of salvage awards.[242]

## Salvage of derelict vessels

The quantum awarded in the case of salvage of abandoned ships or cargo differed from that awarded in the case of ordinary salvage. In the case of an abandoned derelict the only interests involved were the Crown and the salvor. A generous salvage award merely reduced the property interests of the Crown. By contrast with ordinary salvage no private ship owner interests were engaged. The general practice was to remunerate to a higher degree, rewarding the salvor with, at the least, one-third of the value of the vessel saved, or, in cases where the salvage was meritorious, and considerable exertion had been used,[243] one-half of the value of the derelict recovered.[244] However, in the *Berlin*[245] the Court of Delegates, on an appeal from Dr Stock in the Court of Admiralty, held that a strict one-third principle could lead to disproportionate awards in the case of highly valuable vessels, and was erroneous. Instead, the court held that the rule was a flexible one

---

238  *Shipping and Mercantile Gazette*, 28 July 1858.

239  The *Vine* (1825) 2 Hag Adm 1; 166 ER 145.

240  The *Jane* (1831) 2 Hag Adm 338; 166 ER 267. The Irish court was not always consistent in pursuing this principle. In *the Eliza* (1858) 11 Ir Jur 58 the owners of the steamer *Cambria* were held disentitled to an award on account of apprehended damages claims by passengers delayed by the vessel's participation in a salvage operation.

241  (1862) 8 *Law Reporter* 803.          242  The *Mary Stenhouse*, *FJ*, 3 June 1862.

243  The *Sansone* (1847) 3 Ir Jur 258.

244  J. Townsend, *A treatise on the law of salvage in Ireland* (Dublin, 1840), p. 50; the *Elliotta* (1815) 2 Dods 75; 165 ER 1420; *The King (in his office of Admiralty) v. Property Derelict* (1825) 1 Hag Adm 383, 166 ER 136; the *Effort* (1834) 3 Hag Adm 165, 166 ER 367; the *Elizabeth Bibby* (1847) 3 Ir Jur 257; the *Oresund, Mitchell's Maritime Register*, 18 Oct. 1862.

245  (1849) 4 Ir Jur 11.

that might be displaced according to the circumstances of the case. Given the state of the vessel, 'the fair wind and the little danger in which the vessel stood, and the fact that the conduct of some of the salvors appears to have not been very meritorious', the court considered £3,000 rather than £5,000 (the sum due were the moiety principle applied) adequate compensation.[246] Although the court was free to dis-apply the old rules, salvage derelict awards continued to be 'meted out on a more liberal scale than ordinary'.[247] Services which were meritorious, though not of the highest quality, were entitled to proportions of between one-quarter[248] and two-fifths[249] of the value of the vessel. On the other hand, the court might also grant more than a moiety where the proceeds of the salvaged derelict were small, and the salvage meritorious. In the *Castletown*,[250] a decision noted in the leading English text,[251] in which the net proceeds after sale amounted to just £120, the court awarded the entire sum to the salvors.

*Suits in claims by material-men*

One of the most significant comparative doctrinal differences between the Admiralty Courts of England and Ireland continued to be in the relief given to the unpaid provisioners or material-men. After the reign of Queen Anne the English High Court of Admiralty refused to issue *in rem* process against vessels which had been outfitted by unpaid suppliers.[252] In contrast, the Irish court continued to assist unpaid shipwrights or suppliers.

The Irish court never managed to identify a convincing positive justification for operating this remedy beyond the weak excuse that it had long been the practice. In the 1850s Dr Stock rationalized the process as a concession allowed to the Irish Admiralty Court by the courts of common law: 'it is so administered here as a species of indulgence of the temporal courts, who have thought proper not to interfere. We have no instance of a prohibition against the Court of Admiralty in Ireland'.[253] Judge Kelly justified the practice by reference to the fact that the Irish Court of Admiralty Act 1783[254] had created an independent Irish court, free to develop its own jurisprudence:

---

246  The *Berlin* was applied in the *Elizabeth* (1854) 8 Ir Jur 340 and the *Burns* (1869) 3 *ILT & SJ* 483.

247  The *Jane* (1852) 5 Ir Jur 31; the *Empire Queen* (1868) 2 *ILT & SJ* 719.

248  The *Juanita, FJ*, 14 Apr. 1864.

249  The *Sansone* (1847) 3 Ir Jur 258; the *Simpson* (1848) 3 Ir Jur 270; the *Sarah Marie, FJ*, 26 Feb. 1864.

250  (1849) 5 Ir Jur 378; the *Rutland* (1849) 3 Ir Jur 283; the *Miltown Malbay* (1850) 5 Ir Jur 380.

251  C. Abbott, *A treatise of the law relative to merchant ships & seamen* (12th ed., London, 1881), p. 546.

252  Between 1761 and 1835 the English court had allowed unpaid material-men to claim as intervenors (rather than primary parties) out of surplus funds: the *John* (1801) C Rob 288; 165 ER 466. The Privy Council closed that anomalous exception in the *Neptune* (1835) 3 Knapp 94; 12 ER 584. See p. 199 above.

253  The *Shannon* (1852) 6 Ir Jur 82. Judge Kelly delivered a judgment along similar lines in another material-man case, the *Bon Accord, Mitchell's Maritime Register*, 23 Aug. 1857.

254  See p. 175 above.

now in Ireland, which possessed its independent legislature, and possesses its independent municipal courts, the High Court of Admiralty has been permitted to exercise a jurisdiction, carrying out that principle of the *lex mercatoria* namely that a ship is itself liable for repairs, provided only she be a foreign and not a domestic one.[255]

The court operated the jurisdiction diffidently. Relief was confined to the suppliers of defaulting foreign vessels; it was not available to the suppliers of Irish based-vessels. In the *Shannon*[256] repairs had been affected in Arklow on an Irish vessel. The court distinguished an Irish vessel from a foreign vessel. In the case of Irish vessels, the primary remedy of the unpaid supplier was through the *in personam* process of the ordinary common law courts. Redress from the Admiralty Court was restricted to the victims of foreign vessels. This was because a foreign vessel, able to escape, might 'withdraw herself from the notice of justice'; but there was no such emergency where the vessel was Irish-registered and was 'in constant intercourse with the port, going in and out'. Second, the jurisdiction was only made available for services supplied in Ireland. In the *William Creevey* the court refused to act at the suit of a supplier based in Galatz; Kelly held that the jurisdiction was limited to necessaries supplied in British ports and that 'further this court has not yet gone'.[257] Third, the remedy was granted only where it was positively alleged that the repairs or supplies had been provided in return for a promise to make the vessel amenable in case of default, and not where credit had been induced by some other undertaking. In the *Isabella of Glasgow* Judge Kelly dismissed a claim for repairs done at Kingstown on the basis of the petitioners' error in pleading that they had carried out the works on faith of the personal credit of the vessel's owners.[258]

The material-man jurisdiction traditionally exercised by the Irish court was put on a secure foundation by the Court of Admiralty (Ireland) Act 1867: section 30 provided that 'the Court of Admiralty shall have jurisdiction over any claim for the building, equipping or repairing of any ship', while section 31 provided that 'the Court of Admiralty shall have jurisdiction over any claim for necessaries supplied to any ship elsewhere than in the port to which the ship belongs'. The power conferred on the Irish court was slightly wider than that given to the English court. By section 6 of the English Act of 1861, the jurisdiction of the English court to hear claims submitted for the supply of necessaries was subject to the limitation that the owners of the vessels were domiciled in a country other than England or Wales. Under the Irish legislation the process could, after 1867, be exercised against Irish-based vessels.

---

255  *FJ*, 15 Aug. 1857. Judge Kelly repeated the same theory in the *Isabella* (1866) 4 Bar Reports 145.
256  (1852) 6 Ir Jur 82. Foreign vessels included British vessels: the *Isabella* (1866) 4 Bar Reports 145.
257  *FJ*, 15 July 1862.                     258  (1866) 4 Bar Reports 145.

*Freight suits*

The Court of Admiralty in Ireland had a long tradition of stretching the limits of its proper competence, and of accepting jurisdiction in ordinary maritime contract cases.[259] By the mid-nineteenth century the Irish court was adjudicating claims for unpaid freight – an area in which the English court would not intervene. In the *Thorny Close*,[260] Dr Stock accepted jurisdiction in a suit in which a ship-owner claimed unpaid freight. Dr Stock's successor, Thomas Kelly, continued this practice. In the *Venus of Youghal*,[261] in 1858, Kelly was happy to entertain a suit for demurrage taken by the owner of a vessel against a consignee of coal who had delayed in unloading the cargo. In the *Consul*, proceedings were initiated against the consignee of a cargo of wheat who had refused to pay freight when the cargo safely arrived in Dublin from Hamburg.[262] Kelly, in acceding to the master's application, justified this unorthodox jurisdiction by reference to 'the ancient jurisdiction of the court in such cases'. However, in the mid-1860s Kelly shut down this novel jurisdiction. In 1866 he told the Treasury that he had 'declined further to do so except empowered by statute'.[263]

There was international pressure for entrusting a freight jurisdiction to the court. The consuls of France, Greece, Belgium, Brazil, Norway, Denmark, Sweden, Prussia and Italy, in their submissions to the Royal Commission on the Admiralty Court in 1864, all complained of the injustice caused to foreign ship-owners by the non-availability of such a process in the Irish Admiralty Court.[264] The French government had apparently delivered a remonstrance to the government of England on the lack of an Irish admiralty freight jurisdiction.[265] The difficulty was that there was no such jurisdiction in England either. The Royal Commission advised against such an extension in jurisdiction until a similar reform had been made in England. The commissioners were concerned that 'the result would be to give the Court of Admiralty in Ireland a wider jurisdiction than that possessed by the Court of Admiralty in England; and we think the object should be to assimilate the jurisdiction of the courts'.[266] Accordingly no provision for the recovery of freight was made in the Irish Admiralty Court Act 1867.

The failure to include this reform in the 1867 Act drew criticism. The lack of a remedy in the Admiralty Court meant that ship owners were forced to use the common law courts. However, these courts sat too irregularly to provide foreign shipping concerns with an efficient remedy for unpaid freight. The Court of

259  See p. 128 above.                    260  (1851) 5 Ir Jur 251.
261  *FJ*, 18 Sept, 1858; the *Pearl*, *FJ*, 25 Sept. 1858 (demurrage); *Kenneally v. Carville*, *Irish Times*, 18 Aug. 1859.
262  *Shipping and Mercantile Gazette*, 23 Aug. 1858, *FJ*, 9 Aug. 1858; the *William of Waterford*, *FJ*, 24 Mar. 1859 (freight and demurrage).
263  T. Kelly to the Treasury, 6 Apr. 1866 (TNA (PRO), T1/ 6,627A).
264  *Court of Admiralty Commission Report 1864*, Appendix A, pp 41–5.
265  *Irish Times*, 19 Aug. 1861.
266  *Court of Admiralty Commission Report 1864*, p. xiii.

Admiralty, by contrast, sat all the year around and could provide an immediate remedy. A paper read to the Social and Statistical Inquiry Society of Ireland in 1870 identified, as the principal justification for extending freight jurisdiction to the Court of Admiralty, the comparative slowness of proceedings at common law:

> This state of affairs causes delay, which involves hardship, and not infrequently a practical denial of justice, since the Court of Admiralty sits all the year around, while the superior courts of common law only sit at intervals for the trial of such causes. The long vacation extends practically over four months, and during that time no cause can be brought to trial. Even in the other eight months the remedy is very slow and may be so dilatory as to be practically useless. Such cases can only be tried at the sittings of each term, or at assizes (in March and July).[267]

However, the jurisdictional gap was eventually closed by the Court of Admiralty (Ireland) Amendment Act 1876: section 16 gave the court 'jurisdiction to decide all claims arising out of any agreement made for, or in relation to, the use or hire of any ship'. The grant of jurisdiction to Ireland was in advance of developments in England.

*Cargo suits*

For a short period during the late 1850s the court processed petitions concerned with damage to, or non-delivery of, cargo.[268] However, in 1859 it reversed that practice. In the *Luna*, a Tralee merchant (the consignee of a cargo of wheat from the Ukraine) complained that the master had closed the hatches and had refused to release the cargo. The vessel was arrested.[269] Relying on the English admiralty statutes of 1389 and 1391, an objection was made by the ship-owner to the competence of the court.[270] Judge Kelly agreed with the objection, and aborted the proceedings. He premised his judgment on the proposition that the *in rem* process of the court was in all cases conditioned on the petitioner having a maritime lien in the ship: 'a maritime lien in fact is the foundation of the proceeding *in rem* which is the proceeding in the present case'. The unpaid mariner, or the victim of a collision, or the unpaid material-man, all had a maritime lien. However, on a search of English and European maritime law (including the medieval laws of Oleron) he could find no authority for the proposition that the consignee of cargo possessed a lien upon the vessel 'so as to call into operation the admiralty proceeding *in rem*'. The court held that, since there was no lien, there could no arrest or process *in rem*, and dismissed the petition.

---

267 H. Dix Hutton, 'Report on the extension of admiralty jurisdiction in Ireland to cases of freight and demurrage', *Journal of the Social and Statistical Inquiry Society of Ireland* (1870), 212.
268 The *Brig Melora of Hartlepool*, *FJ*, 6 May 1859; the *Jane Spoors*, *FJ*, 30 July 1859.
269 *FJ*, 12 Nov. 1859.     270 13 Ric. II, c. 5 (Eng.), 1389; 15 Ric. II, c. 3 (Eng.), 1391.

In 1867 the Irish Admiralty Court secured, for the first time in its history, a clear grant of authority (wider, in fact, than that conferred on the English court by the Court of Admiralty Act 1861)[271] to process suits for damage to cargo. Section 37 of the Court of Admiralty (Ireland) Act 1867 conferred on the court jurisdiction to hear suits for damage to goods 'carried into any port in Ireland' resulting from 'the negligence or misconduct of, or for any breach of duty or breach of contract on the part of the owner, master or crew of the ship'. Section 37 of the 1867 Act restricted the jurisdiction to 'any goods carried into any port in Ireland'. It did not operate when the damage occurred while the vessel was in transit from Ireland. In 1876 the anomaly was closed. Section 15 of the Court of Admiralty (Ireland) Amendment Act 1876 extended the jurisdiction to include 'goods shipped upon, or carried, or about to be carried upon, or carried by, any ship from any port in Ireland' (giving a consignee a remedy *in rem* against a vessel which had returned having damaged cargo on its outward voyage). The impact of this jurisdictional extension begun to be registered almost immediately. During the maritime boom of the 1870s, Judge Townsend described the jurisdiction given to 'this court in cases of damage to cargo as very important indeed to the mercantile interests of the country',[272] and it was widely used.[273]

### Bottomry

The nineteenth-century international trade in bottomry bonds was the basis of a further source of business for the Irish court. Suppliers of maritime goods and services from all over the world, who had received bottomry bonds in exchange for emergency goods or repairs, would sell those bonds to specialist bond-recovery agents operating from London or Dublin. These agents would execute the bond, by process of arrest from the court, when the vessel returned to Ireland.

Fights for priority between competing bottomry bondholders, and between bond holders and other creditors, were a regular source of legal contest. The English rule, that a bottomry bond holder took precedence over all other creditors except unpaid mariners, was faithfully applied by the Irish court. Wages were regarded as 'sacred liens, and as long as a plank remains, the sailor is entitled, against all other persons, to the proceeds as a security for his wages'.[274] The Irish

---

271  S. 6 of the 1861 Act withdrew this jurisdiction where 'at the time of the institution of the cause any owner or part owner of the ship is domiciled in England or Wales'.

272  The *Fortuna* (1872) 6 *ILT & SJ* 80, 84.

273  The *Energie* (1874) IR 9 Eq 58 (consignee of cargo of timber from Memel complained that the master of the vessel had illegally detained the cargo); the *Austin Friars* (1869) 3 *ILT & SJ* 608 (owner of a cargo of Indian corn which had been carried from Odessa petitioned for damage done to the cargo by hot air generated by the steamer's engine); the *Fortuna* (1872) 6 *ILT & SJ* 80 (owner of a cargo of wheat which had been damaged in transit from Chile to Dublin claimed that the ship had been unseaworthy).

274  Per William Scott in the *Madonna D'Idra* (1811) 1 Dods 32; 165 ER 1224, applied by Dr Stock in the *Carlota* (1849) 4 Ir Jur 237.

court maintained this rule in the face of strong arguments in favour of prioritizing the bottomry holder. In the *Woodman*[275] the bondholder argued for priority on the ground that the bond provided the means by which the earnings were generated: 'these wages were earned prior to the execution of the bottomry bond, and that, therefore, as the latter was the sole means of the safe arrival of the vessel, it should be the first paid'. Judge Kelly, however, reasoned that it was the crew's labour which provided the means of safe arrival of the vessel and of the bondholder's ability to realize his security: 'the ancient and hitherto unbroken rule of the Court of Admiralty has been that the bondholder takes his security subject to seamen's wages, and to certain services as pilotage and towage etc., which are for the benefit of all concerned'.

The governing principle of bottomry was that the bond last given was entitled to priority because the 'last loan furnished the means of preserving the ship, and without it the former lenders would entirely have lost their security'.[276] However, in the *Clytha*,[277] one of the few original doctrinal contributions made by the Irish court,[278] it was held that the later bond holder could lose its normal priority by unconscionable behaviour. In the *Clytha* two bonds had been entered into: the first in Boston secured the ship and freight; the second at St John's, New Brunswick, also secured the ship and freight. The New Brunswick creditor knew that the earlier bond secured only the ship and freight, but, acting to protect the cargo owners (with whom he was in business), deliberately did not secure the cargo. If this had been done the assets would have been marshalled: the later (New Brunswick) bondholder would have been compelled to proceed against the cargo, leaving the earlier (Boston) bondholder to his security against the ship and freight. The vessel was arrested in Galway; the fund realized by the subsequent sale of the vessel and the freight was insufficient to satisfy both bondholders. Dr Stock held that, while the second bondholder normally had priority, this could be lost on equitable principles: 'although the Court of Admiralty is not a court of equity, yet from the nature of the subjects of adjudication in this court, it often happens that it must decide such questions as the present as a court of equity'. Here the second bondholder, who acted as an agent of the consignees of the cargo, had deliberately frustrated the capacity of the prior bondholder to realize its security: there was

275  *Mitchell's Maritime Register*, 8 Aug. 1857; *FJ*, 6 Aug. 1857. In the *Hendrica Gazina* (1860) 2 LT (NS) 139 suits were instituted against a Dutch vessel docked in Cork by a bond holder, by unpaid seamen, and by the suppliers of materials to the vessel. The funds in court, the proceeds of the sale of the vessel and the amount of the freight, were insufficient to meet the claims of both parties. Judge Kelly, rejecting the bottomry holder's argument that absolute priority of sailors' claims over unpaid bondholders was prejudicial to commercial interests and the extension of commercial credit, applied 'the ancient and hitherto unbroken rule of a bondholder taking his security subject to the seamen's wages'.

276  The *Rhadamanthe* (1813) 1 Dods 201, 165 ER 1283; the *Betsey* (1813) 1 Dods 289, 165 ER 1314. C. Abbott, *A treatise of the law relative to merchant ships and seamen* (London, 1827), p. 128.

277  (1849) 5 Ir Jur 317.

278  Abbott, *A treatise of the law relative to merchant ships and seamen*, p. 599.

'sufficient evidence to establish that when the second bond was executed [he] had full knowledge of the prior hypothecation'. Yet, acting in the interests of the Irish cargo consignees, 'he chose deliberately to take his own security not affecting the cargo'.

*Seamen's wages*

The number of cases involving seamen's wages claims declined in the mid-Victorian period.[279] This may have been accounted for by the effects of section 16 of the Merchant Shipping Act 1844 which displaced the Court of Admiralty in favour of magistrates' courts where the value of the claim was less than £20 in value. During the period 1844–67 the court was, as a result, forced to turn away its principal traditional constituency – the unpaid seaman. The Irish court construed this exclusion upon its competence widely, extending beyond cases where the amount of an individual claim was less than £20. In the *Fairy Queen*,[280] the court held that it lost jurisdiction where the amount claimed in a consolidated wages suit taken by a number of crew members exceeded £20, even though none of the promovents claimed the amount of £20 individually. The extent of the exclusion of the Admiralty Court in favour of magistrates' courts was increased by the Merchant Shipping Act 1854 which raised the sum within the exclusive jurisdiction of the magistrates' courts to £50.[281] However, in 1867 Parliament reversed its policy of diverting wages cases to magistrates' courts: section 33 of the Court of Admiralty (Ireland) Act 1867 returned the court's historic wages jurisdiction, giving it jurisdiction over 'any claim' by a seaman for wages.[282]

The 'special contract' doctrine,[283] under which the Court of Admiralty did not have wages jurisdiction where the character of the contract deviated from the ordinary seaman's contract, provided a second exception to the court's jurisdiction.[284] The term 'special contract' had not been precisely defined in the case

279 In 1863 collision and salvage cases had overtaken wages suits as the staple of Irish admiralty business: in 1863 only 5 wages cases were instituted before the court. The number of collision cases was 22 and salvage cases 18: *Court of Admiralty Commission Report, 1864*, Appendix D, pp 62–3.
280 (1847) 3 Ir Jur 283.
281 S. 189. The exclusion of the Court of Admiralty was subject to four exceptions: (i) where the owner of the vessel had been declared bankrupt; (ii) where the vessel was already under arrest or sold; (iii) where magistrates hearing a claim for wages worth less than £50 referred the case to the Court of Admiralty. (In the *Christiana*, *FJ*, 2 Aug. 1859, the presiding magistrate at Capel Street, Dublin had referred a wages case for the opinion of the court). (iv) Where neither the owner nor master resided within twenty miles of the place where the seaman was discharged. (In the *Happy Return*, *FJ*, 26 Aug. 1862, the crew was discharged in Dublin. Since the owners resided in Berwick-upon-Tweed and there was no master, the court held that the case was 'within the exception of the statute' and was entitled to hear a claim for £26.)
282 A provision (s.10) in the English Act of 1861 under which a successful party would lose his entitlement to costs where the amount recovered was less than £50 was not included in the Irish Act.
283 The *Mona* (1840) 1 W Rob 137, 166 ER 524; The *Riby Grove* (1843) 2 W Rob 52, 166 ER 675.
284 *Court of Admiralty Commission Report 1864*, Appendix A, p. 4.

law but in an impressive judgment in the *Black Diamond*,[285] Judge Kelly extracted two underlying strains in the law: (i) cases where the mariner undertook some special function in addition to the routine duties of a sailor, and (ii) cases where the mariner received some extraordinary form of emolument. The *Enterprise of Dundalk*[286] fell within the first of Kelly's categories: the promovent was required to undertake ordinary seaman's functions; but he was also required to provide pilotage. Kelly held that the unorthodox elements relating to pilotage made the agreement a special one, *prima facie* outside the jurisdiction of the court. In the *Trio of Galway*[287] a share fisherman was paid both a wage and a profit share in the catch; the share component of the remuneration was held 'special' and the court was held incompetent. Section 33 of the Court of Admiralty (Ireland) Act 1867 – which gave the court jurisdiction whether wages be due under a 'special contract or otherwise' – finally expunged this exclusionary doctrine.

The jurisdiction of the Court of Admiralty over wages had previously been limited to seamen only. Masters were not entitled to sue in the Court of Admiralty for unpaid wages. That restriction was partly lifted in 1844, by the Merchant Seamen Act 1844.[288] The 1844 Act allowed masters to sue for unpaid wages but only in 'the case of the bankruptcy or insolvency of the owner of the ship'. In the first case in which the 1844 Act was used in Ireland, the *Simon Glover*,[289] a suit was instituted by the master of a vessel who had conducted a voyage between Galatz and Belfast. The ship owner had been declared bankrupt in Scotland. Notwithstanding what Dr Stock described as 'rather flimsy proof' of bankruptcy (the bankruptcy proceedings in Scotland had not been authenticated by a notarial certificate) the court decreed for wages. However, ten years later, by the Merchant Shipping Act 1854,[290] the restriction upon a master's entitlement to sue for wages in the Court of Admiralty, to cases where the owner was bankrupt, was lifted. Section 191 of the Merchant Shipping Act 1854 provided that the master of a ship should have the same 'rights, liens, and remedies for the recovery of his wages' which any ordinary seaman had.

The problem of the comparative priority between unpaid seamen and the victim of a maritime collision – the collision lienor – was considered by the Irish court on a number of occasions, with the court taking inconsistent stances on the same issue of principle. In the *Carlota*,[291] proceedings had been instituted against an American vessel for a collision on the river Shannon. Following a suit in the Court of Admiralty she was then sold by the marshal, and the profits returned to the court. Members of the American crew then presented a petition against the fund in court, and asked for their wages. The problem was that the proceeds in court were insufficient to meet both claims. In a detailed judgment, which included references to American law and the Napoleonic 'Code de Commerce', Dr Stock held that the

285  *FJ*, 18 Nov. 1863.
286  *Mitchell's Maritime Register*, 17 Mar. 1860; 5 Law Reporter 29.
287  *FJ*, 27 May 1864.        288  7 & 8 Vict., c. 112, s. 16.        289  (1848) 3 Ir Jur 284.
290  17 & 18 Vict., c. 104.      291  (1849) 4 Ir Jur 237.

sailors ranked first, and applied the principle that 'in proceeding against the ship
*in specie*, if the value thereof be insufficient to discharge all claims upon it, the
seaman's claim for wages is preferred before all other charges'. A different analysis
of the problem was adopted by Stock's successor. In the *Duna*,[292] Judge Kelly held
that collision lienors were entitled to priority over unpaid sailors. The *Duna* had
run down the *John Bull* in the Black Sea; it had also failed to pay wages to its crew.
Two rationales were offered by Kelly for preferring the collision lienors. The first
was that the crew had been partly responsible for the accident, and that this justified
denying them their ordinary priority. The second was that the unpaid Russian
sailors had a series of alternative remedies in Ireland, including proceedings *in
personam* against the master. The vessel owners of the *John Bull*, on the other hand,
had no effective alternative remedy in Ireland against the Russian owners:

> By the maritime law of all great maritime states the mariner has a threefold
> remedy for the recovery of his wages. He can sue the ship herself, or he can
> sue the owner, or he can sue the master of her. His right to all or any of these
> several remedies is beyond dispute, and he can select any of them which his
> convenience or his necessity may suggest. The petitioners in this cause of
> damage, in which the ship is a foreign one, and sold in this, a foreign country,
> have no other remedy than against the ship, and if that be not abstracted, or
> its value absorbed by other claimants, they are remediless.[293]

*Dissentient part-owners; part-owners' accounts*

Like the English Court of Admiralty,[294] the Irish court regularly[295] provided relief
to dissentient part-owners[296] who had fallen out with their partners and wanted an
order to prevent the other part-owners from undertaking a reckless venture. The

292  (1861) 5 LT (NS) 217.
293  Ibid., p. 218. This section of Kelly J's judgment was recently quoted by David Steel J in the English
     Queens Bench Division in the *Ruta* [2000] 1 WLR 2068 (at p. 2073). The circumstances in the *Ruta*
     were distinguished from those in the *Duna*, and claims of the unpaid sailors were preferred.
294  The source of the jurisdiction was discussed by Lord Stowell in the *Apollo* (1824) 1 Hag Adm
     306, 166 ER 109.
295  The *Maria Ross, Shipping & Mercantile Gazette*, 3 Mar. 1856; the *Sir William Stamer, Shipping &
     Mercantile Gazette*, 15 Dec. 1856; the *Waterwitch, Shipping & Mercantile Gazette*, 13 June 1857; the
     *Snaresbrook, Shipping & Mercantile Gazette*, 2 Nov. 1857; the *Fire Fly, Shipping & Mercantile
     Gazette*, 9 Jan. 1858.
296  In *Haly v. Godson* (1816) 2 Mer 77; 35 ER 870 the lord chancellor of England, Eldon LC,
     distinguished applications for restraint made by part-owners, the extent of whose shares was
     ascertained, and applications by part-owners the extent of whose shares was disputed. In the
     former case the Court of Admiralty had exclusive jurisdiction. In the latter case, the Court of
     Admiralty, having no jurisdiction to determine disputes relating to ownership, the Court of
     Chancery alone had jurisdiction to provide a remedy by way of injunction. The principle that
     jurisdiction was exclusive to the Court of Admiralty in a case where the shares were ascertained
     was applied in *Hallaran v. Donal* (1846) 9 Ir Eq R 217 where the plaintiff, who was the owner of
     a one-eight share of an emigrant passenger vessel, sought an injunction from the Court of

remedy took the form of a rule requiring the majority shareholder to provide security to the minority shareholder for the safe return of the vessel. The dissentient part-owners would, on the other hand, forfeit all profits derived from the journey.[297] A more efficient remedy, where partners' relations had permanently broken down, would have been to order a buy-out. In the *Criterion*,[298] Judge Kelly observed that the jurisdiction to order security was less efficient than the American remedy under which the dissenting part-owner could be directed to sell its shares to the other part-owners. 'In this kingdom', Kelly noted regretfully, the 'jurisdiction of the admiralty is limited to compelling a security'.

The pre-1867 court did not, either, have an official jurisdiction to provide a remedy where a partner had failed to provide his co-partners with accounts. However, once again there were instances of the Irish court apparently exceeding its strict jurisdiction, and providing relief in disputes between co-owners about profits. There was one instance of this in 1856 (during Kelly's early expansionist period) in the *Sir William Stamer*[299] when the court heard a suit by a co-owner claiming that he had not been provided with accounts, or had not been paid profits. However, in the early 1860s the court abandoned this jurisdiction. In the *Margaret and Joseph*, Judge Kelly dismissed on grounds of lack of jurisdiction, an account of profits' dispute between co-owners. He noted that the English court had just been granted such a competence[300] and urged that for 'the sake of the general justice, and the protection of the shipping interests of the United Kingdom, it is to be wished that this and such other anomalies with respect to these two courts no longer existed'.[301] Six years later, section 32 of the Court of Admiralty (Ireland) Act 1867 conferred on the court an account of profits jurisdiction.[302]

### REFORM OF ADMIRALTY PROCEDURE

Between September 1867, when he was officially informed that he was to be appointed judge, and his taking up his appointment in November 1867, Dr Townsend busied himself in formulating a modernized set of rules of court.[303]

Chancery to restrain the defendant taking the vessel out of the port of Dublin. Cusack Smith MR applied *Haly v. Godson* and held that the 'jurisdiction of [the Chancery] Court does not attach except in the case of unascertained shares'. The plaintiff, it was held, was required to proceed to the Court of Admiralty.

297 In the *Graff Arthur Bernstorff* (1854) 2 Sp. Ecc. & Ad. 30; 164 ER 290, Dr Lushington held that the remedy did not apply in the case where a British national was part-owner of a foreign ship.

298 *Mitchell's Maritime Register*, 24 Mar. 1860; *FJ*, 20 Mar. 1860.

299 *Shipping & Mercantile Gazette*, 15 Dec. 1856.

300 S. 8 of the Court of Admiralty Act 1861.                301 *FJ*, 10 Dec. 1861.

302 'The Court of Admiralty shall have jurisdiction to decide all questions arising between co-owners or any of them touching the title to or the ownership, possession, employment and earnings of any ship registered at any port in Ireland, or any share thereof, and may settle all accounts outstanding and unsettled between the parties in relation thereto'.

303 J. Townsend to the earl of Mayo, 16 Nov. 1867 (NAI, CSORP, 1867/21,623).

Those new rules, required by section 40 of the Court of Admiralty (Ireland) Act 1867, came into force on 27 November 1867.[304] The lord chancellor, Abraham Brewster, had directed Dr Townsend to render the new Irish rules as close as possible to the English model,[305] and Townsend's rules made little deviation from the new English code. Prior to 1867 the practice of the Irish court had continued to be based on the late-sixteenth-century model described in Clerke's *Praxis Curiae Admiralitatis*. Underlying most of the 1867 reforms was the objective of re-orientating the procedure of the court from its old Roman law form towards the contemporary practice of the courts of common law.[306]

The most important of these changes was the reform of the law of admiralty evidence. Under the traditional civil law method only written evidence taken from witnesses in the form of depositions was admissible. A registrar of the English Court of Admiralty described the process as a 'mockery of justice':[307] the examination would be carried out in private (by the registrar of the court where the witnesses were in Dublin, or by a specially appointed commissioner where the proceedings were held in an out-port, or even in a foreign country).[308] The opposing party was not allowed to be present. The witness could be cross-examined but only by a laboured process in which questions were prepared by the opposing party in advance of the examination, and then read to the witness by the commissioner.

In fact, Irish practice had, even before the changes of 1867, moved from the old documentary model. In 1848 Dr Stock had introduced a rule that, where both parties consented,[309] proceedings could be heard *viva voce*. By the mid-nineteenth century this had become the standard practice in Ireland.[310] Indeed, the Irish position was well in advance of English practice. There was no precedent in the English court for the reception of *viva voce* evidence before 1855.[311] Orders 92 and 93 of the General Orders of 1867 strengthened Dr Stock's evidential reforms:

304  *ILT & SJ*, 1 (1867), 659.
305  J. Townsend to Upington 12 Nov. 1873 (NAI, CSORP, 1907/15,859).
306  The rules were made widely available by their publication as an appendix to W. Boyd's *The law and practice of the High Court of Admiralty of Ireland* (Dublin, 1868).
307  *Statement by registrar*, p. 5.
308  In the *Duna, FJ*, 27 Mar. 1860, a commission was issued to the British consul at Riga to conduct an examination.
309  A consent order, dated 23 May 1864, read: 'by consent of the respective proctors in this case, testified in open court, it is ordered by the court, that this case be heard by a *viva voce* examination of witnesses; the evidence to be taken by William G. Chamney , esq., barrister at law, as actuary to the registrar, whose notes, when transcribed, are to be taken as the record in the case' (NLI, MS 11,252 (1)).
310  *Court of Admiralty Commission Report, 1864*, Appendix A, p. 13. Exceptionally, affidavit evidence might be admitted; Dr Townsend in his statement prepared for the commissioners stated that the practice 'has not been generally adopted' (ibid.). However, special leave for the admission of affidavit evidence was granted in the *Orisund, FJ*, 7 Oct. 1862 (witnesses resident in New York; prohibitively expensive to issue commissions for depositions to New York).
311  *Statement by registrar*, p.7.

prior to 1867 the Irish court was only entitled to direct that evidence be given *viva voce* where the parties consented; under the 1867 Rules the judge was given the power to direct the form in which proof was to be given regardless of the parties wishes.

The court's ability to establish the truth was further restricted by the civil law rule that two witnesses were required to make legal proof: the testimony of a single witness was regarded as merely half-proof. A typical instance was the wages case, the *Mary of Liverpool*,[312] where the court was forced to dismiss a wages claim because there was only one witness to support the petitioners' claim. Judge Kelly rehearsed the rule that 'by the established law and practice of this court a material fact must be proved by two witnesses, else it fails'. This rule was finally abolished by section 49 of the Admiralty Court (Ireland) Act 1867, which provided that the 'rules of evidence observed in the superior courts of common law were to be observed in the trial of all matters of fact in the Court of Admiralty'. Section 61 of the 1867 Act advanced the process of assimilation with the common law by empowering the court to direct that issues of fact be tried by a jury. However, by an embarrassing drafting oversight, the Act did not invest the judge with coercive powers to summon a jury. In the *Anderida*,[313] a collision case in which there was a factual dispute as to whether the vessel was displaying lights, an application was made that the matter be sent for trial before a jury. Judge Townsend, however, pointed out that while he had 'power to have questions of fact tried before me by a jury, [he had] no power to summon a jury. It is an unaccountable omission in the Act, yet so it is'.

The rules relating to pleadings had also begun to reformed before 1867. Under the older form of simple pleadings, the promovent's case was set out in a long continuous narrative. Judge Kelly had ordered that this be replaced by the more systematic 'articulate' form: under this form the principal elements in the case were clarified by being paragraphed into a series of separate articles.[314] The 1867 Rules formalized Kelly's innovation.[315] By the mid-Victorian period, the time periods regulating the production and exchange of pleadings had been so strictly disciplined as to make the Court of Admiralty amongst the most efficient commercial courts in the Irish judicature: the rule was that just four days were allowed for the exhibition of the pleadings. Failure to comply with this rule would result in the case being dismissed. As soon as the plaintiff's libel had been submitted, four days were allowed for the exhibition of the answer.[316]

---

312  *FJ*, 27 Dec. 1861. The *Orisund*, *FJ*, 9 Oct. 1862          313  (1869) 9 Bar Reports 180.

314  Townsend said that it was Kelly 'to whom the great improvement in present forms of his court is principally to be attributed', *Court of Admiralty Commission Report, 1864*, Appendix A, p. 23.

315  Irish practice had continued to insist that the libel include a recital averring that the event had occurred within the jurisdiction of the court; this requirement was abolished by Order 80 of the General Orders 1867.

316  *Godzun of Copenhagen*, *FJ*, 18 Feb. 1860; the *Jacob*, *FJ*, 28 Jan. 1860.

The process of proceeding in default of appearance was modernized by the General Orders of 1867,[317] while the laws regulating the obtaining of release on bail of vessels arrested by the court had already begun to be reformed by Judge Kelly. Under the old civil law process a vessel owner had to wait for three processes to be completed before he could obtain the release of his vessel on bail: (i) the return in open court of a notice by the marshal that the vessel had been arrested; (ii) a successful motion permitting the defendant to file bail; and (iii) production to the court of the bail bond and stipulation which had been entered into by the defendant. It was only upon the completion of these steps that the court could issue a warrant of release to the marshal.[318] Judge Kelly had already begun dispensing with some of these over-involved rules. Where the marshal had been slow in returning the warrant of arrest, the vessel was released without going through the usual formality of exhibiting the executed warrant.[319] On occasion orders were made directing that the vessel be discharged without the added necessity of the vessel's remaining in custody until the formal production of the bail bond in court.[320] Acknowledging Kelly's reforms, the Belgian consul observed in 1864 that 'the practice in the Irish court' under Judge Kelly 'affords great facilities in getting ships released on bail'.[321] The 1867 General Orders abolished the old bail process: the function of releasing arrested vessels or goods was rationalized, and delegated to the registrar, without reference to the court.[322]

ADMIRALTY APPEALS

Until 1867 admiralty appeals lay, in accordance with section 3 of the Court of Admiralty of Ireland Act 1783, to the Court of Delegates in Ireland.[323] The Court

317 Under the traditional civil law procedure where there had been no appearance by the impugnant, a rule of 'first default decreed' was issued together with a rule of *primum decretum* (though it seems that this latter formality was not always insisted upon in Irish practice). This procedure of decreeing default had to be repeated on three further court days. This plodding process was, as a contemporary observer noted, 'well enough suited to a time when there was not any such public means of intelligence as we now possess through the medium of newspapers' (J. Morris, *Two lectures on the jurisdiction and practice of the High Court of Admiralty of England* (London, 1860), p. 26). By Order 31 of the 1867 General Orders, the newspaper notice replaced the default decree: if within twelve days after the filing of a warrant no entry of appearance had been made, the solicitor for the plaintiff was entitled to take out a notice of sale to be advertised in two 'public journals', publicizing the impending sale in default of appearance; if within a further six days there was no appearance, the plaintiff was entitled to apply to the court to have the vessel sold and the proceeds deposited in the registry. However, again Judge Kelly had anticipated this procedural innovation, and was already requiring newspaper notices: in the *Happy Return*, *FJ*, 28 Aug. 1862, the court ordered that a public notice be placed in the *Day Note* and the *Shipping Gazette* to the effect that, unless an appearance was entered in six days, the court would proceed in default.
318 *Court of Admiralty Commission Report, 1864*, Appendix A, p. 9.
319 The *Queen of the South*, *FJ*, 28 Apr. 1864.
320 The *Swan*, *FJ*, 3 Dec. 1859; the *Cumberland*, *FJ*, 12 Jan. 1860.
321 *Court of Admiralty Commission Report, 1864*, Appendix A, p. 43.     322 General Orders 50–64.
323 See p. 175, above.

of Delegates was usually composed of five judges, comprising two or three judges selected from the four courts of common law and equity, and two senior civilian advocates.[324] However, the Court of Delegates had fallen out of fashion as a suitable model for deciding appeals. In 1832 in England, the appellate jurisdiction of the Court of Delegates had been removed by the Privy Council Appeals Act 1832[325] and transferred to the Privy Council. Particular objection was taken to the custom of having practising civilians sit alongside the common law judges in the Court of Delegates. Having practitioners sitting in appeal from the very court in which they practised carried the danger that the appellate judges would be inhibited against upsetting the trial judge. The problem was alluded to by Lord Ellenborough, who, in introducing the 1832 Privy Council Appeals Bill, argued that the addition of civilian practitioners was 'manifestly a great evil' for 'no men should be placed in a situation like this, one day acting as practising barristers in the court below, and the very next day called from that Bar to decide upon points exactly similar to those which they had been arguing before the judges in that court from whose decision the appeal had been made'.[326] Furthermore, the range of practitioners available to undertake appeals was very small, since the most eminent practitioners were usually engaged in the decision which was being appealed from. The result was that relatively junior practitioners could end up sitting on the Court of Delegates.[327]

In addressing reform of the appellate structure, the 1864 Royal Commission on the Admiralty Court recommended that the jurisdiction of the Court of Delegates over admiralty appeals should be abolished. The Court of Appeal in Chancery,[328] which was already exercising appellate jurisdiction over decisions from the Court of Probate,[329] was regarded as the appropriate replacement for the civil law appellate work previously undertaken by the Court of Delegates. Accordingly, following the recommendations of the commission, section 91 of the Court of Admiralty (Ireland) Act 1867 provided two methods of appeal: (i) an appeal to the Court of Appeal in Chancery in place of the appeal to the Court of Delegates; and (ii) as an alternative to an appeal to the Irish Court of Appeal in Chancery, a direct appeal to the Privy Council in England.

---

324 In the *Nimroud* (1863) 8 *Law Reporter* 803, O'Brien and Hayes JJ together with W.C. Kyle LLD were commissioned as delegates. In the *Berlin* (1849) 4 Ir Jur 11, the common law component of the Court of Delegates was composed of Crampton and Moore JJ, and the civilian element of Sir Thomas Staples and Robert Andrews. In *Hamilton v. Watt* (1851) 4 Ir Jur 253, the delegates were Crampton and Ball JJ and Lefroy B, together with the civilians Sir Henry Meredyth and Robert Andrews QC; in the *Wakefield* (1852) 5 Ir Jur 69 the delegates were Crampton, Jackson and Torrens JJ together with Drs Radcliffe and Darley.

325 2 & 3 Will. IV, c. 92 (Eng.), 1832, 'An Act for Transferring Powers of High Court of Delegates in Ecclesiastical and Maritime Cases to HM in Council'.

326 *Hansard 3*, vol. 14, cols. 79–80 (5 July 1832).                   327 Ibid.

328 J.A. Dowling, 'The Irish Court of Appeal in Chancery, 1857–1877', *Journal of Legal History*, 21 (2000), 83.

329 20 & 21 Vict. c. 79 (Ire.), 1857, s. 45.

The addition of an admiralty jurisdiction to the functions already discharged by the Court of Appeal in Chancery was strongly resisted by the lord chancellor, Abraham Brewster. While the measure was being piloted through Parliament, Brewster made vigorous representations to the attorney general that the proposal be abandoned. Threatening to oppose the measure in the House of Lords, he argued that 'the Court of Appeal in Chancery is likely to have so much business on its hands that the chancellor will hardly have any time at his disposal for the business of his own proper court' and predicted that the increase of business required to be conducted by the lord chancellor 'will soon lead to a clamour for a second vice-chancellor'.[330] Brewster elaborated urbanely on his objections, confessing his total ignorance of the law administered by the Court of Admiralty:

> no one who ever held the great seal in Ireland, or I believe in England, knew anything about admiralty law or practice. I have never set my foot in that court in my life, and know no more about it than of the law of central Africa, and I believe my colleague [Christian LJ], learned though he is, is in the same happy state of ignorance.

He frankly confessed his own ignorance of admiralty law, complaining that it was embarrassing to impose 'on men who are utterly incompetent for the discharge of it ... the task of reversing the decisions of a man who has been trained in this branch of the law, and who could teach them'. The proposal that the court be assisted by assessors would be of no help: Parliament might as well 'add to the sea captains a couple of cavalry captains and it would not be a whit more absurd'. Brewster pleaded with the earl of Mayo to consider diverting the jurisdiction from his court to the judicial committee of the Privy Council of Ireland arguing that 'the judge of the Probate Court is always a member of that body and he has always been an admiralty lawyer and it so happens that the now master of the rolls is one'. Notwithstanding the lord chancellor's protests, admiralty appeals were foisted on the Court of Appeal in Chancery.

The quantum of admiralty business conducted before the Court of Appeal in Chancery was considerably lower than that undertaken by the old Court of Delegates. There appear to have been only seven appeals in admiralty matters taken to the Court of Appeal in Chancery in the period 1867 to 1877. While the 1867 Act gave appellants the alternative of appealing to the English Privy Council only three such appeals were taken directly from the Irish Court to the Privy

---

330  A. Brewster to the earl of Mayo, 17 July 1867 (NLI, MS 11,148(3)). Brewster LC objected that 'it is not usual to force any measure down the throat of a chancellor on a legal subject on which he ought to be as competent to form as correct an opinion' and he informed the chief secretary that 'he had seen Lawson and Sullivan, and they both concurred with me in thinking that my objections are well founded. I also consulted another person whose knowledge and judgment no one will dispute, least of all the attorney general, and he is of opinion that an appeal to the Privy Council would be quite satisfactory'.

Council between 1867 and 1877.[331] Ten years after its introduction, the Judicature (Ireland) Act 1877 abolished this binary system of appeal. The new Court of Appeal was entrusted with admiralty appeals. Section 9 of the Judicature (Ireland) Act 1877 provided that appeals from the Court of Admiralty 'shall lie to the Court of Appeal constituted by this Act in the same manner and in respect of the same proceedings as heretofore to the Court of Appeal in Chancery'.

## THE LATE-NINETEENTH-CENTURY DECLINE OF THE ADMIRALTY COURT

Following the enactment of the 1867 Act, the level of business being processed by the court gradually rose. In 1868 the total number of causes instituted was 66; by 1873 the level of business had risen to its highest ever level of 76 cases; in 1874 the figure was 72 cases;[332] in 1877 the number of causes before the court reached 81, its nineteenth-century peak.[333]

But by the early 1880s the quantum of work undertaken by the court began a steep and irreversible decline. In 1884 only 51 causes were instituted;[334] in 1886, the figure had dropped further to 31 and[335] in 1891 just 29 cases were initiated in the court.[336] The decline in the mid-1890s was even more sudden: in 1896 the total number of admiralty causes instituted was 8[337], and by 1898 the figure was an unimpressive 13.[338] The perception of the 1830s, that the court was a waste of public resources, begun to re-establish itself. The pamphleteer Rhadamanthus in 1890 wrote that 'the suits are so few that the office of judge is almost a sinecure'.[339]

What was the cause of this? Rhadamanthus attributed the decline in the court's activity to Ireland's declining maritime activity:

> There are not enough ships sailing into Irish harbours, and out of them, to come into collision with one another and give rise to admiralty proceedings. Bottomry and *respondentia* are symptoms of a commercial prosperity that

331 *Meidbrodt v. Fitzsimons* 1874 (TNA (PRO), PCAP 1/517); *Bates v. Queenstown Towing Co.* 1874 (TNA (PRO), PCAP 1/537); *Compagnie Generale Transatlantic v. Owen* 1876 (TNA (PRO), PCAP 1/555).

332 'Return of number of causes instituted in, and number of warrants of arrest in proceedings *in rem* issued by, the Court of Admiralty (Ireland) in each year 1868 to 1874' (HC 1875 (202) lxii, 1).

333 *Judicial Statistics (Ireland), 1877*, p. 75 (HC 1878 [C.2152] lxxix, 265).

334 *Judicial Statistics (Ireland), 1884*, p. 123 (HC 1884–85 [C.4554] lxxxvi, 243).

335 *Judicial Statistics (Ireland), 1886*, p. 44 (HC 1886 [C.5177] xc, 241).

336 *Judicial Statistics (Ireland), 1891*, p. 45 (HC 1892 [C.6782] lxxxix, 253). Of these the largest category was, unusually, cases involving necessaries (7). The 1891 figure was actually an increase upon the previous three years, where 30 cases had been instituted in 1890, 36 in 1889 and 34 in 1888, *Judicial Statistics (Ireland), 1890*, p. 24 (1890–91 [C.6511] xciii, 251).

337 *Judicial Statistics (Ireland), 1896*, p. 48 (HC 1897 [C.8617] c, 761).

338 *Judicial Statistics (Ireland), 1898*, p. 47 (HC 1899 [C.9494] cviii, Pt. II, 445).

339 Rhadamanthus, *Our judges* (Dublin, 1890), p. 108.

unhappily does not exist in Ireland; and collisions and salvage, however unfortunate they may be in themselves, are, like bankruptcy, the signs of an active commerce. The poverty of Ireland is symbolized by the meanness of her High Court of Admiralty; her fitful trade in the *dilettante* admiralty bar; the paralysis of her industry in the oft-closed door of Judge Townsend's court.

This may be part of the explanation. The rate of growth of the shipping activity in Ireland certainly had weakened in the late nineteenth century. There had been a sharp acceleration between the 1840s and the 1870s; from the late 1870s the rate of growth decelerated and remained modest until the First World War.[340] But there was a second, wider, factor at work: the rate of admiralty litigation generated by maritime activity was also falling generally. In England shipping activity more than doubled between 1870 and 1900,[341] yet the level of admiralty litigation had stagnated, and even slightly decreased. In 1867,[342] the number of causes instituted in the English court was 594; in 1884 the number had fallen to 506; in 1898 the figure was 532 cases.[343] Shipping activity, though rising, was simply not generating the level of admiralty litigation that it had previously done. The difference between the two jurisdictions was that the English court could compensate for this. Maritime traffic in England had more than doubled. Accordingly, the English court was not so affected by the decline in the rate of shipping-generated litigation. And London had other advantages. It was often the registered home of shipping companies which could be sued in the Admiralty Division of the High Court of England, for collisions occurring not just in England but abroad (including collisions occurring in Ireland). The English court was also located in the city which was the centre of the maritime insurance industry, and insurance claims by injured ship owners against their insurance underwriters were sometimes processed in the Admiralty Division of the High Court in London.

The 1860s and 1870s, and the optimism for the future of the Irish court, had, it turned out, been a false dawn. By the time that the Irish Court of Admiralty had fused with the High Court in 1893 it was well into a process of decline, a process which would see it retreat once more to the fringes of the Irish judicature – the same situation which it had occupied for the greater part of its three-hundred-year history.

340　Solar, 'Shipping and economic development in nineteenth-century Ireland', 717 & 722.
341　In 1876 23,955 foreign steam vessels entered ports in England and Wales; by 1913 the figure was 62,400 (ibid., p. 348). David Starkey, (ed.), *Shipping movements in the ports of the United Kingdom, 1871–1913: a statistical profile* (Exeter, 1999), p. 348.
342　*Judicial Statistics (England & Wales), 1867*, p. xxix (HC 1867–8 [4062], lxvii, 519).
343　*Judicial Statistics (England & Wales), 1884*, p. xxviii (HC 1884–5 [C.4518] lxxxvi, 1); *Judicial Statistics (England & Wales), 1900*, p. 125 (HC 1900 [Cd. 181] ciii, 221).

# CHAPTER SIX

# Admiralty criminal jurisdiction, 1580–1861

## ADMIRALTY CRIMINAL LAW, 1580–1700

*Piracy law, 1580–1614*

Prior to 1614 maritime criminal offences were not accessible to prosecution at common law: crimes committed at sea were 'done out of the jurisdiction of the common law'.[1] As a seventeenth-century Irish lord lieutenant explained to the king, Charles II, 'the ordinary courts of judicature are not empowered to judge marine [criminal] causes'.[2] Maritime offences could only be prosecuted according to civil law. However, trial according to civil law was encumbered by the awkward civil law rules of evidence. One of the most difficult of these civil law rules of evidence was the prohibition against proof by circumstantial evidence. Since circumstantial evidence was inadmissible, witness testimony was required. But, even where a witness could be produced, the testimony of a single witness would not suffice; at least two witnesses were required to make full proof. The result of these evidential rules, the Irish Parliament complained, was to make the successful prosecution of piracy virtually impossible: 'before any judgment of death can be given against the offenders, either they must plainly confess their offences, which they will never do without torture or pains, or else the offences be so plainly and directly proved by witnesses indifferent, such as saw their offences committed, which can seldom be gotten but by chance'.[3] The defects were remedied in England by the enactment of the Piracy Acts 1535–6,[4] which enabled the prosecution of piracy 'after the common course of the laws of the land'.

It was not until 1614 that legislation equivalent to the sixteenth-century English acts was enacted in Ireland.[5] Before 1614 a number of strategies were resorted to in order to fill this jurisdictional deficiency. The first, suggested by Judge Ambrose Forth, was for the Crown, acting under the English Piracy Act 1536, to issue commissions from England extra-territorially to Ireland. In a document entitled

---

1  *The Case of the Admiralty* (1609) 13 Co. Rep. 51; 77 ER 1461.
2  Earl of Essex to Charles II, 23 Sept. 1673 (TNA (PRO), SP 63/334, ff 155–7).
3  Preamble to the Piracy Act (11, 12 & 13 James I, c. 2 (Ire.), 1614). The measure was enacted in Dec. 1614. R. Blundell to R. Wynwood, 17 Dec. 1614 (*Cal. S.P. Ire. 1611–1614*, p. 533).
4  27 Hen. VIII, c. 4 (Eng.), 1535; 28 Hen. VIII, c. 15 (Eng.), 1536.
5  11, 12 & 13 James I, c. 2 (Ire.), 1614.

'doubts to be resolved touching the admiralties' Forth suggested that pirates apprehended in Ireland could be tried under a commission issued from England: 'a commission to be granted from the lord chancellor of England according to the statutes made 27 Henry VIII, c. 4 and 28 Henry VIII, c. 15 [so that] pirates, having committed spoils upon the main seas, and apprehended in Ireland, may be there tried'.[6] However, this strategy was not supported by the law officers, and may never have been implemented. Forth conceded that judicial opinion in Ireland was to the effect that the English Piracy Acts could not be stretched so as to operate in Ireland: 'the statutes made anno. H. VIII. [c.] 27 and anno. H. VIII. [c.] 28 for trial of pirates [are not] of force in Ireland, according the common opinion of justices'.[7]

Second, trial at common law was available when piracy-related offences were committed on land. Although there existed in Ireland no effective power to try offences committed on the high seas according to the common law, courts of assize did have jurisdiction to try piracy-connected offences occurring on land (such as where pirates engaged in inland raids or in dealing in stolen goods). In 1608 lord deputy Chichester described how a raiding party of pirates landing at Baltimore had burnt a dwelling house which in Irish law made them accessible to prosecution for treason; some English settlers who went on board their vessel to treat with them had also been charged with treason, on the ground of conferring with traitors.[8]

In the absence of legislation authorizing the prosecution of pirates at common law, special commissions were issued authorizing the trial of pirates according to the principles of the civil law. In 1573 a commission was directed to the vice-admiral of Ireland, Gerald Fitzgerald, earl of Kildare, together with 'other whom he shall think meet for the determination of certain maters of piracies of divers Scots, being there in prison'. The method of trial was to be 'according to such a form of commission and sentence as before the statute, 28 Henry VIII, which appertained not to Ireland, was accustomed'.[9] In 1587 Ambrose Forth requested the judge of the English court, Sir Julius Caesar, to send over a commission – presumably for trial by civil law – appointing the attorney general, Charles Calthorp, the chief justice and the mayors of Dublin, Waterford, Limerick, Galway and Drogheda, to try pirates.[10] In 1604 Ambrose Forth was named in a piracy commission for Waterford, Cork and Limerick.[11] The difficulties involved in prosecution according to civil law were, Adam Loftus complained, aggravated by the lack of a king's advocate, charged with conducting piracy prosecutions. The absence of a king's advocate meant that the admiralty judge was being forced, at the same time, both to prosecute and to try the prosecution:[12]

---

6　A. Forth to C. Howard, 25 Feb. 1586 (TNA (PRO), SP 63/128, f. 118).　　　　7　Ibid.

8　A. Chichester to Privy Council, 30 Mar. 1608 (*Cal. S.P. Ire. 1606–1608*, p. 445).

9　1 June 1573; *Acts of the Privy Council 1571–1575*, p. 110.

10　A. Forth to J. Caesar, 19 Aug. 1588 (BL, Lansdowne MS 144, f. 418). Forth added that 'if the said commission shall require anything I shall with my thanks defray the same'.

11　TNA (PRO), HCA 1/32/1, no. 68.

12　A. Chichester to the earl of Nottingham, 4 Aug. 1613 ('Letter book of Sir Arthur Chichester', p. 119).

Now forasmuch as he is forced to proceed to the arraigning and executing of pirates after judgment and complains justly of the want of assistance [to] prosecute and enforce evidence in the name of the king or the parties interested, for which he is enforced also to take inquisitions, to examine and give in evidence to accuse and condemn pirates and so to make himself both party and judge (whereof he make a great scruple of conscience).

Loftus 'hath made very earnest request unto me to move your lordships that, after the manner of England, you will be pleased to get one man at least to be allowed for proctor and advocate for the king in this new Court of Admiralty, whose office it may be, for default of others, to prosecute against pirates in the king's name'. Lord deputy Chichester went on to recommend the appointment of the civilian, Dr Thomas Ryves, as king's advocate in Ireland.[13]

A fourth strategy was to employ martial law. The piracy problem, particularly in Munster, had become so acute at the beginning of the seventeenth century that legal process was abandoned altogether in favour of martial law. In 1613 the lord deputy, Arthur Chichester, reported that three former soldiers who had turned to piratical activities had been 'condemned executed by martial law, the rather for example's sake, because they were such', and justified the resort to martial law on the ground that there was no piracy act in Ireland: 'for that we have yet no other law here by which to proceed effectually in that case'.[14] A fifth means of prosecution was to extradite suspected pirates to England for trial by common law there. In 1588 Forth expressed the hope to Sir Julius Caesar that pirates sent over for trial in London 'would learn some bitter lessons in your court'.[15] In 1607 the lord deputy, Arthur Chichester, celebrating the capture of the English pirate, Coward, noted that 'the chiefest of them [would be sent] into England'.[16] The process of extradition was initiated by a warrant from the English court. In 1608 the English Privy Council requested Chichester to assist in the apprehension and extradition of Thomas Crooke, of Baltimore, a 'chief maintainer of pirates', for whose trial in England warrants had been issued by the English Court of Admiralty.[17] The enactment of a Piracy Act in Ireland in 1614 did not end the practice of extradition to England for trial for piracy. After the enactment of the 1614 Act, a system of dual jurisdiction was established with accused pirates apprehended in Ireland prosecuted either, under the Irish Piracy Act, in Ireland, or, following extradition, in England. In 1673 a French pirate named Bienvenue, whose vessel had been arrested for piracy when it arrived in Kinsale, was tried for piracy before Sir Leoline Jenkins in London.[18] However, trial in Ireland was often

13   See biographical note, B. Lavack, *The civil lawyers in England, 1603–1641* (Oxford, 1973), p. 267.
14   A. Chichester to the Privy Council, 30 June 1613, 'Letter Book of Sir Arthur Chichester', *Analecta Hibernica*, 8 (1938), 115.
15   A. Forth to J. Caesar, 19 Aug. 1588 (BL, Lansdowne MS 144, f. 418).
16   A. Chichester to Privy Council, 16 July 1607 (*Cal. S.P. Ire. 1606–1608*, p. 224).
17   Lords of the Council to A. Chichester, 8 Mar. 1608 (*Cal. S.P. Ire. 1606–1608*, pp 433–4).
18   L. Jenkins to Charles II, 21 Apr. 1673, *Life of Jenkins*, ii, p. 772.

the more convenient option. In an opinion written in 1634, the judge of the Admiralty Court of England recommended that a Spanish pirate ('Vicinti Ffita'), who had been apprehended in Galway and who was being detained in Dublin Castle, be prosecuted in Ireland, rather than in England, for it was there that 'his piracies were committed and where the witnesses remain and can give evidence'.[19]

### The Irish Piracy Act 1614

In 1612 the Irish Privy Council transmitted the heads of 'an act against pirates' to London.[20] A memorandum accompanying the heads of bill explained that 'heretofore there was no law in Ireland to bring a pirate to his trial'. The Irish Piracy Act, finally enacted in 1614, was a virtual transcription of the English Act, providing that all 'treasons, felonies, robberies, murders and confederacies' committed at sea were to be tried as if committed on land.

The trial of pirates under the 1614 Act was conducted before a jury. In 1625 William Rankin described how, having been indicted for piracy, he was 'put to his trial by a jury of twelve honest and substantial men out of the city of Dublin'.[21] The 1614 Act required that the piracy trial be conducted before a judge (or judges) drawn from a larger panel of four, or five, commissioners named in a commission for the trial of pirates. The commission was to be composed of the admiral, or his 'deputy' and 'three or four such other substantial persons as shall be nominated or appointed by the lord chancellor of Ireland, for the time being, from time to time, and as often as need shall require, to hear and determine such offences, after the course of the common laws of this realm'. The Act required that one of the appointees be the 'admiral's deputy'. In the early seventeenth century this position was filled by the judge of the Irish Admiralty Court.[22] But it was not necessary that the judge of the Admiralty Court be 'this deputy'. The reference to the admiral's 'deputy' was wide enough to include the provincial vice-admiral, and the judge begun to be excluded from the commission in favour of one of the vice-admirals. In 1670 the vice-admiral of Munster, Robert Southwell, was nominated to the commission to try the Mayo pirate Francis Bodkin.[23] The practice of excluding the admiralty judge continued into the mid-eighteenth century: a commission drafted in 1750 appointed the vice-admiral of Munster, and four others (including the chief baron of the exchequer and the attorney general) but pointedly left out the awkward judge of the Court of Admiralty, Hugh Baillie.[24] Nominations to the panel

19   H. Marten to the commissioners of Admiralty, 18 Nov. 1634 (TNA (PRO), SP 63/254, f. 487).

20   TNA (PRO), SP 63/232, f. 65.

21   'The humble petition of William Rankin', 1625 (TNA (PRO), SP 14/182, f. 130).

22   In a special commission of 1625 the judge of the Irish Admiralty Court, was recorded as presiding at a piracy commission as the 'admiral's deputy', 'The humble petition of William Rankin', 1625 (TNA (PRO), SP 14/182, f. 130).

23   10 Dec. 1670 (TNA (PRO), SP 63/329, f. 286).

24   A commission drafted in July 1750 for a piracy trial in Cork was addressed to the vice-admiral of Munster, Edward Southwell, John Bowes (chief baron of the Court of Exchequer), George

of 'three or four such other substantial persons' sometimes caused internal tensions amongst the commissioners. In 1626 Adam Loftus protested at the appointment by lord deputy Falkland of his rival, Lawrence Parsons. Falkland justified the appointment of Parsons on the ground that 'many pirates being in prison to be tried for their lives, and commission being sent for their trial which could not be exercised without [Parsons'] presence ... delay was both chargeable and dangerous'.[25] The power to hold a trial depended on the continued availability of those who had been appointed admiralty trial commissioners. Where, through death or retirement, the original commissioners could not be summoned, a new commission might have to be drawn up. Legally ineffective commissions were sometimes a cause of difficulty. In 1634 Henry de Laune, who had apprehended a pirate vessel carrying 'Spanish wines and fruits' in Timoleague, enclosed 'a dormant commission issued by the late lords justices for the trial of all pirates that are taken in this county' and sought the advice of the commissioners 'either to confirm this or command a new one to be sent down'.[26]

One of the most high-profile Piracy Act 1614 prosecutions in the late seventeenth century was that of the pirate, Francis Bodkin. Bodkin's operation was well-organized and financed. The earl of Essex reported that merchants based in Sligo and Dingle were subventing the business, and that an army officer, Colonel Fitzpatrick, had assisted in fitting out Bodkin's vessels by procuring arms and ammunition from military stores in Dublin.[27] Bodkin had also taken the precaution of attempting to disguise his activities as legitimate privateering by obtaining a commission of reprisal from the government of Spain; but, as Essex noted, 'it is most certain their whole design was piracy'.[28] In 1670 one of Bodkin's pirate vessels, a cutter named the *St John of Sligo*, seized a vessel from Virginia laden with tobacco off the island of Inishbofin. The raid was particularly vicious, with the crew being flung overboard. He followed this with a second raid upon a Dutch vessel near Ventry in Co. Kerry.[29]

Bodkin's gang was captured when they landed at Dingle looking for supplies. However, all but nine of the crew, including Bodkin himself, escaped from prison before being indicted. Those that remained were tried before an admiralty commission court at Oldcastle, in Cork; six were sentenced to death (but later reprieved by the lord lieutenant, Berkeley). When in 1673 Bodkin was re-arrested, the lord lieutenant wrote to the king seeking a commission under the 1614 Act 'because these crimes being committed upon the sea, being matters relating to the

Caulfield (attorney general), John Mead and Joseph Bennet 'or any four of them' (NLI, MS 15,427).

25  Viscount Falkland to A. Loftus (March [?] 1626) (TNA (PRO), SP 63/242, f. 213; *Cal. S.P. Ire. 1625–1632*, p. 108).
26  H. de Laune to the lord deputy, 22 Jan. 1634 (TNA (PRO), SP 63/254, f. 222).
27  Earl of Essex to Arlington, 30 Sept. 1673 (TNA (PRO), SP 63/334, f. 155).
28  Ibid.
29  Report of Robert Southwell, 10 Dec. 1670 (TNA (PRO), SP 63/329, f. 286).

admiralty, must be tried by special commission, for the ordinary courts of judicature are not empowered to judge marine causes'.[30] Charles II responded with a royal letter directing the issue of a commission under the Act of 1614. Censuring Berkeley for his leniency, the king directed that 'if they be convicted by law that they suffer accordingly'.[31]

The 1614 Act could only be operated where 'treasons, felonies, robberies, murders and confederacies' were committed. Difficulties arose where the acts in question did not correspond to 'treasons, felonies, robberies, murders and confederacies'. In 1675 Sir Leoline Jenkins was asked to report to the king on the Crown's entitlement to issue a 1614 Act admiralty commission in the case of a French privateer, the *Cheline*. The crew of the *Cheline* had seized a Dutch vessel, the *North Caper*, in Dublin bay.[32] Jenkins advised that the raid on the *North Caper* did not involve the commission of a felony. The capture of the Dutch vessel was permitted by the letter of marque granted to the French privateer, the *Cheline*. A privateer did not commit a felony when it acted under a valid letter of marque. On the other hand, the Piracy Act 1614 also enabled the prosecution of 'confederacies'. Jenkins had long regarded the crime of 'confederacy' as including interference with the right of sanctuary in the king's ports: the right of sanctuary was interfered with when foreign privateers hovered outside his majesty's ports in order to surprise vessels.[33] This was precisely what the *Cheline* had been doing, when it was lurking around the entrance to Dublin port. Accordingly, the privateer's conduct could be incriminated as a 'confederacy'. He advised the king, Charles II, that the 'carrying away a ship belonging to a subject of your majesty's allies, out of your majesty's port, and from under your protection … may be enquired of and tried … as a confederacy within the purview of that statute'. It was a 'violation and affront to your majesty's authority, and of the protection due to all mankind'.[34] Second, he suggested that the crew could be indicted for the felony of marine robbery. This was because the *Cheline* had also pillaged two English ships from which it had taken beef, a barrel of butter and a hogshead of wine. This was straightforward piracy; the crew 'may be indicted upon the same statute in the same manner as if this robbery had been committed upon the land'.

Both the English and the Irish piracy acts were compromised by a significant omission: they could not be effectively used to incriminate the accessories and receivers of piracy. Towards the end of the sixteenth century objections begun to be elaborated to the accessibility of accessories and receivers to trial at common law.[35] The matter was finally settled by the chief justices and chief baron of

30   Earl of Essex to Charles II, 23 Sept. 1673 (TNA (PRO), SP 63/334, ff 155–7).
31   20 Feb. 1674 (TNA (PRO), SP 63/335, f.27).
32   L. Jenkins to Charles II, 14 Sept. 1675, *Life of Jenkins*, ii, p. 754.
33   *Life of Jenkins*, i, xci.
34   L. Jenkins to Charles II, 14 Sept. 1675, *Life of Jenkins*, ii, p. 754.
35   *Hale and Fleetwood*, pp cxcii–cxciv.

England in the *Case of the Admiralty* in 1609.³⁶ Piracy was not a felony. It had not been a felony before the enactment of the piracy acts, and those acts did not positively constitute piracy a felony. Since piracy had not been expressly made a felony by the Piracy Act 1536, acting as a receiver or supplier did not constitute the person an accessory: 'seeing the offence is not made felony by the laws of the realm ... there can be no accessory of any felony by the laws of the realm in this case, either before or after the offence, because the principal is no felon by our law, neither doth this Act speak of any accessory'.³⁷ The only method of incrimination was trial by civil law.³⁸ At civil law the receivers of pirates' spoils were liable to be punished by fine or mulct.³⁹ As a result of the gaps in the piracy acts, the civil law provided the only means of dealing with the widespread problem, particularly in Munster, of receivers of pirates. Civil law process was used by Ambrose Forth against piratical victuallers and receivers in 1586: two Dublin merchants who had traded with a pirate were committed to Dublin Castle by the admiralty judge.⁴⁰ In 1632 the Munster Court of Admiralty fined Francis Unick of Ballinskelligs for supplying four gallons of *aqua vitae* to a notorious pirate called Nutt.⁴¹

The Irish Piracy Act 1614 (like the English Piracy Act of 1536) prescribed that convicted persons were to suffer 'pains of death, losses of lands, goods and chattels'. Piracy executions had their own rituals. Following the English practice, pirates were hanged, with minatory intent, by the sea shore.⁴² The English admiralty official, Robert Smith, on a tour of Munster in 1633 reported that six pirates had been hanged near the sea and 'hung upon the gallows three tides'.⁴³ In 1766 four men who had been tried in Dublin for piracy were hanged in chains on the South Wall near Ringsend. The corpses were left to decay for several weeks; two of them fell from the gallows and became impaled on a wooden sea defence works, 'the piles'. Eventually the corpses ('being very disagreeable to the citizens who walk there for amusement and health')⁴⁴ were removed. But the spectacle was not finished yet. The bodies were moved to Dalkey Island, where a new gibbet was specially constructed from which the men were re-strung.

36  (1609) 13 Co Rep. 51; 77 ER 1461.
37  *The case of the Admiralty* (1609) 13 Co Rep 51; *3 Co Inst*, p. 112.
38  'If there be an accessory upon the sea to a piracy, that accessory may be punished by the civil law before the lord admiral, but cannot be punished by this act, because it extendeth not to accessories, nor makes the offence felony' (ibid).
39  Questions put to the common lawyers and the civilians by the English Privy Council in June 1577, reprinted in *Hale and Fleetwood*, pp 363–4.
40  A. Forth to C. Howard, 25 Feb. 1587 (TNA (PRO), SP 63/128, f. 118).
41  T. Harris to Viscount Falkland, 26 Nov. 1632 (TNA (PRO), SP 63/253, f. 245).
42  J.C. Appleby, *Under the bloody flag; pirates of the Tudor age* (Stroud, 2009), p. 126.
43  R. Smith to the commissioners of Admiralty, 1 Nov. 1633 (TNA (PRO), SP 63/254, f. 359).
44  C. Haliday, *The Scandinavian kingdom of Dublin* (Dublin, 1969), p. cxxii.

THE MINOR OFFENCE JURISDICTION OF THE IRISH COURT OF
ADMIRALTY IN THE SEVENTEENTH CENTURY

In addition to its involvement in the trial of piracy, the Court of Admiralty tried a
wide range of minor criminal offences, extending from maritime nuisances, to
fishing offences, to offences against navigation. The criminal side of the court's
business followed the holding of an annual 'court of enquiry', held usually in late
August or September. In the late seventeenth century the practice was to hold
these sessions in Ringsend in Dublin. In September 1662 Dr Edward Cooke
presided at a court held 'at Lazy Hill' near Ringsend'.[45] In the years 1676 and 1677
William Petty processed presentments in Ringsend. A jury was empanelled, with
the function of making presentments, or charges, of navigational obstruction or
irregular fishing in the Dublin port. The jury was traditionally composed of the
'gabbardmen' and fishermen of the port district of Ringsend. Before setting about
its task, the judge would address the jury, instructing it as to the subject matter of
its inquiry. Mimicking the practice of the English admiralty sessions, the judge
would instruct the jury by way of a long formal address. Two of William Petty's
Ringsend grand jury addresses survive.[46] Those discourses, following the practice
of the judges of the English High Court of Admiralty,[47] were divided into two
sections: the first was a highly elaborate eulogy in praise of the lord admiral, the
Court of Admiralty, and the shipping and fishing industry. The second part, 'the
articles', described the offences over which the court had jurisdiction, and invited
the jury to report whether there had been any infringements of these ordinances.
One of the jury's most important investigative functions was to identify persons
causing navigational obstructions:

> the good men of the jury are to enquire what persons do cast out of any ship,
> or other vessel, within any haven, creek, river or channel, flowing, or running
> to any town, any manner of gravel, ballast or other filth, whereby such rivers
> are annoyed and clayed or made unfit for navigation and passage; and you are
> to have a special care that in no navigable rivers or ports within the admiral's
> jurisdiction there be suffered any broken anchors, timbers, stakes, riddles or
> other like impediments to lie ... and you are to see that no inhabitant

45  Ibid.
46  Addresses of 2 Oct. 1676 & 1 Oct. 1677 (BL, Lansdowne MS 1,228, ff 38 & 46).
47  Pepys' *Diary* entry for 17 Mar. 1663 contains a description of the opening of an admiralty
    criminal sessions: 'To St. Margaret's Hill in Southwark, where the judge of the admiralty came
    and the rest of the doctors of civil law, and some other commissioners, whose commission of oyer
    and terminer was read, and then the charge given by Dr Exton, which methought was somewhat
    dull, though he would seem to intend it to be very rhetorical, saying that justice had two wings,
    one of which spread itself over land, the other over the water, which was this Admiralty Court.
    That being done, and the jury called, they broke up, and to dinner in a tavern hard by, where a
    great dinner, and I with them'. *The diary of Samuel Pepys*, ed. R. Latham and W. Matthews
    (London, 1971), iv, p. 76.

dwelling upon, or near, the shore, beneath the bridges, do cast out of their houses, yards, wharfs or quays, any rubbish, soil, sea coal, dirt etc.

The court's concerns extended beyond enquiries into obstructions and nuisances. Petty's very wide understanding was that the Admiralty Court was entitled to regulate all activity carried on upon the sea or navigable waters. In his grand jury address,[48] Petty asked the grand jury to report on the operation of ferry services, and to present persons building houses or quays on the seabed without special licence of the admiral. Some of the matters which Petty invited the Dublin jury to investigate did not feature in the charges to admiralty sessions in England:[49] Petty considered his jurisdiction as extending to the control of immigration, the evasion of customs duties, and the importation of seditious books.[50]

When the address had concluded there was dinner,[51] and an afternoon's drinking for the jury. The grand jury was then required to make a return to the Court of Admiralty within seven days. A note taken in 1680 by Petty's registrar detailed the charges found by the jury and returned by the foreman:

1. That boats and gabbards do bring sand to sell to the builders and lay down their sand upon my Lord Santry's wall and other places upon the Wood Quay and Merchants Quay, so as by leaving it to shore, great part of it falls into the river and they neglect to remove it.

2. There is a house upon the Merchants Quay pulling down and rebuilding, the rubbish whereof is thrown or let fall into the river.

3. Inquiry as to stores and other thrash thrown out at Salmon Pool to the prejudice of shipping etc.

4. Take notice of the sand that grows up upon the east side of the new bridge.

5. Take like notice where the ashes thrown in Sheep Street.[52]

Following the grand jury presentment those identified as offenders were cited and tried. In 1662 Edward Cooke, judge of the Court of Admiralty of Leinster, recorded a conviction against one Arthur Harvey for 'causing ballast to be cast out of his ship and suffering it to remain there in a heap'.[53] John Beaton of Dame Street Dublin was fined 2s. 6d. for 'suffering dung to be cast out of his stable into the millrace to the annoyance of the river'; Robert Cecil was fined for 'casting dirt into the millrace which washed into the river', while Stephen Forest, Faithful Stackpoole and John Price were all fined for 'casting ashes into the river'.[54]

48  2 Oct. 1676 (BL, Lansdowne MS 1,228, f. 38).        49  *Life of Jenkins* (London, 1724), i, xci.
50  W. Petty, memorandum on admiralty jurisdiction, n.d. (BL, Add. MS 7,2893, f. 29).
51  2 Oct. 1676 (BL, Lansdowne MS 1,228, f. 38).
52  9 Aug. 1680 (BL, Lansdowne MS 1,228, f. 56).
53  TNA (PRO), HCA 30/158, f. 219.
54  Casting rubbish into the river Liffey, or any 'common shores' was subsequently made triable by the lord mayor or justices of the peace under the Ballast Act, 1707 (6 Anne, c. 20 (Ire.), 1707, s. 11).

The primary sanction was by way of a fine, usually only a few shillings. Imprisonment was imposed only in default of payment of the fine. In 1663 a legal opinion was prepared by two English civilians for the use of the Leinster Court of Admiralty.[55] The opinion described the criminal sanctions available to the court: 'the judge hath power to impose fines upon offenders and to commit them to prison for [non] payment of those fines'.[56] The power of fine was a useful general deterrent: in 1709 the judge of the Munster Court of Admiralty, Rowland Davies, confessed that 'although I have not yet imposed any [fines], and shall always be very sparing in my doing it, yet I find it necessary sometimes to menace people with it or otherwise the court is not to be supported'.[57] In the 1630s the judge of the Munster Admiralty Court, Henry Gosnold, enquired whether the judge was entitled to retain fines levied by admiralty criminal courts. He was politely advised against treating fines as personal profits: 'consideration might be taken whether it be fit that he that imposed the fine should have it for his own interest [which] may induce him to impose an immoderate fine … or else too little to avoid the scandal'.[58]

In Dublin, at least, this criminal jurisdiction was fragile and under attack from the primary rivals for admiralty jurisdiction in late seventeenth-century Ireland, the municipal corporations. In a note sent to Samuel Pepys,[59] the Irish admiralty judge, William Petty, described five writs of prohibition which had been issued against the Irish Court of Admiralty. The cause of one of these prohibitions was a charge, prosecuted at the 1679 admiralty session, involving the newly constructed Essex Bridge. In November 1677 Petty wrote to the Munster vice-admiral, Robert Southwell:[60] 'You may have heard that there is a new bridge lately built at Dublin, below the old one, without leave of the admiral. This bridge I allow to be a good work, but have questioned the builders for passing by the admiral'. The promoter of this new Essex Bridge,[61] Sir Humphrey Jervis (the Dublin entrepreneur and ship owner, who frequently crossed swords with Petty during his period as judge) then retaliated with a writ of prohibition. Petty wrote 'a bridge hath been made across a navigable river, without the admiralty leave; and a prohibition brought to the suit commenced thereon'.[62]

In the fourth Article of the resolutions agreed at the February 1633 London conference[63] the common law judges conceded that the Admiralty Court was to be allowed jurisdiction over nuisances or obstructions in navigable rivers: 'Likewise the admiral may enquire of, and redress, all annoyances and obstructions in

55  Duke of York to E. Cooke and G. Wentworth, 10 Dec. 1663 (TNA (PRO), ADM 2/1,755). The opinion was drafted by two civilians, Drs W. Turner and D. Budd on whom there are biographical notes in G.D. Squibb, *Doctors' Commons* (Oxford, 1977), pp 176, 179.
56  TNA (PRO), ADM 2/1,755.
57  R. Davis to E. Southwell, 25 Oct. 1709 (BL, Add. MS 38,152, f. 12).
58  'An answer to Judge Gosnold' (n.d.) (Magdalene, Cambridge, Pepys MS 2,872, f. 212).
59  Bodl., Rawlinson MS, A 172, f. 13.
60  W. Petty to R. Southwell, 10 Nov. 1677, *Petty–Southwell Corr.*, p. 39.
61  M. Craig, *Dublin, 1660–1860* (London, 1992), p. 25.
62  W. Petty to R. Southwell, 4 Jan. 1679, *Petty–Southwell Corr.*, p. 66.     63  See p. 37 above.

navigable rivers beneath the first bridges that are any impediments to navigation, or passage to, or from, the sea; and no prohibition is to be granted in such case'. However, by the late seventeenth century the Irish Court of King's Bench had begun disregarding the 1633 rule that no prohibitions be granted in cases of 'annoyances and obstructions of navigable rivers'. In 1679 Petty recorded that a prohibition had issued from the King's Bench 'in the case of a pilot condemned to pay damages for casting away a ship in a gross manner'. He also reported '[a] prohibition in a suit for stopping and annoying a navigable river'.[64]

The preservation of 'the breed of fish' and the punishment of unlawful fishing also fell within the criminal jurisdiction of the court.[65] A memorandum drawn up by Petty in the 1670s included the prosecution of those 'fishing with unlawful nets' as within the court's jurisdiction.[66] Encroachments by French fishermen off the coast of Munster had become a matter of national concern. An Order in Council of 1663 forbade foreign fishermen engaging in pilchard fishing (between the first of June to the end of October); in case they 'presume[d] to offend herein after warning given ... their boats and nets [may be] so seized until, by due course of law, they shall recover the same'.[67] The mayor of Kinsale had complained of the damage to the local fishing industry caused by French fishermen infringing the 1663 Order in Council by fishing close to the shore, using excessively large nets, and fishing during the pilchard fishing season. These infringements were referred for a legal opinion to Dr Edward Cooke, judge of the Court of Admiralty of Leinster. Cooke advised that the judge of the Admiralty Court of Munster, Joshua Boyle, be instructed to enforce the fisheries' ordinances.[68] However, the problem persisted. In 1671 Robert Southwell reported to the lord lieutenant that French vessels were using unlawful nets, and fishing illegally during the closed season between April and October. He requested that permission be given to local fishermen to cut the French fishermen's nets, and that the French offenders be arrested 'to be tried and adjudged according to the rules of the Admiralty'.[69]

## MARITIME CRIMINAL LAW IN THE EIGHTEENTH AND NINETEENTH CENTURIES

### *Admiralty criminal commission courts in the eighteenth and nineteenth centuries*

The post-1782 revision in Irish constitutional theory, and the recognition that Ireland was a distinct kingdom, threatened the very viability of the Piracy Act 1614.[70]

---

64  W. Petty to R. Southwell, 4 Jan. 1679, *Petty–Southwell Corr.*, p. 66.
65  A charge given at a Session of Admiralty within the Cinque Ports, 2 Sept. 1688, *Life of Jenkins*, p. lxxxv.
66  BL, Add. MS 72,893, f. 29.
67  Order in Council, 15 June 1663 (TNA (PRO), SP 63/330, f. 201).
68  James duke of York to the duke of Ormond, 11 July 1663 (TNA (PRO), ADM 1,745, f. 94).
69  R. Southwell to the duke of Ormond, 18 Apr. 1671 (TNA (PRO), SP 63/333, f. 199).
70  See p. 173 above.

The operation of the Piracy Act 1614 was predicated on a criminal commission directed to 'the admiral'. But the identification of 'the admiral' in the post-1782 constitutional dispensation had become problematic. He could not be the admiral of England: a corollary of the theory that Ireland had become a distinct kingdom was that the admiral of the kingdom of England could not constitutionally be the admiral of the kingdom of Ireland. On the other hand, there was no such office as the admiral of the kingdom of Ireland. The problem arose when, in 1782, an Irish privateer, Kelly, acting under letters of marque issued by the French government, had been seizing British vessels. Kelly was captured in Ireland, and the English law officers advised that he be tried for high treason in Ireland under a commission promulgated pursuant to the Act of 1614.[71] But on the Irish side a serious impediment was raised: under the 1614 Act the commission of trial was required to be directed to the 'admiral'. But, there being no admiral of Ireland, a commission could not be issued and there could be no prosecution. In December 1782 the lord lieutenant, Earl Temple, informed his chief secretary, William Grenville, that he had 'stated the question of external legislation in the instance of Kelly and his gang whom we cannot try, as the Irish Act makes the presence of the *admiral* necessary; which admiral in law exists only under our Irish great seal, and, therefore, does not exist in the persons of Lord Keppel and his board'.[72] The Irish Parliament sorted out the problem. Section 4 of the Court of Admiralty of Ireland Act 1783[73] substituted the previous requirement that a commission be issued to the 'admiral' with a new constitutionally-compliant provision: that the commission be directed to 'the judge of the High Court of Admiralty of this kingdom, so to be appointed as aforesaid, and to three or four such other discreet persons as shall be nominated and appointed by the lord chancellor of Ireland'. There was no longer any mention of the 'admiral'.

In the eighteenth century, piracy prosecutions were conducted in Munster in the years 1721 and 1766.[74] There was a long interval before admiralty commissions were issued again. At the start of the nineteenth century, the Irish admiralty lawyer, Arthur Browne, recorded that there had not been 'since my knowledge of this court, to my recollection, any admiralty commission issued in Ireland, under the acts of parliament before-mentioned, to try criminals for offences committed upon the high seas'.[75] However, the process revived in the mid-nineteenth century. Commissions were issued on at least six occasions in the period 1834 to 1860: in the prosecution of a captain for the manslaughter of his mate in 1834;[76] in a murder

71  Opinions of Wynne, Wallace and Harris, 26 Feb. 1782 (TNA (PRO), ADM 7/300, f. 246).

72  21 Dec. 1782, HMC, *Thirteenth Rep., Appendix, Part III, The Manuscripts of B. Fortescue esq* (London, 1892), p. 171.

73  23 & 24 Geo. III, c. 14 (Ire.), 1783.

74  NLI, MS 15,427. W. Lecky, *A history of Ireland in the eighteenth century*, 5 vols (London, 1892), i, p. 419.

75  *A compendious view*, ii, p. 195.

76  *R. v. Drummonds* (NAI, CSORP 1834 A/3011). The deceased had been refused food and had died after the master had tied a rope around his neck. *Belfast Newsletter*, 18 Apr. 1834.

case tried in Waterford at the summer assizes in 1844;[77] in a case of murder on the high seas tried at Galway in 1845;[78] in a murder committed in Galway Bay in 1846;[79] in a trial for robbery on the high seas in 1858;[80] and in a trial for a raid on a vessel in Mayo in 1860.[81] Trials for robbery and murder on the high seas accounted for the majority of these cases. In *R. v. Canavan*[82] the accused was tried in 1845 by an admiralty commission for a murder committed on a turf boat which was being taken between Mann Bay and New Quay in Galway. Although the deceased's body was never found, the accused was convicted following testimony that the accused and the deceased had been arguing earlier. A year later, in *R. v. Mannion*,[83] the accused was convicted of the murder of a woman on a boat in Roundstone Bay. The prisoner argued in the Court of Crown Cases Reserved that the *locus in quo* of the offence was on the cis-marine side of an imaginary line between the two headlands, and, therefore was not in a place 'where the admiral or admirals have or pretend to have power' as required by the 1614 Act. The court (without providing any supporting reasons for its decision) upheld the conviction. In 1855 a ship's mate was convicted of manslaughter at an admiralty commission at Cork for beating the ship's Dutch cook to death.[84] In 1858 a soldier was sentenced to eighteen months' imprisonment for stealing £2 from a drunken fellow recruit on a crossing from Glasgow to Belfast.[85] In *R. v. Browne*[86] in 1858 an admiralty commission was deployed for the prosecution of a master for the manslaughter of a sailor who died on board the *Earl of Lonsdale* as a result of the master's brutal treatment. In the sad case of *R. v. Keane*[87] in 1860 a crowd of about 140 had plundered nearly twenty tons of corn from a Dutch vessel anchored in Blacksod Bay. Evidence was given that before the attack the crowd had assembled and begun to whistle; when asked by the captain what they wanted they had replied 'we want your provisions'. When the captain asked 'is it hunger?' they replied 'it is' and then rushed the ship. The jury found two of the accused guilty, but with a recommendation to mercy on account of the distress in the area. Judge Kelly sentenced them to six months' imprisonment (but, in recognition of the jury's request for leniency, calculated the sentence from the date of their first committal).

The nineteenth-century admiralty criminal commission court opened with the proclamation of the admiralty commission by the clerk of the Crown. A foreman and the grand jury were sworn. The judge would address the grand jury on piracy and maritime criminal law.[88] The Admiralty Court Act 1783 required that the

---

77  NAI, CSORP 1844 A/9022.                    78  NAI, CSORP 1845 O/8810.

79  NAI, CSORP 1846 G/10690.

80  The trial of the prosecution *R. v. Somerville* was postponed at the Antrim lent assizes, when it was discovered that the offence had been committed on the high seas, in order that an admiralty commission could be obtained (*Belfast Newsletter*, 15 Mar. 1858). A trial for a robbery committed on a vessel on the high seas was tried at Munster Summer Assizes, *FJ*, 20 July 1858.

81  *R. v. Keane*, *FJ*, 24 July 1860.        82  *FJ*, 30 July 1845.        83  (1846) 2 Cox C C 158.

84  *R. v. Ford*, *FJ*, 28 Mar. 1855.        85  *FJ*, 20 July 1858.        86  *Clare Journal*, 12 July 1858.

87  *Mitchell's Maritime Register*, 28 July 1860; *FJ*, 24 July 1860.        88  *FJ*, 21 July 1860.

commission[89] be issued to the judge of the Court of Admiralty and 'three or four such other discreet persons as shall be nominated and appointed by the lord chancellor of Ireland'. In practice those 'others' were the two assize judges and two queen's counsel. In an opinion drafted in 1858, the attorney general, James Whiteside, noted that 'according to the ancient usage, this commission is directed, not only to the judge of the Admiralty Court, but also to the two circuit court judges, and two of her majesty's counsel belonging to the circuit'.[90]

The 1783 Act had strengthened the position of the judge of the Admiralty Court in admiralty criminal commissions: under the Act of 1614 the appointee might be the admiral 'or his or their lieutenant general, deputy or deputies'. There was no requirement under the 1614 Act that the judge of the Irish Admiralty Court even be appointed. The 1783 Act, on the other hand, required that the judge be nominated. But while it was essential that the judge of the Admiralty Court be nominated to the commission, it was not strictly necessary that he then actually preside at the trial. The Act permitted an ordinary common law judge to do that. In the early nineteenth century, the general practice was that the admiralty judge would not appear at admiralty criminal commissions. Instead, the trial was conducted by the ordinary assize judge.[91] The law officers considered that the admiralty judge was only under a 'duty so to sit if there were any risk that, for want of his attendance, the commission would remain un-sped'; but the fact that the commission was usually issued to a panel of five meant that 'the risk is very remote that the commission will not be sped'.[92] The reason for the admiralty judges' dereliction was financial: they were not reimbursed their expenses in attending criminal trials, and did not care to discharge this function at their own cost.

However, in the summer of 1858, Judge Kelly resumed sitting at admiralty criminal commissions. Having presided at two trials at Ennis and Belfast he then submitted a claim for an honorarium and expenses based on section 4 of the Judges' Salaries Act 1796.[93] Section 4 authorized the lord lieutenant to order 'such sum of money to be issued, and paid, to any judge, or judges, who shall have any special commission of oyer and terminer and gaol delivery'. Kelly argued that the phrase 'special commission of oyer and terminer' was wide enough to capture an admiralty criminal commission. The law officers, James Whiteside and Edmund Hayes, disagreed: an admiralty commission was not strictly 'a commission of oyer and terminer'.[94] On the other hand, the law officers considered that Kelly did have

---

89  A copy of an 1830s piracy commission survives (NAI, CSORP 1859/4,449).

90  Opinion of James Whiteside and Edmund Hayes, 18 Nov. 1858 (NAI, CSORP 1859/4,449). An 1834 admiralty commission was directed to six commissioners: a justice of the Common Pleas, of the King's Bench, of the Exchequer, Sir Henry Meredyth and two Queen's Counsel.

91  In *R. v. Canavan*, *FJ*, 30 July 1845, the trial was conducted before Lefroy and Jackson JJ; in *R. v. Mannion* (1846) 2 Cox C. C. 158 Ball J., Richards B. and George French QC presided; in *R v. Ford*, *FJ*, 28 Mar. 1855, Henry Martley QC and Sir Colmen O'Loughlen presided.

92  Opinion of James Whiteside and Edmund Hayes, 18 Nov. 1858 (NAI, CSORP 1859/4,449).

93  36 Geo. III, c. 26 (Ire.), 1796.

94  Opinion of Whiteside and Hayes, 18 Nov. 1858 (NAI, CSORP 1858/19,243).

a fair claim to an extra-statutory gratuity, and suggested that 'from the very moderate scale of salary allowed to the judge of the admiralty we think him fairly entitled to consideration in this respect'.

In 1861 the legislature begun the process of eliminating the Admiralty Commission Court. Section 68 of the Offences against the Person Act 1861[95] provided that the offences of murder or assault causing bodily harm committed at sea were to be tried in the ordinary courts. Offences committed on the high seas were deemed to have been committed upon land, and were, therefore, subject to prosecution by ordinary criminal courts (and not by specialist admiralty commissions). Similar clauses were introduced in the Larceny Act 1861 and the Malicious Injury Act 1861.[96] The effect was to integrate the prosecution for offences committed on the high seas into the ordinary criminal process. The old common law rule that offences committed at sea were 'done out of the jurisdiction of the common law', was avoided. After 1861 the institution of an admiralty commission was no more than a remote theoretical possibility. From 1861 onwards, an admiralty commission court would be required only in the case of a felony which the legislature had neglected to provide should be tried by the ordinary criminal courts; it was only in the case of 'offence[s] not comprised in the [consolidation] statutes' that offenders were required to be tried 'in the Commission Court of Admiralty, as before'.[97]

## The prosecution of admiralty misdemeanours

The Piracy Act 1614 made 'treasons, felonies, robberies, murders and confederacies committed on sea' amenable to prosecution at common law. It did not extend to minor offences committed at sea. In 1799 the English parliament enacted the Offences at Sea Act 1799.[98] The 1799 Act extended the jurisdiction of admiralty commissions, appointed under the piracy acts, to misdemeanours as well as felonies. But, as the commissioners of inquiry into the Irish Admiralty Court noted in 1829, 'this enlargement of the criminal jurisdiction has never been extended to Ireland; an omission which has been attended with much inconvenience'.[99] In 1825 the law officers advised that the offence of wearing illegal colours, committed by a vessel master in Dublin, was not amenable to prosecution under the Piracy Act 1614; the offence was a mere misdemeanour:

> We think that no proceeding for wearing illegal colours could be entertained in any Admiralty Court in Ireland – neither by the instance court, inasmuch as this is not a cause 'civil or maritime' within the 8th Article of the Act of Union; nor yet by the commission under the Acts of James 1, and Geo III, inasmuch as these acts do not extend to any misdemeanour except confederacies.[100]

95  24 & 25 Vict., c. 100, s. 36.
96  24 & 25 Vict., c. 96, s. 115; 24 & 25 Vict., c. 97, s. 72.
97  W. Boyd, *The law and practice of the High Court of Admiralty of Ireland* (Dublin, 1868), p. 14.
98  39 Geo. III, c. 37 (Eng.), 1799.          99  *Eighteenth Report*, p. 51.
100 See the opinions of J.S. Copley, C. Wetherell, W.C. Plunket, J.L. Foster, 18 Aug. 1825, W. Forsyth, *Cases and opinions on constitutional law* (London, 1869), p. 104.

There was considerable demand for the extension to Ireland of competence over marine misdemeanours. Sir Henry Meredyth detailed instances of criminal mistreatment of sailors; these offences, because they were misdemeanours, could not be incriminated under Irish law:

> in one of those cases the impugnant had in fact discharged a gun loaded with grapeshot at the promovent, and wounded him in the leg so severely as to produce a mortification, which with difficulty was removed. In another instance, a seaman was disabled for life by a blow upon his arm with an heavy iron ... Instances have also appeared of sending seamen on shore without cause, and without means or clothing, upon deserted or dangerous places, of refusal to receive them back, and of unjustifiable abandonment.[101]

In the absence of criminal jurisdiction over misdemeanours, abused sailors were restricted to the court's civil jurisdiction: in 1827, in the *Russell v. Charlotte of New York*,[102] the king's advocate, in arguing in a civil suit for damages instituted by a sailor who had been assaulted by his master, explained 'that the seaman had been obliged to resort to this mode of redress as, unfortunately for the ends of justice, the Court of Admiralty of Ireland had not a criminal jurisdiction as to minor offences, as the English court had'. However, this omission begun to be closed when it became common in the mid-nineteenth century to include clauses deeming offences committed at sea to have been carried out on land (and therefore accessible to prosecution at common law).[103]

---

101  *Eighteenth Report*, Appendix 5, p. 91.        102  (1827) 1 Law Rec 16.
103  See p. 269 above.

# Appendix

Letters patent granted to Hugh Baillie Doctor of Laws for the office of judge of
the Admiralty in the Kingdom of Ireland follow to wit:

George the Second, by the grace of God of Great Britain, France and Ireland,
king, defender of the faith: to our beloved Hugh Baillie, Doctor of Laws, greeting:
we confiding very much in your fidelity and circumspection and likewise in your
industry in this behalf, do make, constitute and ordain you, the said Hugh Baillie,
doctor of laws, our commissary, deputy and surrogate in, and throughout, our
kingdom of Ireland aforesaid, and maritime parts thereof, and to the same adjacent
whatsoever; with power of taking and receiving all and singular the fees, wages,
profits, salaries, advantages, and commodities whatsoever in any wise belonging and
appertaining, or anciently due and accustomed to the said office; and we do commit
to you our power and authority in all and every the places belonging to our said
kingdom by any means whatsoever; to take congnizance of, and proceed in, all
causes and businesses, civil and maritime, as well of mere office mixt or promoted,
as at the instance of all parties whomsoever, which are now depending, or shall
hereafter depend in the Court of Admiralty in our kingdom of Ireland; and to
receive proofs, swear witnesses, and oblige them to be sworn, and to admit other
sorts of proofs in all such causes and businesses whatsoever; and also to force and
compel such witnesses in case they withdraw themselves for interest, gain, fear,
favour or ill-will, to give evidence to the truth; and to take, accept, and admit,
cautions and sureties and pledges, stipulations and obligations of, and from, all
manner of persons; and duly to punish, mulct, chastise and imprison all
delinquents, rebels and contrarients whomsoever, according to law and justice and
their demerits and misdeeds and the nature of the offence; and the penalties of all
such offenders to mitigate and moderate as to you shall seem meet and expedient;
also duly to search, or inquire of, and concerning all and singular the goods of
traitors, pirates, manslayers, felons, fugitives and felons of themselves and also
concerning those triable as traitors and other delinquents upon the sea, or in any
place over-flown within the ebbing and flowing thereof; and concerning the bodies
of persons drowned, killed or by any other means coming by their death in the sea
or in any ports, rivers, public streams or creeks and places over-flown; and also
concerning maims happening in the aforesaid places; and engines, toils and nets

prohibited and unlawful and the occupiers and exercisers thereof; and moreover concerning fishes royal, to wit, whales, rigs, dolphins, sturgeons, grampuses and all other fishes whatsoever which are of a great or very large bulk or fatness by right or custom any ways used belonging to us, and to the office of our high admiral of England; and also of and concerning all casualties at sea, goods wrecked, flotsam, jetsam, lagan, things cast overboard and wreck of the sea, and all goods taken for, or to be accounted as derelicts, or by chance found, or to be found; and all other transgressions, misdeeds, offences, enormities and maritime crimes whatsoever done and committed, or to be done or committed, as well in, and upon, the high sea as all ports towards the sea, fresh waters and creeks whatsoever, or the shores of the sea and sands within the ebbing and flowing of the sea to high water mark from all first bridges towards the sea of our kingdom of Ireland aforesaid howsoever, whensoever or by what means soever proceeding, and happening; and all such things as are discovered and found out; as also all fines, mulcts, amerciaments and compositions whatsoever, due and to be due in that behalf; to tax, moderate, demand, collect and levy and to cause the same to be demanded, levied and collected and legally to compel and command them to be paid; and to proceed in all such causes and businesses, complaints and offences summarily according to the statutes, ordinances and civil laws, and the legal and laudable customs of our High Court of Admiralty of England anciently used and observed in that behalf, and all such causes and businesses, and all things touching and concerning the same; to hear, examine, discuss and finally determine, and to promulgate all manner of sentences, as well interlocutory as definitive, and to make all decrees in the aforesaid causes and businesses, and every of them, and to put the same in execution; saving nevertheless the right of appealing to the High Court of our Admiralty of England aforesaid, and to the judge and president, to wit, our lieutenant general of the said court for the time being; and saving always the right of our aforesaid High Court of Admiralty of England, and also of the judge and regist[rar] of the said court, from whom or either of them, we will not in any thing detract by these presents; and to do, exercise and expedite all other things in the premises, or that concern the same whatsoever in our abovementioned kingdom of Ireland and maritime coasts thereof, as well within liberties and franchises as without, according to the civil laws and the statutes, ordnances and laudable customs of our High Court of Admiralty of England aforesaid anciently observed; saving the prerogative of our said High Court of Admiralty of England in all things concerning the premises and other affairs whatsoever; with cognizance of whatsoever other causes, civil and maritime which relate to the sea, or which respect or concern the sea or the passage or sailing over the same, or any naval journey or voyage. Also with power of naming, deputing and all such officers, ministers and deputies under you as shall be necessary for the execution of the said office, excepting always the regist[rar] and marshal of the said court, whose nomination and appointment we reserve to our self by these presents, which are to continue only during our pleasure. Further, we do in our name command, and firmly and strictly charge all and singular our governors, knights, justices of the peace, mayors and sheriffs, captains, marshals, bailiffs, keepers of our gaols and prisons, constables and all other our officers and ministers, faithful subjects and liege people in and throughout our whole kingdom of Ireland aforesaid, wheresoever appointed, as well within liberties and franchises as without, that in all and singular the premises and concerning the execution of them, they be aiding, assisting and yield obedience to you and your officers in all things as is fitting under the penalty of contempt, and the peril which will fall thereon.

In witness whereof we have caused the great seal of our High Court of Admiralty of England aforesaid to be affixed to these presents. Given at London in our said court, the fifteenth day of January in the year of our Lord one thousand seven hundred and forty four and in the eighteenth year of our reign.

Samuel Hill Regist[rar]

# Table of statutes

ACTS OF PARLIAMENT OF THE UNITED KINGDOM

# Table of reported cases

# Select bibliography

1. MANUSCRIPT SOURCES

**(a) British Library**

Julius Caesar admiralty papers (Add. MS 12,503)
Julius Caesar admiralty papers (Lansdowne MS 144)
Civil list for Ireland, 1654 (Add. MS 19,833)
Official correspondence of John Ellis (Add. MS 28,887)
Earl of Essex papers, vol. 210 (Stowe MS 210)
Hardwicke papers, 1802–04 (Add. MS 35,761; 35,717)
Letter book of Sir Charles Hedges (Add. MS 24,107)
Leoline Jenkins reports on cases (Add. MS 18,206)
Robert Peel correspondence (Add. MS 40,230; 42,234; 40,320)
William Petty shipping and admiralty papers (Add. MS 72,893)
William Petty's admiralty addresses 1676 & 1677 (Lansdowne MS 1,228)
Petty–Southwell correspondence (Add. MS 72,852)
'The rights and jurisdiction of the lord high admiral of England asserted in Ireland' (Egerton MS 744)
Paul Rycaut letter book 1692–1694 (Add. MS 37,663)
Paul Rycaut's papers (Lansdowne MS 1,153)
Munster Admiralty papers (Add. MS 38,147–38,152)

**(b) The National Archives: Public Record Office**

*High Court of Admiralty records*

High Court of Admiralty, act books, 1569–1749 (HCA 3/13–74)
High Court of Admiralty, assignation books, 1755–65 (HCA 5/124–139)
High Court of Admiralty, exemplars (drafts) files, 1579–1649 (HCA 14/13–14/49)
High Court of Admiralty files of libels, allegations, decrees, sentences (HCA 24/119)
High Court of Admiralty, early instance and prize papers, 1666–1754 (HCA 15/9–15/47)
High Court of Admiralty, warrants for appointments, 1660–72 (HCA 30/821)
Admiralty droits: divers documents (HCA 30/158)
High Court of Admiralty, instance papers, series one (HCA 16)
High Court of Admiralty, warrants (HCA 25/215)
High Court of Admiralty, vice-admiralty courts (HCA 49/106)
High Court of Admiralty, examinations and answers (HCA 13/60)
Prize commissioners appeal papers, War of Austrian Succession (HCA 42/30, HCA 42/35, HCA 42/40, HCA 42/44)
High Court of appeals for prizes, case books, 1750–60 (HCA 45/1–45/6)

*Admiralty records*

Selected orders and letters of the duke of York, 1660–5 (ADM 2/1,725)

Admiralty secretary: civil warrants, letters, 1663–84 (ADM 2/1,755)

Admiralty out-letters; legal correspondence, 1702–81 (ADM 2/1,046; ADM 2/1,049; ADM
    2/1,050; ADM 2/1,052; ADM 2/1,053; ADM 2/1,054; ADM 2/1,055; ADM 2/1,057;
    ADM 2/1,060)

Admiralty Board minutes, 1699–1707 (ADM 3/15–3/22)

Letters from the solicitor of the Admiralty and other Crown legal officers, 1680–1783 (ADM
    1/3,665/; ADM 1/3,666; ADM 1/3,667; ADM 1/3,668; ADM 1/3,670; ADM 1/3,676;
    ADM 1/3,677; ADM 1/3,681; ADM 1/3,699)

Admiralty legal correspondence, 1689–1783 (ADM 2/1,050; ADM 2/1,063)

Doctors' commons, letters from the High Court of Admiralty, 1740–79 (ADM 1/3,880–1/3,885)

Admiralty; miscellaneous Irish in-letters, 1723–90 (ADM 1/3,990)

Admiralty law officers' opinions, 1733–83 (ADM 7/298–7/300)

*Privy Council papers*

Records of the judicial committee of the Privy Council (PCAP)

Miscellaneous unbound papers: memorandum re empowering Court of Prize Appeals to hear
    appeal in prize causes from Ireland (PC 1/5/102)

Miscellaneous unbound papers: committee to hear rival claims re establishment of a Dublin
    ballast office (PC 1/1/72)

Miscellaneous unbound papers: Admiralty report on the pretensions of Galway to admiralty
    jurisdiction (PC 1/2/53)

Privy Council registers, 1665–1755 (PC 2/58; PC 2/62; PC 2/75; PC 2/81; PC 2/102)

*State papers*

Commissioners of Admiralty: minutes of proceedings, 1632 (SP 16/228)

Sir Edward Nicholas' letterbook, 1624–40 (SP 14/215)

State papers, Domestic, Elizabeth I, 1571 (SP 12/83)

State papers, Ireland, 1587–1689 (SP 63/128–351)

State papers, James I, 1615 (SP 14/82)

State papers, Charles I, 1626, 1629, 1633, 1634, 1635 & 1639 (SP 16/36; SP 16/132; SP 16/240;
    SP 16/262; SP 16/264; SP 16/271; SP 16/418)

State papers foreign, Sweden, 1678–81 (SP 95/11)

State papers foreign, Genoa (SP 79/1(3))

*Treasury papers*

Treasury papers, 1759 (T1/397)

Treasury papers, 1866 (T1/6,627A)

*Home Office*

Home Office: Ireland: Correspondence and Papers, 1782–1800 (HO 100/1–100/98)

(c) **National Library of Ireland**

Act of Union papers (MS 887)

Betham transcripts (MS 11,959)
Lyons–Barrington correspondence (MS 1,723)
Naas papers (MS 11,153; 11,155; 11, 252)
Report on private collections no. 226
Admiralty criminal commission (MS 15,427)

### (d) Marsh's Library, Dublin

Dudley Loftus' commonplace book (MS Z. R. 5.14)
Transcription of entries from Leinster Court of Admiralty act book, 1647 (MS Z.3.2.1(3))

### (e) Bodleian Library, Oxford

Carte manuscripts (Carte MSS 7; 14; 22; 23; 24; 28; 29; 34; 36; 39; 45; 47; 51; 144; 152; 168; 169)
Clarendon papers 1666 (Clarendon MS 84)
William Petty papers (Rawlinson A 172; A 186; A 191)

### (f) Trinity College Dublin

H.E. Chatterton biographical sketch (MS 6401/1)
Commonplace book of papers relating to the natural history of Ireland (MS 883/1)
Seventeenth century civilian precedent book (MS 735)
Southwell papers (MS 1,180)

### (g) King's Inns, Dublin

Eighteenth-century manuscript admiralty and ecclesiastical precedent book

### (h) Royal Irish Academy

Haliday notes on the history of Dublin (MS 2/E/2)

### (i) Dublin City Library and Archive

Dublin Corporation financial minutes, 1589 (MR 35)

### (j) Alnwick Castle, Northumberland

Correspondence of Algernon, 10th earl of Northumberland, vol. 14

### (k) Pepys Library, Magdalene College, University of Cambridge

List of vice-admirals 1687 (MS 2,762)
Opinion on ballastage (MS 2,872)

### (l) Osler Library, McGill University

Petty letterbook (MS 7,614)

### (m) National Archives of Ireland

Chief secretaries' official papers, 1790–1830

Chief secretary's registered papers, 1830–80
Calendar of departmental letters and official papers, 1760–88
Dublin Chamber of Commerce records, MS 1,723
Frazer MSS
Miscellaneous state papers (M 2,447)

### (n)  Public Record Office of Northern Ireland

Bedford papers (T/2,915)
FitzGerald papers (T/3,075)
O'Hagan papers (D/2,777)
William Wickham correspondence with Castlereagh (D/3,030)

### (o)  Liverpool Record Office

Edward Stanley papers (920 Der 14)

### (p)  Representative Church Body Library, Dublin

Repertory of leases in chapter books of Christ Church Dublin (C.6.1.17.5)

### (q)  National Archives of Scotland

Erskine papers (GD 124/15/1,555/1)

### (r)  Lambeth Palace Library

Carew papers (MS 619)

## II. PRINTED ORIGINAL SOURCES

*Acts of the Privy Council of England, 1571–1575*, ed. J.R. Dasent (HMSO, 1894)
*Annals of the viscount and the first and second earls of Stair*, ed. J.M. Graham (Edinburgh, 1875)
*Autobiography of Sir John Bramston, K.B.* (Camden Society, London, 1845)
*Calendar of Kinsale documents, vol. 6*, ed. M. Mulcahy (Kinsale, 1998)
*Calendar of material relating to Ireland from the High Court of Admiralty depositions*, ed. J. Appleby (Dublin, 1992)
*Calendar of the ancient records of Dublin*, ed. Sir John and Lady Gilbert, 19 vols (Dublin, 1889–1944)
*Calendar of the Carew manuscripts*, ed. J.S. Brewer & W. Blunden, 6 vols (London, 1871)
*Calendar of the Clarendon state papers*, 5 vols (Oxford, 1869–1970)
*Calendar of the manuscripts of the marquis of Ormonde, K.P., preserved at Kilkenny Castle. New series*, ed. Caesar Litton Falkiner, F. Elrington Ball (HMC, 8 vols, London, 1902–20)
*Calendar of the state papers relating to Ireland in the reign of James 1, 1603–1625*, ed. C.W. Russell and J.P. Prendergast (London, 1872)
*Calendar of the state papers relating to Ireland in the reign of Charles 1*, ed. R.B. Mahaffy (London, 1900)
*Calendar of the state papers relating to Ireland in the reigns of Henry VIII, Edward VI, Mary and Elizabeth*, ed. H. Hamiton, E. Atkinson, R.P. Mahaffy (London, 1860–1912)

*Calendar of the state papers relating to Ireland preserved in the Public Record Office 1660–1670*, ed. R.P. Mahaffy (London, 1905)

*Calendar of Treasury Books, 1669–1672*, ed. J. Redington (London, 1868–1903)

*Calendar of Treasury Books, 1714–1715*, ed. W.A. Shaw and F.H. Slingsby (London, 1957)

*Cases and Opinions on Constitutional Law*, ed. W. Forsyth (London, 1869)

*Complete collection of the treaties and conventions at present subsisting between Great Britain and foreign powers*, ed. L. Hertslet (London, 1820)

*Correspondence of Daniel O'Connell*, ed. M.R. O'Connell, 8 vols (Dublin, 1977)

*Correspondence of Edmund Burke, vol. 1*, ed. T. Copeland (Cambridge, 1958)

*Council Book of the Corporation of Kinsale, 1652–1800*, ed. R. Caulfield (London, 1879)

*Council Book of the Corporation of the City of Cork from 1609 to 1643 and from 1690 to 1800*, ed. R. Caulfield (Guildford, 1876)

*Diary of Samuel Pepys*, ed. R. Latham and W. Matthews (London, 1971)

*Eighteenth-century Irish official papers in Great Britain*, ed. A.P. Malcomson (Belfast, 1990)

*Hale and Fleetwood on admiralty jurisdiction*, ed. M.J. Prichard and D.E.C. Yale (Selden Society, London, 1993)

*Hamilton manuscripts*, ed. T.K. Lowry (Belfast, 1867)

*Inchiquin manuscripts*, ed. J. Ainsworth (Dublin, 1961)

*Law and custom of the sea*, ed. R.G. Marsden, 2 vols (Naval Records Society, London, 1915–16)

'Letter Book of Sir Arthur Chichester', ed. R. Dudley Edwards, *Analecta Hibernica*, 8 (1938), 3

*Letters and dispatches of Thomas Earl of Strafford*, ed. W. Knowler, 2 vols (London, 1739)

*Life of Leoline Jenkins*, ed. W. Wynne (London, 1724)

*Lismore papers*, ed. A.B. Grosart, 2nd ser., 5 vols (London, 1887–8)

'Lord Chancellor Gerard's report on Ireland', ed. C. McNeill, *Analecta Hibernica*, 2 (1931), 93

*Manuscripts of B Fortescue, I, 1698–1790* (HMC, London, 1892)

'Manuscripts of … Lord Emly', *Fourteenth Report, Appendix IX* (HMC, London, 1895)

'Manuscripts of the marquis of Ormonde', *Fourteenth Report, Appendix 7* (HMC, London, 1895)

*Middlesex Pedigrees* (Harleian Society, lxv, London, 1869)

*Notes on four Admiralty registry letter books*, ed. K.C. McGuffie (London, 1964)

*Petty Papers*, ed. marquis of Lansdowne, 2 vols (London, 1927)

*Petty–Southwell Correspondence, 1676–1687*, ed. marquis of Lansdowne (London, 1928)

*Report on the manuscripts of J.B. Fortescue, IX, 1807–1809* (HMC, London, 1915)

'Sir Paul Rycaut's memoranda and letters from Ireland, 1686–1687', ed. P. Melvin, *Analecta Hibernica*, 27 (1972), 123

*State Letters of Henry, earl of Clarendon*, 2 vols (Dublin, 1765)

*Tanner letters: original documents and notices of Irish affairs*, ed. C. McNeill (Dublin, 1941)

*'A volley of execrations': the letters of John FitzGibbon, the earl of Clare, 1772–1802*, ed. D.A. Fleming and A.P.W. Malcomson (IMC, Dublin, 2005)

### III. CONTEMPORARY PRINTED BOOKS

Abbott, C., *A treatise of the law relative to merchant ships and seamen* (5th ed., London, 1827)

Abbott, C., *A treatise of the law relative to merchant ships and seamen* (12th ed., London, 1881)

*Analytical digest of all the reported cases determined by the High Court of Admiralty of England*, ed. W.T. Pritchard (London, 1847)

Anon., *The Georgian era; memoirs of the most eminent persons who have flourished in Great Britain*, 4 vols (London, 1833)

Anon., *Handbook for Travellers in France* (London, 1854)

Anon., 'An unventilated grievance', *ILT & SJ*, 2 (1868), 382

Anster, J., *The Roman Civil Law. Introductory lecture on the study of the Roman Civil Law* (Dublin, 1851)

Baillie, H., *A letter to Dr Shebear: containing a refutation of his arguments concerning the Boston and Quebec Acts of Parliament: and his aspersions upon …* (London, 1775)

Barrington, J., *The rise and fall of the Irish nation* (Paris, 1833)

Boyd, W., *The Law and Practice of the High Court of Admiralty of Ireland* (Dublin, 1868)

Browne, A., *A compendious view of the ecclesiastical law*, 2 vols (Dublin, 1799)

Cleirac, E., *Us et coutumes de la mer* (Rouen, 1661)

Coke, E., *The Third Part of the Institutes of the Laws of England* (London, 1669)

Coke, E., *The Fourth Part of the Institutes of the Laws of England* (London, 1644; repr. Dublin, 1797)

Dix Hutton, H., 'Report on the extension of Admiralty jurisdiction in Ireland to cases of freight and demurrage', *Journal of the Social and Statistical Society of Ireland* (1870), 212

Dunlap, A., *A treatise on the practice of courts of admiralty in civil causes of maritime jurisdiction* (Philadlephia, 1836)

Gilbert, J.T., (ed.), *History of the Irish Confederation and the war in Ireland, 1641–49*, 7 vols (Dublin, 1882–91)

Haliday, C., *The Scandinavian kingdom of Dublin* (Dublin, 1882; repr. Shannon, 1969)

Hardiman, J., *The history of the town and county of the town of Galway* (Dublin, 1820)

Hedges, C., *Reasons for settling admiralty-jurisdiction, and giving encouragement to merchants, owners, commanders, masters of ships, material-men and mariners, humbly offered to the consideration of his majesty, and the two Houses of Parliament* (London, 1690)

Holt, W., *Rules of the road* (London, 1867)

Howard, G., *A treatise of the Exchequer and Revenue of Ireland* (Dublin, 1776)

King, W., *The state of the Protestants of Ireland under the late King James's government* (London, 1691)

*Original works of William King, LL.D.*, ed. J. Nichols, 3 vols (London, 1776)

La Touche, J.D., *Case of Frederick Berg, Master of the Freden of Stockholm* (Dublin, 1752)

La Touche, J.D., *The Humble Petition of James Digges La Touche in behalf of himself and others, the merchants of the city of Dublin* (Dublin, 1751)

*Magna Charta Libertatum Civitatis Waterford*, ed. T. Cunningham (Dublin, 1752)

Marvin, W., *A treatise on the law of wreck and salvage* (Boston, 1858)

Mason, W.M., *The History and Antiquities of the Collegiate and Cathedral Church of St Patrick's* (Dublin, 1819)

McGhee, R., *A sermon on the death of the late lamented John Henry North Esq., M.P., judge of the Admiralty* (Dublin & London, 1831)

Morris, J., *Two lectures on the jurisdiction and practice of the High Court of Admiralty of England* (London, 1860)

Petty, W., *The political anatomy of Ireland* (London, 1691)

Reynolds, T., *The life of Thomas Reynolds*, 2 vols (London, 1839)

Robertson, G., *A genealogical account of the principal families in Ayreshire, more particularly in Cunninghame* (Ayreshire, 1823)

Smith, C.S., *The ancient and present state of the county and city of Cork*, 2 vols (Dublin, 1774)

Thompson, J., *The law of criminal procedure in Ireland* (Dublin, 1899)

Townsend, J.F., *A treatise on the law of salvage in Ireland* (Dublin, 1840)

Watts, R., *Practice of the Court of Admiralty in Ireland and England* (Dublin, 1757)

IV. MODERN WORKS

'Admiralty Business in Ireland', *ILT & SJ*, 44 (1910), 11

Appleby, J. & O'Dowd, M.,'The Irish Admiralty: its organization and development, *c.*1570–1640', *Irish Historical Studies*, 24 (1985), 299

Appleby, J., 'An Irish letter of marque, *1648*', *Irish Sword*, 61 (1983), 218

Aylmer, G., 'Patronage at the court of Charles II' in E. Cruickshanks (ed.), *The Stuart Courts* (Stroud, 2000)

Baker, J.H., *An introduction to English legal history* (London, 2002)

Baker, J.H., *The Oxford history of the laws of England, vol. VI: 1483–1558* (Oxford, 2003)

Barnard, T., *A new anatomy of Ireland: the Irish Protestants, 1649–1770* (Oxford, 2003)

Barnard, T., *Cromwellian Ireland: English government and reform in Ireland, 1649–1660* (Oxford, 1973)

Bennett, D., *The Silver Collection, Trinity College Dublin* (Dublin, 1988)

Bourguignon, H.J., *Sir William Scott, Lord Stowell* (Cambridge, 1987)

Clarke, A., *Prelude to Restoration in Ireland* (Cambridge, 1999)

Craig, M., *Dublin 1660–1860* (London, 1992)

Crawford, J., *Anglicizing the government of Ireland: the Irish Privy Council and the expansion of Tudor rule, 1556–1576* (Dublin, 1997)

Dickson, D. & R. English, 'The La Touche Dynasty' in D. Dickson (ed.), *The gorgeous mask: Dublin 1700–1850* (Dublin, 1987)

Dowling, J.A., 'The Irish Court of Appeal in Chancery, 1857–1877', *Journal of Legal History*, 21 (2000), 83

Duncan, G.I.O., *The High Court of Delegates* (Cambridge, 1971)

Dunlop, R., *Ireland under the Commonwealth*, 2 vols (Manchester, 1913)

Fincham, F.W.X., 'Letters concerning Sir Maurice Eustace, lord chancellor of Ireland', *English Historical Review*, 35 (1920), 251

Fitzmaurice, E.G.P., *The life of Sir William Petty* (London, 1895)

Gibb, A.D., *Judicial corruption in the United Kingdom* (Edinburgh, 1957)

Grose, C., 'The Anglo–Dutch Alliance of 1678', *English Historical Review*, 39 (1924), 349–72, 526–51

Haley, K.H.D., 'The Anglo–Dutch rapprochement of 1677', *English Historical Review*, 73 (1958), 614

Healy, T.M., *Stolen waters: a page in the conquest of Ulster* (London, 1913)

Hunt, W., *The Irish parliament, 1775* (Dublin, 1907)

Jardine L. and A. Stewart, *Hostage to fortune; the troubled life of Francis Bacon* (New York, 1999)

Kavanaugh, A.C., *John FitzGibbon, earl of Clare: Protestant reaction and English authority in late eighteenth-century Ireland* (Dublin, 1997)

Kearney, H., *Strafford in Ireland, 1633–1641* (Cambridge, 1959)

Kelly, J., *Henry Flood: patriots and politics in eighteenth-century Ireland* (Dublin, 1998)

Kenny, C., 'The Four Courts at Christ Church, 1608–1796', in W.N. Osborough (ed.), *Explorations in Law and History* (Dublin, 1995)

Lecky, W., *A history of Ireland in the eighteenth century*, 5 vols (London, 1892)

Levack, B.P., *The Civil Lawyers in England, 1603–1641* (Oxford, 1973)

Marsden, R.G., 'Vice-Admirals of the coast', *English Historical Review*, 23 (1908), 736

Maxwell, C., *A history of Trinity College Dublin, 1592–1892* (Dublin, 1946)

McDowell, R.B. and D.A. Webb, *Trinity College Dublin, 1592–1952* (Cambridge, 1982)

McDowell, R.B., *The Irish administration, 1801–1914* (London, 1964)

Murphy, E., '"No affair before us of greater concern"; the war at sea in Ireland, 1641–1649'
    (PhD, TCD, 2007)
Ó Siochrú, M., *Confederate Ireland, 1642–1649: a constitutional and political analysis* (Dublin,
    1999)
O'Higgins, P., 'William Ridgeway (1765–1817): law reporter', *NILQ*, 18 (1967), 208
Ohlmeyer, J., 'Irish privateers during the Civil War, 1642–1650', *Mariner's Mirror*, 76 (1990),
    119
Rhadamanthus, *Our judges* (Dublin, 1890)
Solar, P., 'Shipping and economic development in nineteenth-century Ireland', *Economic History
    Review*, 69 (2006), 717
Squibb, G.D., *Doctors' Commons* (Oxford, 1977)
Steckley, G.F., 'Bottomry bonds in the seventeenth century Admiralty Court', *American Journal
    of Legal History*, 45 (2001), 256
Sweeney, J.C., 'Admiralty law of Arthur Browne', *Journal of Maritime Law and Commerce*, 25
    (1995), 59
Treadwell, V., *Buckingham and Ireland, 1616–1628* (Dublin, 1998)

## V. WORKS OF REFERENCE

*Alumni Cantabrigienses, part 1*, ed. J. Venn, 4 vols (London, 1922)
*Alumni Dublinenses: a catalogue of the graduates of Trinity College Dublin*, ed. G. Burtchaell and
    T.U. Sadlier (Dublin, 1869)
*Alumni Oxonienses 1500–1714*, ed. J. Foster, 3 vols (London, 1896)
*Athenae Oxonienses, An exact history of all the writers and bishops who have had their education in
    the university of Oxford*, ed. A. Wood (London, 1813)
*British sources for Irish history, 1485–1641*, ed. B. Donovan & D. Edwards (Dublin, 1997)
*City and country calendar; or Irish court registry … 1795* (Dublin, 1795)
*Collection of treaties*, ed. G. Chalmers, 2 vols (London, 1790)
*Complete collection of treaties and conventions at present subsisting between Great Britain and foreign
    powers*, ed. L. Hertslet (London, 1820)
Dix, E.R., *Catalogue of early Dublin printed books*, 3 vols (Dublin, 1898)
*Faculty of advocates in Scotland, 1532–1942*, ed. F.G. Grant (Edinburgh, Scottish Records
    Society, 1944)
*Fasti Ecclesiae Hibernicae*, ed. H. Cotton (Dublin, 1857)
*Handlist of proclamations, George I to Edward VII, 1714–1910* (Wigan, 1913)
*House of Commons 1660–1690 (II) Members C–L*, ed. B.D. Hemming (London, 1983)
James, G.F. and J.J. Sutherland Shaw, 'Admiralty administration and personnel, 1619–1714',
    *Bulletin of Institute of Historical Research*, 14 (1936), 10 & 166
Johnston-Liik, E., *History of the Irish parliament, 1692–1800*, 6 vols (Belfast, 2002)
*King James's Irish army list*, ed. J. D'Alton (reprinted, Missouri, 1997)
*Liber Munerum publicorum Hiberniae*, ed. R. Lascelles (London, 1824)
*Office holders in modern Britain: volume IV, Admiralty Officials, 1660–1870*, ed. J.C. Sainty
    (London, 1975)
*Oxford companion to Irish history*, ed. S.J. Connolly (Dublin, 1998)
*Parliamentary election results in Ireland, 1801–1922*, ed. B. Walker (Dublin, 1978)
*Records of the Honourable Society of Lincoln's Inn: admissions from A.D. 1420 to A.D. 1893, and
    chapel registers*, ed. W.P. Baildon, 2 vols (London, 1896)

*Register of admissions to the Middle Temple*, ed. H.A.C. Sturgess 3 vols (London, 1949)
*Vice-Admirals of the coast*, ed. J.C. Sainty (List and Index Society, London, 2007)
*Watson's Almanack 1777* (Dublin, 1777)
*Watson's Almanack 1831* (Dublin, 1831)
*Watson's Almanack 1836* (Dublin, 1836)
*Who's who of British members of parliament: a biographical dictionary* ... ed. M. Stenton, 4 vols (Sussex, 1976)
*Wilson's Dublin Directories* (Dublin, 1753–1830)


VI. ROYAL COMMISSIONS, SELECT COMMITTEES AND SPECIAL
RETURNS

*Third report of the commissioners of public records, 1813* (HC 1812–13 (337); 1814–15 (342))
*Fourth report of the commissioners on the courts of justice – on offices in the disposal of the Crown* (HC 1818 (140) x. 557)
*First report of the deputy keeper of the public records of Ireland, 1869* (Dublin, 1869)
*Eighteenth Report of the commissioners appointed to inquire into the duties, salaries and emoluments of the officer, clerks and ministers of justice in all temporal and ecclesiastical courts in Ireland – the Court of Admiralty* (HC 1829 (5) xiii. 195)
*Report of the select committee appointed to take into consideration the Eighteenth Report of the commissioners of judicial inquiry in Ireland, together with the depositions forwarded to those commissioners by Sir Jonah Barrington, judge of the High Court of Admiralty in Ireland, and other papers connected with the conduct of Sir Jonah Barrington in the discharge of his judicial functions* (HC 1829 (293) xxii. 359)
*Account of the names and description of causes which have been tried and adjudicated in the Court of Admiralty in Ireland since the 1st day of August last* (HC 1831 (201) xv. 359)
*Report of the commissioners on the practice and jurisdiction of the ecclesiastical courts of England and Wales* (HC 1831–2 (199) xxiv.1)
*Appendix to the report of the commissioners appointed to inquire into municipal corporations in Ireland* (HC 1835 (25) xxvii.1)
*Select committee on legal education* (HC 1846 (686) x.1)
*Return of the number of sittings of the judge of the Court of Admiralty in Ireland and of warrants issued in the said court, in each year, for the seven years ending 31st December 1855 and 1862* (HC 1863 (399) xlix.1)
*Report of the commissioners appointed to inquire into the constitution, establishment, practice, procedure, and fees of the High Court of Admiralty of Ireland* (HC 1864 (3343) xxix. 219)
*Return of number of causes instituted in, and number of warrants of arrest in proceedings in rem issued by the Court of Admiralty (Ireland) in each year 1868 to 1874* (HC 1875 (202) lxii.1)
*Letter addressed to the chief secretary to the lord lieutenant by Mr Murphy, under date April 1875* (HC 1876 (321) lxi. 323)
*Return of number of cases in which the local admiralty courts of Cork and Belfast have, during the years 1877, 1877, 1879 been applied to exercise the powers created by s. 4, of 9 & 40 Vict., c. 28* (HC 1878–79 (349) lix. 327)

## VII. JUDICIAL STATISTICS

*Judicial Statistics (England & Wales), 1867* (HC 1867–8 [4062] lxvii. 519)
*Judicial Statistics (Ireland), 1868* (HC 1868–69 [4203] lviii. 737)
*Judicial Statistics (Ireland), 1870* (HC 1871 [C. 443] lxiv. 231)
*Judicial Statistics (Ireland), 1877* (HC 1878 [C. 2152] lxxix. 265)
*Judicial Statistics (Ireland), 1884* (HC 1884–85 [C. 4554] lxxxvi. 243)
*Judicial Statistics (England & Wales), 1884* (HC 1884–5 [C. 4518] lxxxvi. 1)
*Judicial Statistics (Ireland), 1886* (HC 1886 [C. 5177] xc. 241)
*Judicial Statistics (Ireland), 1890* (HC 1890–91 [C. 6511] xciii. 251)
*Judicial Statistics (Ireland), 1891* (HC 1892 [C. 6782] lxxxix. 253)
*Judicial Statistics (Ireland), 1896* (HC 1897 [C. 8617] c.761)
*Judicial Statistics (Ireland), 1897* (HC 1899 [C. 9249] cviii. Pt. II, 351)
*Judicial Statistics (Ireland), 1898* (HC 1899 [C. 9494] cviii. Pt. II, 445)
*Judicial Statistics (England & Wales), 1900* (HC 1900 [Cd. 181] ciii. 221)

## VIII. NEWSPAPERS

*Belfast Newsletter*
*Clare Journal*
*Examiner*
*Freeman's Journal*
*Gentleman's Magazine*
*Illustrated London News*
*The Times*

*Irish Law Times and Solicitors' Journal*
*Irish Times*
*London Literary Gazette*
*Mitchell's Maritime Register*
*Morning Chronicle*
*Shipping & Mercantile Gazette*

# Index

# Irish Legal History Society

(www.irishlegalhistorysociety.com)

Established in 1988 to encourage the study and advance the knowledge of the history of Irish law, especially by the publication of original documents and of works relating to the history of Irish law, including its institutions, doctrines and personalities, and the reprinting or editing of works of sufficient rarity or importance.

### PATRONS

The Hon. Mr Justice Murray
Chief Justice of Ireland

Rt. Hon. Sir Declan Morgan
Lord Chief Justice of Northern Ireland

### COUNCIL 2010–11

### President

Professor Norma Dawson

### Vice-Presidents

Robert D. Marshall, esq.

The Hon. Sir Donnell Deeny

### Honorary Secretaries

Dr Niamh Howlin

Dr Thomas Mohr

### Honorary Treasurers

John G. Gordon, esq.

Felix M. Larkin, esq.

### Council Members

The Hon. Mr Justice Geoghegan
Daire Hogan, esq.
Judge John Martin
Dr Patrick Geoghegan
Dr Séan Patrick Donlan
Dr Robin Hickey
Yvonne Mullen BL

The Hon. Sir Anthony Hart
John Larkin QC
Professor Desmond Greer QC (hon.)
Dr Kevin Costello
Professor Colum Kenny
James McGuire MRIA
Professor J.O. Ohlmeyer
Dr Kenneth Ferguson